Public Governance as Co-creation

T0384607

We need new governance solutions to help us improve public policies and services, solve complex societal problems, strengthen social communities, and reinvigorate democracy. By changing how government engages with citizens and stakeholders, co-creation provides an attractive and feasible approach to governance that goes beyond the triptych of public bureaucracy, private markets, and self-organized communities. Inspired by the successful use of co-creation for product and service design, this book outlines a broad vision of co-creation as a strategy of public governance. Through the construction of platforms and arenas to facilitate co-creation, this strategy can empower local communities, enhance broad-based participation, mobilize societal resources, and spur public innovation while building ownership for bold solutions to pressing problems and challenges. The book details how to use co-creation to achieve these goals. This exciting and innovative study combines theoretical argument with illustrative empirical examples, visionary thinking, and practical recommendations.

CHRISTOPHER ANSELL is Professor of Political Science at the University of California, Berkeley. He is the author and/or editor of ten books, including *The Protective State* (Cambridge, 2019) and *Pragmatist Democracy* (2011). His research focuses on understanding how organizations, institutions, and communities can engage effectively in democratic governance in the face of conflict, uncertainty, and complexity.

JACOB TORFING is Professor of Politics and Institutions in the Department of Social Sciences and Business, Roskilde University, Denmark, and Professor in the Faculty of Social Sciences, Nord University, Norway. He is the founder and director of the Roskilde School of Governance. He has chaired the Danish Political Science Association, been a member of the Danish Social Science Research Council, and served on the Executive Committee of the European Consortium of Political Research.

Cambridge Studies in Comparative Public Policy

The **Cambridge Studies in Comparative Public Policy** series was established to promote and disseminate comparative research in public policy. The objective of the series is to advance the understanding of public policies through the publication of the results of comparative research into the nature, dynamics and contexts of major policy challenges and responses to them. Works in the series will draw critical insights that enhance policy learning and are generalizable beyond specific policy contexts, sectors and time periods. Such works will also compare the development and application of public policy theory across institutional and cultural settings and examine how policy ideas, institutions and practices shape policies and their outcomes. Manuscripts comparing public policies in two or more cases as well as theoretically informed critical case studies which test more general theories are encouraged. Studies comparing policy development over time are also welcomed.

General Editors:

M. Ramesh, *National University of Singapore*

Xun Wu *Hong Kong University of Science and Technology*

Michael Howlett, *Simon Fraser University, British Columbia and National University of Singapore*

In Defense of Pluralism: Policy Disagreement and Its Media Coverage
By Éric Montpetit
Asia after the Developmental State: Disembedding Autonomy
Edited by Toby Carroll and Darryl S. L. Jarvis
The Politics of Shale Gas in Eastern Europe: Energy Security, Contested Technologies and the Social Licence to Frack
By Andreas Goldthau

Public Governance as Co-creation

A Strategy for Revitalizing the Public Sector and Rejuvenating Democracy

CHRISTOPHER ANSELL
University of California, Berkeley

JACOB TORFING
Roskilde University

CAMBRIDGE
UNIVERSITY PRESS

CAMBRIDGE
UNIVERSITY PRESS

Shaftesbury Road, Cambridge CB2 8EA, United Kingdom

One Liberty Plaza, 20th Floor, New York, NY 10006, USA

477 Williamstown Road, Port Melbourne, VIC 3207, Australia

314–321, 3rd Floor, Plot 3, Splendor Forum, Jasola District Centre, New Delhi – 110025, India

103 Penang Road, #05–06/07, Visioncrest Commercial, Singapore 238467

Cambridge University Press is part of Cambridge University Press & Assessment, a department of the University of Cambridge.

We share the University's mission to contribute to society through the pursuit of education, learning and research at the highest international levels of excellence.

www.cambridge.org
Information on this title: www.cambridge.org/9781009380409

DOI: 10.1017/9781108765381

First published 2021
First paperback edition 2023

A catalogue record for this publication is available from the British Library

Library of Congress Cataloging-in-Publication data
Names: Ansell, Christopher K., 1957– author. | Torfing, Jacob, author.
Title: Public governance as co-creation : a strategy for revitalizing the public sector and rejuvenating democracy / Christopher Ansell, Jacob Torfing.
Description: Cambridge, United Kingdom ; New York, NY : Cambridge University Press, 2021. | Series: Cambridge studies in comparative public policy | Includes bibliographical references and index.
Identifiers: LCCN 2020029343 (print) | LCCN 2020029344 (ebook) | ISBN 9781108487047 (hardback) | ISBN 9781108765381 (ebook)
Subjects: LCSH: Public administration – Decision making. | Public administration – Citizen participation. | Political planning – Citizen participation. | Public-private sector cooperation.
Classification: LCC JF1525.D4 A67 2020 (print) | LCC JF1525.D4 (ebook) | DDC 352.3/67–dc23
LC record available at https://lccn.loc.gov/2020029343
LC ebook record available at https://lccn.loc.gov/2020029344

ISBN   978-1-108-48704-7   Hardback
ISBN   978-1-009-38040-9   Paperback

To all those public, private, and civil society actors who endeavored to co-create innovative solutions in response to the coronavirus crisis that raged through the entire world in 2020 causing sorrow and despair and deepening social and economic problems.

Contents

Figures

Tables

Acknowledgments

One of the joys of academic life is the opportunity it affords to form close and lasting work relationships and friendships with colleagues from other nations. Our homes in Berkeley, California, and Roskilde, Denmark, are separated by a continent and an ocean – they are 8,750 kilometers (5,437 miles) apart. Yet whether working at a corner table in Café Milano in Berkeley or at the kitchen table in Mors, Denmark, or simply by Skype, we have somehow managed to find opportunities to work in the intense way demanded by a sustained book project. Some find it surprising that we work in a very traditional fashion – sitting side by side (physically or virtually) to line-edit each chapter.

Our wives, Suzanne Ryan and Eva Sørensen, have been central to this international camaraderie and have happily joined our downtime adventures – whether collecting fossils on a Danish beach, climbing Camel's Hump in Vermont, or sampling bagels in Montreal.

Eva has also been an essential partner in shaping the overall intellectual agenda that this book carries forward, and her own recent book *Interactive Political Leadership* provides deep complementary insights into the nature of contemporary governance.

In developing this book, we have been influenced and inspired by too many scholars to name them individually. But we would like to especially thank Tony Bovaird, Margaretha Breese, John Bryson, Barbara Crosby, Scott Douglas, Kirk Emerson, Alison Gash, Paul 't Hart, Satoshi Miura, Tina Nabatchi, Asbjørn Røiseland, and M. Ramesh. We would also like to thank the anonymous reviewer and our editors Joe Ng and Gemma Smith at Cambridge University Press. Special thanks to Lillian Ansell for her cover design.

The research conducted by Jacob Torfing in connection with this book has been supported by the EU Horizon project COGOV, grant number 770591.

Abbreviations

AEDs	automated external defibrillators
ARC	Austrian Red Cross
BCCA	British Columbia Citizens' Assembly
EPIM	European Program for Integration and Migration
ESF	European Social Fund
ICT	Information and Communications Technology
NEF	Network of European Foundations
NGOs	nongovernmental organizations
NPCC	National Policy Consensus Center
NPM	New Public Management
OC	online collaborations
UNICEF	United Nations Children's Fund

1 A New Public Governance Based on Co-creation

This book offers a new perspective on how public value can be produced through deliberate efforts at co-creation with the goal of transforming the public sector and improving democratic governance. By bringing politicians, public managers, citizens, and civil society organizations together in cross-boundary collaboration, the aim is to stimulate innovation and build ownership for bold solutions to challenging societal problems. A new public governance based on co-creation will create a new interface between public and private actors and help the public sector out of its current deadlock.

Western societies are governed through a combination of liberal democracy and public bureaucracy. Citizens participate in free and open elections and elect a government that controls a public bureaucracy in charge of implementing policies, regulating society, and delivering services. At the beginning of the 1970s, the successful expansion of liberal democracy and bureaucratic government gradually gave way to mounting criticisms of the long-term sustainability of the public sector (Crozier, Huntington, & Watanuki, 1975), the inefficiency and lack of responsiveness of public bureaucracy (Downs, 1967; Niskanen, 1971), and the failure of liberal democracy to maintain a high level of participation and trust in government and to prevent alienation of large sections of the population (Pateman, 1970; Barber, 1984; Norris, 2011).

The neoliberal response was to privatize or contract out public services, introduce an elaborate system of performance measurement, and turn citizens into customers who could supplement voting with a new ability to "vote with their feet." If they were free to leave a public service provider in favor of another public or private provider, so the theory went, they could hold the public sector accountable for the quality of the services they received (Hood, 1991; Pollitt & Bouckaert, 2004; Torfing & Triantafillou, 2013). However, after thirty years of New Public Management (NPM) reforms, the results seem to be meager (Hood & Dixon, 2015), and despite notable benefits (Osborne & Gaebler, 1992), the pathologies of privatization, contracting out, performance management, and the new service markets have become more and more visible (Dunleavy & Hood, 1994; Behn, 1998; Moynihan, 2008; Hjelmar, Petersen, & Vrangbæk, 2013; Petersen, Hjelmar, & Vrangbæk, 2017).

Advocates of alternatives to NPM have opted for a return either to the virtues of classical bureaucracy (Du Gay, 2000; Pollitt & Bouckaert, 2011) or to communitarian solutions that aim to create self-governing neighborhoods and communities based on active participation and deliberation (Barber, 1984; Hirst, 1994; Pateman, 2012). However, only a few public leaders seem prepared to return to an improved version of the kind of public bureaucracy that preceded NPM, and the call for self-governing communities seems futile in a world of interdependency in which no individual actor – public or private – has the ability to solve the complex problems confronting Western societies (Kooiman, 1993, 2003).

As such, we seem to be stuck in the mud and in need of new governance solutions that can help us to improve public policies and services, solve complex societal problems, strengthen social communities, and reinvigorate democracy. Our claim is that the elevation of co-creation to a core principle of public governance provides an attractive and feasible alternative to the false choice between Weberian bureaucracies based on hierarchical command and control, NPM reforms that run the public sector like a private business, and communitarian dreams of a society based on democratic self-government in small enclosed communities sheltered from the systemic power of the state and the market economy. A more attractive strategy, we argue, is to build a governance system based on cross-boundary collaboration that can spur public innovation while empowering communities and enhancing broad-based and distributed participation in public governance. In short, we need to develop a governance system founded on the co-creation of public value.

During the past decades of neoliberal ascendance, the public sector has suffered from a paralyzing inferiority complex. Advocates of neoliberalism praise private markets because competition incentivizes private companies to produce commodities and services valued by customers. By contrast, they portray the public sector as a parasite squandering the taxpayers' money on wasteful services and policy solutions that seldom solve the problems they are meant to solve. Against this background, it is easy to appreciate how public employees can become demotivated and lose faith in what they are doing. Hardworking and dedicated public employees are constantly being told that the only cure for the problems that weigh down the public sector is to privatize or contract out public services and to subject the remaining public employees to a strict control regime (Osborne & Gaebler, 1992; Barber, 2008).

Fortunately, researchers have gradually come to realize that the public sector – just like the private sector – is a value-producing entity in its own right. It might not produce private value validated by customers in private markets, but it produces public value defined as what adds value to the public sphere and is valued by citizens (Moore, 1995; O'Flynn, 2007; Bennington & Moore, 2011). The new focus on public value production is a game changer because it shifts attention away from insulated public bureaucracies and their auxiliary private for-profit or nonprofit contractors toward a novel appreciation of the manifold ways that public and private actors can contribute to public value production. While this argument is anticipated in the seminal work of Moore (1995), his primary concern is how public managers get the green light from their authorizing environment for new strategic plans for public value production, and how they subsequently build the necessary organizational capacities to implement these plans. As a result, his pathbreaking work has downplayed the role that a wider range of actors may play in public value production. More recently, however, there has been a growing appreciation of how citizens, civil society organizations, interest organizations, and private firms can supplement and assist public authorities and elected politicians in producing public value outcomes (Alford, 2010; Bryson, Crosby, & Bloomberg, 2014; Hartley et al., 2015; Bryson et al., 2017; Crosby, 't Hart, & Torfing, 2017).

In this vision of public value production, public and private actors are not merely working in parallel. Instead, by recognizing their mutual interdependence, they can share knowledge and coordinate their actions to avoid gaps and create synergies. They can exchange and pool their various resources and engage in collaborative interaction based on deliberation in order to identify needs, define problems, create joint solutions, and facilitate implementation. In short, public and private actors can co-create public value outcomes and the public sector can encourage this co-creation of public value by constructing platforms and arenas that allow relevant and affected actors to join forces and collaborate. Building on this insight, we claim that the advancement of co-creation as a core principle of public governance is a desirable and feasible option that will greatly improve the production of public value through its contribution to service improvement, innovative policy making, community building, and democratic renewal.

There has always been an element of co-creation in the public sector, *avant la lettre*. We propose that an expanded agenda for co-creation could become the backbone of a new public governance paradigm, one that initiates and sustains cross-boundary collaboration in order to stimulate public innovation and enhance our collective capacity for societal problem-solving. Turning co-creation into the constitutive principle of a new public governance paradigm will by no means eliminate centralized bureaucratic control and rulemaking or market-driven performance management. These government practices will remain auxiliary tools, but their modus operandi will be transformed so that they are better suited to support processes of co-creation.

By elevating "co-creation" from a sporadic practice taking place on the margins of the public sector to the cornerstone in the future development of public governance, this book offers a fresh perspective on public governance at a time when rising citizens' expectations for public service provision and the proliferation of complex societal problems collide with the public sector's efforts to make ends meet due to economic crisis, public spending cuts, and political unwillingness to raise taxes. Resource mobilization through the engagement of a broad range of public and private actors in the co-creation of public value outcomes offers a way out of this impasse.

For more than thirty years, the public sector has focused on how to use existing resources more efficiently. Rationalization efforts, productivity campaigns, and across-the-board cuts replaced the postwar expansion of the welfare state. Years of cutbacks have eliminated the slack in public service organizations, and further cuts in public expenditure are likely to hurt public employees, reduce service quality, and erode the political and professional capabilities of public authorities. In order to maintain its high ambitions on behalf of society and the economy, the public sector must find new ways of tapping into the resources of societal actors and thus create a new interface with society that can stimulate innovation and the development of new and better solutions through co-creation.

The concept of co-creation originally emerged in the private sector as a strategy for promoting growth and increasing profitability. As noted by several scholars (Osborne, Radnor, & Nasi, 2013; Osborne & Strokosch, 2013), this strategy is also highly relevant for public service delivery. However, the implications of adopting a co-creation perspective on the production of public value outcomes have not yet been fully explored. Despite a growing body of literature on co-production and co-creation in public service delivery (Pestoff & Brandsen, 2008; Brandsen, Steen, & Verschuere, 2018a), only a few authors have sought to broaden the focus from service production to policy making, societal problem-solving, and democratic participation or to elevate co-creation to a new perspective on how public governance is conducted in our complex, fragmented, and multilayered societies (Ansell & Torfing, 2014; Torfing, Sørensen, & Røiseland, 2019). The goal of this book is to provide a scholarly contribution to the academic and political debate on how public governance can mobilize the resources, ideas, and energies needed to co-create solutions to the problems and challenges confronting modern societies. Our book offers a new and comprehensive account of co-creation as a public governance paradigm.

Co-creation is premised on the idea that public organizations can work collaboratively with relevant and affected actors to develop innovative solutions to our most pressing problems. To realize this ambitious agenda, however, we must go beyond the current status of "co-creation" as a magic concept (Pollitt & Hupe, 2011) and explore what it will take for scholars and practitioners to turn it into a realistic strategy for governing contemporary societies. This is precisely what we intend to do by conducting a thorough investigation of the complexities and dynamics of co-creation as a mode of governance.

Our ambition is to write a book that combines scientific rigor with sociological imagination and societal impact. As such, we will draw on state-of-the-art research on interactive, collaborative, and networked governance; recent studies of co-production, co-creation, and co-governance; the new scholarship on open, social, and collaborative innovation and design thinking; and recent developments in collaborative leadership theory. We will combine theoretical studies with experiences from innovation hubs and living labs, empirical illustrations from different parts of the world, and our own studies of co-creation processes in different policy areas. We will explore the limitations of existing research and reflect on how it can be extended and extrapolated in order to imagine what a public sector based on co-creation would look like and what it would take to get there. As such, we aim to discover and enlarge practices, institutions, and forms of leadership and management that are conducive for the advancement of co-creation as an organizing principle for the future development of the public sector. In sum, we believe that this book may be of use for both scholars and students interested in public administration and public policy and for practitioners aiming to pilot public-sector reforms.

1.1 What Is Co-creation?

We have already talked a lot about co-creation without providing a clear definition of the term. Since we provide a more elaborate discussion of how to define co-creation in Chapter 2, we restrict our discussion here to a brief and concise clarification of what co-creation is and what it is not. Co-creation is tentatively defined as *the process through which a broad range of interdependent actors engage in distributed, cross-boundary collaboration in order to define common problems and design and implement new and better solutions*. The actors may be relevant and affected individuals, groups, or organizations either from the public, private for-profit or nonprofit sectors, or from civil society. Recognition of their mutual dependency brings the actors together in collaborative processes that cut across the boundaries between different levels, sectors, and organizations. Ideally, these collaborative processes will involve joint attempts to assess and define problems and challenges; to design and test new solutions; and to select, implement, evaluate, and consolidate the most promising ones. However, in reality, participation in different parts of the co-creation process may vary considerably and be more or less inclusive. In any case, the intention of co-creation is to contribute to public value production. This may occur through continuous improvement of existing practices, the development of innovative solutions that disrupt the common wisdom and practice in a particular area, or the development of empowered participation in new interactive forms of governance that help to build democratic ownership.

As with all other concepts such as governance, innovation, and trust-based management that have been embraced by public-sector entrepreneurs (Pollitt & Hupe, 2011), there is imminent risk that the notion of co-creation will be misunderstood due to its newness and lack of conceptual precision, misconstrued by people who are skeptical toward the idea of a new public governance based on co-creation and thus want to discredit it, or misused by those looking for a way to legitimize what they are doing by dressing it up in a fancy new language. To mitigate the risk of misunderstandings and conceptual abuse, let us briefly point out what co-creation is not.

First of all, while co-creation involves multi-actor collaboration, it cannot be reduced to the collaborative process itself and does not aim to advance collaboration for the sake of collaborating. Collaboration is an increasingly popular term in a public sector suffering from coordination problems rooted in the administrative compartmentalization of the public sector and the contracting out of services to a diverse set of private service providers. Cross-boundary collaboration is called for, but co-creation does more than facilitate knowledge-sharing, coordination, and problem-solving through crosscutting interaction and deliberation. Co-creation uses collaboration as a tool for creating new solutions to challenging problems and needs as well as for fostering resilient communities and new forms of democratic participation and ownership. There is a creative element inherent to co-creation that is not necessarily found in all forms of collaboration.

Second, although co-creation presupposes participation of active citizens and resourceful stakeholders, it does not rest on conventional forms of participatory democracy conducted through citizen panels, town-hall meetings, public hearings, or referenda. Unlike traditional forms of both representative and participatory democracy, co-creation does not presuppose mass participation of the individual members of a unified demos. Instead, it opts for participation of a broad but selective group of relevant and affected actors that together constitute one of many demoi (Bohman, 2005). Moreover, co-creation does not strive to merely enhance societal participation in predesigned or mandated public decision-making processes. Rather, it aims to construct a new interface between the state and the public sphere that harnesses both the public sector's attempt to engage citizens and relevant stakeholders in an open-ended problem-oriented dialogue *and* the effort of citizens and stakeholders to engage public authorities in community-based problem-solving strategies. In short, co-creation goes beyond "citizen engagement" by insisting that both public and private actors can initiate co-creation and invite other relevant and affected actors to participate in processes meant to enhance input and output legitimacy (Skelcher & Torfing, 2010).

Third, contracting out of public services to private firms based on a classical purchaser–provider model and standard principal–agent theory has nothing to do with co-creation. Conceived from the vantage point of standard principal–agent theory, contracts create hierarchical relationships between purchasers and providers and competitive relationships between providers that discourage collaboration and knowledge-sharing. Standard outsourcing contracts tend to define outputs and outcomes in ways that leave little space for a joint search for new and better solutions. However, the growing recognition of the incompleteness of contracts and negative impacts of high-powered incentives has led to a shift toward relational contracting (Jensen & Stonecash, 2005; Brown, Potoski, & Slyke, 2006), where processes, outputs, and outcomes are continuously adjusted through an ongoing collaboration between public and private actors. This shift may occasionally open up for co-creation, especially if the two parties trust each other and are willing to manage the risks associated with an innovative approach to service improvement.

Finally, it would be a grave mistake to infer that political attempts to downsize the public sector by shifting social and economic responsibilities and risks to citizens and local communities have anything to do with co-creation. Although co-creation taps into the resources of citizens and societal actors, and thus may help to cushion the decline of public welfare in times of economic crisis where tax revenues are shrinking, it is not the human face of public spending cuts. Politicians might try to sell public budget cuts as a part of a deliberate strategy to empower citizens and local communities by relying on their capacity to do what the public sector used to do (this was the core idea of the former British prime minister David Cameron's vision of "Big Society"), but abdicating the responsibility for social welfare provision is not the same as co-creating outcomes. By contrast, co-creation presupposes a firm commitment of both public and private actors to work together to enhance the production of public value outcomes.

1.2 Why Is Co-creation a New and Powerful Vision?

When schoolkids do their homework, when patients obediently do the knee-strengthening exercises prescribed by their doctor after surgery, and when parents help kindergarten staff organize the annual excursion to the local zoo, they are in a sense co-creating public services. When citizens volunteer in the local elderly home, the fire brigade, or the hospital, they contribute to the production of services for others. We claim that the concept of co-creation goes a step further. The ambition of co-creation is more expansive. For example, it may engage lead users and frontline personnel in efforts to reform entire service systems to make them more effective and user-friendly; it may encourage citizens and communities to work with planners, local developers, and the police to develop strategies for neighborhood regeneration and crime prevention; and it may bring public and private stakeholders together to formulate and implement new policies and regulatory frameworks in response to pressing societal problems. At the highest level of ambition, co-creation encourages distributed problem-solving through cross-boundary collaboration between relevant and affected actors who together define the problems and design and implement new and creative solutions.

Elevating the status of co-creation from a name for the active involvement of service users in public service production to the core principle for governing modern societies reconfigures the public sector and transforms our understanding of its role and nature. From its status as a "public authority" and a "service provider," the public sector becomes a "platform and arena for co-creation."

In the past, when classical public administration was the primary lens for thinking about and organizing public governance, the public sector was primarily perceived as a "public authority" that uses laws, regulations, and social policies to govern society and the economy. To most citizens and private firms, the public sector appeared as an almighty legal authority capable of prohibiting, prescribing, and sanctioning particular forms of behavior; granting rights, permissions, and access to social services; and keeping order in society through the actual and anticipated display of legitimate physical and symbolic violence. People would contact frontline staff and public-sector professionals when they needed a building permit or wanted to enroll their kid in the local school. The problem with this type of relationship is that it leaves citizens feeling disempowered vis-à-vis the power, authority, and expertise of public professionals such as doctors, schoolteachers, judges, policemen, case managers, and so on. When eventually they were granted certain permissions or given access to particular services and cash benefits, the citizens were expected to be thankful and to readily accept the professional judgment of well-meaning but somewhat paternalistic public employees. As such, there was no doubt about the hierarchy between the powerful public authorities based on a combination of legal rationality and professional expertise and the disempowered population that was relegated to the role of "subjects" and "social clients."

From the late 1960s and onward, the hierarchical relation between citizens and public authorities came under heavy attack. The educational revolution made people more knowledgeable and self-confident, and the antiauthoritarian revolt questioned all forms of authority, including that of public authorities. The subordination of citizens to the exercise of public authority by a steadily growing public sector was criticized by both the left and the right for underestimating the capacities of citizens and giving too much power to public institutions and public professionals. While left-wing intellectuals in Europe subscribed to Habermas' critique of the political and economic systems' colonialization of the citizens' lifeworld (Habermas, 1985), neoliberal politicians and commentators in the Anglophone world criticized the paternalistic "nanny state," sought to roll back the welfare state, and sought to give the citizens a free choice between public and private service providers (Osborne & Gaebler, 1992).

In continental Europe, the neoliberal wave of privatizations and cutbacks hit the bulwark of the highly entrenched welfare state, but the less radical reform discourse of NPM started to spread to most countries, although at an uneven pace and with different levels of impact (Pollitt & Bouckaert, 2004). New Public Management had a new vision of the public sector that changed the relation between citizens and public service organizations. The public sector was no longer viewed as a public authority, but as a "service provider." Citizens were perceived as rational and capable customers who should be able to choose between an array of public and private service providers operating in newly created service markets. The free choice of service provider would empower the service users and help to ensure that their needs were properly served. Competition between the service providers to attract customers would force public service organizations to be more responsive and to cut their costs while improving quality.

To take up the competitive challenge from the private providers of public services, public managers were expected to act strategically and use performance technologies from the private sector and a combination of transactional and transformational leadership to discipline and motivate public professionals to be more service-minded. Le Grand (2003) succinctly captures the transformation of the role of citizens and public employees when he talks about the citizens' transformation from disempowered "pawns" to capable "queens" and the reconceptualization of public professionals from "knights" to "knaves." New Public Management sought to discipline the "knaves" through a combination of marketization and manager-ialism so that they would provide better and less costly service to the "queens."

The citizens who once were conceived as "voters," "legal subjects," and "social clients" were increasingly perceived as "customers" oper-ating in a market with choice and exit options. This transformation of the role of citizens turns out to be the Achilles' heel of NPM. The more citizens begin to act as individualistic and rational customers rather than democratic, community-oriented citizens, the more they will raise their demands and complain about the quality of what they actually get, and the less they will see themselves as a part of the solution and as responsible for the wider community to which they belong. The ultim-ate consequence is that the public sector will participate in a race that it can never win as the demands will rise faster than the available resources. In the long run this will erode the popular support to the public sector and trust in government.

Faced with these negative consequences of NPM and the need to meet social needs and solve complex societal problems such as climate change, gang-related crime, homelessness, and traffic congestion in big cities, the public sector has started to look for a new vision and a new way of conceptualizing and organizing relations between public and private actors. Advocates of new public governance (Osborne, 2006, 2010; Torfing & Triantafillou, 2013; Ansell & Torfing, 2014; Morgan & Cook, 2014) talk about the role of networks, partnerships, and collaborative governance, and they advance a new vision of the public sector as a "platform and arena for co-creation." This vision aims to shift attention away from the public sector's function as a "public authority" and a "service provider." Instead, it focuses on the collaborative interaction between public and private actors and on how this interaction can create new and better services, regulations, policies, and societal solutions while simultaneously empowering citizens, communities, and stakeholders as responsible partners with democratic ownership to joint solutions.

The new vision of the public sector builds upon and critically extends existing practices and traditions of public and private collaboration. While extant forms of corporatism, lobbyism, public contracting, and procurement are based on collaboration between public and private actors, they only involve a few privileged actors and often take the rational pursuit of interests and the need for interest mediation as the point of departure. Perceived as a mode of governance, co-creation aims to broaden the range of participants to include lay actors and to shift the focus in the direction of resource mobilization, creative problem-solving, and democratic decision making.

Such a shift might be difficult to imagine in policy areas dominated by distributive and redistributive struggles in which the social and political actors are locked into particular positions. However, deliberate attempts to disrupt the current political culture and the development of new strategies for reframing problems, agendas and potential outcomes may help to move public governance in a new direction. Thus, the advancement of co-creation hinges on a reorganization of power that seeks to replace narrow, zero-sum games with broader, and positive-sum games. By deepening participation beyond the traditional public and private elites, public solutions can be more effective and capable of producing more winners.

Central to this effort to expand the scope for co-creation is the transformation of the role perceptions of the key participants in co-creation. Ideally, citizens will transform their role perception from "customers" to "active citizens." Public employees will change their role perception from "service providers" to "co-creators." Public managers will transform their role perception from "directors" to "facilitators." Elected politicians will change their role perception from "sovereign decision-makers" to "interactive political leaders." Private firms and interest organizations will convert their role perception from "self-interested lobbyists" to "social partners." Civil society organizations will shift their role perception from "untainted alternative providers" to "co-producers of joint solutions." Such transformations in role perceptions are tough because the old roles provide a guide for how to act appropriately in different contexts (March & Olsen, 1995), but the roles are likely to change if the overall discourse of how to govern and be governed is changing. Ultimately, transformation of the discourse of public governance and changes in role perceptions of key actors are mutually dependent and will have to co-evolve.

The new vision of the public sector as a platform and arena for the co-creation of public value has three important implications: first, it introduces a new focus on synergistic resource mobilization; second, it develops a more generative approach to public governance; and third, it transforms democratic governance in ways that foster more active and direct participation. Let's briefly look at each of these implications in turn.

The *first* implication concerns the need to mobilize resources that can help the public sector achieve its high political and professional ambitions. The basic idea of traditional forms of public bureaucracy is to use public money collected through taxes to hire competent public employees who design and implement public solutions authorized by the political principals and to purchase the necessary facilities and equipment to facilitate goal achievement. Each program and agency typically has a certain number of people and facilities at their disposal when delivering services, regulations, infrastructures, or policies. Resource sharing and resource pooling across departments are rare as programs and agencies compete for scarce funding and are prepared to fight to protect their turf. Consequently, programs and agencies must rely on in-house resources when producing results. Yet rising public expenditure, economic crisis, and political opposition to tax increases make it difficult for the public sector to make ends meet.

New Public Management claimed that competition would help to drive public costs down and quality up and thus to get more for less. Private contractors now supplement the work of public service providers. Evidence of their comparative cost efficiency is inconclusive (Brogaard, Sørensen, & Torfing, 2019), but even if they do help to lower the costs of public service provision, the private contractors do not bring additional resources to the table. Their service provision is paid for by public money that would otherwise have been paid to public service providers doing the same job.

As a result, the public sector remains caught in a cross fire between rising expectations about the availability and quality of public roads, services, and benefits and the increasingly scarce resources of cash-strapped programs and agencies. A systematic effort to co-create public value will help the public sector to escape this predicament. Co-creation mobilizes new and important resources such as experience with problems and current solutions (users), knowledge about causalities (researchers and consultants), creativeness (nongovernmental organizations (NGOs) and social entrepreneurs), access to new business models and technologies (private firms), dedicated manpower (volunteers), organizational support and visions (politicians), leadership skills (public managers) and implementation capacity (frontline staff). Private actors offer their resources voluntarily because they have a stake in the problem, challenge or task, get some personal enjoyment or benefit from exchanging or pooling resources with other actors, or are driven by more altruistic reasons embedded in their socially constructed roles and identities.

The *second* implication concerns the changing modus operandi of the public sector. Although, in principle, co-creation of public value can be initiated by a broad range of public or private actors, it often falls on public leaders and agencies to convene the manifold actors, facilitate collaborative interaction, and drive co-creation processes forward to meet the expectations of the participants. Not only does the public sector have the necessary skills and resources to take the lead, but it also has a huge interest in the resource mobilization that co-creation makes possible.

The effort to initiate and spur co-creation introduces a new way of working in the public sector. Normally, public agencies are in charge of the entire process of public governance from the initial political decision to do something to the final implementation and evaluation of concrete interventions. Co-creation interrupts the flow of communication and action in the public implementation chain by involving relevant and affected actors in a collaborative effort to define and solve problems in new and perhaps more creative, effective, and democratic ways. This move involves deliberative efforts to construct platforms and arenas that can catalyze and support co-creation (Ansell & Gash, 2017). We shall later define platforms and arenas as generative mechanisms that facilitate the emergence of collaborative processes. Making co-creation a core principle of public governance requires a shift toward generativity as a core strategy for stimulating open-ended co-creation processes that are enabled but not controlled by the platforms and arenas that provide their conditions of emergence. In short, this means that the public sector will have to replace its standard "how-can-our agency-do-this" thinking with a new "how-can-our agency-do-this -together with-other-relevant-actors" thinking. In metaphorical terms, the public sector will have to construct coral reefs that attract and nurture ecologies of marine animals that will interact and produce ecosystems with particular impacts on their environment.

The *third* implication concerns the effort to renew and expand democratic governance. Traditional forms of representative democracy through which voters elect politicians to govern on their behalf until the next election are increasingly supplemented by new forms of citizen engagement that aim to bring elected politicians, citizens, and local communities closer together in order to enhance democratic legitimacy. The public sector's attempt to strengthen citizen engagement is often tokenistic, merely relying on conventional forms of citizen engagement based on participation in public meetings and hearings and thin forms of participation based on crowdsourcing and crowdfunding.

Making co-creation a core principle of public governance will boost thick participation that allows politicians, citizens, and a host of other actors to explore problems and solutions through open-ended dialogue that leads to common decisions and actions and produces joint owner-ship over the solutions (Nabatchi & Leighninger 2015: 14). Thick participation moves citizen engagement beyond tokenistic attempts to give citizens in general and intensely affected actors in particular a chance to be heard and state their complaints. It involves a plethora of private actors, including citizens, in public governance in order to shape public outputs and societal outcomes. Private actors are not merely involved because an established democratic norm dictates that affected actors should have a chance to influence public decision mak-ing, but rather because the empowered participation of a broad range of actors will lead to well-informed, smart, and innovative solutions and will build democratic and resilient communities better equipped to meet future challenges. In short, co-creation directly addresses the trade-off between effective and democratic governance.

1.3 The Current Demands and Possibilities for Co-creation

A unique opportunity exists to expand co-creation beyond the extant forms of co-production in public service delivery and the emerging attempts to co-create service systems and planning solutions (Osborne & Strokosch, 2013). The timing is perfect because the public sector is facing four serious problems that a turn toward co-creation will help to solve and because a large number of factors support the development of a new governance paradigm based on co-creation.

The first problem is the *service problem*. Public services aim to meet basic needs for social protection, education, gainful employment, health care, equal opportunities and so on. In countries where the middle class has access to a broad range of public services and benefits and where NPM has turned the population into demanding customers, the expectations about the availability, quality, and individualization of public services is growing. These expectations are probably intensified by the digitalization of markets, which massively customizes and speeds the delivery of private goods and services. At the same time, public money is increasingly scarce and productivity gains are slow due to the labor-intensive character of public service production. This dilemma puts a squeeze on public service provision and raises the perennial question of how to provide an adequate amount of high quality services at low cost.

Even if public money was plentiful, there would be no guarantee that public services would meet the expectations of citizens. Citizens' needs and demands tend to vary and there is no one size that fits all. Judging from recent experiences, neither the discretion of well-intended, paternalistic professionals in schools, hospitals, job centers, and social agencies nor the introduction of new exit mechanisms such as free choice of service providers have ensured a satisfactory alignment of the needs of citizens and local communities and the public provision of welfare and physical infrastructures. As such, the public sector continues to wrestle with the question of how to ensure that public services match citizens' needs and demands. In sum, the service problem consists of finding new ways to facilitate the production of a sufficient supply of low cost, high quality services that actually meet the needs and demands of different groups of citizens. We might not need to reinvent the wheel and create huge innovations to solve the service problem, but we need to develop new ways of working with service production in order to ensure its continuous improvement.

The second problem is the *policy problem*. It is not that we lack policies. Many will agree that we probably have too many policies since we tend to add new policies with a shovel and take them away with a pair of tweezers. The problem is rather that in many areas there is a mismatch between policies and problems as the actual policies fail to address the problems that confront modern societies. The failure to provide robust policy solutions to a broad range of problems such as inner-city poverty, drug abuse, sustainable food security, soaring CO_2 emissions, financial instability, unequal access to health, education, and employment, the spread of multiresistant bacteria, inhuman treatment of animals in factory farming, is caused by political and institutional factors as well as by the nature and character of the problems themselves.

Beginning with political factors, adversarial and ideologically charged politics block creative problem-solving and the search for pragmatic policy solutions (Torfing & Ansell, 2017). In addition, the political nature of problems and the limited capacity of public leaders to find and process evidence of what works in different contexts tend to discourage evidence-based policy making (Howlett, 2009; Ansell & Geyer, 2017). At the same time, bold, forward-looking political leadership is undermined by the development of tunnel vision, decoupling, and insulation (Kjær & Opstrup, 2016). Politicians tend to develop tunnel vision as a result of spending too much time in the sector-specific committee work that is preoccupied with technical details. The decoupling of politicians from policy making is a result of the growing influence of public managers and special policy advisors who have better education, more knowledge and experience and a broader network of contacts with key stakeholders than the politicians. Finally, the insulation of political decision makers from ordinary citizens and relevant stakeholders is a result of the relegation of the elected politicians to the role of a board of directors that seldom engages in detailed policy discussion, but focuses attention on overall goal and framework steering and handling the media to secure their reelection.

Institutional factors further contribute to an explanation of the policy problem. The development of a multilevel governance system and the functional differentiation of policy sectors creates a fragmented polity in which it is not always clear where policy problems are best dealt with and how other levels and sectors can contribute to designing robust policy solutions (Hooghe & Marks, 2001; Bache & Flinders, 2004).

In addition to these political and institutional factors, we must not forget the wicked character of many policy problems, which tends to make them hard to solve (Rittel & Webber, 1973). Wicked problems are difficult to define and their causes are complex, encouraging vague and conflicting goals with solutions that are difficult to measure and where room for failure is limited. Although we must be careful not to overestimate the wickedness of public problems, which tend to differ in their degree of complexity and conflict (Head & Alford, 2015), there seems to be little doubt that many problems cannot be solved simply by having the right knowledge and skills.

For all these reasons, the policy problem consists of a failure to match problems and solutions. There is a shortage of well-designed policies that hit the target and should they eventually emerge, implementation failures might prevent them from having their full impact (Ansell, Sørensen & Torfing, 2017).

The third problem is the *community problem,* which concerns local communities' ability to deal effectively with old and emerging problems by mobilizing local resources and capacities. There is no reason for the public sector to interfere in people's lives if they can sort out their personal, social, and local problems by themselves, but the capacity for personal and collective action depends on the social bonds that people have with each other. This insight is at the core of the research on social capital, defined as the things we can do by drawing on our trustful relations with other people (Putnam, 1995). The problem is that social capital is in decline. Socioeconomic downturns, ongoing individualization processes, changing family structures, new post-materialist dividing lines, and participation in globalized mass consumption – including mass consumption of television, digital streaming services, and online gaming – are frequently quoted as sources of the progressive erosion of the social cohesion of civil society and the decline of social capital (Putnam, 1995; Castiglione, Deth, & Wolleb, 2008).

Social capital involves bonding with members of one's own group, bridging the gulf separating one group from other groups and linking civil society to public decision makers. While bonding capital is susceptible to processes that make us turn inward toward our own personal and domestic life, bridging and linking capital is heavily influenced by democratic forms of governance and particular political-administrative cultures. Some countries give precedence to traditional forms of electoral democracy, which tend to promote a technocratic political culture over participatory and deliberative forms of democracy that encourage different groups in society to communicate. These countries may inadvertently contribute to the decline of bridging and linking capital and thus to the erosion of the capacity of local citizens and civil society to deal with old and emerging problems.

The presence of social capital enhances the collective capacity of local communities to act and find robust solutions to local problems and challenges, but the task of creating spaces for the mobilization of social capital, spurring deliberation, and giving direction to processes of local problem-solving, often falls on civic leaders. Civic leadership (Cuoto, 2014) is exercised outside the realm of the state and often without the leaders having any formal position and authority or capability to use organizational resources and coercive tools to support their leadership. Civic leaders are locally embedded "elites" that lead the development of local communities by getting people to take responsibility and initiative. They are not necessarily recognized as leaders but play a crucial role in catalyzing collective action. Civic leadership is enhanced by education and the rise of social movements and community organizations, but the local elites capable of exercising civic leadership may decline in numbers either because increasing affluence makes it possible for them to move to new high-end neighborhoods (Self, 2005) or because de-location of private corporations, public institutions, or public–private utility companies force them to move (Heying, 1997).

The fourth and last problem is the *democratic problem* related to the present challenges to liberal democracy, defined as a democratic system based on free and equal mass participation that aims to narrow the gap between what people want and what they get. On the one hand, the institutions of liberal democracy appear to be robust enough to withstand the pressures arising from the growing power of the corporate sector, the persistence of policy gridlocks and the rise of authoritarian right-wing populism. On the other hand, liberal democracy is challenged by democratic disenchantment, the rise of anti-politics, greater political polarization, and the development of counter-democracy.

Democratic disenchantment concerns the scale of discontent with and disengagement from formal political processes in established democracies (Dalton, 1999; Stoker, 2006a). This disenchantment is evidenced by the decline of traditional patterns of participation – including voter turnout and party membership – and the decline of trust in government (Warren, 2002; Norris, 2011). While this decline is partly explained by the rise of anti-politics, where citizens turn strongly against the way that politics is conducted by allegedly self-serving politicians engaged in mudslinging and vote catching stunts, it is also explained by the fact that many citizens apparently want more from democracy than the occasional visit to the ballot box (Warren, 2002).

While democratic disenchantment and anti-politics account for the decline in some forms of democratic participation, political polarization provides a different threat to democracy. Political polarization is both happening along traditional ideological, socioeconomic, and racial lines of division and along new antagonistic frontiers based on identity-related issues pertaining to sexual orientation, ethnicity, culture, and lifestyle. While liberal democracy thrives on passionate political debate between groups with different views and opinions, the development of antagonistic conflict – in which the combatants promote their own identity in uncompromising ways and seek to crush their opponents – tends to destroy the democratic conversation that builds on mutual respect (Mouffe, 2000).

A final concern is the gradual development of a counter-democracy in which citizens are cast as veto-players capable of opposing local planning proposals in public hearings, complaining about service quality as members of public user boards, expressing their dissatisfaction with public service provision by exiting their service provider, and attacking politicians via social media. Counter-democracy is partly a result of citizen engagement going bad because political decision makers hesitate to give citizens any real influence by engaging them in public governance debates through thick participation (Rosanvallon, 2008). Counter-democracy turns citizens into distrustful spoilsports and thus prevents political decision makers from learning about real problems and needs and the solutions they may call for. These challenges to liberal democracy do not mean that democracy is terminally ill, but there are signs of an unhealthy development that must be cured.

The four problems that call for the development of new forms of public governance are summarized in Table 1.1.

Our claim is that co-creation provides a solution to these four problems. Co-creation will neither be the only nor the ultimate solution, but it provides a plausible way of tackling the aforementioned problems. The book as a whole intends to explain and substantiate the inherent promise of co-creation. Let us briefly consider the core arguments.

Table 1.1 *Summary of problems that call for new forms of public governance*

Problem type	Problem description
The service problem	The public sector is caught in a cross fire between the citizens' growing and increasingly diversified service expectations and the scarcity of public resources that makes it difficult to meet these expectations
The policy problem	Political and institutional factors prevent governments from providing robust policy solutions to complex societal problems that call for political action
The community problem	The decline of social capital and the progressive erosion of social cohesion and civic leadership prevent civil society and local communities from fostering robust self-organized solutions to pressing problems
The democratic problem	Democratic disenchantment, political polarization, and the development of a new form of resistance democracy undermine the established forms of liberal representative democracy

First, the *service problem* will be greatly alleviated because co-creation brings additional resources to the table and thus helps the public sector to shoulder the burden of the rising expectations from citizens and private stakeholders. Involving citizens, such as volunteers, civil society organizations, and private firms, in the co-creation of public value will not only mobilize new and important resources, but also serve to create more realistic expectations about the public sector's ability to provide services and solve societal problems. Co-creation of service systems and concrete services with users and their relatives also serves to orient public services toward the needs of service recipients. However, it is important to stress that co-creation is not merely about responding to the demands of service users, but about discovering the needs behind these demands and exploring how these are best met. In sum, co-creation will help to ensure continuous improvement of public services in response to the needs of citizens while simultaneously mobilizing resources and making service expectations more realistic.

Second, the *policy problem* will be relieved since co-creation will seek to engage a broad network of actors from different organizations, sectors, and levels in exploring the problems and challenges at hand and in designing matching policy solutions. If elected politicians participate in networked policy deliberations, which will force them to adopt more pragmatic problem-focused behavior, they will gain a deeper knowledge and understanding by being exposed to evidence and narratives presented by relevant and affected actors and by engaging in debates in which they will have to provide reasons in support of their ideas and proposals. The broader the range of actors involved in the process of co-creation, the more depth and nuance it will add to the politicians' understanding of problems and solutions.

In short, co-creation breaks down the insulation of elected politicians from the policy networks controlled by public managers or strong interest groups. The direct and unmediated interaction between politicians, citizens, and stakeholders can foster an interactive political leadership (Torfing & Ansell, 2017) that will not only improve the quality of policy making, but also help to muster support for the implementation of new policy solutions (Ansell, Sørensen, & Torfing, 2017). While the attempt to solve wicked problems benefits from the development of a common knowledge base consisting of widely accepted facts, theories, and experiences, reasoned debate will not lead to an ultimate solution due to inherent complexities and trade-offs. Most often, existing solutions will not do the trick. Wicked problems call for creative problem-solving and innovative solutions, and here co-creation has particular strength. The actors involved in co-creation will tend to disturb the entrenched forms of knowledge, beliefs, and ideas in a given policy area and the cognitive and ideational disruption will stimulate critical and transformative learning and foster innovative policy solutions supported by a strong coalition of actors willing to test and revise the new solutions until they are considered to be good enough and ready for upscaling. In sum, co-creation facilitates the development of more effective and integrated policy solutions that match the nature and character of the problem.

Third, the *community problem* will be mitigated by a turn to public governance based on co-creation as a core principle. Co-creation will neither halt the cultural trends toward a growing individualism and the addictive use of television and other forms of cultural mass consumption nor stop ongoing globalization and recurrent economic slumps. However, co-creation will bring citizens, community organizations, private firms, public employees and managers, and elected politicians closer together in a myriad of mini-publics that sometimes will take on the character of communities of destiny that rise and fall with their ability to deal with the urgent problem or challenge they address.

Co-creation will build bridging and linking capital (Agger & Jensen, 2015) and enhance social cohesion of local communities. The empowerment of local communities through participation in co-creating solutions to pressing problems will tend to enhance their resilience, defined as their ability to bounce back with little or no assistance when they are hit by new and (re-) emerging socioeconomic problems, natural hazards, or cultural threats (Manyena, 2006). Indeed, co-creation will not only strengthen local communities, but also generate broader functional communities by bringing actors from different localities, regions, and countries together in national or global communities for dealing with wicked and unruly problems (Scharpf, 1997; Lasker & Weiss, 2003; Pan & Leidner, 2003). In sum, co-creation will have an important community-building effect.

Finally, the *democratic problem* will be partly resolved by co-creation that provides new venues for thick participation. Co-creation gives citizens the ability to participate more actively and more directly in public governance and value creation. Widening the venues and efficacy of democratic participation is likely to strengthen ownership of both political solutions and democratic institutions. It will also allow politicians to become more visible to the public and demonstrate their commitment to solving pressing problems and their willingness to communicate more directly and responsively with actors that are affected by particular problems and have relevant input to their solution. This might help to combat anti-political sentiments that basically regard politicians as a self-serving menace to society.

Although it may be difficult to expand co-creation in contexts characterized by polarized ideological or identity-related conflicts, co-creation may help to civilize antagonistic conflicts by inviting relevant and affected actors to participate in problem-focused debate on how concrete problems can be solved in pragmatic ways that go beyond the least common denominator. As such, the growing commitment to co-creation as a mode of governance may rebuild and cultivate the kind of democratic conversation that we need today. Such a conversation might help to connect those who have an interest in solving a particular problem with those who have the power to solve it (Bryson, Cunningham, & Lokkesmoe, 2002). As we shall discuss

Table 1.2 *Summary of how co-creation may solve important governance problems*

Problem type	The way that co-creation may solve the problem
The service problem	Co-creation helps to make service expectations more realistic while simultaneously mobilizing societal resources in the production of public services and ensuring that the services delivered meet the needs of the citizens
The policy problem	Co-creation spurs innovationbased on mutual and transformative learning and thus helps foster more effective and integrated policy solutions to wicked policy problems
The community problem	Co-creation brings together a diversity of social actors and thus helps to build bridging and linking capital, enhance social cohesion, and create more resilient communities
The democratic problem	Co-creation widens and deepens democratic participation in deliberative forms of public governance and helps to reconnect elected politicians with the citizens they are supposed to represent

more thoroughly later, co-creation holds the promise of developing an interactive democracy that supplements aggregative democratic procedures for making authoritative decisions with a more integrative view on democracy based on the construction of arenas for democratic participation and deliberation.

Table 1.2 briefly summarizes how co-creation may solve the four governance problems confronting Western societies.

1.4 Enablers of Co-creation

Co-creation is worth studying and expanding because it allows us to address some of the key problems of our time. Seen from the perspective of the predominance of hierarchical government and the recent infatuation with market-based governance, co-creation may appear to be a utopian dream. However, as we shall see, there are already numerous examples of co-creation and growing efforts to advance it. More importantly, the current expansion of co-creation builds on a number of enablers that makes co-created governance a viable future for the public sector. We distinguish five such enablers.

The *first enabler* is the crisis of the predominant governance paradigms known as Classical Public Administration and NPM (Osborne, 2010; Torfing & Triantafillou, 2013) and the growing need for mobilizing societal resources to meet citizens' needs and to solve wicked and unruly problems (Koppenjan & Klijn, 2004; Warren, 2009). While these governance paradigms still have a huge practical and political impact, they are increasingly discredited by their relative inability to spur public innovation and mobilize new resources. As such, political leaders and public managers increasingly recognize the need to involve societal actors in public governance, which leads to a new kind of governance-driven democratization (Warren, 2009).

The *second enabler* is the rise of more assertive citizens with sufficient knowledge, competences, and political self-confidence to engage in dialogue with political and administrative decision makers on a relatively even footing. New generations of citizens are better educated; enlightened by the easy access to knowledge; molded by new anti-authoritarian sentiments; and driven by emancipative values praising gender equality, environmental protection, and equal access to public welfare. They are less allegiant and more assertive than before (Dalton & Welzel, 2014) and are rapidly becoming "everyday makers" that engage in ad hoc activities aiming to improve their living conditions and their quality of life (Bang & Sørensen, 1989).

The *third enabler* is the growth and strengthening of civil society organizations in what is known as the third sector. The number of NGOs has grown, their scope and reach have expanded, they are becoming more and more professional, and there is a growing differentiation among different types of NGOs engaged in different areas (Stiles, 2002; Martens, 2005). In addition, their relations to public agencies are becoming more and more institutionalized. Hence, the prospect for involving them in co-creation of public solutions is increasing. If social movements previously seemed to be heavily engaged in anti-establishment and anti-government struggles, they have become much more constructive, pragmatic, and solution-oriented and keen to engage in local experimentation and social innovation. Hence, it is hardly surprising that the 17th of the United Nations Sustainable Development Goals claims that all the previous goals should be achieved in and through the formation of multi-actor partnerships bringing together government and civil society.

The *fourth enabler* is the rise of new modes of private business mobilization, for example, through the expansion of the Corporate Social Responsibility (CSR) movement. Corporate Social Responsibility has moved from ideology to practice and many firms consider it necessary for defining their roles in society and upholding social and ethical standards in the business (Lindgreen & Swaen, 2010)). Despite the inherent risk of green-washing (Jahdi & Acikdilli, 2009), the idea that private corporations should contribute to the social welfare of their employees and the construction of a sustainable local and global community beyond what is required for profit maximization, creates an opportunity for engaging private firms in co-creation of public value.

The *last enabler* that we want to highlight is the development of new digital technologies that create opportunities for linking citizens and governments in new ways (Dunleavy et al., 2006). Digital technologies connect people with different locations and allow them to communicate electronically in real time. They also allow them to use big data to do sophisticated analysis across programs and policy areas, build and test prototypes, and store and process information. Hence, users, citizens, and stakeholders do not have to meet with government officials face-to-face in order to communicate and use data, software, and information to build new futures. This means that the traditional value-chain in which citizens are placed at the end of a long process of public service production can be completely transformed so that the citizens are engaged as co-creators throughout the process of designing and delivering services and other outputs. The new technologies also help to connect citizens with each other and to learn more about their neighborhood and the problems that call for collective action – the digital platform *Next Door* provides a brilliant example of this. The true power of the new digital technologies lies in their ability to facilitate processes of co-creation (Eggers, 2016: 29–30).

The five enablers of a turn toward co-creation as a core principle of public governance are summarized in Table 1.3.

1.5 Wider Perspectives and Consequences

This book aims to link public administration and governance research with political science. Hence, we are not only interested in how the

Table 1.3 *Five key enablers of a future turn toward co-creation in public governance*

New governance paradigms	Political and administrative leaders are increasingly recognizing the limits of classical forms of bureaucracy and the NPM and are searching for a new governance paradigm that helps foster resource mobilization based on collaboration
New type of citizens	Citizens are becoming more assertive, competent, and critical and want to participate actively in making governance decisions that affect the quality of life
New civil society organizations	Civil society organizations are becoming increasingly professional and diversified and are keen to engage in constructive, pragmatic, and solution-oriented experimentation
New type of business firms	Corporate Social Responsibility has gone from ideology to practice and many private firms are committed to the enhancement of social welfare and sustainable development beyond what is required for profit maximization
New digital technologies	New digital technologies enable citizens to become co-creators of public services, facilitate online dialogue between citizens and public decision makers, and allow local citizens to join forces in dealing with local problems

delivery of services and policies is improved by new ways of organizing and exercising public governance, but also in the wider political, democratic, and societal implications of how we are envisioning and structuring the public sector. In terms of political impact, we think that the development of a public sector based on co-creation as its core principle and practice has two important perspectives.

The first perspective is that it offers an alternative to the binary "state versus market" thinking that has dominated the last three to four decades. There has been a heated political and philosophical debate about whether public bureaucracy or new forms of market governance are the best mechanism for delivering timely, sufficient, cost-efficient high-quality services. However, the attempt to promote co-creation as a mode of governance is founded on a critique of the "in house" thinking of most public and private actors that tend to believe that they must do everything themselves by relying on their own organization, resources and employees. Alternatively, we should aim to combine the resources, ideas, and energies of a broad range of public and private actors in an effort to foster a more synergistic and innovation-enhancing approach to public governance, policy making, and service production. As such, co-creation takes us beyond either/or thinking of both market-oriented neoliberalism and state-oriented welfarism. While the former tends to view the market as the key service-provider and problem-solver with state intervention only to address occasional market failures, the latter tends to perceive the state as the principal provider of public services and solutions with the market playing only a marginal role in correcting the price and quality of public services through the occasional contracting out to private service providers.

In contrast with this binary thinking, our attempt to elevate co-creation from a tool for user-centered service production to a core principle of public governance aims to bring public actors from all levels of government together in problem- and task-focused collaboration with for-profit actors from the private business sector, nonprofit organizations from civil society and citizens in their capacity as users, volunteers, activists, or civic leaders. Cross-boundary collaboration has, for a long time, been advocated by public administration scholars as a solution to specific problems (Ansell & Gash, 2008; Emerson, Nabatchi, & Balogh, 2012; Huxham & Vangen, 2013) and it is now time to take their recommendations one step further and replace the binary governance thinking that dominates most governments with a new governance paradigm based on co-creation.

The second, and closely related, perspective is that co-creation offers an alternative to both right-wing and left-wing ideologies due to its ability to facilitate the mobilization, exchange and pooling of ideas, resources and energies across organizational and sectoral boundaries and to connect public and private actors operating at different levels. Co-creation is neither left nor right. It takes us beyond the false choice between the road to serfdom and the gradual erosion of public responsibility to create a shared responsibility for tackling societal problems and risks. The emphasis on public–private collaboration makes co-creation akin to ideas associated with the Third Way promoted by Giddens (1994) and most visibly pursued by the Blair-government in the United Kingdom (Blair, 1998). However, our view of co-creation as a mode of governance is not based on a de-politicizing belief in everybody behaving nicely and engaging in a harmonious collaboration based on reasoned debate. Instead, we argue that while multi-actor collaboration certainly forms the backbone of co-creation as a mode of governance, collaboration should be perceived as the constructive management of differences in order to find joint solutions to common problems (Gray, 1989).

The co-creation paradigm we advance acknowledges the presence of political conflicts and power struggles that must be handled through negotiation resting on the recognition of mutual dependence, a common grammar of conduct, and a certain degree of agonistic respect among adversaries. Indeed, co-creation thrives on differences in resources, ideas and opinions that both create important complementarities and synergies and spurs conflicts that are productive in so far as they give rise to disturbance and revision of established views and opinions (Ansell, 2011). We shall later return to discuss what happens to power and conflict in the forms of cross-boundary collaboration that co-creation builds upon.

1.6 The Basic Conceptual Model of Co-creation

The argument that we put forth in this book builds on an underlying conceptual model that organizes our way of thinking about co-creation. We have already touched upon some of the components of this model that we present in full in Figure 1.1.

As shown in the conceptual model, we insist that the study of co-creation should always take the *antecedent conditions* into account. The overall political culture, the prevailing public governance regime, the tradition and experience with cross-boundary collaboration, the capacities for organization and leadership and the particularities of the area in which problems, challenges, and tasks are identified will condition the effort to co-create solutions.

The proactive attempt to initiate, support, and give direction to co-creation is captured by the notion of *metagovernance*, which is defined as the deliberate effort to influence processes and outcomes of interactive governance without reverting too much to traditional statist forms of steering based on command and control (Jessop, 2002; Kooiman, 2003; Meuleman, 2008; Torfing et al, 2012). Metagovernance can take the form of either hands-off metagovernance that works through the

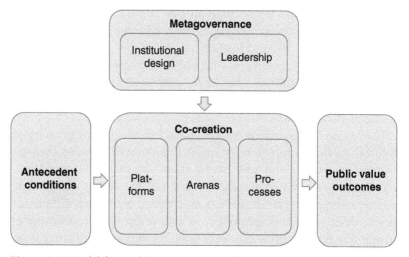

Figure 1.1 Model for studying co-creation of public value outcomes

institutional design of frameworks for public–private interaction or hands-on metagovernance that is basically about *leadership* of collaborative processes with a view toward co-creating public solutions.

Co-creation itself consists of three intrinsically related components: *platforms, arenas, and processes*. Platforms and arenas are both generative mechanisms that facilitate and support the emergence of co-creation processes. Platforms are relatively permanent infrastructures that provide technical and/or physical opportunities for the contingent construction, adaptation, and multiplication of arenas. Arenas are temporary, purpose-built institutionalizations of interaction that comprise a mixture of resources, rules, norms, and procedures that both shape and are shaped by actual processes of collaboration. Co-creation processes are complex articulations of elements of initiation, design, implementation, consolidation, upscaling, and diffusion – often following winding paths with gaps, jumps, iterations, feedback-loops, and so on.

As mentioned earlier, co-creation strives to produce *public value outcomes*. These outcomes may either relate to specific services or policies or more broadly to societal problems and challenges that call for collective action.

In the chapters that follow we will repeatedly refer to this underlying conceptual model when developing our argument.

1.7 Plan for the Book

The programmatic statement in this chapter is followed by Chapter 2 which explores the conceptual and theoretical foundations of co-creation and the movement from co-produced services to co-creation of public value outcomes. This chapter will also present a more elaborate definition of co-creation and discuss its affinity with other similar concepts. The broad range of theories that inform our take on co-creation as a mode of governance will also be briefly introduced.

Chapter 3 discusses the conditions of possibility for co-creation to emerge and argues that co-creation is both everywhere and nowhere. It is everywhere because there seems to be few empirical restrictions on where to find good examples of co-creation, but at the same time nowhere because co-creation is rarely perceived as a comprehensive strategy for public governance.

Chapter 4 introduces and defines the concept of generative governance and more broadly the notion of generativity. It also explains and illustrates the concepts of platforms and arenas and discusses their main differences, how they are related, and how they facilitate co-creation processes.

Chapter 5 looks at the different phases of the dynamic and complex processes of co-creation and identifies relevant drivers and barriers that may affect the process of co-creation. The chapter also provides examples of the tools, methods, and stratagems that are frequently invoked in order to spur processes of co-creation.

Chapter 6 analyzes the public value outcomes that may arise from co-creation. It maps the impact pathways linking co-creation processes to different public value outcomes and reflects upon limiting factors and how they can be removed.

Chapter 7 goes deeper into the democratic implications of a gradual turn toward co-creation and discusses how this turn might help to reinvent democracy in the face of current challenges by providing opportunities for more direct and fulfilling participation that builds democratic ownership and replaces ideological purism with a new focus on pragmatic problem-solving and experimentation.

Chapter 8 assesses the prospect for mainstreaming and scaling co-creation in line with our vision. It reflects on the strategic management of the transition to co-creation and discusses four factors that may help to advance co-creation: new forms of public leadership, development of new institutional designs, strategies for motivating public and private actors to collaborate, and new methods to track and assess results in order to improve performance and goal attainment.

Chapter 9 provides tentative responses to actual and imagined criticisms of co-creation as a mode of governance. The chapter focuses on the unintended negative effects that co-creation might have and how they are avoided, mitigated, or countered.

Chapter 10 aims to take stock of the research on co-creation and its advancement as a new public governance paradigm. The stock-taking results in the advancement of a research agenda for future studies of co-creation and recommendations for the next steps that must be taken to enhance the co-creation of public value outcomes.

This book is written for a wide audience that basically includes everybody interested in what public governance in the post-NPM era might look like. Researchers in the field of public administration, public governance, and public policy might discover a new and interesting perspective on public governance that focuses on generativity. Graduate and postgraduate students may become inspired to study a broad range of co-creation processes and their conditions for success. Public leaders and managers may find ideas that can help them to achieve their goals in new and better ways and with a greater focus on resource mobilization, creative problem-solving, and democratic renewal.

2 | *The Concept of Co-creation*
A Genealogy

This chapter aims to provide the conceptual foundations for discussing the process and impact of co-creation as a mode of governance as developed in subsequent chapters. To do this, the chapter will trace the genealogy of the notion of co-creation, discussing how it has become increasingly central to social science research and defining the concept in ways that distinguish it from similar and related concepts. Building on this genealogical approach, the chapter will also discuss how recently developed theories may contribute to our understanding of the concept of co-creation and support its practical application. Finally, yet critically, the chapter will justify our attempt to elevate the concept from its original narrow focus on service production to a concept that aspires to become a new governance paradigm supplementing and partially supplanting Classical Public Administration and New Public Management.

Although the concept has both public- and private-sector origins, we begin with a discussion of private-sector debates that have inspired the recent surge of interest in co-production and co-creation in the public sector.

2.1 The Emergence of Co-production and Co-creation in the Private Sector

A first major private-sector source of ideas about co-production and co-creation arose from a fundamental rethinking of how firms interact with consumers. Prahalad and Ramaswamy (2002, 2004) were among the first to describe the potential of co-creation as a source of market advantage. They argue that "[t]he interaction between the firm and the consumer is becoming the locus of value creation and value extraction" (2004: 5). Co-creation between firms and consumers has the potential for creating value because value creation is increasingly focused on user experience rather than on the product per se. They describe how the meaning of markets has changed. In the past, the conception was that value was created inside the firm and consumers were only involved at the end stages – at the point of exchange. They classify this view of the market as "company-centric" (2004: 6). However, consumers and consumption have changed. They argue that consumers are now more empowered and are less dependent on information provided by the firm. In addition, there is more consumer-to-consumer communication and consumers are interested in the entire production process. These changes produce new demands for firm–consumer negotiation. At the same time, strong efficiency pressures make it difficult for firms to differentiate their product offerings from other firms on the basis of price. In this new market environment, working closely with consumers to co-create their experience can therefore be a source of competitive advantage.

As an opportunity for achieving competitive advantage, co-creation can be distinguished from previous ideas about firm–consumer relations. Co-creation is not just about being customer-centric or about providing great service. Instead, co-creation requires an authentic dialogue between firms and consumers. The image is one of firms and consumers as "joint problem-solvers" (Prahalad & Ramaswamy, 2004: 9). To have such an authentic dialogue, consumers need to be on a more equal footing with firms, which means that they must have access to information. As a result, the market begins to become more like a *forum* where high-quality discussions and mutual learning can occur. Ind and Coates (2013) add that the move toward co-creation represents a movement toward more "open" conceptions of innovation (e.g., such as "open-source" software) that harness wider inputs.

A second and closely related private-sector source of ideas about co-production and co-creation stems from a rethinking of how firms provide service – an area known as "service science." Vargo, Maglio, and Akaka (2008) argue that a "goods-dominant logic" is characterized by a focus on "value-in-exchange" – that is, firms produce products that they then sell to consumers in the market. From the perspective of this logic, producers and consumers are sharply differentiated (2008: 146). They contrast this logic with a "service-dominant logic" where "the roles of producers and consumers are not distinct," which means that value-in-use is always co-created, jointly and reciprocally (2008: 146). Osborne and Strokosch (2013) draw a similar contrast between a goods-centric and a service-centric logic: Goods are manufactured in one place and sold in another; but for services, production and consumption are not so easily separated and instead occur simultaneously and continuously in ways that are mediated by the service user. In addition, they argue that services are "intangible processes," which makes the experience of consumers central to value creation.

A third source of private-sector ideas about co-production and co-creation arose in the field of design (Degnegaard, 2014). Sanders and Stappers (2008) describe how designers have, since the 1970s, increasingly focused on understanding user needs and experiences in developing designs. This approach has led designers to explore ideas about users as partners and to experiment with participatory approaches to design, where users participate with designers in a process of co-design. They argue that the transition is from designing products to designing in accordance with "people's purposes" (2008: 10). As they write: "We are no longer simply designing products for users. We are designing for the future experiences of people, communities and cultures who now are connected and informed in ways that were unimaginable even 10 years ago" (2008: 10). Users are no longer simply studied through focus groups or consumer surveys in order to understand how they will use particular products. Instead, users become involved in co-design because they are experts on their own experiences.

Sanders and Stappers (2008) ask why "co-creation" has taken so long to develop and suggest four important reasons: first, co-creation can disrupt the authority and power of experts to make unilateral decisions; second, consumption has been understood to be a passive relationship of purchasing and enjoying certain goods and services; third, participatory design has been perceived as an academic enterprise; and fourth, until recently, firms have competed in terms of technological processes and have not seen the need to engage closely with consumers.

These private-sector ideas are important for understanding public-sector co-production and co-creation because the public sector is largely producing services rather than goods and thus lends itself to a transition to a service-centric logic that engages with customers in new ways. Gebauer, Johnson, and Enquist (2010), for example, show how the Swiss Federal Railway was transformed from a "goods-centric" to a "service-centric" logic. In the past, citizens purchased a train ticket as if it were simply a consumer good. But with the adoption of a service-centric orientation, the railway has sought to engage customers in a new way by soliciting inputs and ideas about their service experience.

We note, however, that a public-sector approach to co-creation may be different from a private-sector approach in a number of ways. First, and most obviously, most public-sector agencies are not operating in a market environment where the goal is to achieve market advantage over other public agencies. Although there are competitive dynamics in the public sector, these are typically not the dominant elements driving agency interaction with citizens. The second point is that while there is an element of consumption in public-sector service relationships, the role of citizens can be quite different from the role of consumers. In evaluating and engaging with public service production, citizens have a wider agenda that exceeds the private utility that they receive as consumers. For example, commuters not only might care about timely and reliable rail service but might also want to enhance public transport out of a concern for climate change. A third major difference is that public co-creation relationships are more likely to be collective than individualized. While Prahalad and Ramaswamy (2004) often talk about co-creation as creating a customized individual relationship between the firm and its consumers, public-sector co-creation is more likely to foster customized relations on a collective scale with, say, user groups, neighborhoods, or even organized stakeholders.

Although the private-sector literature on co-production and co-creation is significant, we are also able to draw on a distinguished tradition focusing on the public sector. Within the public sector, both a service-dominant approach and a public-management approach have highlighted the active role of citizens and other stakeholders in contributing to the production of public services and the transformation of public service systems.

2.2 Public-Sector Service Co-production

The earliest work in public administration and public policy relevant to co-creation explicated the idea of "co-production." One of the earliest statements was advanced by Elinor Ostrom (Ostrom et al., 1978) and her colleagues, who focused on how citizens could participate in the co-production of government services. In an early formulation, they defined co-production as follows:

Co-production involves a mixing of the productive efforts of regular and consumer producers. This mixing may occur directly, involving coordinated efforts in the same production process, or indirectly through independent, yet related efforts of regular producers and consumer producers. (Parks et al., 1981: 1002)

By "regular producer," they are referring to public agencies such as police departments that are responsible for the production of a particular service like community policing (Ostrom & Whitaker, 1973). By "consumer producer," they are referring to citizens who not only consume these services but may also contribute to some degree to the production of these services (see also Pestoff, 2006).

In a series of research efforts, Ostrom and her colleagues explored the potential for co-production to enhance service delivery, and they stressed the concept captured an underappreciated relationship between the citizen and the state. They noted, for instance, that "co-production implies that citizens can play an active role in producing public goods and services of consequence to them" (Ostrom, 1996: 1073). They also observed that the concept of co-production breaks with the traditional contrast between state and market provision of services. In her seminal book *Governing the Commons*, Ostrom (1990) goes on to demonstrate how relevant and affected actors may collaborate to successfully address common-pool resource problems.

Another important contributor to the discussion of public co-production, John Alford, referred to the situation where citizens engage with the state in the production of services as "client co-production" (1998: 130). Client co-production, he argued, is necessary where there exists an interdependency between the public agency and citizens such that high-quality products or services cannot be produced or delivered by the agency without the input of citizens. This interdependency may be related to inputs, processes, or outcomes, but in general it requires agencies and citizens to work cooperatively. Similarly, Victor Pestoff draws our attention to the distinction between co-production and "parallel production." While the former requires direct interaction between the service producers and users, the latter "involves services similar to those provided by public agencies, but produced by individuals without contact or co-operation with public agencies" (2006: 507). For example, when citizens comply with public regulations, it helps to achieve public purposes but does not involve interaction with a public agency.

Taking Ostrom's definition as a starting point, we can see that subsequent discussions have sought to either expand or restrict the definition along a number of dimensions. Alford (2014) has argued that Ostrom's conceptualization of co-production is too narrow because it largely focuses on service provision, a focus that limits the potential of co-production. He points out that co-production is not necessarily limited to the involvement of those who consume public services. Moreover, co-production does not just occur in terms of individuals consuming services but can also be a "collective" relationship between communities and the regulations and services provided by governments. Echoing a point made earlier, citizen motivations to participate are varied and not always narrowly self-interested.

Another scholar of co-production, Tony Bovaird (2007), also argues for a wider understanding of who is engaged in co-production, defining user and community co-production "as the provision of services through regular, long-term relationships between professionalized service providers (in any sector) and service users or other members of the community, where all parties make substantial resource contributions" (2007: 847). Joshi and Moore (2004: 40) also emphasize that co-production may be a long-term relationship between state agencies and organized groups of citizens.

Other points of tension in the public administration literature on co-production are related to *who* is doing the co-producing and *what range of activities* it comprises. In an important early account, Brudney and England define co-production in terms of "the degree of overlap between two sets of participants – regular producers (e.g., service agents, public administrators) and consumers (e.g., citizens, neighborhood associations). The resultant overlap represents joint production of services by these two groups, or 'co-production'" (1983: 63).

Brudney and England go on to distinguish three levels of co-production. A first type of co-production, they suggest, operates at the individual level and varies in terms of how voluntary or captured individuals are. For example, in the United States, welfare recipients of food stamps have little choice about whether to co-produce the service, unless they are willing to forego it altogether. In other services, however, citizen voluntarism is high. Volunteering to be a park docent is a good example. A second type of co-production operates at the group level, which they describe as follows: "group co-production involves voluntary, active participation by a number of citizens and may require formal coordination mechanisms between service agents and citizen groups" (1983: 63). They offer neighborhood watch groups as an example. A third type of co-production is "collective co-production," where "co-productive activities result in collective goods whose benefits may be enjoyed by the entire community" (1983: 64). They argue that this type of co-production moves away from a narrow transactional view of services. In this case, the benefits of co-production accrue not only to the volunteering citizen but rather to the community as a collectivity.

More recent treatments of co-production echo these issues. Bovaird observes that "[t]aken together, these references from recent literature in Europe and the United States illustrate that the concept of co-production is not only relevant to the service delivery phase of services management (where it was first discovered in the 1970s) but can also extend across the full value chain of service planning, design, commissioning, managing, delivering, monitoring, and evaluation activities" (2007: 847). Osborne, Radnor, and Strokosch offer a similar definition that stresses that co-creation extends to design, management, and evaluation of public services (2016: 640).

Another point of tension in the co-production literature centers on who is involved in co-production and how. Brandsen and Honingh (2016) argue that co-production refers to a relationship between public agencies and citizens. Although citizens may be operating collectively rather than individually, they distinguish the role of citizens from the role of organizations (cf. Brudney and England, 1983). They also argue that the term "co-production" should be limited to the production or provision of public services. They demarcate this production or provision from citizen advocacy roles. As they observe:

[W]e do not include all inputs by citizens that may affect the overall design and delivery of a service, but focus on the direct input of citizens in the individual design and delivery of a service during the production phase. "Direct" here means that the input by a citizen affects the service individually provided to her or him. (Brandsen & Honingh, 2016: 428)

They suggest that advocacy includes more indirect forms of influence. Based on these assumptions, Brandsen and Honingh identify the essential elements of a co-production definition as follows: "Co-production is a relationship between a paid employee of an organization and (groups of) individual citizens that requires a direct and active contribution from these citizens to the work of the organization" (2016: 431). This dyadic relationship may be more or less voluntary. In some cases, co-production is an inherent element of service – a point made by the "service" literature. However, in some cases, citizens have substantial latitude about whether to contribute to co-production. In the field of education, for example, there is both a voluntary and an involuntary aspect of student co-production of learning.

Brandsen and Pestoff (2006) also interpret co-production restrictively. With a focus on the "third sector" (as an umbrella term for nonstate or nonmarket actors), they distinguish co-production from co-governance and co-management. With co-governance, the third sector participates in the planning and delivery of services. With co-management, the third sector – typically, in the form of organizations – collaborates with the state to produce services. With co-production, citizens as individuals produce, in part, their own services. They acknowledge that this is a restrictive definition.

To summarize the discussion in this section, public administration has discussed the idea of co-production since the early 1970s. Early conceptions stressed that many public services could not be successfully produced without the input and cooperation of citizens. Subsequent discussions have gradually expanded our conception of the scope and relevance of co-production. Co-production is not narrowly restricted to a relationship between service providers and service users. Citizens who are not necessarily the direct consumers of services and whose contributions benefit wider communities may also be participating in co-production. In fact, co-production is not necessarily limited to service delivery at all, though the concept remains rooted in the world of service delivery. Rather, co-production may extend to many different aspects of public problem-solving and policy making. Nor are co-production relationships limited to individual relationships – they may be collective relationships with groups ("collective co-production"). Despite these attempts to broaden the concept of co-production, some scholars prefer to keep the scope of the term co-production more limited.

2.3 Types of Public Service Co-production

Another point of tension in the literature derives from different background assumptions about co-production. Osborne and Strokosch (2013) distinguish between public administration and service traditions in the study of co-production. Tracing its lineage back to the work of Ostrom, the public administration tradition places its emphasis on the "joint working between two parties that typically operate from different places in the production process" (Osborne and Strokosch, 2013: S34). They argue that this tradition has largely seen co-production as something that needs to be designed *in* to public service delivery in order to improve it in various ways. They suggest that the service management literature, by contrast, propose a different starting point, one that views co-production as "the essential and intrinsic process of interaction between any service organization and the service user at the point of production of a service" (Osborne & Strokosch, 2013: S36). From this perspective, co-production is not something designed *in*, but is rather an unavoidable interaction since "you cannot have (public) service delivery without co-production" (Osborne & Strokosch, 2013: S36).

Attempting to integrate these two different streams of thought on co-production, Osborne and Strokosch distinguish between *consumer, participative,* and *enhanced* co-production. First, they argue that the service approach to co-production has an operational focus. From this perspective, co-production is not something to be designed in to the process of interaction between public service organizations and consumers of services. Rather, it is a focus on how "experience and outcomes are negotiated between the service user and the service delivery professional rather than one dominated by the latter professionals alone" (Osborne & Strokosch, 2013: S38). In addition, they argue that the emphasis is on how to empower the service user within this process. They refer to this idea as *consumer co-production*.

Second, they suggest that we can also conceptualize co-production at a more strategic level. The focus here is on design and planning for service delivery – not on the operations of delivery. A design element arises when the focus is on how user experience can be utilized to better design the delivery services in the future. Instead of user empowerment, the goal is to encourage the participation of service users in this design process. We note here that user participation in this context often refers to elite or lead users rather than to broad-based participation (Von Hippel, 1986). Osborne & Strokosch (2013) label this more strategic mode of co-production as *participative co-production*.

Finally, Osborne and Strokosch suggest a third mode of co-production that integrates the service and public administration perspectives – a mode they call *enhanced co-production*. Basically, the idea is that the operational (consumer co-production) and strategic (participative co-production) modes are combined, leading to user-led innovation of public services. What is distinctive here is that service users are conceptualized as critical to the transformative innovation of service delivery. In the private sector, they note, this user-led transformative innovation is called *co-creation*, though they observe that it is undertheorized in the public administration literature. They emphasize that the key to enhanced co-production is to bring the operational and strategic aspects together, such that: "the service organization is proactively seeking to uncover, understand and satisfy 'latent (future) needs', rather than simply reacting to (existing) expressed needs" (Osborne & Strokosch, 2013: S40). To do this, public service organizations need to go beyond simple empowerment or opening up of possibilities for participation.

Other scholars have probed the basic character of co-production and call attention to different types of co-production. Bovaird and Loeffler define co-production as: "the public sector and citizens making better use of each other's assets and resources to achieve better outcomes or improved efficiency" (2012: 3). They note that this definition differs from earlier definitions because it stresses outcomes rather than processes and requires a long-term relationship. They also argue that co-production assumes that citizens are not passive (Brudney & England, 1983). As the limits of provider-centric services become clearer, the focus shifts to a more enabling role. They describe a range of specific types of co-production similar to those described by other authors – co-planning, co-design, co-prioritization, co-financing, co-managing, co-delivery, and co-assessment of services. In other words, co-production encompasses all aspects of service provision including the commissioning, design, and delivery of services.

Despite starting with a narrow definition of service co-production, Brandsen and Honingh (2016) also attempt to identify different types of co-production. Their typology is based on two variables. One key element of variation has to do with whether citizens are involved in the design, or only the implementation, of service production. A second element of variation concerns the extent to which citizens are engaged in co-producing "core tasks" of organizations as opposed to "complementary tasks." Based on these variables, they identify four types of co-production. They call the first type "complementary co-production in implementation," where citizens are involved in the delivery, but not the design, of noncore services. This narrower type of co-production is contrasted with a second type – "co-production in the design and implementation of core services." In this role, citizens are engaged in a wider range of activity and contribute directly to core services. The two intermediate types are, first, "co-production in the implementation of core services," and second, "complementary co-production in service design and implementation" (Brandsen & Honingh, 2016: 432–433).

In their systematic review of the public-sector co-production and co-creation literature, Voorberg, Bekker, and Tummers find that these two terms are not clearly distinguished: "we concluded that in the literature the concepts of co-creation and co-production were often seen as interchangeable. There is empirically no striking difference between both concepts, and within bodies of knowledge different meanings are given to both concepts" (2015: 15). They then distinguish three types of co-production/co-creation: type 1 is where citizens are "co-implementers" of services; type 2 is where they are co-designers of services; and type 3 is where citizens are "co-initiators" of services (Voorberg, Bekker, & Tummers, 2015).

This categorization is similar to the one suggested by Nambisan and Nambisan (2013), who distinguish four different citizen roles in co-creation: the citizen as an "explorer" who helps to identify and analyze problems; the citizen as "ideator" who helps to conceptualize solutions to relatively well-defined problems; the citizen as "designer," which is about operationalizing these solutions concepts; and the citizen as "diffuser" who serves as a catalyst in encouraging the adoption of co-produced programs or ideas.

Most recently, Nabatchi, Sancino, and Sicilia (2017) have suggested a typology of co-production in different phases of the service cycle, which they designate as commissioning, design, delivery, and assessment. This typology is similar to the one advanced by Bovaird and Loeffler (2012), but they also distinguish different levels of co-production, identifying individual, group and collective levels of participation.

These different typologies use somewhat different language and emphasize different points. However, by roughly aligning the ideas expressed by these authors, we can identify a few key distinctions running through their discussions. A first key distinction is between whether citizen input feeds into the operating or implementation phases of service delivery or whether it also extends to the more strategic design of these services. There is also some indication that the citizen role may go even further than providing input into the design of services, to adopt a more innovative role or one that initiates action. These typologies aim to broaden the original definition of co-production which has been focused on the active role that users play in the production of their own services. While these typologies stretch the concept of co-production to cover a wider range of activities, they remain tied to public service production. However, the term 'co' is not limited to service production as it may apply to societal problem-solving and even to policymaking. Since continuing to stretch the concept yields declining returns, we propose to sharpen the distinction between co-production and co-creation.

2.4 Co-creation and Broader Conceptions of Public Value

As we see from the discussion earlier, there have been a number of attempts to expand the meaning of co-production. Although the terms "co-production" and "co-creation" are sometimes used interchangeably, the term "co-creation" begins to have a more distinctive meaning if we become more reflective about where and how value is created (Degnegaard, 2014). Building on the distinction Osborne and Strokosch (2013) drew between a public administration and service management approach to co-production, Osborne, Radnor, and Strokosch (2016) observe that while public administration remains wedded to a more top-down managerial view of service delivery, the service management approach sees users as partially creating their own experience of service delivery. Thus, users "co-create" the value of a service. In other words, the value of a service is not produced in a top-down way, but rather emerges through the interaction of providers and users in such a way that value is jointly produced.

Osborne, Radnor, and Strokosch also draw a key distinction between whether this "co-creation" improves the service in question (either at the level of an individual service or at the level of the service system as a whole), enhances "the sense of well-being that results from this real-time activity," or potentially facilitates "the evolution of individual and community capacity to respond independently to social needs in the future" (2016: 645). An important feature of this discussion is that it begins to focus on co-production as a locus of the creation of value.

Mark Moore's (1995) original concept of "public value" was managerial, but scholars have also re-envisioned it in a multi-agent world (Bryson et al., 2017). Benington argues that a key aspect of "public" value is that "value is being added to the public sphere, not through arms-length market demand and supply, but through closer linking of users and producers in creative joint development of products and services tailor-made to meet unmet human need – in a process of co-creation of public value" (2009: 236). A key point he makes is that public value is not only created by public-sector agencies or managers, but it can also be created by private and nonprofit stakeholders and by citizens themselves. Building on this point, Alford defines public value as the "goals and aspirations citizens have for the society as a whole" (2010: 144) and draws the important conclusion that public value creation is not the exclusive responsibility of public managers, but can also be created by private firms, nonprofit organizations, civic organizations, and individual citizens.

While this discussion has already been advanced in the literature on private sector co-production (Prahalad & Ramaswamy, 2002, 2004; Vargo, Maglio, & Akaka, 2008; Grönroos, 2011), Osborne, Radnor, and Strokosch suggest that the co-production of public services can also be the locus of value creation. Bovaird and Loeffler (2012) argue that the public value potentially created by co-production goes beyond the traditional private sector understanding of user value to also include value to wider groups, social value, environmental value, and political value. As they note, this wider range of public values may change the motivations that users have to participate in co-production processes and mitigate the feeling among politicians that co-production is risky. In other words, shifting from co-production of services to the co-creation of public value entails expanding the range of relevant public and private actors.

Thus, we see that a more expansive conception of co-production – as discussed in Section 2.2 – joins together with a focus on value creation to result in a more distinctive understanding of "co-creation." Co-creation can be elevated from a concept that designates a certain mode of user-involving service delivery to one that describes a participatory and capacity-enhancing mode of governance in which not only services but also plans, strategies, and policies are co-created. To justify the fruitfulness of this conceptual move, we will briefly demonstrate what co-creation as a mode of governance looks like and what it may achieve in terms of public value production. The idea of co-created public value opens itself up to a wider discussion of public innovation (Bason, 2010; Alves, 2013; Lund 2018). A key point is that co-creation, as a driver of innovation, does not only begin with predefined problems but also involves relevant and affected actors in defining problems that call for collective action (Crosby, 't Hart, & Torfing, 2017).

Torfing, Sørensen, and Røiseland (2019) distinguish between co-production and co-creation. They argue that co-production in the public sector refers to the interactive process through which the providers and users of public services apply their different resources and capabilities in the production and delivery of these services. This understanding of co-production restricts it to a situation where two types of stakeholders (service providers and service users) jointly produce a predefined public service. Although co-production may incrementally improve services from this perspective, it does not entail engaging in broader innovation of the services themselves. By contrast, they define co-creation as:

[A] process through which two or more public and private actors attempt to solve a shared problem, challenge, or task through a constructive exchange of different kinds of knowledge, resources, competences, and ideas that enhance the production of public value in terms of visions, plans, policies, strategies, regulatory frameworks, or services, either through a continuous improvement of outputs or outcomes or through innovative step-changes that transform the understanding of the problem or task at hand and lead to new ways of solving it. (2019: 802)

Thus, they envision co-creation as moving beyond a service logic to encompass "public and private actors" (not just providers and users of public services) engaged in a more fundamentally creative or innovative set of activities (e.g., "attempt to solve a shared problem, challenge, or task") that may include, but may also definitely go beyond, services (e.g., "visions, plans, policies, strategies, regulatory frameworks, or services"). Moreover, co-creation entails not just incremental change ("continuous improvement of outputs or outcomes"), but also more transformative innovation.

In widening the scope of the relationship between citizens and the state beyond a narrow transactional view, the possibility emerges that co-creation can contribute to a broader social and democratic agenda. For instance, citizen co-creation may be able to contribute to social solidarity (Bovaird & Loeffler, 2012), to citizen trust in government (Fledderus, Brandsen, & Honingh, 2014) or the co-creation of knowledge (Greenhalgh et al., 2016)

While this account suggests a positive view of public value creation, we must keep in mind that this positive view is not true by definition. In a salutary alternative account, Williams et al. (2016) note that co-creation may lead to "public value failures" if public values are subverted through the process of co-creation. They argue that this can result from the "misuse of resources during the interaction between service providers and service users" (2016: 708).

One conclusion of this discussion is that although co-production and co-creation are often used as synonyms, we argue that we should reserve the term "co-production" for enlisting users in the production and delivery of a given service and use "co-creation" to denote the wider attempts to involve a plethora of actors in developing and innovating public service systems and public solutions more generally.

2.5 Comparing Public Value Co-creation to Similar Concepts

As discussed earlier, the concept of co-creation overlaps with a number of key concepts in public administration and public policy, including citizen participation, deliberative publics, network governance, and social innovation. These concepts are often used as synonyms and often go together in practice (Poocharoen & Ting, 2015). However, it is important to distinguish them because they often have a different focus and scope and different conceptual entailments (Ansell, 2019).

A first cognate concept to consider is "citizen participation," which has a long tradition in public administration (Arnstein, 1969). Public participation can take a wide variety of forms. Most local governments are now using some form of "participative technology" to engage more directly with citizens (Welch, 2012). Many scholars have also examined the possibilities for greater deliberative democracy associated with some forms of participation (Fung & Wright, 2003). However, as Arnstein points out in her "ladder of participation," participation may be quite limited and require limited engagement of citizens with other citizens. Quick and Feldman (2011) have made this point nicely in their distinction between "participation" and "inclusion." They argue that participation and inclusion are two different dimensions of the wider category "public engagement." They summarize the difference as follows:

Participation practices entail efforts to increase public input oriented primarily to the content of programs and policies. Inclusion practices entail continuously creating a community involved in co-producing processes, policies, and programs for defining and addressing public issues. (2011: 272)

As this distinction suggests, participation may be simply about increasing input into decisions made by others. Consider a public hearing. The public may be invited to ask questions and make statements regarding their views of a particular policy issue. This type of participation may increase information available to decision makers that allows them to gauge past decisions or to make future decisions. But, in this example, there is no "co-creation," no interaction to jointly define and produce solutions. Co-creation envisions something much closer to what Quick and Feldman call "inclusion." It implies interaction between citizens and the state and between citizens to create particular outcomes. Quick and Feldman note that participation and inclusion are independent of one another, such that it is possible to have high participation but low inclusion, and vice versa. "Interaction to create" is one important entailment of the concept of co-creation.

Another concept related to citizen engagement that overlaps with co-creation is "deliberative publics." Here the key concept is "deliberative" and it implies discussion and dialogue about issues. Deliberative conceptions of democracy differ from merely aggregative conceptions. Hence, like Quick and Feldman's conception of inclusion, a deliberative public is expected to be interactive. Typically, deliberative publics aim to address certain issues or problems. But the focus is on the fact that participants in a public are advancing and defending political arguments and are prepared to revise their position in the face of new evidence or counterarguments (Öberg, 2016). A successful deliberation may simply result in the participants having a better understanding of an issue or of the positions of others. The concept of co-creation tends to imply that citizens and public actors engage in deliberation. However, while "deliberation" is obviously central to the concept of deliberative publics, it is secondary (or implicit) in the concept of co-creation. Reciprocally, "creation" is a primary entailment of co-creation, but only secondary or implicit for deliberative publics.

A third cognate concept is "network governance." Like co-creation, network governance is a form of governance in which the inputs come from a distributed group of actors, who may come from the public, private, or nonprofit sectors. The concept "network" often has structural connotations. For example, Provan and Kenis define networks as "groups of three or more legally autonomous organizations that work together to achieve not only their own goals but also a collective goal" (2008, 3). Like the term "co-creation," network governance implies a processual element and a significant degree of interaction among the involved parties. However, network governance stresses the need for groups of autonomous actors to work together in a coordinative, cooperative, or collaborative fashion toward "collective goals" (Keast, Brown, & Mandell, 2007). Although networks may be informal, much of the literature on network governance tends to stress that they are partially institutionalized and may aspire to form an organization. Moreover, the literature tends to emphasize that network governance is a solution to collective action problems in contexts where hierarchies or markets are insufficient. Although co-creation may occur in networks, we think it is often equally useful to think of co-creation as occurring in arenas, a point we shall return to in Chapter 4.

A fourth cognate concept is "social innovation," which may take many different forms. One meaning of social innovation is innovation by social entrepreneurs who aim to have social impact. In such a case it does not necessarily imply anything about co-creating innovations since the social entrepreneur may be working alone. Similarly, Torfing, Sørensen, and Røiseland (2019) argue that the concept of co-creation differs from the concept of social innovation because the latter focuses on efforts of civil society to address and solve problems, while co-creation focuses on the joint interaction of public and private actors. The concept of "open innovation" is also sometimes related to co-creation. Mergel (2017), for instance, describes how open innovation attempts to enable broad-based, distributed inputs from citizens. However, these inputs might simply entail a form of crowdsourcing that is limited to harvesting multiple inputs rather than engaging in a process of co-creation.

Thus, while the concept of co-creation overlaps in many respects with a number of other cognate concepts, it has a specific set of meanings that distinguish it in important ways from these concepts. When looking at co-creation as a mode of governance, as we do in this book, there remains a question of how co-creation differs from other collaborative regime forms. Section 2.6 argues that co-creation can be viewed as a third generation type of collaboration that expands and deepens the agenda for collaboration as the result of experiential learning by scholars and practitioners.

2.6 Co-creation – A Third Generation Type of Collaboration

This book describes co-creation as a collaborative mode of governance. Therefore, it is important to discuss how co-creation differs from, but also extends, other widely known modes of governance that center on collaboration. In this section, we contrast co-creation with corporatism and collaborative governance. Our argument is that co-creation not only builds upon these earlier modes of governance but also introduces a new distinctive logic. Hence, we claim that co-creation can be understood as a third-generation type of collaboration.

A traditional mode of governance that relies on collaboration between state and societal actors is democratic corporatism, which gained momentum in many European countries after the Second World War (Schmitter, 1974; Lehmbruch & Schmitter, 1979). Corporatism developed as part of the postwar settlement and was conducive to spurring economic growth and the expansion of the welfare state. A central goal of corporatism is to avoid potentially damaging conflict between trade unions and employer associations, transforming it into a more positive and constructive relationship between "social partners." Democratic corporatism differs from state corporatism because it respects the autonomy of labor market organizations while at the same time giving them enhanced influence over relevant policy and labor market regulations. Central state organizations play a central role in convening tripartite negotiations between the social partners and serve as an arbiter in these negotiations.

Corporatism depended on the strong hierarchical peak associations of both unions and employers that could control their members and deliver support for compromises hammered out in centralized bargaining. Countries with more pluralist interest representation were generally unable to establish the monopolistic peak association of employers and employees necessary for effective corporatist bargains.

Corporatism was a system of interest intermediation that aimed to maintain crucial balances between increases in nominal wages and productivity, forming the so-called Fordist compromise that combined mass production and mass consumption, thus triggering unprecedented economic growth (Jessop, 2002). As a mode of governance, corporatism relied on a degree of state co-optation of the peak associations, but decision making depended on hard-nosed bargaining between the social partners where each pursued predefined interests and could veto cooperative outcomes. An important product of corporatist bargaining was an elaborate system of institutional arrangements to facilitate labor market regulation and to provide welfare benefits and services to wider segments of the public. In sum, the functional outcome of the first-generation mode of collaboration was the formation of social and economic infrastructures that enjoyed strong support from the social partners. Corporatist compromises depended on continued economic growth in order to generate win-win solutions. As the long period of postwar economic growth slowed, in part due to the exhaustion of the economic potential of Fordist technologies of mass production, the corporatist system eroded and only survived in modified form.

Although corporatism declined, there was significant learning during its heyday. Learning occurred in at least three ways. First, it gradually became clear that the involvement of peak associations was important not only for the formulation of policies and wage agreements but also in their implementation. In some countries, for instance, the social partners were heavily involved in implementing labor market education. Second, it was learned that corporatist arrangements could also benefit many types of associations and not simply trade unions and employers. These associations encompass sectors as diverse as agriculture, transport, and health where looser forms of negotiation and cooperation emerged. Third, it was learned that corporatism could function not only at the macro-level of the national state but also at the meso-level of policy sectors and even the micro-level of local government and workplaces. As corporatism has evolved, it has widened the scope of interest intermediation, the range of actors involved, and the relevant levels of governance to which it applies (Cawson, 1985). The erosion of the classical forms of corporatism and the expansion of more varied forms has paved the way to a new era of collaborative governance.

One of the key developments in the evolution of governance in the later third of the twentieth century was the expansion and development of the role of networks of public or private actors involved in policy formation and implementation (Heclo, 1978; Marin & Mayntz, 1991; Marsh & Rhodes, 1992). This literature stresses the interdependency of these actors rather than their co-optation into the state, which has inspired the development of research into how these networks contribute to public governance (Kickert, Klijn, & Koppenjan, 1997; Provan & Milward, 2001; Sørensen & Torfing, 2007). Theories of network governance have gradually given way to a new focus on collaborative governance that pays more attention to the drivers and barriers of effective collaboration than to the structure of interest representation (Ansell & Gash, 2008; Emerson, Nabatchi, & Balogh, 2012).

In the new era of collaborative governance, public agencies at multiple levels convene collaboration with relevant and affected stakeholders from the public, private, and non-sectors. These efforts typically reflect the agencies' recognition that they cannot successfully achieve their specific policy objectives unilaterally and must instead create multilateral collaboration. Collaborative governance enables agencies to expand their reach into realms controlled by other agencies or non-state actors. For example, a forestry agency seeking to promote sustainable forest development is partially dependent on collaboration with a range of stakeholders who own, exploit, or want access to the forest. Hence, there is a "collaborative advantage" when dealing with targeted problem-solving (Huxham & Vangen, 2013). The role of agencies within collaborative modes of governance is to align the perspective and actions of relevant and affected actors in a certain problem domain so as to facilitate negative and positive coordination (Scharpf, 1994). When collaborative governance succeeds, it tends to enhance agency problem-solving capacity through improved coordination and joint learning.

In contrast with politicians who have democratic legitimacy because they are elected, agencies often suffer from weak legitimacy and seek to compensate for this weakness by collaborating directly with stake-holders and by facilitating solutions that reflect their diverse perspectives and interests. As such, the second generation of collaboration is less interested in building societal infrastructures and more focused on enhancing the input and output legitimacy of public governance (Scharpf, 1999).

While agencies initially ventured into collaborative governance when managerial or adversarial modes of governance failed, they increasingly recognized the value of collaboration to improve their own agendas and outcomes. The growing appreciation of collaborative governance as a key governing tool builds on at least three types of learning. Initially, agencies approached collaborative governance cautiously and with a high degree of skepticism, fearing that stakeholders would not cooperate and would only pursue their own narrow interests and that the agency could lose control over outcomes. What they learned from successful collaboration is that stakeholders are capable of transcending their narrow interests in order to pursue public value outcomes. They also learned that positive outcomes such as innovation could sometimes emerge from the collective interaction with a more open agenda and less agency control. In addition, they came to appreciate that lay actors, including service users and citizens, could be successfully incorporated into collaborative processes, bringing new information about needs and wants. Finally, the participating stakeholders realized that engagement with other stakeholders could sometimes yield important information and ideas that could improve outcomes. A key implication of this last point is that agencies learned that they could also benefit from participating in collaborative arenas initiated by stakeholders. Thus, the learning achieved through decades of collaborative governance has expanded the scope of and participation in collaboration as a mode of governance far beyond what even the broadest conception of neo-corporatism imagined.

Co-creation is an even more decentered version of collaboration than collaborative governance. Public agencies are one among many actors involved in distributed forms of collaboration, which might be initiated by either public agencies, stakeholder groups, or even by groups of citizens concerned by issues such as neighborhood crime, equal access to health care, or environmental concerns. Co-creation is often co-initiated through the interaction of multiple actors, which means that the agenda for collaboration is set jointly by co-initiating participants. The purpose of co-creation is often to leverage resources from the public and private sectors in order to engage in transformative problem-solving, which is enabled by the capacity to mobilize diverse and complementary resources. While public agencies contribute authority and financing and organized stakeholders provide specialized knowledge and experience, citizens may contribute relevant experience, new ideas, and manpower.

As a collaborative process, co-creation tends to shift the mode of action from fostering alignment between different perspectives and interests to proactively searching for continuous improvement and innovative outcomes that break with the status quo. Often this requires more than simply meeting the existing demands formulated by interest groups; the co-creation process encourages the actors involved to give up narrow control over agenda-setting in order to pursue agendas and solutions that emerge from collaborative interaction based on transformative learning seeking to problematize established patterns and routines. We refer to co-creation as a third-generation mode of collaboration because it goes beyond the agency-centric need to ensure legitimate governance in its efforts to mobilize societal resources in the search for innovative and robust solutions to old and emerging challenges.

As summarized in Table 2.1, our account in this section clarifies what is distinctive about co-creation as a mode of collaboration. While co-creation bears a family resemblance to both corporatism and collaborative governance, it reveals a distinctive logic that extends beyond either of those concepts. By building on, but also extending these ideas about societal collaboration, the concept of co-creation points to new possibilities for governing our contemporary societies. Based on the contrasts we draw in Table 2.1, we now offer the following definition of our key concept:

Co-creation is a distributed and collaborative pattern of creative problem-solving that proactively mobilizes public and private resources to jointly define problems and design and implement solutions that are emergent and seek to generate public value.

Like corporatism and collaborative governance, co-creation is a collaborative process. However, the definition adds five crucial features that are constitutive of co-creation. First, co-creation is a form of

Table 2.1 *Comparing corporatism, collaborative governance, and co-creation*

	Corporatism	Collaborative governance	Co-creation
Role of state	Central state institutions convene and mediate collaboration	Public agencies convene and facilitate collaboration with relevant and affected actors	Public agencies are one among many actors involved in distributed, collaborative interaction
Participating actors	Peak associations from the economic sector	Stakeholders within a certain policy domain, including civil society organizations	Organized and lay actors including citizens with relevant experiences, ideas, and resources
Purpose	Interest intermediation to avoid destructive conflict and create balanced solutions	Targeted problem-solving that expands the reach of agencies	Societal resource mobilization to enhance transformative capacity
Mode of action	Bargaining between actors with veto-power	Alignment of perspectives and actions to facilitate negative and positive coordination	Proactive search for continuous improvement and innovative solutions
Outcomes	Compromises based on predefined interests	Enhanced problem-solving capacity based on improved	Emergent responses to present

Table 2.1 (*cont.*)

	Corporatism	Collaborative governance	Co-creation
Changing governance perspectives	First generation – search for solutions supported by social partners	alignment and joint learning Second generation – search for input and output legitimacy	problems and future needs Third generation – search for innovative and robust solutions to societal challenges

distributed problem-solving that can be initiated by different kinds of actors, whether public, private, or nonprofit. Second, the definition stresses that co-creation is a process of *creative problem-solving*. The actors are drawn together by common concerns to tackle specific issues by jointly crafting solutions. These solutions are always customized and require the involved actors to go beyond their initial interests, perspectives, and knowledge. Third, co-creation entails *proactive mobilization* of the public and public resources in that it deliberatively tries to tap into and leverage resources, ideas, and knowledge in order to achieve goals that no single actor could unilaterally accomplish. Fourth, co-creation is an *emergent* process, which means that the agenda is relatively open and develops out of the interaction of the participants who are also capable of influencing the design and implementation of solutions. Finally, co-creation aspires to produce *public value* for both the participants and for society at large. It does not just bring together a group of participants to benefit themselves.

Co-creation defined in this manner can vary in its scope and ambition. To characterize this variation, Section 2.7 portrays a ladder of co-creation, with each ascending step realizing greater ambition and scope.

2.7 The Ladder of Co-creation

Not all efforts at co-creation need to be or can be equally ambitious. They may start as small, local initiatives focusing on service delivery, but they may then develop greater scale and grander objectives over time. By illuminating gradations in scale and ambition, it becomes clearer how co-creation might start with limited efforts, and perhaps develop more ambition over time. Introducing a ladder of co-creation allows us to locate and compare various efforts at co-creation across sectors, levels, and contexts. As such, the ladder demonstrates how co-creation can be a continuous rather than a dichotomous variable.

Torfing, Sørensen, & Røiseland (2019) draw an analogy between Arnstein's (1969) classic ladder of public participation and a similar ladder of co-creation. At the lowest rung of their co-creation ladder, "public agencies aim to empower citizens to enhance their capacity to master their own lives and encourage them to co-create the services they are offered by the public sector" (2019: 804). At the next higher rung of the ladder, "citizens are not only co-producing their own welfare services, but also engage in creating value for other citizens through voluntary work carried out in close cooperation with public employees and thereby improving existing services through continuous adjustments and the creation of synergies" (2019: 804). At the third step in the ladder, "individual[s] or organized groups of citizens provide input into the design of new tasks and solutions through crowdsourcing, focus-group interviews, written consultations, and public hearings that only allow a limited dialogue" (2019: 804–805). On a fourth rung of the ladder, "public and private actors engage in a mutual dialogue at ad hoc meetings aimed at designing new and better solutions and coordinating their implementation" (2019: 805). Finally, at the highest step of the ladder of co-creation, "relevant and affected actors from the public and private sector participate in institutional arenas that facilitate collaborative innovation based on joint agenda-setting and problem definition, joint design and testing of new and untried solutions, and coordinated implementation drawing on public and private solutions" (2019: 805). This ladder of co-creation assumes an increasing ambition with regard to objectives, an expanding scope of participation, and an ascending intensification of interaction.

Laitinen, Kinder, & Stenvall (2018) offer a similar conception of levels of participation in public service co-design that identifies four levels of user involvement. *Passive* users have a low level of interactivity and bilateral communication, with learning primarily at the individual level. *Voice* refers to greater interactivity in small focus groups, but the service provider's voice dominates. *Participant* implies more intensive two-way communication where users are full members of design teams and have a status equal to providers. Finally, *champions* work closely with providers on an equal basis, but also communicate the goals of the co-design process to the external public. At the lowest level of this ladder, service providers control the agenda and limit the influence and interaction of users. As we progress up the ladder, users become equal partners and their communication and interaction intensifies. Note, however, that this ladder remains limited to service redesign.

We can further elaborate on these models by suggesting that the ladder of co-creation varies from limited, "one-off" idea solicitation where the problem or design parameters (the agenda) is pre-defined or set, to more extensive, on-going problem-solving where the participants co-construct the operative knowledge and the agenda. Table 2.2 summarizes the ladder of co-creation by distinguishing the ambition, scope, and interaction characterizing each of its five steps.

Table 2.2 *The ladder of co-creation*

LEVEL 1:

Ambition	Public agencies solicit ideas, comments, or feedback from users, citizens, and/or stakeholders for limited and well-defined input into program and service design
Scope	Individual users or citizens and/or organized stakeholders provide this input through crowdsourcing, focus-group interviews, written consultations, and public hearings
Interaction	Almost no interaction between citizens or stakeholders themselves and limited interaction between public authorities and citizens and stakeholders

LEVEL 2:

Ambition	Public agencies engage users, citizens, and stakeholder groups in focused design processes addressing specific problems or striving to achieve specific agency goals or tasks

Table 2.2 (*cont.*)

LEVEL 2:	
Scope	Users, citizens, or stakeholder groups participate in common arenas that enable them to meet together on a limited or ad hoc basis
Interaction	Participants interact regularly with one another and with the public agencies who play a key role in setting the agenda and orchestrating the co-creation process

LEVEL 3:	
Ambition	Public agencies work with users, citizens, and stakeholders to identify opportunities to create public value, either through innovation, problem-solving, or joint action
Scope	Users, citizens, and stakeholders provide significant input over time to help agencies identify opportunities, analyze problems. and creatively develop solutions within the scope of the agencies' current practice and jurisdiction
Interaction	Public agencies continue to set the basic agenda, but their role becomes less directive and more facilitative; these processes require deeper and more sustained dialogue among participants

LEVEL 4:	
Ambition	Public agencies, citizens, and stakeholders seek to identify opportunities for public value creation across boundaries and beyond agency objectives
Scope	Public and private actors engage on an equal footing in agenda-setting aimed at identifying common problems or designing new and better solutions
Interaction	Public agencies may sponsor, facilitate, and empower the co-creation process, but agendas emerge through interaction among all parties

LEVEL 5:	
Ambition	Co-creation becomes reflexive, as public agencies, users, citizens, and stakeholders together seek to co-govern and perhaps even innovate the very institutions and practices needed to make co-creation more effective and universally applied
Scope	Arenas take on the role as drivers of co-creation and promote opportunities for further co-creation
Interaction	A wider ecology of co-creation develops, with many overlapping and nested interaction arenas, some of which use the same platform

At the bottom of the ladder, the ambition for co-creation is limited and agencies use the co-creation process to marginally improve the performance of existing services and programs. The agenda is clearly set by the agency and the scope of participation and the degree of interaction are both quite limited. This level is at the boundary of what our definition would even count as co-creation. As one ascends the ladder, however, co-creation becomes more ambitious, extending to a more systematic redesign of services and programs. In addition, co-creation adopts a more proactive agenda that transcends existing services and programs in order to engage in problem-solving that goes beyond the confines of agency mandates and public jurisdictions. The agenda also becomes more open and emergent, developing through a more intense and sustained interaction of participants. Simultaneously, agency leadership becomes more facilitative than directive and the initiative for co-creation may come from outside the public sector. As co-creation extends toward the top of the ladder, it becomes more reflexive about co-creation itself and more attentive to creating the conditions under which co-creation can expand and flourish. Participation and interaction extend beyond specific co-creation arenas set up to achieve specific tasks, with participants engaging in multiple reinforcing arenas and building platforms that support the formation, multiplication, and adaptation of future arenas of co-creation.

One important issue that this ladder does not fully capture is where co-creation will be found. We might expect that it will first appear where public sector organizations interact directly with citizens or stakeholders with the goal of ensuring that services meet social needs. However, co-creation could also be used at the executive administrative or political levels to engage in strategic planning, crisis management, or policy formulation. Although these levels may be more reluctant to engage in co-creation due their concern about authority and accountability, there are certainly opportunities for these levels to benefit from co-creation in relation to complex problem-solving and policy making.

2.8 What Theoretical Perspectives Can We Draw upon to Elaborate Our Ideas?

As a body of theoretical and practical ideas, co-creation does not stand alone. Rather, the conceptualization and practical application of co-creation may benefit from insights drawn from a range of related discussions. In addition to the cognate concepts described earlier (citizen participation, deliberative publics, network governance, and social innovation), there are a number of other contemporary bodies of theory that we can draw upon to construct a more full-fledged theory of co-creation. We briefly introduce these theoretical perspectives here.

Design thinking is a body of work that has emerged in the last decade or so to apply design concepts to the reorganization of services and programs and to societal problem-solving more generally (Brown, 2008; Bason, 2010). A key principle of design thinking is user-centered design, which emphasizes that design must begin with a deep understanding of and empathy for the experiences that service users and program clients have as they utilize services and engage with programs. A related principle is that good design begins with a thorough investigation of the problems created by existing services and programs. In addition, design thinking encourages a process of problem-solving in which preliminary designs are prototyped and then further evaluated in a process of ongoing inquiry and iterative rounds of experimentation and redesign in conjunction with users and clients. These principles imply a bottom-up and emergent process of ongoing interaction and inquiry (Ansell & Torfing, 2014).

Collective impact is a concept that has recently been advanced in the philanthropic literature to understand how foundations and nonprofit organizations can be more effective in addressing societal problems and issues (Kania & Kramer, 2011, 2013; Flood et al., 2015). Rather than making grants to individual organizations, the collective impact literature stresses the importance of mobilizing the distributed resources and combined commitment of many groups in order to focus efforts on more transformational change. Kania and Kramer (2011) outline five basic principles for achieving collective impact: the formation of a common agenda, the development of a shared measurement system to evaluate progress, the development of mutually reinforcing activities by the various stakeholders, the development of continuous communications among these stakeholders, and the importance of "backbone organizations" that enable and facilitate this collaboration. Kania and Kramer (2013) particularly emphasize the importance of understanding transformational change as an emergent process.

A literature on *living labs* has developed over the last decade or so to encourage user-oriented innovation (Niitamo et al., 2006; Franz,

Tausz, & Thiel, 2015; Gascó, 2017). Living labs provide a framework and a set of resources enabling users to experiment with new innovations. They are often, but not necessarily, associated with user-oriented creation of digital technologies for use at the community level, particularly in urban areas. Bergvall-Kåreborn et al. (2009) suggest that living labs are built around five principles: first, *openness* to the resources and perspectives of a wide group of stakeholders; second, a recognition of the right of different stakeholders to *influence* the outcome of experimentation processes; third, appreciation of *real-world* constraints on innovation; fourth, a focus on creating *value*; and, finally, acknowledging the importance of being *accountable* to a wider community. One of the strengths of the literature on living labs is that it offers concrete guidance about how to organize user-centric co-creation in practice.

Crowdsourcing takes advantage of internet connectivity to mobilize inputs from highly distributed communities. Brabham defines crowdsourcing as an "online distributed problem-solving and production model that leverages the collective intelligence of online communities to serve specific organizational goals" (2013: xix). Although crowdsourcing may mobilize distributed communities to conduct a range of specific tasks, it can also be used to aggregate and harvest input on problem-solving from a wide range of actors. Crowdsourcing is often connected with the literature on *open innovation*, which stresses that innovation processes must open themselves to varied and distributed inputs (Hilgers & Ihl, 2010).

The literature on *public innovation* focuses on identifying drivers and barriers that allow the public sector to be more innovative. Although this literature has lagged behind the literature on private-sector innovation, it has begun to stress the value of both collaboration and design for producing innovation (Ansell & Torfing, 2014; Torfing & Triantafillou, 2016). This literature is also closely related to a body of literature on *public sector organizational change*, which stresses the importance of mobilizing input and support from frontline employees and external stakeholders in organizational change processes (Fernandez & Rainey, 2006). The distinction in this literature between planned and emergent change is particularly useful for our purposes (Van der Voet, Groeneveld, & Kuipers, 2014).

Finally, the literature on *democratic experimentalism* investigates institutional designs that allow many different stakeholders to engage in deliberative forums (Dorf & Sabel, 1998; Sabel & Zeitlin, 2010). This literature argues that experimentalist regimes have at least five key elements that foster deliberation and cooperation among stakeholders. First, stakeholders engage in deliberation to produce a common understanding of the relevant issue. Second, they develop a general framework with broadly defined goals for addressing this issue. Third, the responsibility for achieving these goals is delegated to local actors with an understanding of the implementation context. Fourth, these local actors provide feedback that allows monitoring of progress toward goal achievement and learning from best practices. Fifth, this feedback is used to periodically revise the overall framework and goals. Sabel and Zeitlin (2010) describe many examples of this type of regime in the European Union, such as the Open Method of Coordination.

2.9 Conclusion

This chapter has provided an overview of the concept of co-creation. A key progenitor of the concept of co-creation is the idea of co-production, which has been developed in both the private and public sectors. In both sectors, the concept of co-production has focused on the involvement of consumers or users in the production of basic services. In the private sector literature, this focus has arisen from an appreciation of the importance of understanding consumer experience in the provision of services to increase the value for both firms and consumers. This literature perceives the service sector as distinct from the manufacturing sector because consumers are inevitably involved in the production and consumption of services and thus play an active role as co-producers. The recognition that consumers are the experts of their own experience has led firms to appreciate that service production should be more interactive than top-down and unilateral. The public-sector literature has also come to recognize that users or clients who receive public services often participate actively in service production and are increasingly expected to do so.

Originally, these literatures focused rather narrowly on the participation of consumers or users in the production of services. However, by acknowledging the interactive (as opposed to linear), nature of the relationship with consumers and citizens, firms and public agencies have come to understand that this interaction can be creative rather than simply productive. In other words, consumers and citizens can provide critical creative inputs into wider processes of problem-solving. Although this expanded notion of co-creation (as opposed to co-production) bears some similarity with concepts like citizen participation, deliberative publics, network governance, and social innovation, we have emphasized its distinctive contribution to our understanding of citizen and stakeholder engagement.

To further distinguish co-creation from other collaborative modes of governance, we offered a systematic comparison of corporatism, collaborative governance, and co-creation. This comparison led us to emphasize the role of co-creation in creative problem-solving through the proactive mobilization of societal resources and through emergent processes of collaboration involving organized stakeholders and lay-actors such as users, citizens and community groups. We captured these distinctive features in our definition of co-creation.

The chapter also argued that co-creation can be understood as a continuous variable with gradations of ambition, scope, and intensity of interaction. To capture these gradations, we constructed a ladder of co-creation that describes the various forms that co-creation might take in the public sector. At the highest rung of this ladder, co-creation becomes a self-reflexive process that is concerned with extending and deepening processes of co-creation in the public sector.

Finally, we have concluded the chapter by examining related theoretical and practical discussions that can help to supplement our analysis of co-creation in subsequent chapters. These discussions include work on design thinking, collective impact, living labs, crowdsourcing, public innovation, public sector organizational change, and democratic experimentalism.

Now that we have established an understanding of the concept of co-creation, Chapter 3 will explore the prevalence of co-creation across sectors, countries, and levels of government.

3 | Co-creation Is Everywhere and Nowhere

Chapter 2 argued that co-creation builds on and extends a collaborative strategy previously embodied by the concepts of corporatism and collaborative governance. Whereas corporatism tends to restrict collaboration to peak economic interest groups engaged in economic bargaining, collaborative governance is typically a method utilized by public agencies to better manage their own agenda through collaboration with critical stakeholders. Co-creation further extends collaboration by widening the scope of who participates and what they strive to achieve. While traditional accounts of participatory governance have emphasized the importance of citizen and stakeholder involvement in governance and the value of democratic deliberation about joint outputs, co-creation goes a step further in emphasizing the role of relevant and affected actors in defining problems, designing, and testing solutions and contributing to their implementation and adaptation. In short, co-creation stresses the role of citizens or stakeholders in *creating* innovative public value outcomes.

Another aspect of co-creation brought out in Chapter 2 is that the initiative for public value creation can arise from both the public and the private sector. Whereas the collaborative governance literature tends to see the state as initiating collaboration and the social innovation literature regards innovation as arising from the initiative of social entrepreneurs (rather than the state), co-creation can be envisioned to some degree as a marriage between collaborative governance and social innovation. While either state agencies or social entrepreneurs may take the lead in initiating co-creation, the activity is understood to be a joint enterprise that mobilizes the energies, resources, and perspectives of both sectors.

A third aspect of our vision for co-creation is that it seeks to address public problems in an innovative and problem-solving fashion. Here, again, the concept straddles the existing literatures on public innovation and social innovation. Co-creation is not merely public innovation fostered by creative public agencies and public employees. Nor is it "social innovation" created by lone "social entrepreneurs." Rather, it is innovation by public actors working together with private actors and citizens to devise innovative solutions to shared public–private problems.

As expressed in the definition set out in Chapter 2, co-creation emphasizes *distributed and collaborative* processes of *creative problem-solving* that seek to *mobilize public and private resources* to foster *emergent solutions* in order to produce *public value*. If co-creation were established as a core principle of public governance, how would it change the way the public sector undertakes its business? Building on the conceptualization of co-creation set out in Chapter 2, we will draw out the implications that co-creation has for the public sector and its attempts to govern society and economy. Although co-creation can be layered on as an additional practice on top of existing public sector paradigms and routines, a more systematic and far-reaching reorientation of existing governance strategies would have to be realized to place co-creation at the center of the public agenda.

3.1 Breaking with a Linear Conception of Governance and Management

One way to imagine the implications of co-creation for public governance is that it requires transforming governance from a model of linear inputs and outputs into an interactive ecosystem. Our traditional models of the democratic process and of public management envision governance as a sequential set of steps in which public authority or managerial will is first translated into administrative conduct and then into service consumption or regulatory compliance by citizens. As everyone appreciates, this linear imagery is a gross simplification of what actually occurs in politics and governance. But it does characterize how public governance and management are often conceptualized. Consider, for instance, New Public Management. It conceives of governance and management as a linear sequence of principal–agent relationships linking politicians to agency managers, agency managers to employees, and employees to the citizens as service customers. From this perspective, public input in and through co-creation can only be conceived of as contributing to or disrupting this linear top-down principal–agent chain.

To think about why co-creation is different, it is useful to adopt what we will call an ecosystem perspective. From this perspective, an issue, problem, or policy domain contains a great number of activities and actors who are interacting in complex ways – that is, as an ecosystem. This is easy to imagine if you think of a hospital. There is the emergency room, the critical care unit, the nurses' union, the faculty of medical doctors, the patients themselves, their families, ambulance drivers, and so on. A hospital is easily imagined to be a complex ecosystem of interacting and interdependent people and activities. A common feature of such a system is that each of the groups and activities develops its own perspectives and interests, advancing them when and where possible. If the hospital is a single hierarchical organization, all these moving parts may be coordinated by a single overarching authority that can orchestrate their actions and ensure their harmony. However, as social, political, and economic ecosystems become more complex, as a result of their moving parts becoming more numerous, independent, and oriented toward external parties, hierarchical organization becomes increasingly difficult to maintain and impose. Co-creation seeks to exploit the polycentricity of the ecosystem to enhance value production while limiting the role of hierarchical control, thus embracing the idea of a distributed leadership. Even when co-creation is initiated by a single hierarchical organization, like a public agency or a hospital, it will typically require that the organization adopt an ecosystem-centric rather than an organization-centric perspective on governance in order to mobilize resources and spur innovation.

This ecosystem-centric perspective has increasingly been recognized in the area of "service-dominant systems," which think about the relationship of "service ecosystems" and "value co-creation" (Vargo & Lusch, 2016). Innovation is also increasingly thought about in "ecosystem" terms (Autio & Thomas, 2014). Co-creation, as Gouillart and Hallett (2015) note, requires a shift in perspective from a linear transactional view to an interdependent ecosystem view. They note that this transformation has important implications for how co-creation works. A key point is that co-creation systems evolve relatively organically over time. As Gouillart and Billings claim: "[b]uilding [a co-creation system] is like putting together a jigsaw puzzle: You need to construct it gradually by assembling pieces in various corners of the puzzle and then identifying emerging patterns." (2015: 3)

We can illustrate the interactive ecosystem logic of co-creation with an example from the Swedish city of Malmö, which created a *Building and Living Dialogue* to encourage the upgrading of building energy standards. The process worked on a neighborhood basis through a series of experimental efforts, each learning from and building on previous efforts. The process not only brought groups of stakeholders together but also engaged citizens in some of Sweden's most diverse neighborhoods directly in the planning process. Fitzgerald and Lenhart provide a good description of the interactive rather than linear nature of this process:

> To address challenges, Malmö initiated a participatory planning process, started by Malmö Municipal Housing Company (MKB Housing) and city representatives who met with Augustenborg's residents to discuss ideas for the redevelopment. City officials focused on energy efficiency and seasonal flooding. But residents also wanted solar panels like they saw in Western Harbour. Although solar panels were not part of the original plan, they were added in response to resident input. Planners learned how to initiate and implement participatory planning, including how to compromise, or clarify final decisions with residents. . . . (2016: 373)

As this description suggests, co-creation requires city planners to be truly willing to change their strategies in interaction with participants. Another feature of the Malmö program called out by Fitzgerald and Lenhart is that city agencies must be willing to engage in more horizontal coordination among themselves, breaking down traditional sectoral divisions of labor. They must also be willing to engage in projects on a more experimental basis and to take advantage of cumulative learning. Although such processes appear messy from the perspective of a more traditional top-down model of rational planning, the *Building and Living Dialogue* has been quite successful in upgrading Malmö's sustainability standards.

As an interactive process, co-creation also requires that leadership be conceived in new ways. For example, in the study of an effort to co-create an innovative green agenda in the city of Grand Rapids Michigan, Quick (2017) finds that leadership is itself emergent: "The history of leadership developing in Grand Rapids has this quality of emergence: it was marked by open-endedness, novelty, and change, yet there was cohesive momentum rather than chaotic disorder" (Quick, 2017: 464). The dynamic and diverse character of co-creation often

heightens the importance of "intermediaries" for integrating the different parts of the ecosystem. Although the designers of co-creation
processes may serve this go-between and boundary-spanning role,
a feature of co-creation processes is that intermediaries (persons or
organizations) may emerge from within and during the process of co-
creation (Moss et al., 2009). These intermediaries may be ad hoc and
there may be several such intermediaries in a co-creation process spe-
cializing in different aspects of bridging, aligning, and mediating.
Scholars have also emphasized the importance of "systemic" intermediaries who bundle several such roles together (Lente et al., 2003).

The attempt to link and integrate different parts of the ecosystem
requires "interactive empathy" between different parties and places
a premium on active learning among the participants (Laitinen,
Kinder, & Stenvall, 2018: 73). A move to co-creation also transforms
the character of knowledge production. Whereas the linear model
builds on the translation of expert knowledge to users (so-called
mode 1 knowledge production), co-creation typically calls for more
context-specific knowledge constructed together with the user (so-
called mode 2 knowledge production) (Greenhalgh et al., 2016). Co-
creation, however, is not about replacing professional expertise with
input from lay actors. Rather, it is about bringing professional expertise together with citizen input (Osborne & Strokosch, 2013). In fact,
co-creation transforms the whole thinking about the functioning of the
political-administrative system: it requires different kinds of forums for
citizen interaction on the input side, arenas for co-decision making to
facilitate throughput processes, opportunities for co-delivery and co-
production on the output side, and processes of co-evaluation at the
feedback stage. In short, the political-administrative system is not
divorced from society, but rather continuously interacts with it.

Given that co-creation has rather far-reaching implications for how
public governance functions, one might easily conclude that it is
unlikely to be embraced as a core strategy of governance. In a public
sector traditionally dominated by linear, centralized, and insulated
bureaucracies and subject to more recent reforms that stress manager-
ialism and market-based contracting, the move to co-creation is surely
a daunting one. Although they may have a lot to gain, central decision
makers face undeniable risks in departing from their well-established
systems and practices. We approach this issue in a number of ways.
First, we demonstrate that co-creation is already being experimented

with as a mode of public governance across many policy sectors and many countries. Next, we demonstrate that while this experimentation is extensive, the scale and scope of co-creation still remains limited. To understand why, we examine the barriers that co-creation may face in becoming mainstreamed. We then explore the contingent nature of these barriers and the strategies for overcoming them to achieve the wider application of co-creation.

3.2 Co-creation Is Everywhere

As we noted in Chapter 2, the concept of co-creation builds in part upon the earlier work of scholars on the co-production of services. Ostrom's early formation of the idea of co-production was inspired by policing, since she and her colleagues observed that the police cannot operate effectively without extensive interaction with citizens (Ostrom, et al. 1978; Alford, 2014). As scholars examined co-production more closely, they began to see that it was operating in many places where public services were being provided, including public safety (Eijk, Steen, & Verschuere, 2017), child care (Pestoff, 2006), immigration (Osborne & Strokosch, 2013), homelessness (Farr, 2016), health care (Steen, Manschot, & De Koning, 2011; Nederhand & Meerkerk, 2017), climate change (Homsy & Warner, 2013; Conrad, 2015), and schooling. (Palumbo et al., 2018)

Co-production has also been a geographically widespread phenomenon, extending well beyond developed democratic nations. Ostrom (1996) argues that co-production may even be more relevant for developing countries, though the operational challenges of successful co-production may be greater as well. In fact, Joshi and Moore (2004) have argued that what they call "institutionalized co-production" is common in the developing world. They provide a number of different examples, but point to irrigation as a particularly prominent case of co-production. Noting that successful examples of irrigation typically work through institutionalized co-production, they point out that irrigation delivery is difficult to achieve without co-production for a number of reasons. First, large numbers of small farmers make it difficult for irrigation agencies to successfully engage with them on an individual basis. Second, these farmers face an enormous variety of different contextual situations and irrigation agencies find it difficult to successfully manage for these contextual nuances. Finally, and compounding points one and two, formal irrigation agencies often lack the capacity to work closely with farmers one by one. These circumstances spur public agencies to co-produce irrigation services with farmers, thus making problem-solving a collective endeavor.

We have argued that co-creation goes beyond co-production in envisioning a role for citizens and stakeholders as creators – and not simply producers – of services. Although co-production is narrower in terms of the range of participating actors and their potential achievement, co-creation nevertheless depends on a productive interaction between public and private actors. Thus, the extensiveness of co-production tells us something about the potential for co-creation. If anything, co-creation has even more potential because it is not necessarily limited to service production, but extends to the design of a wide range of policies, programs, and planning strategies as well as to a broad set of societal problem-solving efforts. Indeed, Torfing, Sørensen, and Røiseland (2019) argue that co-creation already operates across policy sectors and in different countries. Although the concept of co-creation is of relatively recent coinage in the field of public governance, Tables 3.1 and 3.2 demonstrate that co-creation has rapidly become a widespread phenomenon both cross-sectorally and cross-nationally.

While acknowledging that this is not a representative sample and that certain communities of scholars (national, regional, or sectoral) may be more likely to pick up and run with certain concepts, our canvassing of the published literature suggests that co-creation has been particularly developed in the urban planning and health sectors and, regionally, in Northern Europe. However, the tables establish that co-creation is being utilized across many policy sectors and in all regions of the world.

For several reasons, we feel quite certain that these tables greatly *underestimate* the degree to which co-creation is already being utilized. First, in constructing these tables, we primarily relied on published journal articles and did not venture far into edited volumes, the grey literature, or project websites. Second, to assemble this literature, we primarily restricted our search term to "co-creation." As noted, this term is of relatively recent origin, particularly in the public sector. There may be numerous cases of co-creation that do not actually use this term. Third, we did not search the terms "collaboration" or "collaborative governance" or "social innovation." Although we think these searches would have yielded additional examples of co-creation,

Table 3.1 *Co-creation cases by policy sector*

Policy sector	Citation of co-creation cases
Agriculture	Sell et al. (2018)
Financial policy making and public budgeting	Siebers and Torfing (2018); Mikheeva and Tõnurist (2019); Woo (2019)
Open government data	Mulder (2012; Khayyat (2017), McBride et al. (2018, 2019)
Smart city development	Oksman, Väätänen, and Ylikauppila (2014); Mayangsari and Novani 2015; Pellicano et al. (2018)
Urban planning and community development	Mulder (2012); Yasuoka and Sakurai (2012); Stangel and Szóstek (2015); Bartenberger and Sześciło (2016); Kemp and Scholl (2016); Wang, Bryan-Kinns, and Ji (2016); Davis and Andrew (2017); Gascó and Eijk (2018); McMullin (2018); Menny, Palgan, and McCormick (2018); Mosquera (2018); Teder (2018); Bisschops and Beunen (2019); Rosen and Painter (2019)
Transportation	Gebauer, Johnson, and Enquist (2010); Fleischmann, Hielscher, and Merritt (2016); Leendertse et al. (2016); Sopjani et al. (2017); Won, Young-jun, and Jong-bae (2018); Nalmpantis et al. (2019); Pappers, Keserü, and Macharis (2019)
Park design	Ahn (2007); Klok (2013); Handberg, Mygind, and, Johansen (2018)
Waste management	Watson (1995); Ostrom (1996)
Community and public health	Bovaird and Loeffler (2012); Cepiku and Giordano (2014); Greenhalgh et al. (2016); Campos-Matos, Chrysou, and Ashton (2017); Leask et al. (2017); Heerik et al. (2017); De Winter (2018); Leask et al. (2019)
Health care	Cottam and Leadbeater (2004); Bowen et al. (2013); Eijk and Steen (2014); Donetto et al. (2015); Hardyman, Daunt, and Kitchener (2015); Windrum et al. (2016); Israilov and Cho (2017); Rantamäki (2017)

Table 3.1 (*cont.*)

Policy sector	Citation of co-creation cases
Elderly care	Jetté and Vaillancourt (2011); Laitinen, Kinder, and Stenvall (2018); Sørensen and Torfing (2018)
Disabilty	Handberg, Mygind, and Johansen (2018)
Education	Voorberg et al. (2017b)
Housing	Brandsen and Helderman (2012); Tortzen (2018); Galuszka (2019)
Immigration	Fanjoy and Bragg (2019)
Policing	Degnegaard, Degnegaard, and Coughlan (2015)
Sustainability	Fitzgerald and Lenhart (2016); Sopjani et al. (2017); Frantzeskaki and Rok (2018); Horsbøl (2018); Miller and Wyborn (2018); Puerari et al. (2018)
Climate change	Nambisan and Nambisan (2013); Conrad (2015)
Fisheries management	Molen et al. (2015); Pope et al. (2019)
Water management	Dobre, Ranzato, and Moretto (2019); Buuren, Meerkerk, and Tortajada (2019)
Coastal hazards	Kench et al. (2018)

Table 3.2 *Co-creation cases by country*

Country	Citations of co-creation cases
Australia	Davis and Andrew (2017)
Austria	Bartenberger and Sześciło (2016); Windrum et al. (2016)
Belgium	De Winter (2018); Dobre, Ranzato, and Moretto (2019); Pappers, Keserü, and Macharis (2019)
Brazil	Watson (1995); Ostrom (1999)
Canada	Jetté and Vaillancourt (2011); Fanjoy and Bragg (2019)
China	Yin et al. (2017); Wang, Bryan-Kinns, and Ji (2016)
Denmark	Nambisan and Nambisan (2013); Degnegaard, Degnegaard, and Coughlan (2015); Handberg, Mygind, and Johansen (2018); Horsbøl (2018); Siebers and Torfing (2018); Tortzen (2018)
Estonia	Voorberg et al. (2015); Voorberg et al. (2017a)
Ethiopia	Sell et al. (2018)

Table 3.2 (*cont.*)

Country	Citations of co-creation cases
Finland	Oksman, Väätänen, and Ylikauppila (2014); Pirinen (2016); Rantamäki (2017); Laitinen, Kinder, and Stenvall (2018)
France	Mcmullin (2018)
Germany	Voorberg et al. (2017a); Menny, Palgan, and McCormick (2018); Teder (2018); Nalmpantis et al. (2019)
Ghana	Koo and Ahn (2018)
Greece	Genitsaris et al. (2017)
Indonesia	Mayangsari and Novani (2015)
Ireland	Khayyat (2017)
Italy	Palumbo et al. (2018); Pellicano et al. (2018); Nalmpantis et al. (2019)
Japan	Yasuoka and Sakurai (2012)
Korea	Ahn (2007); Won, Young-jun, and Jong-bae (2018); Koo and Ahn (2018)
Mozambique	Beran et al. (2018)
Nepal	Beran et al. (2018)
Netherlands	Mulder (2012); Kemp and Scholl (2016); Leendertse et al. (2016); Heerik et al. (2017); Voorberg et al. (2017b); Puerari et al. (2018); Siebers and Torfing (2018); Bisschops and Beunen (2019); Nalmpantis et al. (2019)
New Zealand	Kench et al. (2018)
Nicaragua	Klok (2013)
Norway	Mogstad, Høiseth, and Pettersen (2018)
Peru	Beran et al. (2018)
Philippines	Galuszka (2019)
Poland	Stangel and Szóstek (2015); Gawlowski (2018); Wiktorska-Święcka (2018)
Portugal	Fleischmann, Hielscher, and Merritt (2016)
Singapore	Mikheeva and Tõnurist (2019); Woo (2019)
Slovakia	Nemec et al. (2016); Voorberg et al. (2015)
South Africa	Biljohn and Lues (2019)
Spain	Gascó and Eijk (2018)
Sweden	Fitzgerald and Lenhart (2016); Sopjani et al. (2017); Horsbøl (2018); Menny, Palgan, and McCormick (2018)
Switzerland	Gebauer, Johnson, and Enquist (2010)
United Kingdom	Cottam and Leadbeater (2004); Bowen et al. (2013); Gouillart and Hallett (2015); Campos-Matos, Chrysou, and Ashton (2017); Laitinen, Kinder, and Stenvall (2018)
United States	Conrad (2015); McBride et al. (2018); Rosen and Painter (2019)

our search task would have also been endless. We did, however, conduct some limited searches using the term "participatory design." Fourth, we largely excluded cases that primarily focused on the co-production of knowledge (which are numerous in the field of environmental governance) or on the technical aspects of software and other tools designed to support co-creation. Finally, we only cite actual cases of co-creation in the tables and not theoretical discussions about the prospective use of co-creation in a sector or country. The result is that this is certainly a very conservative list of co-creation cases.

Although these two tables demonstrate the breadth of the application of co-creation across sectors and nations, they do not provide as much insight into the extensiveness of co-creation within any particular public sector. Although it may be an outlier, we did find one article about a Korean Citizens Policy Design Group that encourages co-creation of policy. Koo and Ahn report that: "Since 2014, 26 government agencies and 10 metropolitan cities have piloted the 'Citizens Policy Design Group'. In 2016, 382 policy projects for consumer-oriented policy services employed the initiative, involving 44 central government agencies and 338 municipalities." (2018: 290)

Another study that gives some sense of the extensiveness of co-creation within a particular public sector comes from a survey of Australian local governments. The survey found that 26.3 percent of Australian local governments currently use co-design processes, while 26.9 percent report the intention to use them in the future (Christensen & McQuestin, 2019: 465). In Denmark, a report from the Center of Public Innovation finds that 79 percent of all public innovations have resulted from collaboration with one or more external partners (Lykkebo, Jakobsen, & Sauer, 2018).

The tables also do not fully illustrate the possibility for co-creation to scale across different levels of governance (Ansell & Torfing, 2018). Much of the focus of co-production has been on the municipal and residential level (Brudney & England, 1983; Percy, 1984; Pestoff, 2006) and the emerging interest in co-creation has had a similar focus. Most of the cases in Tables 3.1 and 3.2 are local in scale, although some of these local efforts are being promoted by national governments. The prominence of the local level in examples of co-creation is probably in part due to the proximity of local governments to citizens. Many government services are delivered locally where users and citizens have easier access to and a clear interest in participation.

There is reason to believe, however, that co-creation is not merely a local phenomenon. To illustrate, the national public health authority in the Netherlands recently developed and applied a co-creation approach to public health planning. The process involved more than 100 stakeholders in identifying future challenges and developing normative scenarios, thus enabling policy makers to make sound and well-informed choices about the development of Dutch health care (Leask et al., 2019). We also note the example of the United Nations Children's Fund (UNICEF), which has made co-creation a central feature of its mission. The UNICEF program UPLIFT, for example, has embraced co-creation as a central strategy for youth empowerment (Shinya, 2017). Driven by UNICEF's Office of Innovation, this international organization is experimenting with co-creation in many parts of the world. Thus, while co-creation may be the most prominent at the local level, it is certainly possible to imagine its expansion at the national and international levels.

3.3 Co-creation Is Nowhere

Although Tables 3.1 and 3.2 clearly demonstrate that co-creation is bubbling up as a strategy for service design, problem-solving, and policy making, we cannot claim that it has been mainstreamed as a core practice of public governance. Far from it. Nederhand and Meerkerk (2017) study Dutch government documents for a shift in governing logic with respect to citizens and the provision of care. They find that the dominant narrative logic (in the period between 2012 and 2015) is still "citizen as client," although the narrative logic of "citizen as co-producer" has expanded significantly. We expect this finding to hold elsewhere as well. Co-production and co-creation may be in fashion, but their actual extension appears limited.

The examples identified in the tables have several limitations that prevent us from claiming that co-creation has been widely or systematically embraced. A first reason is that many of the examples of co-creation provided have a relatively experimental nature and can be understood as early efforts to determine whether co-creation is a fruitful approach to public governance. Second, these co-creation cases are not yet mainstreamed within public organizations. As Pirinen observes in a review of the drivers and barriers of co-creation, "one-off co-design workshops or short-term projects were more typical than the construction of continuous co-design practices" (2016: 37). A third reason is that although some of the cases extend to problem-solving and policy making, many of them remain focused on relatively specific service delivery issues. While service design is an important and legitimate area of co-creation, we see fewer cases associated with more ambitious applications of co-creation in the field of planning, program innovation, and policy making (but see also Bason, 2010). A final reason that these examples do not amount to a comprehensive strategy is that many of them might be characterized as add-ons to current governing practices rather than as fundamental transformations of core practices.

Thus, while we see co-creation bubbling up everywhere, we rarely see it as a comprehensive strategy or mainstream practice. Co-creation is on the march in some local municipalities and government agencies, but nowhere has co-creation established itself as the dominant strategy at the national and sectoral levels, although the United Nations embraces co-creation as a global strategy for reaching the Sustainable Development Goals.

To understand why co-creation has not yet achieved its potential, it is worth considering some of the challenges it confronts. We have argued above that co-creation builds naturally on situations where the co-production of services is found. So it is worth beginning our analysis by examining what scholars have suggested about the drivers and barriers of co-production. Ostrom (1996), for example, argues that for successful co-production to occur, technologies, resources, and motivations must be synergistic – that is, both public agencies and citizens (or stakeholders) must control aspects of production that are complementary when brought together. Moreover, legal frameworks must allow for customization of production. Additionally, the state and citizens must make a credible commitment to one another. And finally, both the state and citizens must have an incentive to contribute to co-production. Bovaird and Loeffler (2012) suggest the existence of a number of barriers to effective co-production, including the short-term or narrow objectives of funders or commissioners of services, the difficulty of providing evidence of the value of co-production due to the long term or complex nature of out-comes, limits in the available skills to carry out co-production, and the unwillingness of the state and professions to give up control.

Encompassing insights from both the co-production and co-creation literatures, Voorberg, Bekkers, and Tummers (2015) identify a number of potentially limiting factors, including incompatible organizational structures, negative attitudes toward citizens, risk averse administrative cultures, and unclear incentives. On the citizen side, the lack of citizen interest in participating or the weakness of skills necessary to participate can limit co-production and co-creation. Communities may also lack the social capital to participate effectively. Finally, citizens may lack trust in the co-production or co-creation process. Similarly, Gouillart and Hallett (2015) describe a number of obstacles to effective public sector co-creation, including legal and regulatory requirements that make the administrative process rigid; political and partisan divisions that undermine collaboration; and the problems with scaling up co-creation.

Building on these analyses, we can identify political, legal, institutional, and social factors that stand in the way of making co-creation a more comprehensive and mainstream strategy. Politically, a key challenge is that government change brings new political parties to power, which can make long-term commitments to co-creation difficult (Baptista, Alves, & Matos, 2019). Another political challenge arises from the tensions between government responsibility and citizen influence. This challenge is well described by Buuren, Meerkerk, and Tortajada (2019) in their analysis of co-creation in water governance: "To summarize, the Achilles' heel of invited forms of participation is the difficult tradeoff between the public responsibility to provide water-related goods and services and the ambition to give stakeholders real influence in this domain" (2019, 376). They argue that this challenge is particularly impactful in countries where the legal order is critical for determining outcomes, thus leaving little room for citizens or stakeholders to provide input and shape outcomes.

A third political challenge is that co-creation may require some degree of citizen demand in order to sustain it. In a cross-national study of water governance, for example, Graversgaard et al. found that "when stakes are high and clear" participation in co-governance was more forthcoming (2018: 12). This point is important because without a degree of civic mobilization, co-creation may have a tendency to slide back into a ritualized consultation practice, as Rantamäki (2017) found in an analysis of a Finnish co-creation strategy to reform welfare services.

Legal and institutional factors can also pose a challenge. Voorberg et al. (2017a) argue that the success of co-creation depends on whether state and governance traditions are oriented toward the sharing of authority and consulting with the public. More authoritarian states and state institutions that consider decisions about the public interest to be their prerogative are not as amenable to co-creation as more plural and consultative state systems. Legal concerns may also constrain the public sector from engaging with citizens in co-creation. For example, American public managers viewed the idea of crowdsourced problem-solving via the platform Challenge.gov as legally risky for a number of specific reasons (Mergel, 2017). Alternatively, co-creation initiatives may have to wrestle with regulatory constraints, as a case study of urban redevelopment in the Netherlands discovered (Bisschops & Beunen, 2019). However, administrative law may enable, as well as prevent co-creation (Sześciło, 2018). For example, open data laws and legal norms about consultation of affected parties may encourage co-creation.

In other cases, the challenge can be attributed to institutionalized patterns of thought. Public officials may simply not have a very favorable attitude toward co-creation (Voorberg et al., 2015). In a survey of Italian municipalities, for example, Magno and Cassia (2015) found that mayors were not yet ready to embrace citizen co-creation. In another Italian survey, 30.8 percent of municipal waste offices reported that they did not think that involvement of citizens in co-design could improve the efficiency or effectiveness of waste services, while 42.3 percent reported that they favored citizen involvement in general, but not in the design stage (Landi and Russo, 2019).

Even in countries with strong traditions of civic engagement, political institutions may not yet be oriented toward cultivating co-creation (but see Voorberg et al., 2017b). In a study of municipal climate adaptation in Sweden, for example, Brink and Wamsler found that municipalities "rarely promote pro-active (i.e. anticipatory) citizen engagement or ownership of adaptation" (2018: 92). In many contexts, experts are often loath to give up control over decision making (Parrado et al., 2013; Pirenen, 2016), although the issue may also be – as found in cross-national focus groups – that civil servants lack the skills to engage in collaboration with the public. In any case, Torfing, Sørensen, and Røiseland conclude that, "some significant mental shifts are required to get the various public and private actors to embrace the new arenas of co-creation." (2019: 812)

As these examples suggest, challenges may arise from the limitations of existing institutional arrangements that constrain efforts to undertake co-creation. However, a somewhat different institutional challenge may arise from the failure or inability to craft new purpose-built institutions for co-creation. For example, Graversgaard et al. find that a "key enabling factor for effective water co-governance is creating an institutional and administrative framework within which stakeholders with different interests can discuss and agree to cooperate and coordinate their actions" (2018: 14). The knowledge and capacity to create such frameworks may not be readily available or slow to emerge.

Incentive problems may also represent a challenge to effective co-creation. These incentive problems may arise for both government agencies and for citizens (Voorberg et al., 2015). On the government side, co-creation may appear to be risky, to result in loss of influence, and to be costly to undertake. On the citizen side, all the well-known challenges of engaging in collective action are present. On both sides, these incentive problems may be magnified by lack of time and resources (Pirinen, 2016) and by financial constraints (Dobre, Ranzato, & Moretto, 2019).

Not all of these challenges can be easily addressed. Some political systems are likely to remain more resistant to adopting strategies of co-creation than others. However, we think there are three broad ways to increase the salience of co-creation strategies – to increase the demand, to reduce the relative costs, and to demonstrate the potential of co-creation.

The first way to mainstream co-creation is to increase the demand for it. Even in unlikely contexts for co-creation, the interaction of social movements and entrepreneurial state officials may produce demand for it, as Rossi (1994) has shown for urban regeneration in the Italian city of Naples where existing political and administrative institutions were not necessarily conducive to co-creation. Similarly, in a study of urban housing in the Philippines, Galuszka (2019) found that the scaling up of co-creation required the citywide political mobilization of the urban poor. Political mobilization helped the urban poor to keep the housing issue on the political agenda and reinforced the demand for continued participation.

Beyond social movement mobilization, however, we might also consider how citizen motivations to participate in co-creation processes can be enhanced. A number of studies have established relevant findings. Parrado et al. (2013) have found in a survey that personal efficacy is consistently important in explaining motivation to participate in coproduction. Participation in co-creation depends on a feeling of being able to make a difference and a sense of ownership over the process (Voorberg et al., 2015). A study of urban planning in Finland also found that citizens wanted to be informed about how their inputs were used and suggested that real-time feedback could improve participation (Oksman, Väätänen, & Ylikauppila, 2014).

The type of motivation also matters. Eijk and Steen (2014) discovered that community-centered motivations are more important than egocentric motivations in explaining participation in coproduction. Motivation to participate may also depend in part upon the social nature of participation – that is, the feeling of belonging to a collective process (Voorberg et al., 2015). Relationships are also important for recruitment to co-creation projects and direct and personal recruitment strategies can spur citizen engagement (Marschall, 2004). Careful design of co-creation processes may help to increase motivation to participate, particularly if incentives for participation can be targeted to different groups (Brandsen, Steen, & Verschuere, 2018). Some want to participate because they broaden their social contacts; others want to be impactful; and still others want to enhance their skills by participating in co-creation.

A second way to enhance co-creation is to reduce the relative costs it imposes on both government and on citizens (Voorberg, Bekkers, & Tummers, 2015). On the government side, this will typically mean working out design templates for co-creation that can be easily deployed. An example might be the use of urban "living labs," which have been proliferating in Europe. Although these urban platforms have to be adapted to local contexts, their design has become more standard and arguably less costly to implement for local governments. According to Gouillart and Hallett, "scaling up occurs through the peer-to-peer sharing of locally generated ideas and practices" (2015: 46). Hence, templates developed in one jurisdiction may be used in another.

On the citizen side, new digital technologies show promise for reducing the cost of engaging in co-creation. Nambisan and Nambisan argue that "the availability of new technologies (e.g., social media) has radically lowered the cost of collaboration and the distance between government agencies and the citizens they serve" (2013: 8; see also Halmos, Misuraca, & Viscusi, 2019). However, other scholars are more skeptical about the ability of digital technologies to facilitate citizen participation in co-creation and note that they may distract citizens from engaging in face-to-face participation (Lember, Brandsen, & Tõnurist, 2019). Some research though suggests that citizens may prefer co-creation via digital platforms because these permit flexible use of time (Neulen, 2016). Further experimentation is necessary to discover what kinds of digital technologies are more or less useful for facilitating co-creation.

Finally, we think that co-creation can be mainstreamed as government agencies, citizens and stakeholders come to recognize its potential for service improvement, problem-solving and policymaking. To some extent, the value of co-creation can be learned from pilot and demonstration projects that are currently on-going and may leave a legacy that deserves to be emulated. Brandsen, Steen, and Verschuere (2018) argue that these experiments need to be strategically well-focused and structured in order to demonstrate their potential and should not over-promise. Another strategy, however, is to enable participants in co-creation to learn-by-doing. As actors engage in co-creation, their ambition and their role can expand over time as a result of experiential learning (Horsbøl, 2018). In an analysis of several co-creation cases, Voorberg et al. (2017a) find that both citizens and public officials can become more favorable over time toward the value of co-creation through participating in its processes.

3.4 Five Strategies for Developing Co-creation as a Central Governance Tool

This chapter has established that co-creation is already being used in many countries and sectors. However, we have also found that co-creation is somewhat limited in its application and has not yet fully penetrated the public sector at the strategic and operational level. In the last section, we identified some of the barriers and challenges to the fuller expansion of co-creation. To conclude the chapter on a slightly more optimistic note, we have extracted five strategies from our review of the empirical literature on co-production and co-creation that may permit co-creation to become a more central governance tool. To illustrate each strategy, we provide an example showing how they might work in practice.

3.4.1 Governments and Civil Society Actors at All Levels Can Undertake Strategically Focused Co-creation Experiments in Order to Fully Demonstrate "Proof of Concept" and to Engage in Learning-by-Doing

An example of a relatively large-scale co-creation effort is provided by Danish police reform (Degnegaard, Degnegaard, & Coughlan, 2015). The effort included bringing together a group of professionals and external stakeholders to consider how the police should address two major issues – organized crime in vulnerable neighborhoods and burglaries of private homes. The effort was carefully organized to use design principles such as storytelling, brainstorming, and proto-typing in order to develop better solutions for these issues. The project enjoyed the active support of the Police Commissioner, Helle Kyndesen, who stated that "[w]e need to work with society outside the police force to solve these challenges and we need help to see how to do it" (quoted by Degnegaard, Degnegaard, & Coughlan, 2015: 17).

The design workshop ultimately produced eight different ideas for how to respond to the two major issues. Degnegaard, Degnegaard, and Coughlan (2015) observe that these ideas allowed the Commissioner to ultimately reframe the police's approach to those issues. Importantly, the researchers also note that this large-scale co-design effort encouraged both problem-solving and "problem-finding," since it allowed for a deep investigation of the issues and facilitated iterative reformulation of the problems themselves. This co-creation project demonstrated "proof of concept" (that a co-design approach was viable) and a capacity for learning-by-doing. Together with other strategically focused experiments with collaborative problem-solving, the Danish police have made co-creation a core operational principle and provided tools for working with co-created problem-solving in all police precincts.

3.4.2 Governments, Private Foundations, Nonprofit Agencies, Social Movements, and Citizen Associations Can Provide Authorization and Support for Undertaking Co-creation Experiments and Create Incentives for Their Own Staff and External Actors to Engage in These Experiments

An example of how private foundations can support co-creation comes from an anti-poverty campaign in the Coachella Valley of California. The campaign began when four civic organizations – FIND Food Bank, United Way of the Desert, the Regional Access Project Foundation, and the Desert Healthcare District – came together to brainstorm about the challenges they faced in providing adequate food supplies to impoverished families in the Valley. The organizations formed a partnership that was then funded by the *Collaborating for Clients* initiative sponsored by The Laura and John Arnold Foundation. The funding allowed the partnership to engage in strategic planning and to convene a series of workshops to address food insecurity. Over time, the partnership adopted a more inclusive co-creation strategy prompted by its increasing recognition of how deeply rooted and complex the problem of food insecurity was in the Valley's Latinx community. To do so, it began to build collective action networks to implement its pilot programs and initiated a series of focus groups and listening sessions in order to deepen its engagement with the community. This work eventually led the partnership to receive additional funding from the Robert Wood Johnson Foundation. The initiative that grew out of this funding led to the creation of an organization named *Lift to Rise*, which partnered with the County of Riverside Economic Development Agency. Additional funding was then forthcoming. Rosen and Painter summarize how this program gradually expanded into a major co-creation project:

> ... [T]he initiative has created multiple opportunities to attract significant new investment and establish new relationships with some of the largest national foundations within a historically disinvested region. This reflects the initiative's intentional strategy to create bridges to financial and technical resources to build local capacity and power. Fundamentally, their success at catalyzing new investment from national funders reflects the initiative's strong external networks, leveraged to draw in new resources for residents and organizations to catalyze beneficial new investment... At the same time, the initiative is developing a resident table to institutionalize and empower

residents to participate and gain decision-making influence and is hiring additional staff from the community. The work of connecting residents to power and developing their influential local control is ongoing but has evolved considerably since the initiative's beginning. (2019: 344)

A key point made by Rosen and Painter is that it is not sufficient to simply encourage community participation. The promise of co-creation, as they develop it, is that it connects community participation to sources of power and resources. This case demonstrates how foundations have provided critical support for co-creation efforts in the US context, but also illustrates how co-creation has helped to elicit and deepen that support. The Coachella Valley campaign was not a single one-off effort, but a project that developed into an ongoing co-creation enterprise.

3.4.3 Platforms, Templates, and Digital Technologies Can Be Further Developed to Reduce the Costs of Participation and Collaboration and to Increase the Motivation of Governments, Citizens, and Stakeholders to Engage in High Quality Co-creation

A range of tools can be created to lower the cost and increase the quality of co-creation. An innovative participatory land-use planning framework developed for use in less developed regions and tested on six villages in Laos provides a good example of the value of such tools (Bourgoin et al., 2012). The research team collected data on village land use patterns in conjunction with village representatives. The team then helped to establish village management committees and trained these committees in using a unique game that enabled the committees to explore zoning options in a low-cost fashion. A three-dimensional landscape model as well as Geographic Information System (GIS) maps were then used to help the management committees visualize preliminary zoning strategies. Simulation and visualization tools like these provide a one example of how the costs of co-creation can be reduced for local communities and they may also help to improve the quality of the outputs and outcomes of co-creation. To the extent that these tools are reusable elsewhere, they can also be deployed in several locations to leverage the cost of developing them.

3.4.4 Large Scale Public and Private Organizations Can Provide the Organizational Infrastructure for Realizing a More Ambitious Co-creation Agenda

A case study of the Austrian nationwide public access defibrillation program illustrates how a nonprofit organization can become the backbone of an extended co-creation effort by using its own network to initiate local co-creation (Windrum et al., 2016). The program was designed to encourage the diffusion of portable automated external defibrillators (AEDs) in conjunction with laypeople who were trained in the use of these AEDs. To encourage this diffusion, the Austrian Red Cross (ARC) took the lead role in developing an innovation network in which they served as the intermediary between citizens, medical professionals, politicians, and firms to ensure the proper supply and demand for the AEDs. In doing this, ARC utilized its own resources and competences and its Austrian-wide organizational network to facilitate the mobilization of citizens and other stakeholders.

3.4.5 Co-creation Can Be Deployed as a General Framework at Larger Scales, Such as Entire Cities or Regions, to Support Multiple Co-creation Efforts

An example of how co-creation might scale from single- to multi-project efforts is provided by the strategy of Mayor Rees of Bristol, United Kingdom, to initiate a broad place-based agenda for co-creation. The program was called "One City," and Hambleton (2019) describes it as having six component features. First, the Mayor convened periodic and inclusive "city gatherings" to encourage people to come together in conversations across sectors. Second, he created a dedicated "innovation zone" to provide space for people to come together and develop urban innovations. Third, he encouraged various civic groups and city agencies to develop specific collaborative projects to address concrete issues. Fourth, a One City plan was developed to provide overall strategic direction to the project. Fifth, the program provided leadership training to individuals and civic groups to encourage them to take up problem-solving initiatives. Finally, One City created a funding board to find innovative ways of funding these collaborative projects. In contrast with many one-off co-creation projects, the One City agenda sought to provide a framework for multiple projects at the scale of an entire city.

These and other strategies will be further elucidated in later chapters of the book. Chapter 4 explores and explains how platforms can generate co-creation arenas.

4 | Co-creation as Generative Governance

One of the distinctive features of co-creation is that it is an emergent, interactive process. Citizens, stakeholders, politicians, and public officials engage and deliberate with one another and out of this interaction emerges something new – a new policy, program, or strategy, an innovative societal solution, or improved conditions for future collaboration. While politics and administration have always been and always will be emergent and interactive processes (at least for small groups of decision makers), co-creation extends, deepens, and broadens the scope of this process. It extends participation to a wider group of stakeholders, deepening its application within any specific policy domain, and broadening its scope to a larger set of issues (Boivard, 2007; Paskaleva, Cooper, & Concilo, 2018). A unique attribute of co-creation is that both public and private actors can initiate it and that leadership is distributed rather than centralized.

Distributed innovation has to emerge through the interaction of multiple parties "without the planning of a managerial mastermind" (Kornberger, 2017: 181). As a result, the interactive and emergent character of co-creation creates new opportunities and new challenges that call for an understanding of the distinctive social dynamics at work in co-creation processes and the particular features of institutions designed to direct and enable these social dynamics. Bovaird describes such social dynamics in the context of co-production: "Relationship building in multipurpose, multiagency, multilevel partnerships is likely to be relatively self-organized and less amenable to linear social engineering interventions" (2007: 857). Yet, we cannot expect these relationships to emerge spontaneously or to be completely self-governing; some mechanisms and institutions are needed to generate co-creation without dictating the outcomes.

In this chapter, we refer to these distinctive mechanisms and institutional features that facilitate co-creation as "generative governance."

To put it very simply, when political and administrative processes are interactive and emergent, we need to pay particular attention to how they can be stimulated, supported, and accelerated without predetermining their form, content, and outcomes (Fleming, Mingo, & Chen, 2007).

To be successful, co-creation demands a greater tolerance for the open-ended and sometimes vexing nature of interactive and emergent processes. Sanders and Stappers express this point; co-design and co-creation processes have a "fuzzy front end" (2008: 6) in the sense that specific problems, goals, and solutions are not predetermined at the outset, but subject to negotiation, expansive learning, and chance discoveries. Co-creation is by no means alone in encountering this situation. Many complex and non-linear processes of creativity and innovation confront this basic challenge. Consider the following description of "online collaborations" (OCs):

Tensions in an OC will flare up. Passionate emotions will become inflamed. Time will pressure people into making statements that might appear harmful to the community. Ideas may become cryptic and not helpful to the community. Temporary and incomplete convergence may lead to such disorganization that participants cannot find ideas, threads of ideas, or ways to enter into a topic to be able to make a valuable contribution. The negative consequences of social ambiguity may take hold to such an extent that deception and uncivilized behavior prevails. (Faraj, Jarvenpaa, & Majchrzak, 2011: 1231)

The authors of this study argue that this type of exchange cannot be successfully managed solely by formal structural mechanisms. In other words, the negative features in these interactions cannot be eliminated by retreating to a hierarchical imposition of order, since that would crush the open and creative features of the interaction and stifle the process of collaborative innovation. Instead, they argue, the strategy must be a "generative" one that harnesses the tensions inherent in any interactive, emergent situation through dynamic processes of role-playing, channeling participation, shaping boundaries, and providing "affordances."

In this chapter, we argue that co-creation requires what we will call "generative governance." We will first explore the meaning of the term "generative" and the concept of "generativity." Then we consider some key components of generative governance and how they relate to co-creation. Our main argument is that generative governance involves the formation of platforms that in turn foster arenas where co-creation processes can unfold.

4.1 What Does "Generative" Mean?

In ordinary language, "generative" simply means *tending to generate*. The term has been used in a number of different fields to capture attempts to enable open-ended processes of productive transformation. For example, the field of linguistics uses the concept of "generative grammar" to describe how a limited number of linguistic elements and rules can be used to produce an unlimited number of meanings (Corballis, 1992). Another well-known example comes from psychology, where Erickson used the term "generativity" to describe a life stage in which people become concerned with cultivating the next generation (Erikson 1950). A third usage can be traced to critical realism and the philosopher Bhaskar's description of "generative mechanisms" as causal mechanisms that generate "...the flux of phenomena that constitute the actual" (2008; 37; see also Henfridsson & Bygstad, 2013). The term "generative theory" has also been used in social psychology and organization theory to describe how theory can "expand the realm of the possible" by pointing to alternative ideas and conceptions that can enhance the possibility of change (Gergen, 1978; Bushe & Paranjpey, 2015, 309).

While "generative" is used as a descriptor in a variety of domains, we believe that the usage of the term closest in spirit to the one we advance comes from debates about how to regulate the Internet. Zittrain has argued that the power of the Internet is that it embodies the property of *generativity*, which he argues "...denotes a technology's overall capacity to produce unprompted change driven by large, varied, and uncoordinated audiences" (2006: 1980). Zittrain argues that generative technologies have a "capacity for leverage across a range of tasks" and are easily adapted and mastered. The Internet allows users to easily find and process widely distributed resources and data and also to create their own websites and communication structures. In other words, the generativity of the Internet stems from its capacity to enable "... users to generate new, valuable uses that are easy to distribute and are in turn sources of further innovation" (Zittrain, 2006; see also Post, 2009). The literature observes that digital technologies create generativity because of their features of reprogrammability and their knock-on effects (waves of innovation) and because of the number of "traces" they leave, upon which additional innovations can be built (Yoo et al,. 2012; Foerderer, Kude, Schütz, & Heinzl, 2014).

Like the Internet, co-creation is also a form of distributed action that aims to bring multiple parties together to engage in productive transformation. While scholars have described different forms of co-production and co-creation, they have not sufficiently investigated the triggering mechanisms that allow co-creation to emerge, expand the frontiers of possibility, and ultimately produce public value outcomes. To understand these triggering mechanisms, we import and adapt the concept of generativity to the domains of public governance and co-creation.

On a general level, we define generative governance as:

Governance that facilitates and enables the emergence of productive interaction among distributed actors.

There are several well-known examples of generative governance. One is the idea of reflexive law, which creates processes and procedures of legal interaction rather than prescribing legal outcomes (Teubner, 1982). Another well-known example is the concept of quasi-markets, whereby public purchasers attempt to generate efficient outcomes by creating procedures for service providers to compete for contracts. A third example is devolution, where a higher-order jurisdiction empowers lower-order jurisdictions to undertake particular actions. Co-creation is also a type of generative governance, but it differs in the sense that it does not take a legal form, it facilitates collaboration rather than competition, and it does not take place between different levels of a hierarchy. As a form of generative governance, co-creation involves the creation of interactive spaces where distributed actors can come together to work collaboratively to solve jointly defined problems.

Based on this new perspective on co-creation as a form of generative governance, it is useful to analytically focus on four different aspects of generativity:

Generative interaction refers to the attitudes and behavioral patterns of participants that enable and facilitate their capacity and motivation to creatively contribute to problem-solving and the production of public value (Hopkins, Tidd, & Nightingale 2014). Trust, synergy, and mutual respect are prominent examples of factors that are conducive to stimulating successful co-creation.

Generative tools are devices or technologies that allow actors involved in co-creation to easily produce new knowledge, ideas, products, solutions, and so on (Sanders 2000). Examples of generative tools include computer simulations and physical models that help actors to visualize, concretize, and evaluate future options.

Generative processes are structured procedures that allow groups of actors to arrive at conclusions about joint action by passing through a number of stages or steps. Processes like "scenario planning" or "design thinking" are good examples of what we mean by generative processes.

Generative institutions are the infrastructures that create the spaces and opportunities for co-creation to emerge, develop, and adapt. We will argue for the importance of two types of generative institutions for co-creation: platforms and arenas.

Building on this preliminary discussion, we now explore each of these forms of generativity in turn.

4.2 Generative Interaction

An obvious point is that people have to connect and communicate with one another in order to engage in co-creation. In the context of private-sector co-creation, Prahalad and Ramaswamy (2004) argue that there are four building blocks of productive interactions between firms and their customers. The first is a *dialogue*, which in turn requires that "...the firm and the consumer must become equal and joint problem solvers" and that there be clear rules of engagement (2004: 9). Effective dialogue also depends on *access* and *transparency*, which are the second and third building blocks. Consumers must have access to transparent information for effective joint dialogue and problem-solving. To provide these building blocks, firms must move away from their tendency to create information asymmetries for their customers. The fourth building block is *customized exchange* with customers that share the risks and benefits of the exchange. Although the authors do not use the term "generative" to describe these building blocks, they are intended to facilitate and enable generative interaction between the firm and its customers. We think these four building blocks are equally relevant for understanding generative interaction in the public-sector.

Many accounts of co-creation stress that it thrives on synergies derived from bringing different knowledge, information, perspectives, skills, or resources together in a fruitful way. One consideration for understanding generative interaction is that social creativity builds on, but is distinct from, individual creativity. Fischer et al. (2005) advance a "fish-scale" model of collaboration over a division-of-labor model for encouraging social creativity. In the context of co-creation, fish-scales refer to the fact that actors are not working in siloed or segmented ways each applying their particular knowledge to the problem, but rather in a manner that combines their respective skills and resources in order to facilitate mutual learning.

From this perspective, a first important step toward collaborative interaction is simply to foster connections among citizens or stakeholders who have different backgrounds, vocabularies, and worldviews that might make it difficult for them to communicate, let alone act together (Gouillart and Hallett, 2015). Brokers or mediators can help to bridge these differences and facilitate collaborative interaction (Obstfeld, 2005; Fleming, Mingo, & Chen, 2007; Sele & Grand, 2016). However, it is not enough to simply connect people. Interaction can be negative and anomic and drive people away as London and Sessa write:

When groups are engaged in generative interaction processes, they seek and discover information proactively, acquire new knowledge and skills, and then apply the information, knowledge, and skills. The group gathers information, seeks alternatives, reflects on work processes, tests assumptions, obtains different opinions, and adopts new routines. (2007: 358)

Trust and social learning are often described as important ingredients of productive interaction. Trust is widely viewed as an essential factor for stimulating productive social interactions (McEvily, Perrone, & Zaheer, 2003). It is particularly important for generating social learning, as people must trust one another in order to openly share their perspectives (Sol, Beers, & Wals, 2013). Social learning and co-creation may in turn result in the enhancement of trust, thus creating a virtuous cycle (Fledderus, Brandsen, & Honingh, 2014).

Research on private-sector co-creation also suggests that interactions will be more sustainable and productive if they are "sociable" and "hedonic" – that is, if participants enjoy interacting with one another and find their mutual engagement stimulating and pleasurable

(Nambisan & Nambisan, 2008). Kohler et al. (2011) describe the attitude that helps to produce a hedonic experience as "playfulness." Perhaps the broader lesson is that it is important to consider the experience that participants have in the co-creation process. Some research suggests that this experience is most motivating when it fosters a sense of competence, autonomy, and task enjoyment (Dahl & Moreau, 2007). Cross-national survey research finds that citizens are most likely to participate in co-production when they feel a sense of personal efficacy – that is, when they believe that ordinary people can make a difference in the political process (Parrado et al., 2013).

A number of authors stress the importance of learning in co-creation (Voorberg et al., 2017b). Although the connection has not been previously made, it is possible to link co-creation to the concept of "generative learning," which McGill, Slocum, and Lei describe as "...continuous experimentation and feedback in an ongoing examination of the very way organizations go about defining and solving problems" (1992: 5). Lewis, Pea, and Rosen describe generative learning as a relational activity and point out that the main characteristics of what they call "generative learning communities" are an expanding number of participants, greater engagement among these participants, and knowledge creation by and for these participants (2010: 358).

It is important to note, however, that "generative learning" has been distinguished from "transformative learning" (Mezirow 1991). In generative learning, groups proactively explore new ideas and ways of working together, but they do so based on their prior roles, identities, experiences, and perspectives. Transformative learning goes one step further. London and Sessa (2007) explain that generative learning builds on prior group experiences, while transformative learning changes the character of the group and its perceptions. Generative learning, they argue, provides a stepping-stone for transformative learning.

4.3 Generative Tools

One key strategy for generative co-creation is to put useful tools in the hands of the participants. Toolkits can enable and facilitate user participation in co-creation by making it easy for different actors to undertake productive tasks and explore competing options and scenarios (Graaf, 2018). This strategy reflects Zittrain's basic idea about why the Internet is so generative. The Internet makes a set of easily masterable and adaptable tools readily available to a distributed public and allows them to connect and interact in complex and productive ways. To illustrate, consider the various tools used in a collaborative water resource project:

> In the SLIM project, various tools have been used to assist facilitation and have shown their importance in learning processes: mapping and diagramming techniques based on systems approaches...; media technologies like GIS...; intermediary objects and concepts...; performance arts like theatre events...or even metaphor exploration. ... (Steyaert & Jiggins, 2007: 580–581)

Today, it is common for urban planners to use a variety of digital or physical simulation tools that allow planners, researchers, politicians, and citizens to imagine alternative planning scenarios and reflect on their different impacts. Such tools can not only help participants explore and visualize complex planning issues, but they also serve as "boundary objects" that help facilitate collaboration between different stakeholders (Star & Griesemer, 1989; Nicolini, Mengis, & Swan, 2012).

Information and Communication Technology (ICT) is another important tool for supporting collaborative interaction. Information and Communication Technologies that facilitate participation, for instance, have a range of functional capabilities that allow crowdsourcing of ideas, real-time on-line deliberation, and ranking of policy alternatives (Nelimarkka et al., 2014; Boudjelida, Mellouli, & Lee 2016; Aragon et al., 2017). In the context of thinking about co-creation, "data" can also be understood as a generative tool. Many co-creation processes are triggered by open access to public data, which may be generated by the "internet of things" (Mulder, 2012; Toots et al., 2017). OrganiCity, an EU demonstration project, provides a good example of how open data can serve as a generative tool for co-creation (https://organicity.eu/).

4.4 Generative Processes

"Design thinking" can be understood as a generative process that can be used to support co-creation (Bason, 2010). Design thinking advocates a "user-centric" perspective that encourages the sponsors of a co-creation process to begin by empathetically investigating the needs, perspectives, and desires of end users. One of the key process aspects associated with design thinking is "prototyping," which allows the development and testing of early versions of a product or solution. In co-creation, prototyping can help participants imagine possibilities and provide a low-cost test of a solution's attractiveness and viability (Mulder, 2012).

Design experiments are another example of a generative process (Stoker & John, 2009). Unlike randomized controlled experiments, design experiments tend to take place in real-life settings and aim to develop in situ knowledge about what works in practice in these settings. Design experiments encourage innovators to follow a number of steps, each of which must be carefully negotiated and endorsed by the relevant stakeholders. First, the innovators agree on a diagnosis of the problem at hand and on the criteria by which they will collectively judge the outcome of the experiment. Second, they develop or draw on theory to articulate hypotheses about the kind of intervention that might ameliorate the problem or produce improvement in outcomes. Third, they conduct the experimental intervention and rigorously evaluate the results. In the early stages of the process, this intervention may be merely an approximation of the ultimate solution. However, fourth, and critically, the innovators continue to iterate through steps 1–3, improving the intervention until a satisfactory outcome has been achieved. This design-redesign cycle is generative in the sense that it sets up a procedure for collaborative innovation and public value production.

4.5 Generative Institutions

Institutions provide the meta-framework for action and interaction. What is distinctive about generative institutions, as we conceive of them, is that they are not static structures or rule systems, but frameworks that bring together or assemble generative interactions, tools and processes in order to support co-creation and co-created outcomes. Since generative institutions can to some degree be designed, we are particularly concerned with how the design of such institutions can support the transition to co-creation.

We nominate two types of generative institutions that can provide support for co-creation: arenas and platforms. The term "arena" builds on the work of Bryson and Crosby (1993), who draw a clear distinction between forums of communication and deliberation and arenas for decision making and joint action. We acknowledge this distinction in theory, but in practice, they tend to be hard to distinguish. Decision making tends to be preceded by deliberation, and deliberation tends to be motivated by a desire to reach an agreement, which ultimately implies decision making. In particular, deliberation is often central to what arenas do (Bobbio 2003; Barnes, Newman, & Sullivan 2006). Arenas are created to enable participants to both communicate and act.

In what sense are arenas generative? As noted, arenas are spaces for participation, communication, and joint action. A key generative feature of arenas is that they can call a "public" into existence (Bryson et al., 2017: 649). That is, by enabling a group of citizens, stakeholders, and public agencies to communicate with each other and act together on a particular issue or in a particular domain, arenas "frame" how people come together in a process of joint problem solving, thus forming publics. For example, in a study of social housing, Needham (2008) found that the relationship between public servants and social-housing occupants shifted when they were placed in a position of collectively deliberating and co-creating housing services.

Participatory arenas can facilitate the creation of new political subjectivities by involving a particular set of actors in collaborative problem-solving (Cornwall & Coelho, 2007). In doing so, arenas potentially create and sustain citizenship. Arenas can also be used to expand topics of deliberation beyond narrow technical discussions that only public managers and policy experts participate in. However, the emergent character of problem-focused deliberations also means they can lead in unexpected directions. In his analysis of deliberative arenas, Bobbio writes that "by definition, deliberation is an unconstrained process and therefore cannot be excessively regimented. Deliberative arenas thus frequently tend to cast doubt on the issue assigned them and to redefine the nature of the problems they are faced with." (2003: 345)

Co-creation arenas may run into problems of lack of participation or interest. As one city professional in Tampere, Finland observed: "Everyone was meaning well, but the meetings just weren´t interesting enough for the local residents to take part" (Tuurnas 2015, 17). Moynihan argues that effective management of participatory forums can overcome the traditional limitations of public hearings, though this management may require a considerable public investment (Moynihan, 2003). Effective stakeholder engagement often has a spatial basis – like a neighborhood or region – because people are bound together by communities of fate and by civic pride. (Paskaleva, Cooper, & Concilo, 2018: 128)

While arenas create relatively self-governing and self-sustaining space for communicative interaction and problem-solving, platforms provide a broader generative framework that aims to strategically facilitate and align action at a systemic level. Collaborative platforms serve as infrastructures and opportunity structures for supporting multiple collaborative partnerships, projects, and networks through the provision of dedicated competences, templates, and resources. Collaborative platforms facilitate the creation, multiplication, and adaptation of collaborative arenas that support co-creation (Ansell & Gash 2017; Ansell & Miura 2019).

Ansell and Gash (2017) describe a wide range of platforms used to promote collaboration. They note that these platforms often use a franchising strategy to develop a range of parallel but sometimes interdependent collaborations. By franchising, they mean that the platform encourages different user communities to use and appropriate similar templates, tools, and processes but to adapt them to their own local purposes. For example, the French anti-obesity organization EPODE has established a standard process for organizing local anti-obesity campaigns using a social marketing approach. Each local community customizes these templates, tools, and processes for its own local needs. To put this in terms of our generative framework, the platform – EPODE – provides templates, tools, and processes that local campaigns use to create generative interactions.

Nambisan (2009) describes three types of collaboration platforms: *exploration platforms* that define problems and connect problem-solvers; *experimentation platforms* that enable distributed actors to develop problem solutions, often through prototyping; and *execution platforms* that build templates and make them available for the joint implementation of problem solutions. From this perspective, EPODE is an execution platform. Innovation platforms often cut across these distinctions, combining them in practice. For example, Anttiroiko (2016) suggests that urban innovation platforms allow citizens to engage in exploration, experimentation, and execution of new urban policies and programs.

One source of platform generativity arises from the way that platforms may facilitate easy reconfigurability or reusability of component parts or processes (Foerderer et al., 2014). Other scholars emphasize the reusability, recombinability, or reprogrammability of assets provided by platforms. A broader lesson to take away from this discussion is that platforms create the conditions for easy, flexible, or low cost distributed and emergent innovation.

Modularity is one such strategy for creating easy ways of combining and recombining platform resources. A system is modular when changes in one module do not have consequences for other elements of the system (Tiwana et al., 2010: 678). Using the Lego system as an illustration, Kornberger describes how modularity relates to generativity:

Lego provides a good example of how a simple system that adheres to modularity, granularity, and low integration costs can provide the grammar for open-ended creative expression. Indeed, Lego blocks can be understood as a language that allows, through grammar and vocabulary, the creation of complex artifacts and experiences. (2017: 182)

A related design component of platforms is that they organize flexible "interfaces" that facilitate easy combinations of customized templates, tools, and processes. An interface can be defined as "a medium that organizes the exchange between two or more heterarchically distributed elements" (Kornberger, 2017:180). The easy-to-use interfaces between different modules allow a network of co-creators to scale their efforts and transform and diversify their agenda.

Returning to the EPODE example further illustrates how templates, tools, and processes represent a modular form of platform organization. Local EPODE franchises can appropriate and utilize the parent platform's templates, tools, and processes and customize them for their own local purposes. By reusing these tools and processes across many local campaigns, the EPODE strategy reduces the costs of organizing for local anti-obesity groups. At the same time, the ability of local franchises to recombine a standard set of generative templates, tools, and processes allows them to take very different paths. The advantage of platforms is that they combine efficiency (through the reuse of a standard repertoire of modules) with local scaling and customization (because this repertoire can be combined and tailored to different purposes).

Platforms can also be generative by scaffolding generative processes. For example, platforms can provide a supportive basis for experimentation.

On the one hand, they can support individual experiments. On the other hand, platforms can serve as frameworks for many experiments operating either in parallel or sequentially. Living labs and smart city platforms offer one example of platforms that try to expand the number and scope of experiments conducted by citizens and local stakeholders (Ansell & Bartenberger, 2016).

Platforms can also be understood as generative at an "ecosystem" level – that is, they help to foster positive interdependence between a diverse group of stakeholders (Anttiroiko, 2016). The development of agricultural innovation platforms offers a good example of what this can mean. Earlier attempts to develop agricultural "technology transfer" programs in developing countries were conceptualized in a technocratic fashion as agricultural experts transferring their knowledge to local farmers. Knowledge flowed in one direction from experts to farmers. Yet, local farmers often ignored these efforts because experts were often poorly informed about local conditions. Therefore, a two-way flow of interaction was next envisioned. Experts would collaborate with farmers to develop more effective transfer programs by learning about the farmers' local situation. This model, however, ran into the additional problem that even where knowledge was successfully transferred, the farmers encountered problems in accessing needed services or achieving access to markets where they could sell their surplus production. In the most recent refinement of this strategy, agricultural innovation platforms have been conceived of as strategies to capture the multilateral character of expert-farmer-supplier-market interactions. In other words, agricultural innovation platforms foster not only two-way interaction but also relations with upstream suppliers and downstream markets. Thus, the innovation platform becomes the center of a multilateral web of interactions, as it connects an entire innovation ecosystem (Adekunle & Fatunbi, 2012).

A similar way to characterize platforms is that they operate as "systemic intermediaries," a concept used to describe an emerging role in innovation systems (Lente et al., 2003). As with the discussion of aforementioned agricultural innovation systems, Smits and Kuhlman (2004) describe "the end of the linear [innovation] model," which acknowledges the need for more interaction between designers and users. As a result of this and other developments, a more heterogeneous group of actors becomes engaged in the innovation process, creating a need to manage the "system" of interactions. In addition, innovation processes become more uncertain in character (a point that is similar to the argument we make at the beginning of the chapter about indeterminant "emergent" processes), which then demands the use of a wider range of tools and greater stress on learning.

Smits and Kuhlman go on to argue that innovation in this context requires a distinctive approach to orchestrating five distinctive tasks: (1) the management of interfaces; (2) building and organizing innovation systems; (3) providing a platform for learning and experimentation; (4) providing an infrastructure for strategic intelligence; and (5) stimulating demand articulation, strategy, and vision development (2004: 11–12). It is important to perform these tasks in order to facilitate the productive exchange between the stakeholders who are involved in innovation. Lente et al. (2003) use the California Fuel Cell Partnership as an example of an institution that contributes "systemic intermediation" for the purpose of developing a clean transport system. In our terms, we would characterize this partnership as a "platform."

To summarize the work of platforms, they are doing a number of things that encourage and support co-creation (Ansell & Miura, 2019). Typically, platforms organize the public's attention by advertising their existence and creating storylines that attract participation. They also establish visible contact points that direct and channel participation. They sometimes impose access rules that determine who can participate, how they participate, and toward what ends. Platforms will provide resources and adaptive communication systems that can lower the transaction costs of interaction and support or subsidize the costs of collective action. Platforms also provide procedures, routines, and templates that make it easier to initiate co-creation and to create spin-off collaborations. They may also provide advice, assistance, and facilitation with how to conduct activities and develop innovative strategies and products. These elements suggest the general platform components that designers may consider when building platforms.

4.6 Putting Arenas and Platforms Together for Co-creation

The basic point in this chapter is that platforms can generate arenas that are, in turn, generative for co-creation. We acknowledge that the pattern of invention can flow in the other direction as well – from arenas to platforms. However, for the purpose of envisioning

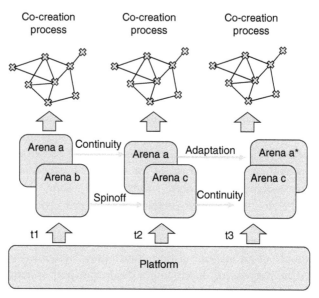

Figure 4.1 Generative relationships between platforms, arenas, and co-creation

how co-creation can be promoted, we stress the lineage from platforms to arenas. Figure 4.1 schematically illustrates how a single platform can generate several arenas, which may coexist at a particular point in time. Part of what platforms do is to help these arenas organize in the first place and adapt over time to changing conditions. Platforms may also help to scale and multiply arenas, as necessary to meet changing needs, demands, and conditions. Arenas that are created and sustained by platforms may, in turn, create the conditions for co-creation by providing the space and the governance arrangements through which distributed actors can interact and innovate. Often, arenas will produce spin-off projects and activities that platforms may help to mobilize in new arenas. New and old arenas may have shared or overlapping membership.

Current discussions sometimes fudge together the concept of a platform with the concept of arenas. For example, Gouillart and Hallett (2015) describe the creation of a local "engagement platform" to help the dispersed Somali community liaise with public services, while Aragon et al. (2017) describe Decidim Barcelona as an online platform developed by the Barcelona City Council to encourage citizens to discuss and elaborate ideas for the city's strategic city plan. In these cases, platforms are arenas for co-creation.

We want to preserve the distinction between platforms and arenas because we want to emphasize that platforms specialize in the creation of arenas. Table 4.1 summarizes the key difference between platforms and arenas. Since a single platform can often give rise to multiple arenas, platforms tend to be fewer in number than arenas. In addition, platforms tend to provide long-term resources for organizing arenas that have a more temporary status. Arenas are similar, in this sense, to projects that organizations temporarily create to achieve certain goals. The role of platforms and arenas also tends to differ. The platform role emphasizes strategic intermediation that brings together and aligns distributed action to achieve general goals. Arenas tend to have more specific purposes and focus on facilitating public value production through joint action. Most importantly, platforms are generative of arenas, while arenas are generative of co-creation.

The Internet has facilitated the creation of participation arenas, including arenas for deliberation and policy making. Desouza and Bhagwatar (2014), for example, describe web-based platforms like Textizen and Urban Mechanics that allow citizens to discuss issues, engage with public agencies, and develop new ideas. These "technology-enabled participatory platforms" are available in a number of mid-sized and large US cities. They also describe the example of a virtual platform used in the city of Santa Cruz, California to generate ideas and gauge public opinion on how to deal with a serious budget shortfall. At an even greater scale, CONSUL provides a free, secure, and customizable digital

Table 4.1 *Conceptual comparison of platforms and arenas*

	Platform	Arena
Number	Few	Many
Endurance	Relatively permanent	More temporary
Role	Strategic intermediation	Facilitation of value production
Generative Focus	Creating arenas	Fostering co-creation

platform for collaborative interaction between citizens and public agencies. It is used in 22 countries and by 130 public agencies and millions of citizens all over the world (see http://consulproject.org).

Not all platforms, however, are digital. Many platforms may also be physical in the sense that they provide a meeting ground for entrepreneurs who want to probe ideas, identify potential collaborators, and launch new collaborative projects. Many cities now have sites that serve as incubators for civic ideas, collaboration, and experiments. Municipal civic centers, urban living labs, foundations, local universities, and even public libraries may serve this incubator role. In our terminology, these conventional organizations may act as platforms.

Platforms perform a strategic scaffolding role for co-creation arenas. This point is consistent with Ramaswamy and Ozcan's recent conceptualization of interactive platforms as "affording a multiplicity of interactive system-environments through which interactional creation occur" (2018: 197). However, this perspective raises a critical challenge for our discussion of generative governance. Platform generativity is produced in part by the openness of the platform. As Parker and Alstyne write: "A platform is more "open" to the extent that it places fewer restrictions on participation, development, or use across its distinct roles, whether for developer or end user" (2018: 4). Yet, they also regulate activity and interaction in order to produce fruitful engagement and facilitate goal achievement. The challenge is how to strike the right balance between openness and control – too much control can stifle generativity; too little control produces fragmentation (Boudreau, 2010; Yoo et al., 2012; Janssen & Estevez, 2013; Foerderer et al., 2014).

We suggest that for co-creation platforms, a key issue that goes to the heart of this trade-off between control and openness relates to rules about who can participate. Access rules are particularly important design features of platforms, in the same way that rules of engagement are critical to arenas (Bryson & Crosby, 1993). While more open access rules can produce generative outcomes by expanding the diversity of perspectives, skills, and resources involved, such openness may also accentuate power asymmetries or produce deliberative confusion. Just as with more conventional participation processes, innovation platforms confront the challenges of managing power asymmetries between participants. For example, Cullen et al. (2014) describe the failure of open innovation platforms in Ethiopia to generate authentic participation by farmers due to their negative power relationship with the government.

Nevertheless, platforms are all about opening up governing processes to more widely distributed groups through the creation of arenas. From the perspective of strategic scaffolding of generative interaction, they are about spotting or experimentally identifying opportunities for productive alignment and linkage. Therefore, they are quite often about opening up governing processes that were traditionally much more restrictive in terms of participation. In some cases, governments who have ventured to engage more directly with the public have been surprised by the interest they have received (Mergel, 2017: 10). This public interest could serve as a positive feedback to encourage greater openness.

An example of a platform that works in part by enabling arenas is the Network of European Foundations (NEF), which describes its mission "...as enabling better and more strategic collaboration between foundations" (www.nef-europe.org/who-we-are). The Network of European Foundations serves as a broker that supports the development and launch of transnational partnerships/joint ventures and it does so, in part, by creating arenas for generative interaction. For example, Wilkinson, Mayer, and Ringle (2014) describe how NEF developed a visioning and foresight exercise on the future of Europe. The Network of European Foundations imagined this exercise as diverging from a traditional conference, emphasizing the quality of interaction among a carefully selected but highly diverse group of participants. Hosting the "unconventional summit" in a distinctive venue – a Benedictine monastery – NEF sought to "...create a space for a generative high-power dialogue" by organizing "a combination of interactive exhibition spaces, plenary and small group discussions and various "*markets for ideas*" (2014: 6–7). It also used design and visualization techniques to facilitate these interactions.

The Network of European Foundations also creates arenas. A good example is the European Program for Integration and Migration (EPIM). By pooling funds from many foundations and then reallocating them in order to build effective European collaboration on issues related to migration, EPIM creates an arena for co-creation. The European Program for Integration and Migration is governed by Steering and Executive Committees and administered by a small secretariat that facilitates the work of six sub funds. These sub funds support pilot projects and manage "their own strategy, priorities, budget, grantees and evaluations" (Network of European Foundations, 2017: 14), a strategy that helps to attract a wider range of foundations to NEF. Although EPIM is in one sense a conventional grant funding mechanism, it describes its strategy as "funding plus" because it uses this funding to encourage collaboration and build capacity. It clearly acts as a "systemic intermediary" to facilitate the creation of a European "ecosystem" of collaborating foundations.

On a larger scale, the European Social Fund (ESF) functions as a platform to promote local collaboration, networks, and partnerships in order to enhance employment opportunities in Europe, particularly among vulnerable groups (http://ec.europa.eu/esf/home.jsp). The ESF proactively defines goals and provides tools and templates for local authorities, social partners, and nongovernmental organizations to work together on employment-generating projects. The ESF support for employment initiatives represents approximately 10 percent of the entire European Union budget.

As platforms develop arenas for collaboration, they must be sensitive to the local context in which arenas must operate. The social embedding of platforms can be challenging because the generic features of the platform must be adapted to the specific social, political, and economic conditions on the ground in order to support the formation of co-creation arenas. Over time, generative platforms – like arenas – can learn and adapt to the feedback they receive from socially embedded processes and experiences (Ansell, Sørensen, & Torfing, 2020). Due to the emergent character of co-creation, action in local arenas can deviate from the goals, expectations, and procedures initially promoted by the platform. New possibilities for co-creation may be discovered in local arenas and ultimately feedback to transform the agenda of the platform. Hence, there is a dialectical relationship between platforms and arenas.

In conclusion, this chapter has introduced the idea of generativity and demonstrated its relevance for understanding public governance based on co-creation. It has also described the functionality of platforms that allows them to generate arenas where co-creation process can unfold. Chapter 5 delves more deeply into the different phases of co-creation processes.

5 | *The Complex and Dynamic Process of Co-creating Public Value*

Public value, defined as an outcome that has value for and is valued by the public, is typically produced by public bureaucracies inhabited by professionally trained public managers and employees. Sometimes governments invite private contractors to bid for public service production and if they are awarded a contract, the contractors either replace or complement the efforts of public service organizations. Co-creation, however, offers an interesting alternative that suspends the public sector's choice between making and buying public services (Brown, Potoski, & Slyke, 2006). Instead of relying either on bureaucratic or market-based service provision, co-creation engages relevant and affected actors in the exploration of needs; the definition of goals; and the creation, testing, and delivery of public solutions.

Co-creation offers a number of advantages to the public sector. A first advantage lies in its ability to narrow the gap between needs and service provision as well as between problems and policy solutions. A second advantage is that co-creation can mobilize private resources in the process of designing and implementing solutions and thus help increase the capacity of the public sector to fulfill its high ambitions. A third advantage is that the interaction between the public and private actors tends to spur innovation and create joint ownership over the new solutions. A final advantage is that co-creation may also help to build more resilient communities and widen democratic participation. As such, there are many good reasons to explore how co-creation can complement and perhaps even rearticulate the traditional tools of government and thus renew democratic governance.

In Chapter 6, we look at how co-creation may produce different public value outcomes. Before doing that, we need to get a deeper understanding of what the process of co-creation entails. Toward that end, this chapter aims to open the black box of co-creation, look at its constituent parts and inner mechanics, identify the drivers of and barriers to different parts of the process, and highlight the tools that may support and facilitate the co-creation of public value. To provide a baseline for subsequent analysis, this chapter establishes an analytical framework for studying processes of co-creation.

While recognizing that the dynamic processes of co-creation are often extremely complex and full of gaps, overlaps, jumps, feedback loops, and iterations, it makes sense for heuristic reasons to speak of four phases in the process of co-creating public solutions: (1) initiation; (2) design, (3) implementation; and (4) consolidation, upscaling, and diffusion. Each of these phases can be broken down into three interlacing sub-phases.

This chapter carefully elaborates what goes on in the different phases and sub-phases of co-creation and identifies relevant drivers and barriers that may affect the internal dynamics of these phases and sub-phases. Drawing on network analysis, design theory, and other relevant contributions, the chapter provides examples of the tools, methods, probes, and stratagems that are invoked to organize, facilitate, and spur processes of co-creation. Chapter 4 referred to these as generative tools and processes.

5.1 The Initiation Phase

Co-creation processes are more than a one-off meeting between elected councilors and local citizens to discuss a new plan for urban regeneration and more than an administrative consultation with a range of stakeholders over watershed management. Co-creation processes involve relatively enduring interactions that unfold across time and space. They often run through several iterations and may give rise to other, related processes with a slightly different focus, though they may also fizzle out due to a series of obstacles or the lack of commitment. While this makes it difficult to identify the end point of co-creation processes, they certainly have a beginning in so far as they are initiated by public and/or private actors who invite other actors to participate in a collaborative endeavor to co-create a certain solution.

In principle, the right and ability to initiate co-creation is shared by a broad range of public and private actors. While single individuals with a clear and appealing cause sometimes succeed in convening a broad spectrum of actors (see Sørensen & Torfing, 2018), collectively organized groups of actors often have a greater convening power as they tend to command the resources and have the necessary contacts needed to initiate co-creation processes. Social entrepreneurs, civil society organizations, interest organizations, and private firms are examples of private actors who under normal circumstances are capable of initiating co-creation processes. However, it often falls to public organizations to (co-)initiate co-creation. Not only do they have the necessary resources and capacities, they also have the authority and legitimacy needed to initiate co-creation because they are positioned and perceived as guardians of public interests.

Hence, whereas private actors may risk being accused of having a hidden private agenda and merely acting in their own interest when inviting other actors to co-create a solution to a particular problem, public actors are often trusted to have a broader agenda and to act in the interest of the common good, although they are sometimes suspected of trying to shift public responsibilities onto private actors. Public actors have both the resources and authority needed for initiating co-creation and must often initiate co-creation in situations where private actors are too weak to take on the convener role and where the potential benefits from it solutions are significant and other governance strategies have been tried and found wanting.

The initiation of co-creation has three important elements: (1) describing the problems, challenges, or tasks that call for a co-created solution; (2) identifying relevant and affected actors and motivating them to participate and interact; and (3) building trust and facilitating collaboration through the constructive management of differences.

5.1.1 Describing the Problem, Challenge or Task That Calls for a Co-created Solution

Co-creation is a problem-driven process engaging two or more actors in the creation of emergent understandings, ideas, and solutions that have public value. Hence, co-creation is initiated by inviting relevant and affected actors from different organizations, sectors, and perhaps also levels, to collaborate in solving a particular problem, responding to an emerging challenge, or carrying out a complex task that requires collaboration.

Problems that call for co-created solutions are often described as wicked in the sense that they have a number of challenging characteristics, such as the lack of a definite problem definition, a unique character, linkage to other problems, multiple and contradictory goals, and emergent solutions that are neither true nor false but rather good or bad (Rittel & Webber, 1973; Head & Alford, 2015). Wicked problems are difficult to solve due to the presence of cognitive constraints that prevent a linear problem-solving strategy from being used to address problems occurring in open social systems. In addition, there might also be a number of political constraints or temporal dynamics that make wicked problems unruly. These political constraints include the misalignment of problems with capacity and authority, divergent interests, the discounting of the future, and the tendency to settle on symbolic and inefficient solutions (Hofstad & Torfing, 2017). The temporal dynamics include the unexpected emergence of problems, their unpredictable variation in intensity and magnitude, and their delayed, cumulative, spillover, or contagious effects (Ansell & Bartenberger, 2017). Both public bureaucracy and private contractors tend to give up on wicked and unruly problems requiring the mobilization of specialized knowledge, multi-actor negotiation, mutual learning, creative thinking, and the development of the widespread social and political support necessary to formulate and implement innovative solutions (Roberts, 2000). In short, wicked and unruly problems often beg for the initiation of co-creation processes.

Whereas sizeable and pressing problems tend to push us down the road toward co-creation, positive and ambitious challenges daring us to realize our dreams or exploit new opportunities for improving living conditions tend to pull us in the direction of co-creation. New knowledge, experiences, technologies, political conditions, and socioeconomic developments may make it possible to do new things that fulfill our dreams and aspirations about the future. Exploiting new and hopeful situations often calls for a concerted effort to transform abstract possibilities and vague dreams into concrete solutions and outcomes. New knowledge about how to combat a particular disease may bring public and private actors together in the hope that public health will be improved through the development of new health programs. New digital technologies might be exploited to empower chronically ill patients to better master their predicament, but may require collaboration between technicians, health personnel, patient organizations, and prospective users in order to design a digital tool that works in practice. Finally, globalization of trade may open up new possibilities for a poor rural community to increase the value of their local crops by processing them into new products that can be exported to other countries, especially if the farmers work together with agro-technicians, investors, manufacturers, public education and training institutions, national trade agencies, and so on.

Co-creation is not only triggered by more or less spectacular problems and challenges. While some tasks are simple and can be carried out by following a manual, other tasks require adaptation, reinvention, coordination, and resource exchange. We live in a turbulent world in which the achievement of core tasks, such as waste collection, preventive health care, or integration of immigrants, constantly has to be reconfigured in order to meet new demands. The public or private actors that have the responsibility for such tasks, or depend on their solution, will benefit from initiating co-creation processes that bring together relevant and affected actors.

Particular kinds of problems, challenges, and tasks tend to drive the initiation of co-creation processes. Often there is a fierce competition to get other actors' attention and to place a problem, challenge, or task sufficiently high on the public agenda to stir action. Hence, the framing of problems as "significant," "intense," and "urgent"; the discursive construction of challenges as "grand," "strategic," or "irresistible"; and the description of tasks as "important," "necessary," and "challenging" is essential for the attempt to initiate co-creation (Torfing, 2016). The right framing, however, is not enough. Initiation of co-creation also requires legitimate, energetic, and persuasive entrepreneurs that can get the ball rolling in terms of steering people's attention toward particular problems, challenges, and tasks and making the case for a co-created response (Kingdon, 1984; Doig & Hargrove, 1990; Mintrom & Norman, 2009). This endeavor requires a good sense of timing, a considerable amount of social capital, and rhetorical skill to convince people that this particular problem, challenge, and task calls for a co-created solution that will produce a desirable public value outcome.

Responsibility for, or ownership of, problems, challenges, and tasks drives public and private actors to use their entrepreneurial skills to initiate co-creation. However, the problem is that the public sphere of modern mass communication is fragmented, overloaded, and almost impossible to control, making it difficult to draw attention to problems, challenges, and tasks that do not lend themselves to scandalous or life-threatening dramatization. Public and private entrepreneurs have to use strategies other than mass communication to draw attention to a cause that prompts joint action and co-creation of public value. Hence, networking, perhaps supported by communication via social media, is a common way of drawing attention to an important issue and may allow rapid, cascading dissemination even when actors have limited power resources. Viral advertising techniques might provide a source of inspiration (Scott, 2015).

If the networking activities succeed to get elected politicians interested in the issue at stake, they might be persuaded to use mass media to draw attention to the problem, challenge, or task at hand and support the need for action. Sometimes politicians happen to be the main entrepreneurs and initiators of co-creation and use mass media, political party meetings, parliamentary assemblies, and political committees as instruments to broadcast problems, challenges, and tasks as a way of exercising their political leadership (Tucker, 1995). The result of this process might be a formal mandating of the formation of platforms, arenas, and processes of co-creation.

5.1.2 Identifying and Inviting Potential Actors and Motivating Them to Participate

The initial description of the problem, challenge, or task that sets the co-creation into motion paves the way for the attempt to identify and invite potential participants. Co-creation builds on multi-actor collaboration, but who should be invited to participate? The brief answer is to look for the relevant and affected actors (Torfing, 2016). The affected actors are those social and political actors who are facing the consequences of the current and future predicaments and stand to benefit, or perhaps suffer, from the development of a new co-created solution. Affected actors are important to include in a co-creation process because they have a clear interest in the issues at stake and because they are experts in their own lives and can help to uncover basic needs, understand the problems and limits of the current predicament, bring new ideas to the table, and assess the potential impact of co-created solutions. However, the forms of expertise needed in the processes of co-creation go beyond the experiences, ideas, and assessments of the affected actors. As such, we should also look for a broader set of relevant actors defined as those social and political actors whose knowledge, competences, resources, and ideas are essential for understanding the problem, challenge, or task at hand and for designing and implementing a creative solution through cross-boundary collaboration.

The list of relevant and affected actors quickly gets very long, and while there is no set limit for how many participants there can be in a co-creation process, the inclusion of all potential participants will often be extremely demanding in terms of logistics, communication, and leadership. Therefore, in most cases, some of the many relevant and affected actors will have to be included while others will have to be excluded. Sometimes the inclusion and exclusion of relevant and affected actors is a result of a bottom-up process in which one actor invites another, who in turn invites others in a snowballing process. In other cases, the conveners will base their invitation of relevant and affected actors on a careful stakeholder analysis that aims to discern key stakeholders. In relation to co-creation processes, stakeholder analysis must (1) determine the resources of the potential participants; (2) analyze their power and interests; (3) reflect on which part of the co-creation process different actors should participate in; and (4) determine what to do with potential veto actors. Let us look at each of these four aspects of stakeholder analysis in turn.

First, a stakeholder analysis must analyze the kind of resources that each of the potential participants will bring to the table in order to make sure that between them the group of actual participants have all the skills and resources needed to solve the problem, respond to the challenge, or carry out the task that brings the actors together. The shopping list is long since there will be great need for knowledge, cognitive skills, social capital, empathy, creativity, courage, stamina, authority, implementation capacity, and so on. The question here is how to select a relatively small and manageable group of public and private actors that together possess all, or at least most, of these co-creation assets.

Second, the stakeholder analysis should analyze the interest and power of the stakeholders (Eden & Ackermann, 1998; Bryson, 2004; Ackerman & Eden, 2011; Bryson, Patton, & Bowman, 2011), who may have varying degrees of interest in solving the problem at hand and varying degrees of formal or informal power that enables them to do something to solve the problem. For example, Bryson, Cunningham, and Lokkesmoe (2002) used a "power versus interest grid" to array stakeholders in terms of their interest in and power to achieve better health outcomes for African-American men in Minneapolis. The analysis draws attention to the asymmetry between interest-holders and power-holders. Many of the actors with the power to improve outcomes for African-American men had little interest in the issue and there was not sufficient power in the African-American community to produce the desired change. The stakeholder analysis makes it clear that both the African-American community and the wider business community had to be mobilized if the health of African-American men was going to be improved.

Third, the analysis of the resources, interests, and power of different stakeholders may result in a high number of actors that somehow should be included in the co-creation of public value outcomes. In order to make the inclusion of a large number of stakeholders more manageable, the conveners might consider which of the later phases of the co-creation process the different relevant and affected actors should be involved in. Straus (2002) recommends the use of a "process map" that lists the number of relevant and affected actors and determines which part of the process they should be a part of in order to optimize their contribution while ensuring that they get the influence they expect. The process map ensures that relevant and affected actors' participation is need-based. Some core actors may participate in all parts of the co-creation process in order to ensure continuation while others may only participate in and contribute to one or two phases. Transparency about the inclusion and exclusion of different actors in different phases is important in order to avoid accusations of illegitimate exclusion of particular actors.

Fourth, there is always a risk that some of the relevant and affected actors are known to be spoilsports who are likely to block or veto the development and implementation of new, bold, co-created solutions, either out of concern for their short or long-term interests or because they easily get offended and feel that they are bypassed by other actors. If their participation in co-creation will stall the collaborative process and prevent an open-ended search for new and better solutions, then it is probably better to exclude them. However, if the antagonistic actors can be persuaded to participate in and influence the joint solutions rather than trying to block them, then including them is probably a good idea as their critical stance might force other actors to reconsider their arguments and opinions (Torfing, 2016: 133).

The selection of a broad-based team of co-creators may also be influenced by the concern for not creating a high degree of power asymmetry. Large power asymmetries may discourage weaker participants from joining the team because they suspect that they will become steamrolled by the stronger actors because the strong actors may threaten to opt out and go it alone if their particular interests are not considered. While huge power asymmetries are problematic, co-creation processes may be more tolerant of unequal power distributions than we might expect. Unequal power distributions are more acceptable if stronger actors recognize their dependence on the resources held by weaker actors and refrain from flexing their muscles and scaring weaker actors away. In addition, it may be more interesting for weaker actors to participate in a co-creation process if they can influence actors that are more powerful than themselves to invest in the co-creation of new and better solutions.

Nevertheless, large power asymmetries can be a problem (Gray, 1989: 250) and thus call for deliberate strategies to empower the weaker actors and disempower or constrain the stronger actors (Torfing, 2016: 141–146). Weaker parties must develop their capabilities as stakeholders to match the power of other actors – for example, by developing complementary skills, resources, and forms of knowledge that other actors will need and want to share, or by being allocated an informal right to veto joint solutions that make other actors keen to listen to them and include them in agreements. By the same token, stronger actors should be disempowered relative to other actors by ensuring that their resources are more widely shared and perhaps dispersed for a more even distribution.

When careful stakeholder analysis has produced a shortlist of relevant and affected actors that will be good to include in the co-creation process, the problem becomes how to motivate them to participate (Torfing, 2016: 135–137). Most public and private actors are busy, overburdened and risk averse and it might require a strong and patient effort to get them on board. The key tool of persuasion involves emphasizing the urgency of the problem and the strong need for a solution followed by praise for the decisive resources that each of the actors will be able to bring to the table. Pointing out the potential short-term and long-term gains from collaborating for society at large and the individual participant is also helpful and so is the explanation of why co-creation is a preferred strategy and perhaps the lender of last resort.

Some of the potential participants that are approached will be very concerned about how demanding it will be to participate and thus need to be convinced that even a small, initial contribution to the process is welcomed and that overall the benefits from participating will exceed the transaction costs. Other would-be participants will dread that their influence will be limited compared to the other actors and fear that stronger actors will dominate the process and steal the show. Clarification of the processes, mechanisms, and ground rules that will help to ensure fairness in terms of equal possibilities for being heard and influencing outcomes may ameliorate actual power asymmetries. Most actors, however, are likely to be reached through an appeal to shared values, public spiritedness, and positive past experiences with co-creation. No matter whether the actors invited to participate in co-creation are elected politicians, professional public employees, local businessmen, and so on, they are all citizens and part of the same social and political community and thus tend to subscribe to many of the same core beliefs and hopes for a better future. The ability to tap into people's personal aspirations to do the right thing and to help create a better society is a key motivating factor.

5.1.3 Building Trust and Facilitating Collaboration

Conveners might succeed to seat a broad range of actors from different organizations, sectors, and levels around the same table and get them to talk to each other. However, getting them to work together over a longer period of time in order to craft new and creative solutions to complex problems, challenges, and tasks is not easy. The actors' decisions about whether to invest time and energy in cross-boundary collaboration will rest on a series of judgments, including whether the other participants will agree to collaborate, whether they will share or pool their resources, whether they will listen with an open mind to new ideas and proposals, whether emerging conflicts can be overcome, whether collaboration will lead to a positive outcome, and whether there is enough parity and structure to the process to ensure a fair agreement.

At the core of these judgments is the question about whether the actors trust each other enough to open up and accept the risks associated with multi-actor collaboration, creative problem-solving and innovation (Nooteboom, 2002). Trust is based on a calculation of the likelihood that other actors will refrain from exploiting a given situation to achieve a one-sided advantage at the expense of the other actors. This calculation is either informed by past observations of the actual behavior of other actors or by the perceived quality of the relation with other actors. Trust is built through positive spirals whereby trust-based expectations are confirmed by the behavior of other actors, which in turn feeds the growth of trust-based expectations in the future. Positive trust-building spirals can be started by social interaction through which the actors get acquainted with each other and bond with each other and the spirals are sustained by joint mechanisms for punishing actors that act in a distrustful and self-serving manner. Since positive trust spirals are easily demolished by severe or repeated breaches of trust relations, the actors will need a rapid response system to deal with such breaches.

When the level of trust is sufficiently high, the actors invited to co-create public value outcomes are likely to engage in cross-boundary collaboration. Collaboration is often associated with a cumbersome search for unanimous consent that leaves no room for opposition or dissent. However, in the absence of a unifying common good or a universal normative code for reasoned debate, a total consensus tends to be out of reach or to be predicated on least common denominator agreements, which is not what co-creation aims to achieve.

Co-creation aims to produce public value outcomes through an open-ended search for innovative yet feasible solutions, and the tool is collaboration, which is defined as a temporal social arrangement through which a plurality of actors work together in an organized way to transform joint problems and opportunities into joint solutions that rest on provisional agreements robust enough to tolerate some degree of opposition and dissent (Torfing, 2016: 64). In short, we perceive collaboration not as an attempt to deny or eradicate the presence of diverging views and interests among the participating actors, but as an attempt to construct a common ground for the constructive management of differences in order to find joint solutions to common problems, challenges, and tasks (Gray, 1989).

Boundary spanners and the construction of boundary objects may contribute to the constructive management of differences. Co-creation is a learning-based exploration and design of joint futures, and diversity is a key asset for such an endeavor. However, actors with different backgrounds, worldviews, and vantage points may be unable to engage in high-quality communication and high-intensity interaction and the risk of creating a dialogue of the deaf looms over the process. To avoid this risk, it is essential to recruit a number of intermediaries in the form of boundary spanners who are capable of linking and translating different forms of knowledge and ideas and thereby creating synergistic collaboration. Boundary spanners are competent people, often with an interdisciplinary or cross-sector background, who have a general knowledge of the field, a high capacity for empathy and an extensive toolbox that enables them to mediate between different actors, discourses, and forms of knowledge (Williams, 2002; Long, Cunningham, & Braithwaite, 2013; Meerkerk & Edelenbos, 2018). Boundary spanners sometimes use boundary objects to focus the attention of diverse actors in a collaborative process. Boundary objects are transmutable objects that lend themselves to different interpretations, but contain enough immutable content to maintain their distinctive identity and integrity. Specimens, field notes, reports, maps, physical, or digital models, and so on may be used as joint objects to discuss common problems and to design and implement new solutions.

Attention steering instigated by boundary spanners' use of boundary objects might not be sufficient to spur collaboration between actors with different presuppositions, ideas, and interests. Centrifugal forces associated with unilateralism, free riding, and dissent may prevail over the centripetal forces aiming to construct a common ground for joint problem-solving through dialogue and joint action. To change this balance in favor of collaborative interaction, the participating actors must be brought to recognize and appreciate their mutual dependence on resource exchange, knowledge sharing, and the pooling of ideas. They must understand that no one person has all the requisite skills and resources needed to engage in large-scale transformations of services, policies, or societal solutions and that they need each other to share the workload (Roberts & King, 1996: 93). Boundary spanners and other facilitators play a crucial role in clarifying and reinforcing the mutual dependencies between the manifold actors and they may use different tools to enhance recognition of interdependency.

Drawing on network theory, facilitators may use game structuration to create incentives for the actors to collaborate with each other. The promise of immediate or future rewards can be tied to successful collaboration and joint agreement (Scharpf, 1993; Hertting, 2007) and the interaction between the actors can be segmented to avoid tension and conflict (O'Toole, 1997). If the centrifugal forces are unabated, it might be a good idea to remind actors who contemplate leaving the collaborative process that the alternative to nonagreement is often worse than that of the co-created solutions that can be obtained through continued collaboration. Hence, reliance on hierarchical forms of government, anarchistic market competition, or adversarial conflict resolution in the courts is seldom a preferred alternative to a negotiated solution that aims to unleash the innovative potential of co-creation (Gray, 1989).

Collaboration involves more than a trust-based exchange of knowledge, resources, and ideas. It involves mutual learning and the formulation of a mutual agreement that can guide future action. It can be quite a challenge to get all the different actors to agree on a joint course of action. It involves the construction of a winning argument that finds support from most actors, and here, Bryson, Cunningham, & Lokkesmoe (2002) offer some good advice. A collaborative leadership team may identify the different goals and interests articulated by each of the core actors and map the causal relationships between them. Such a mapping will enable the identification of overlapping goals and interests and determine which set of mutually connected goals and interests can garner support across a wider spectrum of actors. The interconnected goals and interests that enjoy broad support can be put together in a "winning argument" that allows a community of actors to coalesce and co-align in the further pursuit of public value production. In a similar manner, Hajer (2009) emphasizes the importance of story lines, defined as condensed statements summarizing complex narratives linking problems, solutions, and goals. Defining problems, solutions, and goals in broad and somewhat ambiguous terms may allow people with diverging interests to join forces in filling in the blanks.

Turbulence is a key driver of collaboration because it tends to generate an urgent need to enhance the collective capacity for responding to rapid structural changes (Gray, 1989). A second driver is tradition and positive experience, which can encourage social and political actors to work together (Ansell & Gash, 2008). A third driver is social capital, in terms of both strong and weak ties between actors, which can facilitate communication and joint action (Granovetter, 1973). Finally, collaboration thrives on the social and political role perceptions that privilege public spiritedness over self-interested action (Torfing, 2016).

The absence of these aforementioned drivers does not erect the only barrier to collaboration. Another set of barriers includes the presence of uncertainty, interest conflicts, and the fear of losing control when outcomes are a result of negotiation and joint action. If the process and outcome of collaboration is uncertain, participants may not want to get involved because they dread that it might be a waste of time. In this case, more than transparent institutional design and process management are called for (Kickert, Klijn, & Koppenjan, 1997). Interest conflicts are a constant threat to collaboration, and conflict mediation is strictly necessary and may involve shared fact-finding missions where conflicting actors go on a joint excursion to establish a common understanding of the facts that may provide a stepping-stone to an agreement to work together to solve the problem, challenge, or task in question (Koppenjan & Klijn, 2004). Loss of control is a frequent barrier for public leaders to engage in multi-actor collaboration, which often appears as complex, chaotic, and difficult to steer. However, as we shall discuss in a later chapter, new forms of leadership and management show how public leaders may loosen the reins when participating in multi-actor collaboration without losing control. This is the core idea of metagovernance defined as the governance of tendentially self-organizing interactive governance processes (Peters, 2010).

5.2 The Design Phase

After relevant and affected actors are brought together in the initiation phase, the design phase begins. Design can be defined as a deliberate attempt to create solutions in response to particular needs, complex problems, intriguing challenges, and urgent tasks (Simon, 1996). As such, design processes typically involve framing, researching, brainstorming, prototyping, learning, and so on. In the past, design was considered a downstream step in product development that added aesthetic quality and attractiveness to the product. Today, design is viewed as an upstream practice that shapes the outputs and outcomes of complex collaborative processes (Serrat, 2010). It is no longer tied to commodity production, but involves attempts to solve societal problems and create new futures (Banerjee, 2010).

For strictly analytical reasons, we divide the design phase into three components: (1) exploring and redefining the problem, challenge, or task at hand; (2) designing tentative solutions through processes of mutual learning; and (3) selecting and testing the most promising solution(s) through experimentation.

5.2.1 *Exploring and Redefining the Problem, Challenge, or Task at Hand*

The problems, challenges, and tasks that trigger the co-creation process and motivate the participants to collaborate are often defined in broad and ambiguous terms, and the underlying causes and conditions are unknown. Further exploration of their nature, character, manifestations, context, and sources is necessary in order to be able to deal with them and design appropriate solutions. The exploration process may combine fact finding, observation of real-time phenomena, processes or events, collection and analysis of a wide variety of experiences, commissioning of expert opinions and consultation of experts. In the exploration phase, the actors aim to learn more about the problem in order to delimit, understand, and explain it. In line with social constructivist learning theory, we assert that social and political actors actively seek to build new concepts and ideas based on new and existing knowledge when exploring the problem they are trying to solve. As such, the design phase begins with reconfiguration or reframing of the problem (Schön & Rein, 1995; Spinosa, Flores, & Dreyfus, 1997).

Trust-based, collaborative interaction between actors with different backgrounds and vantage points is a key driver of the learning-based reframing of problems, challenges, and tasks (Jehn, Northcraft, and Neale, 1997). A multidisciplinary exploration may stimulate learning and reframing, but there are many reports about how disciplinary groups evaluate their own contribution in positive terms and the contributions of other groups more negatively, thus impairing the exchange of information, knowledge, and ideas (Gray & Ren, 2014). While user involvement is crucial for understanding how different groups are affected by problems, challenges, and tasks (Hargadon & Bechky, 2006; Bason, 2010), many professionals strongly resist the idea that users possess a particular expertise that is essential for understanding problems, challenges, and tasks (Rutter et al., 2004; Tait & Lester, 2005). Here again there is a crucial role for boundary spanners to act as intermediaries and to facilitate mutual learning across professional groups and between public and private actors.

5.2.2 Designing Tentative Solutions through Processes of Mutual Learning

The exploration process aims to get a handle on problems, challenges, and tasks to make them amenable to problem-solving. Creative problem-solving then aims to design improved or innovative solutions through the circulation, cross-fertilization, critical revision, and integration of ideas, views, and suggestions. Design processes begin with an empathic exploration and understanding of basic needs and aim to generate, enrich, disrupt, and evaluate a broad range of potential solutions vis-à-vis the formulated goals and the observable constraints. At first, it is a matter of generating and circulating as many ideas as possible without thinking too much about feasibility and constraints; then comes the process of enriching, problematizing, and integrating ideas as viable agendas; and finally the effort to concretize and operationalize the most promising solutions.

It is in this design phase that co-creation demonstrates its value. The attempt to generate, combine, and integrate the ideas of different relevant and affected actors has the potential to produce a synergistic and creative result that would be impossible for the participants to achieve on their own (Straus, 2002; Bommert, 2010; Ansell & Torfing, 2014). Co-creation mobilizes and harnesses the ideas and suggestions of a variety of social and political actors and aims to build on and transform the best ideas through iterative rounds of joint evaluation in which new ideas are tested against goals and constraints. Hence, the question of "What if we tried to …?" is followed by the question of "Does this fulfill goals and needs?" and finally the question "Is this feasible?".

While collaborative processes may mobilize and harness a plurality of ideas, the development of tunnel vision or group think is a constant risk. The collaborative endeavor may round up the "usual suspects" that have collaborated many times before and over time developed similar worldviews that prevent them from developing new ideas

(Skilton & Dooley, 2010). Instead, they recycle old litanies about how bad things have become and confirm each other's skepticism toward the possibility of changing things for the better. The cure for the development of tunnel vision or group think is to broaden the group of participants; disrupt the collaborative arena by incorporating new inspiring information, knowledge, and experience; and perhaps changing the venue of the meetings, inviting different guests, organizing excursions and using future workshops, brainstorming, and scenario building. The use of such tools calls for the exercise of catalyzing leadership that aims to produce an appropriate disturbance that triggers creative problem-solving (Ansell & Gash, 2012).

5.2.3 Selecting and Testing the Most Promising Solution through Experimentation

When the field of possible solutions is narrowed down to perhaps a handful of options, it is time for the actors to select the most promising ones, to develop and test prototypes through experimental processes to see if they work in practice. The rationalistic approach to selecting a preferred solution based on calculations of costs and benefits does not seem to be an attractive decision-making tool in co-creation processes. Cost-benefit analysis will be hampered by cognitive constraints (Simon, 1957), chaotic processes where problems, goals, and solutions influence each other (Kingdon, 1984) and the presence of uncertain, intangible, and context-dependent effects of the newly co-created solutions (Stacey, Griffon, & Shaw, 2000). Cost-benefit analysis also tends to disregard the fact that co-creation processes are pervaded by political conflicts and subtle power struggles that mean that the optimal solution is not an option.

Dreyfus and Dreyfus (1986) recommend that we move from a calculative rationality, which aims to predict outcomes based on data analysis and rule following, to a deliberative rationality that seeks to make practical judgments about what is likely to work in a particular context based on a combination of experience, intuition, and collective reasoning. As such, deliberation in collaborative arenas will engage actors with different backgrounds who will use heuristic rather than analytical tools to select their preferred solution. The alternatives to rationalistic analysis include: continued talk based on individual expertise and the collective intelligence of the group;

argumentation that appeals either to logic or common experiences and values; attempts to signal emotional sympathies and antipathies rooted in identities and traditions; disagreements that force the participating actors to clarify and revise their views; and persuasive rhetoric that aims to foster agreement.

The deliberative model does not prevent intelligent change. Hence, it has been suggested that "among the instruments of intelligent decision-making that have been discovered as a result of the disappointments with rationality none is more prominent than learning from experience" (March & Olsen, 1995: 199). Co-creators may learn from experience by testing one or more of the preferred solutions through small-scale experimentation. Processes of trial and error will help to reduce the costs of initial failures and enable fast learning and adaptation that is likely to improve performance and enhance desirable outcomes while reducing externalities. Experiential learning through experimentation involves risk-taking and applying strategies of risk management. Risk management is not simply a question of minimizing risks and developing contingency plans for how they are contained, counteracted, and compensated. Indeed, co-creators should avoid a one-sided focus on risks and the damage they might cause, since often they will be willing to bear a certain level of risk in exchange for particular benefits (Renn, 2008). Hence, determining and choosing between acceptable risk-benefit trade-offs provide a good alternative to risk minimization (Osborne & Brown, 2011).

The impact of an experiment often causes considerable confusion because the actors may judge its effects differently depending on their past experiences and goal preferences. However, deliberation will enable the actors to draw inferences from the experiment and discover how they are going to proceed in the future. Hence, arguably, deliberation and experiential learning goes hand in hand in collaborative decision-making processes (Ansell, 2016).

5.3 The Implementation Phase

Experimental testing of new designs tends to blur the line of demarcation between design and implementation. However, at some point, the actors may agree that iterative rounds of small-scale testing have demonstrated the potential impact of a co-created solution and that, with a few revisions, it is "good enough," and therefore ready for major investment and a full-scale rollout. Hence, the search for a new design is considered to be over for the time being and the new solution must now show its worth outside the more or less artificial, exceptional, and sheltered space of experimentation and test-driving.

At this moment, it might dawn on both participants and external actors that a more or less disruptive change is underway and that resources must be committed, rules and procedures must be altered, and a new division of labor must be established in order to implement the new solution. The implementation phase is a very delicate and vulnerable aspect of the co-creation process. First, the positive energy associated with the invention and discovery of a new and promising solution to an urgent problem is replaced with the hard work of mobilizing resources, creating new routines, and motivating actors to deliver what they are supposed to deliver. Second, the group of actors involved in the development of the new solutions might differ significantly from the group of actors responsible for implementing them, especially if frontline personnel in public service organizations are supposed to play a major role in implementation and were not invited to participate in the prototyping. Hence, there is a risk that the co-creation process will lose momentum and support when entering the implementation phase.

Public administration and management research has studied the risk that implementation may result in a considerable gap between planned and actual results and finds that implementation problems are common. The classical explanations of implementation problems either focus on the negative impact of distorted communication and veto players in the long bureaucratic implementation chains (Pressman & Wildavsky, 1973) or on the effect of coping strategies developed by self-protective street-level bureaucrats who are capable of exerting considerable discretion in the provision of services to users (Lipsky, 1980). New research argues that implementation problems may also emanate from bad and ill-founded designs that may be difficult to implement for even the most competent and committed employees or from the failure to adjust designs to local conditions and emerging problems (Ansell, Sørensen, & Torfing, 2017). Hence, it is argued that co-creation of new service or policy designs may help to mitigate many of these problems by facilitating collaboration between upstream and downstream actors in both the design and implementation phase and by encouraging adaptive implementation. However, the implementation phase may still be perilous because resistance to new solutions may arise if, and when, people feel the solutions are disruptive or harmful to their interests.

To further explore what happens in the implementation phase, we shall look at three sub-phases: (1) mobilizing resources and routinizing new behaviors; (2) establishing a new division of labor and coordinating actions; and (3) dealing with opposition and integrating new solutions with existing ones.

5.3.1 Mobilizing Resources and Routinizing New Behaviors

Implementation of co-created solutions requires resource mobilization and construction of rules, norms, and routines that support the new behaviors and practices. Sometimes co-creation processes are sponsored by a resourceful actor capable of funding the implementation of a new solution. In the absence of such a sponsor, actors may have to deliver the solution themselves and thus commit their own resources to its implementation. Contracts are often used to establish the obligations of different participants in a public–private partnership, but co-creation processes involve users, citizens, and civil society organizations in loosely coupled networks that tend to rely on informal agreements and everybody keeping their word.

Sometimes the resources to finance co-created solutions are neither provided up front by a sponsor nor provided by the participating actors who all chip in their own resources. In this situation, fundraising applications to public or private foundations and crowdfunding via local collections or established websites such as Gofundme, Kickstarter, and Indiegogo are required to make ends meet. Success will depend on the ability to present a simple solution to a complex problem and to produce important public value outcomes.

Resource mobilization in the implementation phase is facilitated by the participation of relevant and affected actors in the previous phases of the co-creation process. Participation in the design phase builds ownership over the solution, which in turn creates a strong commitment to contribute resources to its implementation. Celebration of results and achievements may further the motivation to commit scarce resources such as time, energy, and money to the implementation process. Of course, classical collective action problems such as free riding may occur, but in a trust-based network of co-creators the scope for this will be minimal as egotistical behavior will be seen as a serious breach of trust and a cause for exclusion from the network.

When funding is secured, and sufficient resources are mobilized, an important roadblock is lifted and the co-creating partners can embark on the implementation journey that will turn the prototype into the new normal. When the new solution merely attempts to optimize existing practices, the behavioral changes of key actors will only be marginal. If the new solution is innovative, however, and tends to disrupt the common wisdom and established practice, implementation will involve setting up new rules, norms, and procedures that will help to routinize and institutionalize new patterns of behavior that hopefully will generate new positive effects. While recognizing the importance of flexible adjustment of the co-created solutions to the conditions on the ground, implementation of new solutions still depends on the formation of clear rules, norms, and procedures that ensure the stable delivery of high-quality and high-impact solutions within the available budget. As such, a certain degree of institutionalization that creates standards for appropriate action is necessary (March & Olsen, 1995), but it should not create rigidities that prevent adaptation and future innovation. Hence, the goal is a robust institutionalization that ensures a stable implementation of the new solution in the face of turbulence, while keeping future options open. Ideally, milestones should provide stepping-stones for future solutions, and the new best practice should be leveraged to create next practice.

The development of new routines is based on a combination of adaptive planning and processes of trial and error. The rules, norms, and routines that support the new practices cannot be thought out at the desktop, but emerge in the implementation process when involved actors reflect on how things are done in the best and most effective way. Still, it is important for these actors to come together to discuss and evaluate the emerging routines and make sure that they support the goals. Service blueprints provide a suitable tool for this. Service blueprints create a visual schematic – for example, in the form of a comic strip – that incorporates the perspectives of users, providers, and other relevant actors and specifies every aspect of the service from the point of user contact to behind-the-scenes processes (Stickdorn & Schneider, 2011; Radnor et al., 2014). Blueprints result from collaborative processes in interorganizational communities of practice in which minor obstacles and new opportunities are detected and reflected upon and routines are adjusted accordingly. The collaborative process constructs a living document that supports the coherence, flow, and direction of the implementation process.

5.3.2 Establishing a New Division of Labor and Coordinating Actions

Disruptive co-creation processes not only provide a new solution that is supposed to outperform the exiting solution, but also unravel and transform the division of labor between the actors involved in implementation. Bringing new actors into the implementation process in order to make a solution more holistic or user-friendly is often a key feature of co-created solutions. One example is when programs designed to move people at the margins of the labor market into gainful employment rely on teams from different departments to provide cross-disciplinary training and counseling activities in order to address the whole set of interconnected problems that prevent labor-market participation. Another example is when local-training programs seeking to help the elderly acquire valuable Information and Communication Technology (ICT) skills recruit other elderly ICT-users as teachers because they teach at a pace and in a way that suits the learners.

The involvement of an increasing number of actors from different organizations and sectors calls for the creation of a clear division of labor that eliminates gaps and overlaps and creates synergies. It also calls for efforts to coordinate action. Rather than involving top-down allocation of responsibilities and tasks or competition between an infinite number of customers and providers, coordination will be pluricentric in the sense that it relies on mutual adjustments obtained through negotiation between different actors that play a central role in the implementation process (Pedersen, Sehested, & Sørensen, 2011). Again, service blueprints may come in handy as they provide a visual expression of the roles that different actors play in delivering services, policy programs, or societal solutions. Service blueprints are boundary objects facilitating discussion of the division of labor and the need for coordinating action.

5.3.3 Dealing with Opposition and Integrating New Solutions with Existing Ones

Continuous motivation of co-creators to contribute valuable resources to the implementation of joint solutions is important, not least because the new solutions are likely to generate resistance. A first source of resistance comes from external actors who have not been involved or feel that they have had insufficient influence in the design phase (Evans, 1996). A second source of resistance arises in implementation contexts characterized by a high degree of inertia and path-dependency that results from people having learned to master existing technologies and institutions and from the high costs of transforming the status quo (Pierson, 2000, 2011).

Opposition to new solutions often emerges in the implementation phase when different groups of actors realize what the new solution entails. If the opposing actors are necessary for implementing the solutions, there is a need for the exercise of "soft power" based on persuasion and encouragement (Nye, 2008). Providing reasons for the new solutions and explaining the background and intentions behind them may calm oppositional actors. In addition, the eventual losses faced by these actors might be compensated and the construction of the right incentives may ensure compliance. However, the implementers may also realize that the criticisms are fair and square and the objections worth listening to. It is seldom too late to involve critics in making marginal adjustments of the softshell around the hard kernel of solution strategies in order to remove opposition to implementation.

Dealing with problems related to institutional inertia and path-dependency also calls for adaptation of new solutions so that they work in existing environments. There is always a risk that the forces in favor of preserving the status quo are stronger than those in favor of change. The new practices might not be supported by or compatible with the old practices and sentiments. In this situation, deliberate attempts to disrupt and change the existing modus operandi are necessary for advancing implementation. When old and new practices clash, it is important to precisely diagnose the problem and name the elephant in the room so that everybody can see what impedes the implementation of the new solution and discern the norms and values driving the behavior behind the problem (Heifetz, Grashow, & Linsky, 2009). Having carefully diagnosed the obstacles, the implementers can now consider how to intervene to remove them through a combination of institutional reform, reinforcement of the purpose for change, and expansion of political alliances. Sticking to the plan while allowing concessions and adaptation requires strong support beyond the group of co-creators who designed the new solution.

5.4 The Consolidation, Upscaling and Diffusion Phase

The failure rate of intended improvements and innovative solutions is often high. The new solution may not be fully implemented as planned or needs to be adjusted to local conditions on the ground to work properly and produce the desired results. The implementers may not be fully trained and the new solution might not be well-integrated with other solutions. As such, there are many sources of initial disappointment that call for efforts to consolidate the new solutions and enhance their positive impact through learning and incremental adjustments. If and when a co-created solution is consolidated and begins to deliver on its promises, it should be scaled up to enhance the number of beneficiaries in the present context and diffused to other contexts so as to increase the scope of its impact. Those who believe that successful implementation of the initial prototype of a solution is enough and shy away from the hard work of consolidating, upscaling, and diffusing co-created solutions, will never see their full impact. The sprout will never come to maturity if it is not properly nursed and it will never spread its seeds beyond the local habitat if there is no carrier.

In order to explore how co-creation processes can realize their full impact, we shall look at three sub-phases in the consolidation, upscaling, and diffusion phase: (1) evaluating outcomes and adjusting the course of action to enhance impact; (2) upscaling successful solutions through expansion of their scope; and (3) diffusing co-created solutions through networking.

5.4.1 Evaluating Outcomes and Adjusting the Course of Action to Enhance Impact

Co-creation is often thought of as a creative process with emergent goals, strategies, and activities that defy evaluation. Outputs and outcomes will emerge and change in the course of interaction. As a result, attempts to measure whether activities and progress follow a predetermined schedule to reach particular goals is often considered a futile waste of resources by social innovators. Still, there is a need for evaluating outputs and outcomes in order to help co-creating actors see whether they are actually solving the problem they set out to solve and learn whether they can improve upon the results. Co-creation is not about having a nice collaborative process with well-intended stakeholders, but is a goal- and utility-oriented change process that aims to greatly improve or transform the current system, and if the actors have no knowledge of whether they are going in the right direction, they will never arrive at their destination. As such, the participants in co-creation must constantly test their actions and assumptions against reality to succeed in their endeavor to produce public value outcomes.

As we shall further discuss in Chapter 8, developmental evaluation (Patton, 2011) based on single- and double-loop learning (Argyris & Schön, 1978) is a useful tool for evaluating emergent co-creation processes. In single-loop learning, people adjust their course of action as they evaluate the difference between desired and actual outcomes and reflect on how they can improve goal attainment. They detect emerging problems and correct their actions to enhance impact. In double-loop learning, the involved actors go beyond single-loop learning and critically examine and question the assumptions, values, policies, change theory, and methods that inform and guide their actions in order to make more profound systemic changes that keep them on track and solve the problems or tasks they came together and agreed to solve.

In developmental evaluation, the actors test whether their causal assumptions about the problem and its sources and negative effects hold up by consulting experts and involving those affected by and close to the problem. They test whether the new procedures are working well, whether the new solutions produce the expected effects, and whether emerging problems and new developments are responded to in a swift and adequate manner. Finally, they interpret possible signs that the problem is diminished, the challenges are met, and the task is done.

Developmental evaluation raises two problems. First, it is not easy to get busy and action-driven co-creators to spend time reflecting on goal attainment and the need to modify the initial solution. Second, it is difficult for them to integrate and synthesize multiple and conflicting data sources (Patton, 2011). A plausible response to these challenges would be to call upon supporting actors with adequate resources and analytical capacity to help organize evaluation workshops. Involving relevant researchers from local or regional universities to evaluate processes and outcomes can also be a solution. What is important is to find someone who can evaluate emergent co-creation processes without falling back on checklists and other standardized evaluation procedures.

5.4.2 Upscaling Successful Solutions through Expansion of Their Scope

The common wisdom to "start small, evaluate outcomes and scale up when the new solution works" also applies to co-creation of public value outcomes. If more people can benefit from scaling up co-created solutions, upscaling should be pursued. Upscaling may occur in three different ways. First, the target group may be expanded so that more people can use and benefit from the new solution. Second, new qualities and functionalities may be added to the new solution so that its applicability is enhanced. Third, the area in which the new solution is applied may be expanded by using its core principles to solve a wider set of related problems, challenges, and tasks.

There is often a lot of hype around new and innovative strategies that disrupt existing environments and provide new and smarter solutions. They are expected to do wonderful things and cannot be scaled up fast enough to meet the demand. Here a pro-innovation bias may kick in as there are many examples of innovative solutions that are not properly tested before they are scaled up, thus expanding the use of erroneous solutions that fail to do what they are supposed to do (Abrahamson, 1991; Park & Berry, 2014). To prevent this from happening, decisions to upscale co-created solutions must build on clear documentation of results and a prognosis that upscaling will generate positive results at a wider scale.

5.4.3 Diffusing of Co-created Solutions through Networking

Co-created solutions that work well and produce desirable public value outcomes in one context should be diffused to other contexts and localities that are capable of reaping the same fruits from the new solutions. Broadcasting and adopting new co-created solutions is a moral imperative as it is impossible to justify that people in other contexts, and localities should not be able to benefit from what appears to be a better solution that generates more public value. However, diffusion rarely involves "copy and paste" of ready-made solutions with a universal applicability. More often, diffusion of innovative solutions involves translation, modification, and even reinvention of the new solutions to fit the specific demands and conditions in the new environment (Torfing, 2016). The appropriate metaphor is not to "copy and paste" new solutions, but to "graft and grow" them so that they can thrive in the new and different environment (Hartley & Benington, 2006). Hence, instead of talking of "adoption" of new solutions that are developed elsewhere, we should talk about "adoption and adaptation" of new solutions.

Whether or not a new solution is adopted and adapted to fit a new context or environment depends on the nature and character of the solution, the would-be adopters, and the wider context of adoption. The relative advantage of a new solution, defined in terms of a well-documented public value outcome, is an important diffusion driver. Other attributes of a solution that increase its chances of being diffused are compatibility with social, political, and professional norms in the new context, a low degree of complexity, the possibility of experimenting with the new solution at a limited scale to see how it works, and its discursive construction as promising, feasible, and politically legitimate (Rogers, 1995: 219–265; Greenhalgh et al., 2004: 594–598). The potential adopters are social entrepreneurs who are open-minded, visionary, and risk-taking and are based in organizations with a strong strategic leadership and a broad range of external contacts (Greenhalgh et al., 2004: 606–607). Adoption tends to occur where there is the political will to search for new solutions, a public discourse that focuses on the need to respond to turbulence, and a healthy rivalry between local agencies, organizations, and communities seeking to achieve or maintain a competitive advantage by trying out new solutions (Greenhalgh et al., 2004: 610).

Networks that supplement digital communication with face-to-face contact are the primary medium for diffusion of new co-created solutions (Roger, 1995; Rashman and Hartley, 2002; Dobbin, Simmons, & Garrett, 2007; Ansell, Lundin, & Öberg, 2017). Networks with strong ties tend to enable high-quality communication, while weak ties enable the spread of solutions over long distances and across highly different contexts (Granovetter, 1973). A major barrier to diffusion of co-created solutions between broadcasters and potential adopters is that the potential adopters have little ownership over the new solution and might end up rejecting it because they have not been involved in its development and fear that it will not work in their particular context. The solution is to encourage potential adopters to reinvent the new solution by treating it as input to a local co-creation process that will tailor the solution to the local conditions by transforming both its softshell and its hard kernel (Denis et al., 2002). A co-created reinvention of solutions will build local ownership and enthusiasm that fuels the implementation process and optimizes the result and impact.

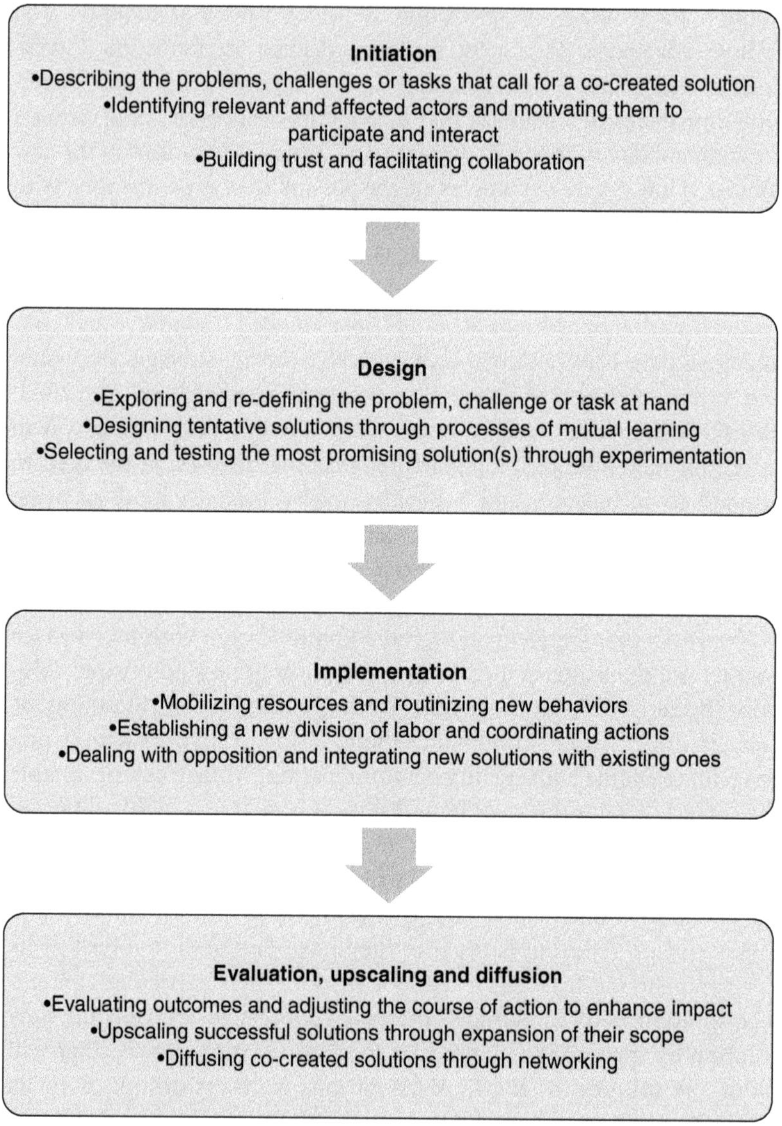

Initiation
•Describing the problems, challenges or tasks that call for a co-created solution
•Identifying relevant and affected actors and motivating them to participate and interact
•Building trust and facilitating collaboration

Design
•Exploring and re-defining the problem, challenge or task at hand
•Designing tentative solutions through processes of mutual learning
•Selecting and testing the most promising solution(s) through experimentation

Implementation
•Mobilizing resources and routinizing new behaviors
•Establishing a new division of labor and coordinating actions
•Dealing with opposition and integrating new solutions with existing ones

Evaluation, upscaling and diffusion
•Evaluating outcomes and adjusting the course of action to enhance impact
•Upscaling successful solutions through expansion of their scope
•Diffusing co-created solutions through networking

Figure 5.1 The co-creation process

5.5 Concluding Remarks

This chapter has mapped the co-creation process from the initiation phase through the design and implementation to the consolidation, upscaling, and diffusion of new solutions. The full process is depicted in Figure 5.1.

The linear logic of presentation should not obscure the complex and potentially chaotic character of co-creation as it moves back and forth between different phases and sub-phases in the search for innovative yet feasible solutions that enjoy sufficient support to ensure robust implementation and consolidation. There are drivers and barriers that may either accelerate or impede collaborative interaction and agreement on problem definitions, solutions, implementation, and consolidation, but a broad array of tools and strategies may be called upon to overcome, or at least mitigate, these barriers and reinforce the drivers. A complete inventory of supportive tools and strategies is beyond the scope of this book, and even the longest list of tools will not alter the fact that the synergies and joy derived from fruitful collaboration and discovery of new and promising solutions tends to be matched by conflicts and barriers to further advancement of the co-creation process. Co-creators are likely to react differently when facing bigger or smaller roadblocks. Quitters will leave the process in the face of unsurmountable obstacles, and campers will slow down, partly withdraw and wait to see if the weather conditions improve. By contrast, climbers will try to describe the obstacles as "creative constraints" (Ibbotson, 2008) and turn them into "opportunities" (Stoltz, 1997). Successful co-creation depends on the climbers' ability to convince quitters and campers to continue the journey.

6 | *Pathways to Co-created Public Value Outcomes*

This chapter examines the outcomes and limitations of co-creation. Promotors of co-creation are sometimes satisfied with having stimulated civic voluntarism and created processes that are gratifying for the participants, but it is also paramount to consider the collective impact of co-creation on societal problems and challenges. A systematic literature review reveals that while the drivers and dynamics of co-creation have been the subject of numerous studies, the outcomes of co-creation have received scant attention (Voorberg, Bekkers, & Tummers, 2015). To compensate for this neglect, this chapter aims to explain what kinds of outcomes we should expect from co-creation. Since co-creation is intrinsically linked to value production (Gebauer, Johnson, & Enquist, 2010), we discuss the outcomes of co-creation in terms of public value outcomes. This discussion is balanced against a consideration of some of the obvious problems and limitations associated with collaborative processes of co-creation.

Processes of co-creation are complex and contingent and not always carried to fruition, at least not in the first iteration. However, when successful, co-creation processes will not only mobilize relevant resources and improve the quality of existing service solutions but also help to foster innovative, resilient, and legitimate responses to wicked and unruly problems and the growing experience of turbulence. As such, we propose that co-creation enhances the problem-solving capacity of modern societies.

To better understand the production of outcomes, this chapter identifies and describes impact pathways leading from co-creating platforms, arenas, and processes to desirable public value outcomes, including: (1) production of a needs-based and cost-effective service improvement; (2) development of innovative solutions to wicked and unruly policy problems; (3) generation of resilient communities capable of finding robust solutions to recurring and emerging problems; and (4) enhancement of input and output legitimacy (see Loeffler & Bovaird, 2018).

Service quality was at the heart of the original research on co-production (Sharp, 1980; Brudney, 1984; Levine & Fischer, 1984; Percy, 1984), although the focus was more on improving individual services rather than the entire system of public service production. Service improvement is also the main focus of the recent literature on co-creation (Voorberg, Bekkers, & Tummers, 2015) and some scholars note that co-creation may have a positive systemic effect on service delivery (Osborne & Strokosch, 2013). From a public governance perspective, however, co-creation is not merely a tool for service improvement but also a lever for developing innovative solutions to complex societal problems that are hard to solve through top-down government or market competition. In the process of improving public service solutions and enhancing the capability for dealing with intractable problems, co-creation may also have a more indirect and long-term effect on enhancing the ability of local and regional communities to bounce back in the face of crisis and turbulence either by returning to the former equilibrium (static resilience) or by creating a new equilibrium (dynamic resilience, or robustness) (Ansell & Trondal, 2017). Finally, while public service improvement, societal problem solving, and the enhancement of resilience are public value outcomes that improve the governing of society and the economy, the last public value outcome that we will consider concerns the production of the legitimacy necessary for securing the sustainability of the political system. The argument is that co-creation tends to enhance popular support for public governance by fostering efficient, effective, and equitable responses to unfulfilled needs and pressing problems and by involving a broad range of citizens and private stakeholders in decision making (Skelcher & Torfing, 2010; Meijer, 2011). As such, co-creation may enhance both the input and output legitimacy of the political system.

Co-creation also tends to democratize public governance by creating venues for active and direct participation, stimulating public deliberation between a plethora of social and political actors, and building democratic ownership of societal solutions. The impact of a systematic turn to co-creation on the transformation and deepening of democracy is further explored in Chapter 7.

6.1 Impact Pathways to Improved Service Production

The bulk of public budgets is spent on public service provision. The cost of education, social welfare, and health services is steadily rising due to citizens' increasing expectations and growing public ambitions, as well as exciting possibilities for curing diseases, mitigating environmental problems, and enhancing the quality of life (Dunston et al., 2009). The scarcity of public funds makes it increasingly difficult to make ends meet and political and administrative frustration grows in the face of reports that costly public services do not meet the needs of target groups. Hence, it is a crucial task for public governance to provide a needs-based and cost-efficient quality improvement of public services.

Involving individual users in the co-production of the services they receive helps to mobilize societal resources, improve the quality and outcomes of service provision, and increase the prospect of meeting the actual needs of the recipients (Alford, 2009). Co-creation takes us one step further by involving public delivery agencies, services users, volunteers, community organizations, private firms, and so on in redesigning the production and delivery of services either at the institutional, system, or policy making levels (Brandsen & Pestoff, 2006; Bason, 2010; Osborne & Strokosch, 2013). Co-creation of the content, goals, and delivery of public services may help to make service provision more needs-based and cost-efficient while simultaneously improving service quality. While the service users may participate in co-creation in order to enhance the private value of the particular services they are receiving, research shows that intrinsic rewards in terms of doing the job and doing it well, sociality defined as group belonging and group solidarity, and expressive values such as civic duty, altruism and the attainment of worthwhile goals are also crucial factors in motivating participation in the co-creation of services (Alford, 2002; Eijk & Steen, 2016).

Co-creation involves a sustained interaction between relevant and affected actors aiming to find joint solutions to common problems. It may spur the development of efficient service production systems that satisfy the needs of the users through the provision of high-quality services (Ostrom, 1996; Andrews, Boyne, & Walker, 2006; Vamstad, 2012). While there are many empirical examples of successful cases of co-created services (Merickova, Nemec, & Svidronova, 2015; Sørensen

& Torfing, 2018), we need a clearer understanding of the impact pathways that connect co-creation to improved service production (Morris et al., 2007).

The concept of impact pathways enables us to map the intermediate steps and factors that connect co-creation with different public value outcomes. Impact pathways are based on cumulative causation, and feedback loops may occur (Maru et al., 2018). Our attempt to reconstruct the multiple impact pathways that lead to the production of the four different public value outcomes draws on existing research in order to identify the different mechanisms that produce a particular outcome. Future research may contribute to revising and expanding the hypothetical impact pathways we have identified and may also help to determine their scope conditions. As such, the endeavor to show why and how co-creation may produce particular public service outcomes is an open-ended work in progress.

Studies show that co-creation in the field of service provision may produce desirable outcomes. To deepen our understanding of the causal mechanisms that connect co-creation to service improvement, we have mapped several impact pathways that are presented in Figure 6.1.

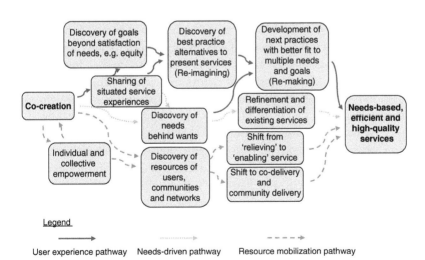

Figure 6.1 Impact pathways connecting co-creation to improved service production

Figure 6.1 reveals three different impact pathways (marked with different arrows) beginning on the left side with co-creation, defined as a process through which relevant and affected actors collaborate to jointly improve public services. The *first impact pathway* involves reimagining and remaking public services (Dunston et al., 2009). As a first step, co-creation facilitates the sharing of situated service experiences between users, professionals, and other relevant actors (Radnor et al., 2014), for example, by mapping how different users travel through the service system and listening to their experiences along the way. A careful discussion of user experiences with existing services may stimulate the discovery of best practice alternatives to the existing service provision, which in turn may create more positive experiences for users (Dunston et al., 2009). A focus on user experiences may also help to discover important public goals such as empowerment, equity, and accountability that go beyond the immediate fulfillment of the social needs of the user group (Pestoff, 2012) and that might in turn fuel the search for best practice alternatives to the present services. Having identified a number of alternative service solutions, the next step may be to develop and test new service designs that provide a better fit between needs and services and enhance the impact of public services on multiple goals. This step takes us from reimagining to remaking services and contributes to improving service quality and making public services more needs-based.

The *second impact pathway* begins with the discovery of the needs behind the wants. While service users are often keen to flag their wants and expectations vis-a-vis particular services, sustained dialogue with professionals and other relevant actors and joint evaluation of the users' experiences with the services that they are offered will help to discover the needs that lie behind their wants and expectations (Alford, 2009; Wiewiora, Keast, & Brown, 2016. Hence, the unemployed may want larger cash benefits and less systemic control, but what they really need is help to get proper education and training so that they can get sustained employment and better living conditions. Moreover, they need training that develops the skills that are in high demand in the labor market. Discovery of these needs may trigger a further differentiation and refinement of the existing services. As a result, services will become better at targeting social needs.

The *third impact pathway* takes as its point of departure the observation that co-creation empowers citizens by enhancing their self-worth and strengthens private organizations by sharpening their profile and expanding their membership basis (Mitlin, 2008). This empowerment will tend to produce positive feedback on the motivation and capacity of citizens and civil society organizations to participate in co-creation. It will also stimulate the discovery of the manifold resources of users, citizens, and organizations operating in a particular service field. This is an important discovery since users, citizens, and local communities should be viewed as "hidden resources, not drains on the system" since "no service that ignores this resource can be efficient" (Boyle & Harris, 2009: 11). While users and citizens can often play a much more active role in public service production and are highly motivated to do so in order to be able to take care of themselves, civil society organizations, voluntary groups, and private firms may offer to contribute to the production and delivery of services, perhaps even new and better services that complement the existing services. Hence, the discovery of resources outside the public sector may transform the public system of service production by shifting the emphasis from relieving to enabling services (Bovaird, 2007) and by enhancing co-delivery and community delivery of services (Ostrom, 1996). The latter may not only lead to better coverage in some areas but also help to reduce public expenditure.

The three hypothetical impact pathways uncover the dynamic flow of events that may be triggered by co-creation and may lead to improved services. An empirical example may serve to illustrate some of the causal mechanisms implicit to the hypothetical impact pathways.

In the Canadian province of Quebec, the discovery of the resources of nongovernment actors led to the creation of a hundred or so domestic help social economy enterprises that complement the services that the public sector delivers to elderly people. The social enterprises help to provide services to elderly in rural areas and enable them to stay longer in their own homes rather than being transferred to an expensive elderly care institution. There are also examples of the social enterprises having added to the basket of services provided for the elderly by identifying and responding to their need for social contact (Jetté & Vaillancourt, 2011). These examples suggest the presence of a link between co-delivery and the development of new and better services.

The three impact pathways explain why and how co-creation can improve public service provision. However, the analysis of the positive impact of co-creation in the field of public service production must not blind us to potential problems and limiting factors connected to co-created service production. The fiscal pressure on government means that there is a risk that governments will be tempted to dump daunting service tasks and complex problems on users and communities that may not be able to shoulder the burden and solve the problems (Bovaird, 2007). Government may save public money by doing so, but the service might not be produced or may be of poor quality. Governments that give priority to enhanced cost efficiency over quality improvement and needs-orientation may also be reluctant to engage users and community actors in co-created service production because they fear that it may drive up costs. However, these problems simply bear witness to the fact that successful co-creation presupposes a mutual will and capacity for addressing problems that are defined as common. Co-creation is a two-way street.

Another set of problems relates to the participation of users and citizens in the co-creation of public services. While their participation may strengthen accountability of public service providers, it may also blur the boundary and division of labor between the public and private sector, thus making it more difficult for voters to hold their political representatives to account for service provision (Joshi & Moore, 2002; Mayo & Moore, 2002). In the case of co-delivery or community delivery, it is hard to tell who is responsible for service gaps or wasteful service duplication. In the final instance, elected politicians hold the ultimate responsibility for the entire system of service provision, but we need to find ways of holding the actors involved in co-creation collectively responsible.

While contract termination is an option where services are contracted out to private providers, it is more difficult to hold private, community actors, and citizens engaged in noncontractual co-creation accountable for bad outcomes. Moreover, while co-creation may offer a new venue of participation for people who distrust political parties, interest groups and old grassroots movements but still want to be involved in "small politics" (Bang, 2005), participation may tend to favor the well-educated and resourceful middle classes that may aim to reshape service provision to cater to their specific needs, thus undermining equity in service production (Bovaird, 2007). This problem calls for political and administrative efforts to secure a seat at the table for less resourceful and organized groups. A combination of socioeconomic, political, and organizational empowerment strategies –

that for instance may help a poor minority group to organize – and appointment of participants based on their different experiences and needs rather than on their self-selection may offer a solution to this problem.

Service users and citizens may have an individual interest in service improvement. However, it is not always clear what public managers can learn from spending time listening to citizens' experiences and judgments or how these inputs can be translated into service improvements without increasing public expenditure (Kouzmin et al., 1999). Moreover, as Ryzin and Immerwahr (2007) argue, the users are sometimes unaware of, or perhaps unwilling to, confess their true preferences. There might also be professional resistance to co-creation of public service systems. Many professional groups assume that gains in status among co-creating users, citizens, and organizations might come at their expense (Crawford, Rutter, & Thelwall, 2004). As such, they are often reluctant to hand over discretion to service users and their support networks because they do not trust them to behave responsibly (Barnes, 1999). In many cases, the professionals also lack the skills and methods to work closely with users and community actors (Schachter & Aliaga, 2003).

For these reasons, the active involvement of public managers and professionals in the co-creation of service improvement may appear an uphill struggle. That being said, there is only one way to learn about the needs and experiences of different target groups and to discover why the existing services either are unwanted or inappropriate, and that is to involve users and other relevant and affected actors in discussion about the problems at hand and the ways they can be solved. The methods and techniques for orchestrating that kind of conversation are already well developed, and public managers and professional groups can remove a major obstacle to their engagement in co-creation by reflecting on the contingency of their own knowledge and expertise. Recognizing the multiple sources of knowledge about public service systems and the value of pragmatic experimentation based on multi-actor collaboration is an important first step toward co-creation.

6.2 Impact Pathways to Innovative Problem-Solving

Public managers and professionals work hard to ensure continuous improvement of public services and policies, but the pervasiveness of wicked and unruly problems and the turbulence surrounding the public sector tend to put innovation high on the public sector agenda. Far from being a goal in itself, innovation is an instrument for disrupting underperforming service organizations, breaking policy deadlocks, and creating smart solutions to intractable societal problems and rapidly changing socioeconomic conditions (OECD, 2017).

Unlike co-production, there is strong evidence for the innovative impact of co-creation (Torfing, 2016; Torfing, Krogh, & Ejrnæs, 2020). Co-creation permits a broad range of actors to explore and redefine problems and challenges, design, and test new and bold solutions and build broad-based ownership for implementation and consolidation (Bommert, 2010; Hartley, Sørensen, & Torfing, 2013). Hence, innovation is a frequent public value outcome of co-creation. To deepen our understanding of why and how co-creation leads to disruptive change and innovative transformations, Figure 6.2 maps two hypothetical impact pathways linking co-creation to public innovation outcomes.

The *first impact pathway* begins with the positive impact that co-creation has on the perception of self-efficacy and the social interaction that it engenders. Being part of the creative processes of co-creation will tend to empower the participating actors and heighten their confidence in their individual capacity to influence their surroundings and achieve results. It will also generate a lot of informal social interaction. Both the

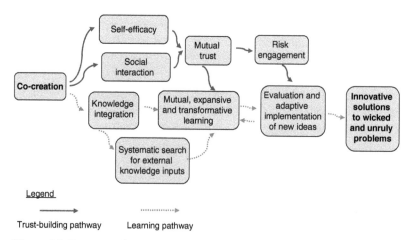

Figure 6.2 Impact pathways connecting co-creation to public innovation

feeling of being capable of doing great things and the informal social communication through which the actors get to know each other will tend to build mutual trust relations (Fledderus, Brandsen, & Honigh, 2014).

Trust relations are important for stimulating mutual learning that requires that the actors are prepared to open up and admit that they might not have all the answers and that their current way of thinking is inadequate and needs revision through a questioning of their tacit and explicit knowledge and perhaps even its underlying paradigm (Edmondson, 1999). Trust is also important for the development of joint strategies for risk engagement that in turn will tend to stimulate real-life testing of new and bold ideas and engagement in adaptive implementation through iterative rounds of application, evaluation, and revision (Renn, 2008; Osborne & Brown, 2011). It is in the testing and implementation phase that things often go wrong and where it is critical that stakeholders are willing to engage in joint risks. If you do not trust other actors to help in preventing and mitigating risk, bring out countervailing benefits, and distribute costs and benefits fairly, it is unlikely that actors will accept the risks that innovation requires. Therefore, mutual trust is a prerequisite for handling the risks of innovation.

The *second impact pathway* looks at how co-creation may stimulate knowledge integration with a view to promoting mutual learning and advancing problem-solving capacity (Edelenbos, Buuren, & Schie, 2011; Maiello et al., 2013; Molen et al., 2015). Mutual learning is based on knowledge sharing and knowledge integration. In most cases, none of the participating actors will have all the knowledge needed to produce an innovative solution to the problem or challenge at hand, but each of them may hold a piece of the puzzle. Piecing together more or less compatible bits of knowledge into a joint picture that advances the collective understanding of the problem and offers a new perspective on its solution is an important step toward innovation. Knowledge integration may sometimes reveal gaps in existing knowledge. The actors may realize that a new type of solution is needed, but lack concrete ideas about what the solution looks like in practice. The identification of such gaps may trigger a systematic search for external knowledge inputs in the shape of successful solutions from elsewhere (Dobbin, Simmons, & Garrett, 2007), which, may in turn further stimulate the process of mutual learning as new ideas are evaluated, translated, and perhaps reinvented.

Not all forms of learning, however, are equally effective when it comes to stimulating innovation (Torfing, 2016). Some forms of learning are reproductive in the sense that they use the current repertoire of tools and ideas to solve minor problems in an instrumental way through processes of trial and error that aim to match tools to problems. Other forms of learning are expansive because they reframe problems and solutions and search for concepts, narratives, and ways of thinking that can give meaning to the unknown and thus extend our previous knowledge (Engeström, 1987, 2008). Expansive learning – similar to the notion of generative learning referred to in Chapter 4 – has a high potential for stimulating innovation. However, there is a risk that the new knowledge will be continuous with the past and result in an affirmative worldview that preserves rather than transforms the status quo.

To unlock innovation, transformative learning (Mezirow, 2000) emphasizes the need for critical reflections that may challenge and transform the taken-for-granted frames of reference within which the co-creating actors operate. The critical transformation of the joint frame of reference will also tend to change the role perceptions of the actors and give them a new understanding of how they can contribute to joint problem-solving. The collective processes of mutual, expansive, and transformative learning spur the development of new ideas that need testing, careful selection, and adaptive implementation in order for the new solutions to work in the context of existing solutions and formats (Heifetz, Linsky, & Grashow, 2009). The result of this endeavor will be public innovation defined as the development and implementation of new ideas that disrupt common wisdom and established practices (Ansell & Torfing, 2014).

The two hypothetical impact pathways show why and how co-creation may result in innovative solutions to wicked and unruly problems. An empirical illustration of pathways leading to innovative problem-solving is provided by Gray & Ren (2014) who studied how trust-based integration of cognitive schemas helped to overcome the initial failure of two team subgroups to collaborate in designing an innovate software database for a high-profile US space program. The diverging organizational heritages of the two groups of experts had given rise to conflicting understandings of how to design the database and how to apply the different forms of expertise that were available. Development of mutual trust enabled knowledge integration and agreement of key constructs that in turn spurred the development of an innovative solution to the design of the database.

As we have seen, co-creation may not only spur continuous service improvement, but can also enhance the production of innovative solutions to wicked and unruly problems (Hartley, 2006; Sørensen & Torfing, 2011). However, these outcomes may not be as easy to achieve as the hypothetical impact pathways suggest. First of all, it is sometimes difficult to get citizens to participate in public problem-solving when there are no immediate gains in terms of benefits from improved service delivery that speak directly to their self-interest. That being said, Marschall (2004) shows that the context-dependent perception of societal problems as serious and urgent stimulates civic participation and that the attempt of public officials to appeal to and contact citizens directly has a clear mobilizing effect (for the effect of direct contact see also Rosenstone & Hansen, 1993; Ostrom, 1996).

Second, Fenwick & McMillan (2013) note that the co-creation of new and innovative public solutions requires that the participating actors spend a lot of time, energy, and resources in the initial diagnostic stage; display a high level of trust; and have a high tolerance for ambiguity. This requirement is not always met in reality and thus might prevent the development of a common understanding of the problem or challenge at hand. The problem can be solved by relying on a small and tightly knit core group that has already developed a high degree of trust, though this solution prevents crowdsourcing of the experiences, suggestions, and ideas of a larger group of actors. Digital solutions might be helpful here. Meijer (2011) shows that digital platforms provide an inexpensive tool for sharing knowledge about problems and building positive relations between public and private actors and among peers. In a later work, Meijer (2012) concludes that digital technology facilitates new practices of co-creation as new online media lower the costs of large scale and dispersed interactions, and therefore enables practices of co-creation with a broad range of actors that are hardly possible offline.

Third, when the involved actors have jointly diagnosed the problem or challenge that calls for a co-created solution, they need to exchange and integrate their different forms of knowledge in order to stimulate mutual learning. The problem here is that the knowledge of public managers and scientific experts may fit well together, but it is often difficult to integrate these forms of knowledge with the knowledge produced by stakeholders motivated by narrow organizational interests (Edelenbos, Buuren, & Schie, 2011). In addition, professional knowledge is not always compatible with the knowledge of users, citizens, and other lay actors (Maiello et al., 2013). While some of the participating actors may speak the same scientific language when presenting and validating their knowledge, others may base their knowledge claims on personal impressions and intuitions and normative assertions. Knowledge integration in co-creation processes may, therefore, be prevented by conflicts over the origin and content of knowledge. However, Molen et al. (2015) maintain that knowledge is both a core aspect of conflict within collaborative governance as well as a key to its resolution. As such, integration of knowledge in the face of conflict is likely to benefit from: 1) the collective formulation of research questions, dialogue on the interpretation of results, and, subsequently, collective decision making based on the results; 2) a focus on data and knowledge with a "fact-like" character that contributes to curtailing knowledge disputes in governance settings; and 3) involvement of experts who are closely connected to the governance practice and whose expertise is valued and trusted by all parties involved.

Fourth, the conversion of collaborative governance into expansive and transformative learning and the development and testing of new and bold solutions may be hampered either by tunnel vision developed by a group of the "usual suspects" who over time have developed similar worldviews and, therefore, cannot disturb and inspire each other (Skilton & Dooley, 2010) or by veto players that seek to block new solutions that are perceived as going against their interests (Gray, 1989; Scharpf, 1994). While actors suffering from tunnel vision need to be disturbed by new and disruptive knowledge or by actors who catalyze creative out-of-box thinking, veto actors must either be persuaded by side-payments or be convinced that the solution on the table is better than no solution.

Finally, adaptive implementation of innovative solutions may be hampered by the lack of clear responsibilities and stable procedures for implementation in collaborative settings (O'Toole, 1997) or by institutional inertia supported by strong path dependencies (Pierson, 2000). The cure for these problems may be to focus on pluricentric coordination of the efforts of the different public and private actors in the implementation phase (Pedersen, Sehested, & Sørensen, 2011) or to build a strong network coalition behind the innovative solution that can overcome institutional inertia (Considine, 2013).

6.3 Impact Pathways to Resilient and Robust Communities

Global economic transformations, natural disasters, man-made environmental problems, disruptive innovations in technology, social interaction and public programs will from time to time disrupt local and regional communities and expose the inhabitants and their way of living to considerable risks. Resilience describes the ability of communities to function during and after the events that cause disruption by means of negotiating, managing, and adapting to the dislocation (Windle, 2011). When faced with disruptive events and continuous stress, healthy and strong communities will seek to mobilize their knowledge, resources, and energies in an attempt to bounce back and restore the former equilibrium (static resilience) or to create a new equilibrium that takes the source of disruption into account (dynamic resilience) (Ansell & Trondal, 2017).

A recent report from the US National Academy of Sciences (2011) concludes that public and private collaboration stimulates the ability of local communities to prepare for, respond to, and recover from setbacks, crises, and disasters. When actors from the public and private sectors work together in community-wide networks and use their complementary skills, competences, and resources to monitor change, prepare for emergencies, and respond to emerging challenges, the community's capacity for dealing with and recovering from crises, shocks and disasters is significantly increased. Public and private actors will typically engage in joint reflection, planning, coordination, and action that allows the community to deal with dislocating events through a combination of reactive and proactive measures. In fragmented communities with few and weak ties between public and private actors, the ability to bounce back or create new futures will be severely constrained; in communities where public actors exchange key resources with each other and co-create solutions to actual problems and perceived challenges, resilience will tend to be higher.

An important conclusion we can draw from the National Academy report is that co-creation does not only lead to immediate, visible, and tangible results in terms of improved public service production and the creation of innovative solutions to wicked problems; it also produces more indirect, long-term results by building stronger and more resilient communities that are prepared for future emergency action, disaster management, and future community-building. Promoting co-creation as a core principle of governance allows communities to come together to meet emerging challenges with adaptive and transformative strategies. In order to gain a better understanding of how and why co-creation enhances resilience, Figure 6.3 maps the hypothetical impact pathways connecting co-creation to resilience.

The point of departure is the ensemble of community-wide co-creation processes through which public and private actors aim to ensure continuous improvement and enhance innovation. Resilience involves more than effective disaster response and thus begins as a more or less explicit dimension of a large number of co-creation projects that bring together public and private actors (National Academy of Sciences, 2011). Three different impact pathways link the ecology of co-creation to resilience in a particular domain.

The *first impact pathway* starts off by highlighting the positive effect of co-creation on the physical and psychological well-being of social and political actors. Co-creation not only improves the well-being of the people who *receive* co-created social services but also enhances the well-being of those who *participate* in the co-creation process. The later process may enhance their participation and attract further participants. For example, it has been shown that when people become volunteers late in life, it tends to lead to improved life quality,

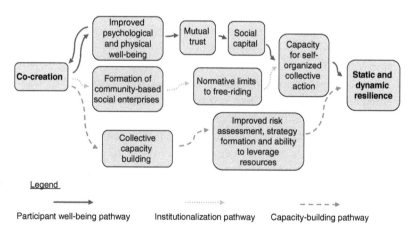

Figure 6.3 Impact pathways connecting co-creation to resilience

psychological well-being and functioning, better self-reported health, and a sense of purpose, belonging, and value within society (e.g. Greenfield & Marks, 2004; for a review, see Warburton, 2006). Moreover, individuals with improved physical and psychological well-being and a growing sense of social belonging can be expected to develop a high level of trust in other community members and institutions they work with that will tend to enhance their social capital (Putnam, 1995), defined as the things they can accomplish through their relations with others. Co-creation allows people to bond with people from their local community and bridge the social and cultural differences that may separate them from other groups. However, it also permits them to forge linkages with public actors from organizations with different kinds of authority and resources. The private actors work together with public actors to solve problems and meet old and emerging challenges. They get to know each other and it gradually becomes easier for them to contact each other and draw on each other's resources when something happens (Sørensen & Torfing, 2003). The accumulation of social capital enhances the ability of communities to take joint action when they are hit by shocks, crises, disasters, and other stress factors. Their capacity for self-organized collective action is increased and this tends to make them more resilient.

The *second impact pathway* plays an auxiliary role in relation to the first pathway as it takes a slightly different road to enhancing the capacity for self-organized collective action and improving resilience. It begins with the observation that co-creation processes sometimes become institutionalized by the formation of community-based social enterprises that provide social services and opportunities for interaction (Munoz, Steiner, & Farmer, 2014). Community-based social enterprises are nonprofit business structures based on voluntarism. They aim to develop sustainable services with a broad reach and they often create spin-offs in terms of collaborative projects of co-creation that involve a new and different set of actors. By improving the well-being of the voluntary actors involved in their activities and the trust-based interactions among a growing number of actors, social enterprises will tend to add to the accumulation of social capital. The social enterprises also play a role in curbing the free-riding that presents one of the key obstacles to collective action. Free-riding is mitigated by creating an environment with enough social and normative control to encourage individuals to sacrifice their short-term personal interests in favor of the pursuit of collective goals (Olsen, 1965, 1970). Ostrom (2000) has shown that in institutional settings with strong normative pressures, people are willing to contribute to collective goal achievement either if they believe that others will reciprocate or if joint action is rewarded and shirking is frowned upon. This finding is important because the reduction of classical collective action problems will further enhance the capacity for self-regulated collective action (Pestoff, 2012).

The *third impact pathway* is another spin-off of co-creation. The proliferation of co-creation can often stimulate collective capacity building. Initiation and facilitation of community-wide co-creation processes and the need for coordination between different projects and processes spurs the construction of communication mechanisms enabling information and knowledge sharing, the development of training programs enhancing collaborative skills and building leadership competences, and the formulation of overarching guidelines and procedures facilitating collaboration, decision making, and tracking of results (Academy of Sciences, 2014). This type of collective capacity building will gradually improve risk assessment and the ability to formulate strategic responses to different kinds of threats and leverage the resources of relevant and affected actors based on their interdependencies (Academy of Sciences, 2014). These are all important components of the attempt to enhance resilience that feeds on the ability to provide a strategic response to risks and mobilize the resources that are needed on the ground.

Hermansson (2017) provides an illustrative example of how the mechanisms captured by the three hypothetical impact pathways work in practice. Her study looks at how cross-sectoral collaboration between the Turkish government and local civil society organizations influenced the ability to perform key disaster management activities such as damage assessment, search, rescue and aid distribution. In response to the critique of the insufficient government response to the 1999 earthquake, the Turkish disaster management system was reformed in 2009. A new agency, the Disaster and Emergency Management Presidency (AFAD), was created and charged with responsibility for all matters pertaining to disasters. Based on past experiences, the new agency came to the conclusion that local NGOs provide an effective and efficient response when disaster hits, especially if they are provided with sufficient training and resources and their efforts are coordinated with professional disaster management person-nel. As a result, AFAD began to arrange joint workshops, training sessions, and planning meetings with local NGOs during non-disaster periods. The increased interaction between AFAD and the local NGOs built mutual trust, improved cross-sectoral working relations, and clarified the division of labor and the role of the various actors, thus enhancing the capacity for collective action. At the same time, the training sessions and the institutionalized knowledge-sharing improved the ability to identify and deal with risks and mobilize local resources when needed.

The new collaborative system of disaster management was put to the test in the 2011 earthquake. The empirical analysis shows that government distrust in local NGOs and political tension between the Turkish government and the Kurdish separatist movement continued to prevent much-needed collaboration between professional disaster management teams and local NGOs. However, the analysis also shows that in those areas where pre-disaster collaboration had built trust and enhanced local skills and competences, the local ability to deal with the damage caused by the earthquake was much higher, especially in the field of search and rescue. In sum, while the attempt to expand cross-sectoral collaboration and build social capital and local capacities was no panacea, it contributed to reducing suboptimal disaster response.

The study conducted by Hermansson (2017) points to some import-ant limiting factors that may prevent collaboration from leading to a higher degree of resilience. Collaboration may not thrive and co-creation may not flourish if there are deep-seated ethnic, political, or socioeconomic conflicts that create mutual distrust and undermine the capacity for self-organized collective action. In addition, if government agencies continue to distrust local actors and are reluctant to provide the resources and guidance they need, it will reduce the ability of the local actors to use their local knowledge and skills to deal with the impact of the disaster. In both cases, mutual learning that takes into account the positive contribution of cross-sectoral collaboration may gradually remove these barriers.

Another problem is that the growth of community-based social enterprises is hampered by the lack of investment and business support (applies to for-profit enterprises) and stable financing (applies to non-profit enterprises) (Hines, 2005; Philips, 2006). Social enterprises share financial problems with other small businesses, but the problem is exacerbated by their complex, value-based, and mission-driven character that tends to limit their fundraising capacity. The solution could be to devise new government programs aiming to spur growth in and by social enterprises. However, the problem is that many of them find growth problematic rather than attractive (Phillips, 2006). Creation of self-organized networks between social enterprises is perhaps the way forward since flexible collaboration and co-funding may enhance their sustainability. Also crowdfunding seems to be a growing option in the future. The risk associated with crowdfunding a small and unknown social enterprise might be reduced if government actors are a part of the social enterprise.

A final problem is that in some geographical areas such as remote rural regions, there is a very small pool of people with the personal resources needed to enhance participation in collaborative activities, form social enterprises and engage in collective capacity building (Munoz et al., 2014). Those who are capable of participating are already actively engaged in co-creation, or need further motivation in order to become an asset for local resilience. The new emphasis on voluntarism and the actual demonstration of how co-creation may enhance the influence of people in local affairs may serve as factors for further mobilization.

6.4 Impact Pathways to Input and Output Legitimacy

There are other reasons for recognizing the importance of co-creation that go beyond managerial concerns for efficiency and social concerns for effectiveness (Ryan, 2012). There are also political reasons that derive from the legitimacy of public solutions produced through processes of co-creation (Alford, 2009; Bourgon, 2009; Boyle & Harris 2009; OECD, 2011). The stability of a political order does not rest solely on its efficiency and effectiveness but ultimately depends on the obedience of citizens to collectively binding rules and norms (Börzel & Panke, 2007). The sociologist Max Weber identified three sources of obedience: self-interest, fear, and legitimacy. In the long run, legitimacy is the preferred source of obedience in liberal democracy because it is impossible to satisfy all the personal interests of citizens and because coercion is very costly, generates fierce resistance, and clashes with liberal values. Legitimacy can either be generated on the input- or output-side of the political system (Scharpf, 1999). Input legitimacy is defined as political support derived from responsiveness to citizens as a result of their participation in policy making. Output legitimacy is defined as political support derived from the effectiveness of public solutions as a result of their ability to solve the problems they are meant to solve. Schmidt (2013) also adds a third form of legitimacy that she calls "throughput" legitimacy, which refers to legitimacy derived from the procedural fairness of public decision making.

Network theorists insist that the co-creation of public services and policy solutions helps to ensure a high degree of input and output legitimacy (Skelcher & Torfing, 2010). Input legitimacy is ensured when a wide range of actors are invited to participate in shaping the solution. Joint deliberations and the efforts to test and revise promising ideas tend to create a broad ownership over the ultimate solution even if the influence of each actor is marginal. Output legitimacy is ensured when manifold actors help to produce a deeper and more nuanced understanding of the problem at hand, bring forth a plurality of ideas and insights that inform the formulation, testing, and revision of a joint solution and coordinate their actions in the implementation phase in order to make sure that the solution has maximum impact. Drawing on the insights in the previous sections and adding new ones, we have identified the hypothetical impact pathways that connect co-creation to input and output legitimacy. These are presented in Figure 6.4.

The *first impact pathway* builds on insights generated above. We have shown that co-creation might lead to continuous improvement of

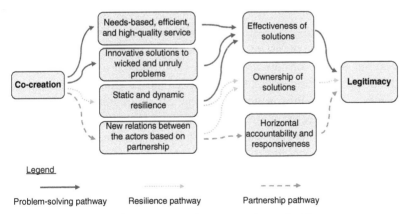

Figure 6.4 Impact pathways connecting co-creation to legitimacy

public services, innovative solutions to wicked and unruly problems, and static and dynamic forms of resilience. Improvement of services, innovative designs, and resilience based on multi-actor collaboration will tend to make the public solutions more effective when it comes to satisfying needs, solving problems, and responding to disruptive situations of crisis and disaster. Better solutions that hit the target will enjoy heightened popularity and political support and thus will increase the output legitimacy of the political system.

The *second impact pathway* highlights the fact that co-creation tends to build more resilient communities. When a broad array of public and private actors are involved in risk assessment and disaster management, they will tend to feel that the solution is their solution. Hence, rather than opposing the attempt of external government agencies to securitize the disaster area or impose expert solutions to local problems, the citizens will work with government agencies to implement solutions that they are supporting and feel responsibility for achieving them. In short, co-creation for resilience tends to enhance input legitimacy.

The *third impact pathway* focuses on the transformation of relations between public and private actors. When public actors engage in co-creation they have to give up the idea of drawing exclusively on their own professional knowledge and authority and of going-it-alone. They must open up and listen to the private actors who in turn play a much more active role when co-creating public solutions. Private actors thereby cease to be passive clients who are acted upon and offered services and provided solutions they have no part in and no responsibility for. They become actively engaged in public value creation and are expected to commit resources, time, and energy to the co-creation process. As such, co-creation radically transforms the hierarchical relations between public and private actors into horizontal partnership relations based on interdependence and mutual respect (Pestoff, Osborne, & Brandsen, 2006; Boyle & Harris, 2009). Co-creation fosters a partnership in which, ideally, all the involved actors have influence over decisions and solution designs.

The new partnership relations provide new possibilities for citizens and private stakeholders to hold public decision makers to account for their actions and inactions and forces the latter to become more responsive (Boyne & Walker, 2004). Indeed, co-creation brings forth a new kind of horizontal accountability in which the participating public and private actors become accountable to each other, creating a mutual responsiveness that curtails freewheeling and narrow-minded pursuit of personal interests. The design of public solutions through a collaborative process between public and private partners that holds participants accountable to each other for results and ensures a high degree of responsiveness will tend to make the solutions more legitimate. Here, it is not the actual content of the solutions, but the normative quality of the procedures through which they are designed that make people accept them as right and proper. To illustrate this point, Jetté & Vaillancourt (2011) show how social enterprises – through their closeness to communities, reciprocity with individuals, and emphasis on democratic participation – places them in a good position to foster dynamics and values that tend to be scarce in the public and private sectors. Thus, co-creation can also contribute to throughput legitimacy.

Bressers (2014) offers an illustrative example of how the hypothetical pathways interact to enhance the legitimacy of water management. The city of Rotterdam is not only threatened by flooding when the water level of the river Meuse runs too high or sea-water levels rise due to storm surges, but also by heavy cloud-burst rain that cannot be absorbed by the ill-equipped urban water management system. To deal with this problem, a dull public square surrounded by schools, businesses, and other buildings was transformed via a co-creation process in which city planners, architects, and about twenty-five local stakeholders were actively involved. The result was an innovative way of dealing with excessive amounts of rain water by temporarily storing the water in a redesigned square with greatly improved aesthetic and recreational qualities. While this innovative solution enjoyed wide support because it solved two problems with one stone, the legitimacy of the solution was also secured by the high-intensity involvement of citizens and private stakeholders and the high degree of fairness and adaptivity in the collaborative design process.

There are, of course, some dangers involved in the attempt to involve citizens and stakeholders in co-creation. Although civic engagement is often motivated by the need to enhance legitimacy and secure support for the implementation of new and bold solutions, there is a risk of tokenistic involvement of citizens and stakeholders that may backfire and create widespread dissatisfaction and conflict. Citizens may be invited to participate in the design of public solutions, but their input is overlooked and not taken seriously by professional planners who rely on their own ideas. Hence, co-creation is not really about improving services, spurring innovation, or building resilience but about looking good in the eyes of the public. As Cockburn (2007) maintains, an accommodating and pluralistic arena for co-creation must avoid patronizing or tokenistic participation. Bressers (2014) suggests that this can be accomplished by taking the demands and needs of citizens, rather than the supply of new public solutions, as the point of departure for co-creating innovative solutions.

The legitimacy effect of co-creation may also be reduced by the lack of transparency. Although the co-creation process may be transparent to those who are involved, it might not be clear to the wider public who is involved, how they worked together and why they reached a particular result. The lack of transparency may prevent the public from realizing that the solution was shaped by a broad range of public and private actors through a responsive and adaptive process that helped to ensure that the outcome reflects different needs and a variety of public values and concerns. It may even create the unsettling idea that important public decisions are taken behind closed doors in smoke-filled rooms by an unknown conspiracy of actors. The solution to this problem is openness and communication. Bressers (2014) insists that communication about collaborative innovation should begin at the point where ideas are first generated and should continue throughout the process to the execution phase.

6.5 An Integrated View of the Impact Pathways and the Core Challenges to Production of Co-created Outcomes

The previous sections have mapped the impact pathways that link co-creation to different public value outcomes. The discussion identified four major outcomes of co-creation: service improvement, public innovation, enhanced resilience, and legitimacy. We do not observe any strong trade-off between these four outcomes. To some extent, there is a choice between whether the aim of co-creation is merely to improve the quality of service systems, or whether it is to bring about more radical forms of innovation. However, both continuous improvement and innovation are oriented toward finding better strategies for meeting social needs and solving public problems. Although the enhancement of resilience can be an explicit goal of co-creation, in many cases it will be more of a by-product of co-created service improvement or public innovation. This means that even if a co-creation process fails to improve services or create innovative solutions, it might still build local capacities and enhance the resilience of communities. In this sense, the first three goals that we have discussed can be conceived as complementary rather than alternative co-creation outcomes. Finally, service improvement, public innovation, and resilience would all seem to contribute to raising the level of legitimacy, particularly output legitimacy. Resilience may also broaden the range of actors involved in public problem-solving and hence contribute to input legitimacy.

We also observe a pattern of relationships between the key mechanisms associated with the pathways we identified for each of the public value outcomes. First, we note that resource mobilization and capacity-building are common themes in many of the pathways, thus providing critical overarching concepts for understanding the work that co-creation does. Second, we observe that many of the mechanisms associated with the different pathways are really describing generativity, which was defined in Chapter 4 as governance processes that facilitate and enable the emergence of productive interaction among distributed actors. The different forms of generativity discussed in Chapter 4 reappear in the pathways described earlier. Trust building and participant well-being are examples of generative interaction. Procedures for risk management and mutual knowledge-sharing are examples of generative tools. The attempt to draw on user experience and discover the needs behind the wants are important generative processes. Finally, partnerships and attempts to institutionalize interaction are crucial aspects of generative institutions.

Our discussion of the challenges confronting co-creation discovers a number of common themes. One of the most important themes is the motivation of actors to participate. Absence of immediate gains, professional reluctance, and the shortage of time and energy to engage in demanding co-creation process are all likely to hinder effective co-creation. There may also be unfavorable starting conditions, such as deep-seated conflict or lack of participants in certain geographical areas. Co-creation processes may also lack adequate support from government, who may only see co-creation as a way of off-loading responsibilities on to citizens and stakeholders, or who may only be willing to engage in tokenistic co-creation. Finally, the co-creation process itself may create certain problems of accountability, transparency, or uncertain division of responsibilities. Although these limiting factors are all serious concerns, they can be addressed through a combination of leadership, institutional design, and attention to generative mechanisms.

7 | Co-creation as the Reinvention of Democracy

This chapter aims to flesh out the democratic implications of a strategic and systemic turn to co-creation in public governance. While there is an imminent danger that co-creation strengthens the influence of the resourceful and articulate middle-class at the expense of less advantaged groups, we contend that co-creation carries the potential for developing and revitalizing democracy in response to democratic challenges such as democratic disenchantment, anti-politics, ideological polarization, and counter-democracy.

Our claim is that co-creation can lead to a much-needed reinvention of democracy. Co-creation offers new ways of connecting public leaders with citizens who today seem less inclined to become members of political parties and vote for them in regular elections. Co-creation transforms the way an increasingly competent and assertive citizenry interacts with the state and provides opportunities for a more direct and fulfilling role in public governance that allows ordinary citizens to influence the conditions that determine their quality of life. Co-creation tends to enhance citizens' and private stakeholders' democratic ownership over public policy, deepen their understanding of why it is so hard to solve complex public problems, and enhance their appreciation of the efforts that public leaders put into the production of public value outcomes. Co-creation counters ideological purism by focusing on pragmatic problem-solving and experimentation based on dialogue, compromise formation, and creative processes of trial and error. Finally, yet critically, co-creation replaces the unsustainable "counter-democracy", which has developed over the last forty years in response to the call for more active and inclusive participation, with a new form of "interactive democracy" that involves citizens and relevant stakeholders in the constructive formulation and implementation of public solutions.

The turn toward co-creation in the public sector is primarily motivated by social and political concerns for improving public governance and producing specific public value outcomes. However, co-creation tends to expand and transform democracy as a side-product of its effort to improve the capacity for public problem-solving. It develops new forms of democracy that take us beyond the ballot box by insisting that democratic participation should not be reduced to voting every fourth year or so and by facilitating direct participation in ongoing deliberations about the nature of societal problems and challenges, their appropriate solutions, and how these solutions can then be implemented and adapted in ways that lead to fair, equitable, sustainable, and robust outcomes.

Co-creation also provides a method for involving a broad range of social and political actors in rethinking and redesigning democracy. As such, it offers a potent strategy for spurring democratic innovation in response to new and changing conditions of the twenty-first century. Currently, there are several accounts of the contemporary crisis of democracy (Reich, 2012; Levitsky & Ziblatt, 2018; Runciman, 2018) and the urgent need to develop a new set of democratic institutions that can reconnect the people and the political elites and break political deadlocks. Many of these accounts have surprisingly little to say about what new forms of democracy may look like and how they are brought about. A public governance perspective based on co-creation offers both a new democratic vision and a method for securing democratic renewal through joint discussion and experimentation.

Co-creation holds out a promise for democratic reinvention by introducing a new kind of interactive democracy whereby political solutions are not merely designed for and by the people but also *with* the people (Neblo, Esterling, & Lazer, 2018). However, at least two challenges remain in relation to co-creation and democracy.

First, it is difficult to ensure democratic accountability when shifting constellations of public and private actors participate in defining problems, designing solutions, and implementing them in practice. Who took which decisions and who is to blame when things go wrong? How do we sanction bad judgments, outright blunders, and serious neglect? The accountability problem needs to be solved, or at least put to rest, by finding suitable ways to think about how accountability can be ensured in relation to co-created outputs and outcomes.

Second, the new forms of participatory and deliberative democracy that are promoted by co-creation must somehow be combined with traditional forms of representative democracy. For many years, critics of liberal representative democracy praised the development of alternative forms of democracy based on direct participation and open-ended deliberation. However, recent reports on democratic backsliding in Western, Central, and Eastern Europe (Sedelmeier, 2014) and North and South America (Smith & Ziegler, 2008; Levitsky & Ziblatt, 2018) create growing concern about the fate of representative democracy in the Western world. As such, it is perhaps time to give up the idea that we should either preserve the traditional forms of representative democracy *or* develop new forms of participatory and deliberative democracy. Instead, we should think about how we can create a well-functioning hybrid democracy that combines representative democracy with participatory and deliberative forms of democracy in ways that bring out the merits of the two forms of democracy while suppressing, or compensating, for their disadvantages.

Our investigation of the democratic implications of co-creation proceeds in the following way. The first part of the chapter presents four widely debated challenges to the current forms of liberal democracy in order to envision how co-creation may provide an adequate response to underlying democratic problems and thus help to reinvigorate and expand democratic governance. The second part of the chapter revisits the accountability problem that arises in relation to public governance based on co-creation and reflects on how new forms of democracy advanced by co-creation practices can be integrated with representative democracy to form a new hybrid democracy. The final section discusses how co-creation can secure and perhaps even democratize the future development of democracy.

7.1 Democratic Disenchantment

Democracy is based on a norm of collective self-rule that holds that all citizens should have a free and equal right to influence decisions that affect them. The Democratic Revolution began some 250 years ago with the American and French revolutions, and it has been highly successful in dismantling *ancien regimes* based on despotic rule, problematizing pre-established hierarchies, and promoting democratic government based on civil rights, universal suffrage, regular elections, and political competition. However, the Democratic Revolution is still to be considered as a "work-in-progress" as economic inequalities continue to undermine the idea of free and equal political influence (Macpherson, 1978). Democratic rule has failed to penetrate important sectors such as private business and public bureaucracy, and the participatory ideal inherent to collective self-rule has been pushed to the margins of liberal democratic theory and is frequently reduced to the act of voting for competing parties and candidates on election day. (Warren, 2002)

The Democratic Revolution is one of the most potent political imaginaries in modern times (Laclau & Mouffe, 1985), and it has gradually transformed political rule and social life in all parts of the world. Yet, scholars have voiced increasing concern about the rising disenchantment with democracy in the most established western democracies and even in some of the new democracies (Munck, 1993; Cruz-Coke, 2001; Warren, 2002; Dalton, 2004; Flinders, 2012). According to Freedom House (2018), the paradox is that while more countries than ever have democratic political regimes based on elections with universal suffrage and party competition (Warren, 2002), the last decades have seen a growing dissatisfaction among citizens with democratic institutions and their political performance, not least in the most established democracies.

After a comprehensive empirical study of advanced industrial democracies, Dalton concluded that citizens "have grown distrustful of politicians, skeptical about democratic institutions, and disillusioned about how the democratic process functions" (Dalton, 2004: 1). Some of the indications of this kind of "democratic disenchantment" are the decline in voter turnout, party membership, and membership activity (Pharr, Putnam, & Dalton, 2000; Stoker, 2006a), and the fact that citizens are increasingly seeking to manage the complexities of politics without taking their cues from political parties (Dalton, 2007).

There is a clear downward trend in voter turnout in general elections at a global level, but the decline of voter turnout is strongest in the European countries where it has dipped 10 percentage points since 1980. In the post-communist countries in Europe, it has declined as much as 20 percentage points since the establishment of the new democracies after the fall of the Berlin Wall (IDEA, 2016). Voter turnout fluctuates between elections, but most European countries have set a new record of low voter turnout within the last three decades, indicating a massive withdrawal from conventional democratic practices (Mair, 2013). Both in Europe and the United States the decline in voter turnout is particularly strong among young people.

The fall in voter turnout is accompanied by a dramatic decline in party membership that means that we can no longer talk about mass political parties (Delwit, 2011). Party membership has dropped both relative to the electorate and in absolute terms. In most European countries, political parties have only retained about one-third of the members they had in the early 1960s. From 1980 to 2009 alone, the average loss of party members in the established European countries varied between 27 and 66 percent (Mair, 2013: 41). Recently, the exodus from the political parties has stopped, but the membership basis of political parties has also shrunk so much that "it is almost impossible to imagine further decline in absolute numbers without this signaling the wholesale collapse of the party organizations" (Mair, 2013, 40). In Europe as a whole, fewer than 4 percent of the citizens were party members in 2002.

Political parties have fewer members and the remaining party members are less active. As such, party activities have declined so that today only about a third of the party members are active while two-thirds report that they are not (Whitely, 2010). Among the nonparty members, voter identification with a particular political party is in decline (Dalton, 2002), and citizens increasingly tend to learn about political issues and form a political opinion about them without guidance from the political parties (Dalton, 2007). As such, political parties seem to be losing their grip on the formation of citizens' political views and ideas.

The standard explanation of democratic disenchantment points to a growing apathy among the citizens who no longer care about politics and society and sit passively at home on the couch binging on television shows from different streaming services. However, Warren (2002) warns us that it is more complicated than that. People have not necessarily become less interested in society and politics or less active, engaged, and willing to participate in social and political activities. There are deep concerns among people in most countries about big societal issues such as global warming, large streams of refugees, and the failure to provide the basic social and economic conditions for everyone to thrive as human beings. So, as opposed to being apathetic, people in the most established democracies may simply be disaffected from their political institutions, in the sense that they hold increasingly critical evaluations of government and democratic political institutions.

Citizens expect more from democracy than it often delivers. However, while this could signify that government is performing worse and is less democratic, there is growing evidence that it is expectations that are rising. After the educational and anti-authoritarian revolutions of the 1960s onward, and galvanized by new and often positive experiences with civic engagement in social movements and local forms of democracy, citizens have become more competent, critical, and assertive (Nye, 2008; Norris, 1999, 2011; Dalton & Wetzel, 2014). This development is well-captured by Bang & Sørensen's (1999) notion of "everyday makers" who are citizens deeply concerned about the everyday conditions that influence their quality-of-life and who seek to influence these conditions through active and direct participation in various ad hoc activities. The bottom line is that there is a more popular demand for active and direct participation than the standard procedures of liberal democracy tend to allow.

We believe that the credo of turning co-creation into a mode of governance provides a solution to rising democratic discontent as it aims to fulfill the new and changing expectations that citizens have for democratic participation. A public sector based on co-creation welcomes active and direct participation in service production, creative problem-solving, strategy development, and policy design. It constructs physical and digital platforms that support the formation and multiplication of arenas for collaborative governance where active, competent, and critical citizens and organized stakeholders can work together with public officials to address public problems and challenges. It provides opportunities for public and private actors to engage with crosscutting political problems and social issues that are not delimited to particular political institutions, sectors, jurisdictions, or territories and to participate in the initiation, formulation, and implementation of joint solutions that aim to improve the life quality of broad segments of the population, including those who are less assertive and less inclined to participate in the co-creation of public solutions. Instead of merely asking people to stick to traditional forms of participation to make themselves heard – like writing a letter to the editor or joining a political party – the co-creation perspective offers a new and different channel for democratic participation on the output side of the political system where services are delivered; problems are solved; and policies are formulated, implemented, and adjusted to the needs of society.

To illustrate the point, a young guy in Copenhagen regretted seeing how elderly people in the local care center could only walk to the corner and back with the aid of a walking frame. Limited mobility and access to outdoor life can seriously reduce their quality of life. Instead of writing to his favorite party or the city council, he went out to rent a rickshaw for the week, drove it down to the elderly care center, and asked one of the care workers whether she thought that one of the residents would care for a ride around town in the rickshaw. Gertrud, an elderly woman of 88 years, happily volunteered and together with the care worker, they rode around town visiting places Gertrud had not seen for a long time. It was a huge success and after having offered rides to several other residents, the elderly care center and rickshaw pilot contacted the municipality in order to get them to buy a rickshaw. After some negotiation, the municipality offered to buy two rickshaws for each elderly care center in the city if the pilot would organize a network of volunteers to drive them. The offer was accepted and that led to the formation of Cycling Without Age, which is now present in more than half of all the Danish municipalities and in 1,200 cities in 40 countries (https://cyclingwithoutage.org). The volunteer rickshaw pilots are trained by local captains and they work closely together with local elderly care centers to improve the quality of life of the elderly based on the slogan that "everybody has the right to wind in their hair." Citizens and care workers co-create welfare solutions together with the elderly who exchange their life stories in return for the volunteer pilots' pedaling power. The rickshaw pilots, the care workers, and the elderly all get to influence everyday public service production in new and meaningful ways and thus become active and engaged democratic citizens between the elections (Sørensen & Torfing, 2018).

7.2 Anti-politics

With the dramatic rise of populist governments in Europe and the United States, the research on democratic disenchantment has given way to new research on anti-politics (Stoker, 2006a, 2011, 2019; Fawcett et al., 2017; Clarke et al., 2018). Whereas the literature on democratic disenchantment focuses on citizens' disaffection with democratic political institutions, the new literature on anti-politics aims to explain the rise of populism with reference to the growing dissatisfaction with the way that formal politics is carried out by elected politicians. As such, anti-politics occurs when citizens turn strongly against the failure of established politicians to fulfill popular expectations and against the perception of politics as dominated by mudslinging, vote-catching stunts, and empty rhetoric (Stoker, 2006a).

The prevailing negative popular image of elected politicians is one of self-serving elites who launch personal and insulting attacks at each other on a daily basis, prioritize short-term political gains over long-term problem-solving, and seem willing to give up their political integrity and opportunistically adopt a new political standpoint if it helps them to get reelected. Politicians frequently do things that play into this negative popular image and increasingly cynical mass-media commentators are quick to point out the self-seeking behavior of elected officials. Moreover, the way that news stories are choreographed today actively contributes to the personification and dramatization of politics. As a result, our democratic leaders are portrayed as more concerned with point scoring and personal victories and defeats than with solving important policy problems and producing public value.

At a somewhat deeper level, anti-politics is a result of changing and unfulfilled expectations on the part of citizens. An ambitious quantitative and qualitative study of British citizens' changing expectations about elected politicians reveals that the popular image of the good politician has shifted considerably from the mid-twentieth century to the beginning of the twenty-first century (Clarke et al., 2018). Earlier, citizens expected politicians to be sincere, hardworking, strong, able, and moderate and thus to possess and display a noble and elevated set of political competences that separated them from the ordinary citizens. Today, citizens increasingly expect politicians to be all of the above while at the same time they expect them to be "normal" and "in touch" with reality and ordinary people. The latter expectation is new and makes it very difficult for the politicians to live up to citizens' expectations. To be simultaneously a strong and able politician *for* the people and a genuine and authentic politician *of* the people comes close to a performative contradiction.

To make things worse, two empirical trends make it increasingly difficult for politicians to appear as a "man or woman of the people" (Clarke et al., 2018). First, politics has become professionalized in the sense that politicians are recruited from a relatively homogenous class of well-educated people, seemingly detached from the rest of the population. Second, the mode of interaction between citizens and politicians is dominated by mass media and professionalized campaigning that make it difficult for politicians to perform their political virtues and for citizens to judge their behavior and feel the kind of intimacy, warmth, and authenticity that they expect from politicians. The result of the politicians' failure to fulfill the citizens' expectations is dwindling trust in elected government and, in some countries, a strong resentment against everything that has to do with politics and elected politicians.

The co-creation answer to anti-politics is to rebuild the connection between citizens and elected politicians, thus seeking to advance an interactive political leadership where politicians are developing much-needed policy solutions to pressing problems in and through sustained dialogue with citizens and stakeholders (Torfing & Ansell, 2017). A problem-focused interaction between politicians and citizens, either through online dialogue or in physical face-to-face meetings, will allow citizens to come closer to and "feel" the elected politicians. It will also allow them to see how committed many politicians are to solving societal problems and producing public value outcomes, while simultaneously revealing how difficult it is to solve complex problems that are often ridden by cognitive uncertainties and political goal conflicts. Citizens' participation in interactive arenas in which politicians co-create solutions based on input from and dialogue with citizens and other relevant actors will tend to create a greater proximity between citizens and politicians and contribute to changing the negative popular image of how politics is carried out.

Here some people will argue that inducing citizens to participate in interactive processes of co-created policy making would run counter to their instincts and preferences and just create more resentment. Such a skeptical argument is voiced by Hibbing and Theiss-Morse in their highly acclaimed book *Stealth Democracy* (2002) that claims that Americans dislike politics and prefer to leave public governance to authoritarian populists and technocrats. When citizens do reluctantly participate in politics, it is typically to defend public interests against corrupt politicians and not because they are genuinely interested in politics.

Neblo, Esterling, and Lazer (2018) take issue with this pessimistic account of the apparent nonparticipation of US citizens. As such, they claim that today's nonparticipation is rooted in disaffection with the available participatory options. Citizens are turned off by what they see as an unresponsive, distant, and corrupt system and bitterly partisan forms of politics, but that does not mean that they would lack motivation for participating in interactive political processes through which they get a chance to communicate directly with elected politicians and are invited to co-create joint solutions to common problems. In short, "it is frustration rather than apathy that alienates people from politics" (Neblo, Esterling, & Lazer, 2018: 55). A survey administered to a large representative sample of US citizens aimed to test the hypothetical willingness to participate in more interactive political arenas. People were asked about their willingness to participate in politics under different circumstances. The main findings are that: the willingness to participate in interactive "town-hall" meetings is much more widespread than expected; those people who are less likely to participate in traditional forms of politics are precisely those who are most interested in new forms of participation; and the people attracted to new and more interactive forms of participation tend to view these as a welcome alternative to "politics as usual" (Neblo, Esterling, & Lazer, 2018: 55).

Fortunately, new forms of participation in interactive political processes are already under way and are propagated by parliaments, public innovation agencies, private think tanks, and consultancy houses. The National Policy Consensus Center (NPCC) at Portland State University is a good example of how institutional support to interactive policy making can be provided by public actors. Each of the programs at NPCC promotes participation in collaborative policy making in some way. *Oregon Consensus* convenes key stakeholders at the behest of the governor and encourages them to come up with consensus decisions about contentious policy issues. *Oregon Solutions* brings community leaders and stakeholders together at the direction of the governor in order to implement public policies where there is no clear public leadership to steer the process, and *Oregon's Kitchen Table* is an online consultation with a broad cross-section of community members asked to weigh in on policy concepts. The National Policy Consensus Center is far from alone in supporting collaborative processes that bring politicians and citizens together in co-creation of public solutions. Policy innovation labs and collaborative policy platforms are mushrooming all over the world, thus making politics and political leadership more interactive (Sørensen, 2020).

7.3 Ideological Polarization

In recent years, national political discourse has come to be pervaded by strong ideological polarization that seems to suppress democratic participation and prevent democratic decision making based on a constructive management of differences and the formation of political compromise about long-term solutions. The rise of left- and right-wing populism has polarized the political parties. This is clearly visible in most European countries where the political rhetoric in party programs and election campaigns has sharpened and antagonistic clashes over value-laden questions such as immigration, abortion, discrimination, and regional autonomy have come to the fore. However, there is perhaps no country where ideological polarization is more evident than the United States (Iyengar, 2016). The difference between the Republican Party and the Democratic Party when measured on a left-right dimension is growing, and studies of political platforms, interest group ratings of legislators, and the sentiments of party activists confirm the picture of an intensified ideological polarization (Layman, 1999; Stonecash, Brewer, & Mariani; 2003; Layman, Carsey, & Horowitz, 2006).

In the postwar era, ideological polarization is a relatively new thing. Not long ago, political parties were accused of being too center seeking and having almost identical political views and opinions, making it hard for the voters to distinguish between them and to choose which one to vote for. Today, this picture has changed dramatically as the political parties are pulling apart and are busy grinding their ideological axes before clashing on the political battleground. Many countries have seen the rise of right-moving parties being matched by the rise of left-moving parties. The political clash between the Conservative leader Prime Minister Boris Johnson and the former leader of the Labour Party Jeremy Corbyn in the 2019 election in the United Kingdom is a case in point.

The first steps toward ideological polarization occurred in the 1980s when the rise of neoliberalism fostered a dogmatic turn to economic liberalism, elevating the market as the standard solution to all problems, praising economic inequality as a motivational driver of hard work, and recommending that the public sector be run like a private business. After the fall of the Berlin wall, and under the influence of expanding globalization, social-democratic parties in Europe came under the sway of the new neoliberal consensus. In an anti-ideological gesture, Tony Blair's labour government denied the relevance of both left- and right-wing ideology and insisted that there is no alternative to a politics based on market-conformity. The turn to neoliberal dogmatism, combined with fatal political decisions such as support for the second Gulf war in Iraq, gradually alienated the voters that had brought the social-democratic governments into power in Germany, Denmark, and the United Kingdom. In the United States, the personal popularity of President Bill Clinton could not prevent the Democrats from losing power to the Republicans who offered the real neoliberal deal.

The neoliberal consensus was gradually challenged by an anti-neoliberalist movement, most notably evidenced by the Occupy Wall Street initiative, environmentalists opposing neoliberal climate change deniers, and Bernie Sanders' bold advocacy for "Nordic socialism" as a possible political future for the United States. At the same time, a wave of political correctness hit center-left politics and imposed considerable limits on public expression by creating a purist gold standard – in terms of a completely anti-discriminatory, egalitarian, sustainable, and community-oriented living – against which all political solutions were found wanting. Both neoliberalism and the political correctness discourse of the center-left tend to make the totalizing demand for perfection a sworn enemy of the good.

More recently, ideological polarization has been fueled by the rise of left-wing and right-wing populism that combines populism with some version of anti-corporate "socialism" or anti-immigrant "nationalism," respectively (Mudde, 2006; Mudde & Kaltwasser, 2017). Working partly within the confines of democracy, the present forms of populism assume that democracy can lead to a better world if only the people are given the power and opportunity to take control of their lives (Canovan, 1999). As such, populist ideology is based on a politics of faith as it believes that the world can be a better place if people find a strong, dedicated, or charismatic leader who can work for them with passion and commitment (Stoker, 2019). The view is that corrupt and failing political elites and their corporate- or media-based allies must be driven out of government offices so that new authentic political leaders can "tell it as it is" and help the pure, homogenous, and sovereign people to prosper and blossom. As such, populism builds on a divisive "Us" versus "Them" antagonism that portrays the opposition as an "enemy" rather than a political "competitor" or "adversary" (for empirical evidence of the growing tendency of US. Congress members to portray oppositional parties as extreme, see Iyengar, Sood, & Lelkes, 2012).

Clear ideological dividing lines may help to stimulate passionate political debate, which is important in order to preserve a vibrant democracy (Mouffe, 2005). However, a strong and uncompromising ideological polarization may also constitute a political and democratic problem to the extent that it undermines democratic norms and procedures and erodes the common ground for political negotiation and compromise formation by dividing society into two antagonistic camps (Laclau, 2005). As such, routine legislative measures such as extending the debt ceiling or nominating cabinet members or judicial nominees tend to drag on and become political battlegrounds (Goldman, 2003). Laws are enacted only when the governing party or coalition imposes its will on the opposition, with the losing side then engaging in relentless delegitimization of the policies passed by the majority (Mann & Ornstein, 2016). With the lack of compromise and joint ownership, public policies lose their efficiency and robustness, as they become targets of ongoing political and legal battles. The overall effect of the continuous contestation of new legislation is that political leadership becomes dysfunctional (Iyengar, 2016).

Another democratic downside of ideological polarization is that it may suppress democratic participation. As such, Hayes, Scheufele, & Huge (2006) find that in a polarized ideological climate, some people may refrain from participating in publicly observable political activities that make them vulnerable to scrutiny and criticism by others who hold opinions that differ from their own. Analysis of a representative sample of US citizens shows that people who are likely to censor themselves in a polarized opinion climate are likely to participate less in public political activities compared to those less willing to censor their own opinions.

Co-creation may offer an antidote to this ideological polarization that risks generating a dialogue of the deaf where equally purist parties and voters fail to communicate and constructively manage their differences and insist on dividing the political space into "friends" and "enemies". A turn to co-creation in public governance will gradually change the public political culture, thus bringing it closer to a consensus democracy than to a majoritarian democracy (Lijphart, 1984). Co-creation calls for a pragmatist approach to democratic governance that aims to turn antagonist conflicts into a respectful agonistic clash between competing views, ideas, and solutions and that spurs problem-driven experiential learning, engaged democratic debate, and agreement based on compromise formation (see Ansell, 2011).

Co-creation focuses on problems and challenges that are shared by different groups of people across a wide political spectrum; it recognizes the potential contribution of manifold public and private actors and relies on their mutual feeling of dependency in order to foster collaboration; and it combines creative problem-solving based on mutual learning with social and political experimentation based on trial and error in order to develop robust and grounded solutions that solve the problems at hand. The pragmatist focus on public problem-solving, mutual dependency, and experiential learning implicit in co-creation will help to break down or put aside ideological concerns for upholding totalizing fantasies about the right, principled, and ideal solutions. Instead of pursuing principled perfection, co-creation looks for solutions that are good because they work well in the specific context, enjoy widespread support, and are flexible enough to be adapted to new and emerging trends and events.

A greater emphasis on co-creation in public governance does not aim to abolish public bureaucracy, but rather seeks to turn it into a builder of social and political communities engaged in creative problem-solving based on a constructive management of difference (Ansell, 2011). In an ideologically polarized environment, the expansion of platforms and arenas for co-creation of public solutions may appear as a tall order. In support for the feasibility of this endeavor, it should be noted that co-creation is an attractive strategy because it facilitates rather than suppresses political participation that will eventually enable people to improve their living conditions, and because in the long run it is reasonable to expect that people will prefer good, robust, and grounded solutions to pressing problems over adherence to ideological dogmas and purist ideas about perfection.

Co-creation recognizes that trust-based learning and pragmatic experimentation and problem-solving take place in a context of political conflicts and unequal power games. The kind of "pragmatist consensus democracy" that we envision does not rely on universal acceptance of the common good, but on political agreement between different actors with different interests, basic views, and opinions. The process of coming into agreement through sustained deliberation entails revision of standpoints, compromise formation through combination and integration of different positions and tacit dissent. As such, co-creation of joint solutions readily assumes the presence of conflict, but insists that conflicts are dynamic and can be solved, at least partly and provisionally, if the pressure and willingness to find a solution is big enough. Indeed, the presence of conflict is not only assumed, but welcomed since it forces the participants to reevaluate facts, arguments, and proposed solutions in search for precision, relevance, and impact.

7.4 Counter-Democracy

Co-creation carries the promise of producing a qualitative shift in citizen participation by replacing the present "counter-democracy" with a new form of "interactive democracy" (see Rosanvallon, 2008, 2011). What we shall here refer to as "counter-democracy" developed when, from the 1960s onward, the electoral channels of representative democracy were gradually supplemented by new alternative channels of citizen participation that enabled intensely affected citizens or organized interest groups to influence political decisions and public governance.

The new participatory channels were created in three successive waves. The first wave, from the 1930s onward, focused on the socioeconomic interests of citizens, and introduced a new system of corporatist representation that allowed organized stakeholders to pursue a particular set of interests via state-sponsored negotiations. The attempts to influence social and economic reforms through negotiation were sometimes backed by demonstrations, strikes, and other mass political manifestations. The second wave, from the 1960s onward, introduced the right for citizens affected by public planning decisions to be consulted in local hearings and town-hall meetings. The formal right to participate in consultative hearings was often supplemented by informal forms of participation through petitions, donations, happenings, occupations, sit-down strikes, and so on. The third wave, from the 1980s onward, has aimed to enhance the responsiveness of the public sector to citizens' needs and wants by introducing a combination of free service choice (exit) and participation in local user boards and user satisfaction surveys (voice).

All these new forms of citizen participation tend to place citizens in the role of critical veto actors that are mainly empowered to criticize, resist, oppose, or reject public solutions without necessarily taking any responsibility for providing an appropriate solution and making a collective impact. People can participate between regular elections by advancing and defending their different particularistic interests without weighing them up against competing ideas about the common interest and the public good. Hence, while these new forms of citizen participation have deepened democracy, they have created a "counter-democracy" in which citizens can resist or block public policy and governance leading to policy deadlocks and frustrated talk about the ungovernability of society.

Co-creation provides a possible way out of this impasse. The construction of platforms and arenas for co-creation of public value outcomes tends to turn the present "counter-democracy" into a new type of "interactive democracy" in which citizens and private stakeholders are not merely supposed to reject or endorse policy solutions devised and promoted by political and administrative leaders, but invited to collaborate with public actors in defining the problems and challenges at hand, designing new solutions, and implementing them in practice (Rosanvallon, 2011). Whereas protesting within the confines of a counter-democracy tends to be based on one-way communication, the endeavor to co-create joint solutions within an interactive democracy calls for two-way communication. Interactive democracy is both participatory and deliberative as it aims to stimulate active participation in dialogical processes that enable people to engage in mutual learning, joint decision making based on reasoned debate and shared efforts to implement new and bold solutions in practice and achieve the desired outcomes.

According to Rosanvallon (2011), citizens increasingly expect political leaders to listen and respond to their experiences, ideas, and demands and to justify their political decisions in the light of the input they receive. This situation calls for an enhanced proximity between citizens and political leaders. Proximity is not defined in spatial terms, but in terms of a mutual accessibility, openness, and receptiveness. For citizens, enhanced proximity means that they feel empowered to engage in and monitor public policy making, and for political leaders, it provides a valuable resource for governing society and the economy, especially if they can avoid being captured by strong advocacy groups when interacting with citizens and local communities. A key task for political leaders is, therefore, to build institutional arenas that facilitate the exchange of inputs from citizens and societal actors for political justification of the final policy decisions.

There are good reasons to expect that the construction of institutional arenas supporting the development of interactive democracy is far easier at the local level where the distance between citizens and elected politicians is relatively close than at the national or supranational level where the distance is greater. Nevertheless, the directly elected Members of the European Parliament (MEPs) have stepped up their efforts to interact with European populations in relation to EU policy making. The European Citizens' Consultation (ECC) in 2009 provides an ambitious and pioneering example of this trend.

The question posed to European populations at the initiation of the ECC was as follows: what can the European Union do to shape our social and economic future in a globalized world? The question was very broad and unfocused, but seems to have been well suited to stimulating broad-based participation and deliberation, which may inform and shape future policy agendas. As a part of the ECC, 1,635 randomly selected citizens from twenty-seven countries participated in national consultations that were prepared and supported by websites and online debate forums and concluded with a discussion between citizens and a panel of politicians consisting of national MEPs and candidates in the upcoming elections. Participation by the wider public was facilitated during the interim online phase that led up to the European Citizens' Summit, at which the 270 national recommendations were discussed and reduced to fifteen proposals that were further debated with political and administrative leaders from key EU institutions.

A research-based evaluation (Leyenaar & Niemöller, 2010) concluded that participation in the ECC was based on fair conditions and equal opportunities; that the participants had a solid information base and were well-qualified for participating in joint deliberations; that rules and procedures regarding participation and deliberation were openly communicated; and that the time, money, and energy invested in the participation were commensurate with the results. While media coverage of the process was disappointing, a large majority of the participating citizens claimed that they had learned a lot about the European Union and that their support for EU institutions had increased. However, they had rather low expectations about their chances of influencing policy making. The participating EU parliamentarians thought that the ECC provided a useful forum for interaction with citizens and helped to strengthen their role as political representatives. However, they thought that the advisory function of the ECC was limited, perhaps because the initial question was too broadly formulated, thus making it difficult for the MEPs to translate the final recommendations into new EU policies.

A recent experiment in the United States shows how democratic policy interaction can be carried out in a smaller and simpler way that is easy to reproduce elsewhere. In a pilot experiment, Neblo, Esterling, & Lazer (2018) recruited thirteen members of congress to participate in separate online town-hall meetings where they answered questions about contentious issues posed by a random sample of citizens from each of their local constituencies. Both the citizens and the congress members thought that the pilot was highly successful and helped to bring politicians and citizens closer. The participating citizens felt that they had been heard and respected by the politicians; and that, overall, they had received nuanced answers to their questions that they learned a lot from. The congressmen thought that the meetings provided a good opportunity for them to explain themselves and to get a better sense of what was important for the voters.

7.5 The Challenges of Democratic Accountability

While an increasing reliance on co-creation in public governance provides a timely response to important democratic challenges of our time, it also creates a fundamental democratic problem: it is not clear how platforms and arenas of co-creation are to be held democratically accountable for their processes, outputs, and outcomes. From the 1960s onward, there has been a growing demand for public accountability and this demand becomes even more acute when nonelected social, economic, and political actors take part in producing, or perhaps even destroying, public value.

Accountability is basically about "answerability towards others with a legitimate claim to demand an account" (Bovens, Goodin, & Schilleman, 2014). Public accountability implies the rendering of a transparent account for matters of public interest, or perhaps more precisely, matters pertaining to the exercise of public duties and responsibilities. In representative democracies "accountability usually means that voters know, or can make good inferences about, what parties have done in office and reward and punish them conditional on these actions" (Stokes, 2005: 316). This kind of democratic accountability whereby the voters in their capacity as political principals hold their elected political agents to account for their actions and inactions stems from the early days of "protective democracy" where the taxpaying citizens wanted to be able to monitor and control how elected officials spent tax revenues in order to prevent squander and abuse of power (Macpherson, 1978).

Since elected politicians in modern representative democracies tend to leave the responsibility for implementing political decisions with public bureaucracy, the democratic accountability of the politicians is supplemented by bureaucratic accountability whereby government holds civil servants to account for their effort to implement policies and deliver public services within the constraints of the budget and the legal framework. Hence, whenever a principal is delegating power and authority to an agent, the latter is called upon to account for how this delegated power is exercised (Warren, 2014). Although this framing of accountability in terms of principal–agent relations tends to oversimplify accountability relationships and to overemphasize the control and sanction aspect, it helps us to understand the importance of the access to information allowing proper scrutiny and to reflect on the costs of retrieving and assessing this information.

As a mechanism for ensuring control with delegated power, accountability has three basic components (Bovens, Goodin, & Schilleman, 2014: 9). First, there must be an account-giving based on the agent's obligation to inform a legitimate forum about his or her conduct. Second, there must be an opportunity for this forum to question the adequacy of the account and the legitimacy of the conduct. Third, the forum must be able to pass a judgment on the conduct of the agent. A negative judgment may lead to the imposition of sanctions, while a positive judgment may result in the agent receiving a reward. Hence, while accountability is essential to democracy, it places high demands on both principals and agents who must produce and scrutinize accounts and impose and accept different kinds of sanctions. In this sense, accountability can be said to come with costs that must be weighed against the harms that it addresses (Warren, 2014: 44).

In representative democracy, voting in competitive elections provides a low-cost accountability mechanism that enables citizens to acquire information about the conduct of elected politicians, to participate in scrutinizing public debates about the performance of both government and opposition and finally to pass a judgment by means of either reelecting or removing the political representatives. Although electoral participation is commonly assumed to provide little direct citizen control over government, it helps to align policies with the preferences of the median voter, at least over longer time periods (Przeworski, 2010).

In an interactive democracy based on active participation of public and private actors in co-creation of public value outcomes, accountability relationships become messy because there is no clearly identifiable "people" or "government" (Benz & Papadopoulos, 2006). A selective group of citizens, civil society organizations, and/or business firms may be involved in policy formulation, service delivery, or processes of creative problem-solving, in and through which they collaborate with elected politicians, public managers, and public employees. In such collaborative forms of networked governance there is no separation between the civic principals from the government agents. As co-creators of public solutions, citizens and organized stakeholders become co-responsible for the jointly created solutions and their societal impact (Damgaard & Lewis, 2014). The same blurring of roles occurs between the political principals and the administrative agents who may all participate in processes of collaborative problem-solving that cuts across levels, organizations, and sectors.

That accountability becomes muddied in processes of co-creation does not mean that there can be no accountability at all. Instead, it seems to take many different forms. First of all, in co-creation networks where there is no formal hierarchy between public and private actors and no formal obligation to produce accounts, the participants may still try to hold each other to account for their views and actions. Common concerns with ensuring that everybody contributes toward joint solutions and with maintaining good working relations with one another will tend to make network actors exchange and share knowledge about individual and joint actions and engage in joint discussions about how their different resources, competences, and energies have been and can be exploited to enhance outputs and outcomes. Such a discussion between different social and political actors standing on an equal footing has been referred to as horizontal accountability (Bovens, 2007a). Yet, as a method of ensuring accountability of co-creation processes, horizontal accountability is limited. While horizontal deliberations among a group of co-creators may enhance responsibility and improve future performance and results, these processes will still lack external accountability. Without an external accountability forum, it is difficult to see how horizontally related actors can pass binding judgments on one another, sanction bad decisions, and ultimately ensure control or prevent abuse.

The actors participating in co-creation networks may be held accountable by the organization or group that they claim to represent (Klijn & Koppenjan, 2014). Public managers are accountable to their superiors, which include both administrative and political leaders. This upward accountability is a straightforward bureaucratic accountability (though not necessarily simple to achieve). Public employees will also sometimes be held accountable to their professional organizations, their professional peers, and the norms and values shared by their profession. Private stakeholders are accountable to their organization or association, and citizens are accountable to the community, neighbourhood, or group they reside in or belong to. There is typically a principal–agent relationship inherent in these accountability relations. However, the problem is that top-down accountability holders have limited oversight, control, and influence due to the self-organizing character of co-creation arenas and to the fact that the participants in co-creation processes may not answer to the same accountability holder.

That leaves us with a dual accountability challenge: (1) the challenge of ensuring accountability between the co-creation network as a whole and the elected government or public authorities that may have played a role in initiating, mandating, and supporting the co-creation network; and (2) the challenge of ensuring accountability between the co-creation network as a whole and the citizens affected by the solutions produced by the network. Whether the accountability forum consists of elected politicians and government officials, or it consists of affected citizens, critical publics, and local media, there are several problems when it comes to holding the co-creation network as a whole to account for its actions and inactions.

The first problem is that networks are characterized by being relatively closed (Klijn & Koppenjan, 2014), with deliberations benefitting from seclusion (Torfing et al., 2012), and they often have no formal obligation to give accounts to anybody. In cases where account-giving is mandatory for a network, the account is often presented in a technical or specialized language that is difficult for outsiders to understand.

The second problem is that it is often difficult to establish who in a network of co-creating actors is responsible for what since there are often few formal decisions and the responsibility for the implementation of new and bold solutions is often shared with bureaucratic agencies. This problem is known as "the problem of many hands" (Bovens, 2007b). Decisions about what the problem is, how it is going to be solved, and how the solution is to be delivered pass through many hands and it is virtually impossible to pin down who has done what, how, when, and to what effect.

The third problem concerns the difficulties with sanctioning networks of co-creating actors that may have failed to act or have produced an inadequate or inappropriate solution. Since the actors participating in co-creation are often (self-) appointed rather than elected, they cannot be voted out of office; and since they often possess indispensable knowledge, resources, and authority for co-creating solutions to pressing problems, it is difficult to exclude actors that have proposed or supported failing solutions.

As a result of these three problems, metagoverning politicians trying to hold a whole co-creation network to account for its efforts to solve a complex problem or challenge are left with few options other than to politely ask the network to produce accessible narrative accounts of how they have perceived the problem, why they chose a particular solution, and how they assess its impact. Such a request is more likely to be met if there is a public network manager who answers to elected politicians. When it comes to ensuring the answerability of the network participants, there is no other way than to engage the "many hands" in a forward-looking dialogue about what can be done to improve the co-created solution in the light of new experiences and to eliminate negative externalities. Instances of direct incompetence, neglect, or abuse leading to bad outcomes may be sanctioned by withdrawal of public support. But if there is no public money involved in financing the co-created solution or in sponsoring the collaborative arena that produces this solution, the only way that the co-creation network can be penalized for making bad choices or creating negative externalities is through naming and shaming, which carries the risk of creating a hostile atmosphere that will prevent future attempts to mobilize relevant and affected actors in the co-creation of joint solutions.

One potentially fruitful accountability strategy for co-creation processes is to enable accountability forums composed of users, citizens, civil society organizations, and other stakeholders to request, scrutinize, and pass judgments on regular accounts from co-creation networks (Sørensen & Torfing, 2020) – a strategy sometimes referred to as "social accountability" (Bovens, 2007a; Fox 2015). Direct communication between co-creation arenas and relevant external forums of users, citizens, and civil society organizations can create a public space for nontechnical account-giving (Schillemans, Twist, & Vanhommerig, 2013). These forums can demand transparency and ensure access to data that can be used to further facilitate account-giving and that can in turn provide opportunities for critical debate among intensely affected users and citizens, relevant stakeholders, and interested publics. Well-functioning third-party accountability forums can enhance democratic control and prevent the abuse of power and public means, while simultaneously stimulating learning and promoting effective governance (Schillemans, Twist, & Vanhommerig, 2013).

A social accountability strategy carries its own challenges. An accountability forum composed of users, citizens, and critical publics may lack the authority and resources to compel high-quality account-giving and the sanctions that such forums can bring to bear may have limited effects. However, these forums can become more effective if their critical assessment is relayed to public authorities that are superior to the collaborative governance arena, thus triggering further scrutiny and corrective measures from above. In short, "relatively powerless forms of accountability can become influential because they operate 'in the shadow of hierarchy'" (Schillemans, 2008: 178). When combined, public authority and third-party social accountability may provide a mutually reinforcing mechanism, with each side compensating for the weakness of the other (Braithwaite, 2006). Negatively affected users, citizens, stakeholders, and publics may be keenly interested in voicing their discontent and holding the co-creation arenas to account, but they may lack formal, hierarchical authority, and means of sanctioning beyond public criticism. Conversely, metagoverning public authorities have formal power to back soft sanctions with harder ones, but they may lack access to adequate information about the co-created solutions and interest in the outcomes, or at least their finer details. In sum, the local communities and central authorities need each other, since, as Fox (2015: 357) puts it, "voice needs teeth to have bite - but teeth may not bite without voice".

Still, a third party accountability forum must have the necessary capacity to hold co-creation networks accountable and to raise the occasional fire alarm. Hence, a strategic approach to social accountability is important to help 'voice' and 'teeth' to become mutually empowering (Fox, 2015).

The conclusion from this attempt to solve the accountability problem is that accountability in relation to co-creation arenas is messy and complicated but not impossible since the right mixture of horizontal, bureaucratic, professional, and whole-network accountability may establish a sufficient level of democratic accountability. More rigorous attempts of governments to ensure accountability through formal contracting with networks of private firms and voluntary groups (see Goldsmith & Eggers, 2004) may raise the level of accountability but may also increase transaction costs and may not be entirely meaningful since such attempts seek to subject informal processes of creative problem-solving to formal guidelines and checklists that presuppose a linear governance strategy (Bovens & Schilleman, 2014).

7.6 Towards a Hybrid Democracy

Co-creation aims to involve active and engaged citizens in deliberative processes of creative problem-solving in order to enhance the production of public value outcomes and thus tends to push democracy in the direction of a more participatory and deliberative model. The new interactive forms of democracy, which are advanced by co-creation, build on active and direct participation in deliberative processes. In democratic societies, however, the expansion of these forms of interactive democracy takes place within the overarching frame of representative democracy. Therefore, the big challenge is to combine the preexisting model of representative democracy with a new interactive model of democracy based on participation in deliberative processes. Both models of democracy have merits and the development of a hybrid democracy may help to harness their respective merits and thus create important democratic synergies.

Although there have always been small pockets of participatory and deliberative democracy – for example, in self-governing work places, educational institutions, and cooperative housing associations and as a part of recent experiments with participatory budgeting (Pateman, 1970, 2012; Mansbridge, 1983) – there are surprisingly few attempts to integrate participatory and deliberative democracy with representative democracy. Parliamentary assemblies, and especially their permanent political committees, provide considerable room for deliberation (Bächtiger, 2014), but citizens are seldom a part of these deliberations (but see Hendriks, 2016). Hence, there is no popular mass participation in parliamentary deliberations. Representative democracy is sometimes combined with direct democracy based on mass participation, as exemplified by the frequent use of referendums in Switzerland (Trechsel & Kriesi, 1996) and California (Bowler & Glazer, 2008), but decision making in these referendums is based on majority rule rather than deliberation. In sum, while representative democracy is frequently combined with elements of *either* deliberation or direct participation, it is rarely combined with *both* of these elements at the same time in a form of hybrid democracy.

Before demonstrating and exemplifying what a hybrid democracy may look like, we shall first explain how participatory and deliberative democracy is connected and then compare the merits and weaknesses of representative democracy with the merits and weaknesses of participatory and deliberative democracy.

A core argument of the original advocates of participatory democracy such as Rousseau and Cole is that direct participation educates people and empowers them to influence the political decisions that affect their lives (Warren, 1996; Fung & Wright, 2003). In the 1960s and 1970s, theories of direct participatory democracy resurfaced (Pateman, 1970; Macpherson, 1977). Liberal democracy was criticized for giving people far too little influence over their lives (Pateman, 1970) and for its inability to combat the growing inequalities in capitalist societies that threatened to undermine the sovereignty of the people (Macpherson, 1978). In this situation, participatory democracy was seen as a way of strengthening popular control through the expansion of the capacity for self-determination. However, in most cases the goal of the participatory democrats was neither to overturn nor reform the institutions of representative democracy, but rather to supplement these with participatory forms of democracy in relatively confined spaces where direct participation would enable people to influence their own living and working conditions.

In recent years, researchers have emphasized that the kind of direct and active participation favored by participatory democrats is about participating in deliberative processes through which public decisions are reached through a joint exploration of problems and solutions that allows the participants to revise their opinions and come to agreement about what to do (Roberts, 2004; Floridia, 2017). Hence, despite the fact that 'participation' and 'deliberation' build on different normative assumptions – that is, the idea that power should be equally shared (participation) and the idea that identifying the common good requires reasoned debate (deliberation) that goes beyond mere aggregation of private interests – they are frequently linked in both theory and practice.

A theoretical linkage between participation and deliberation is found in Manin's notion of inclusive deliberation (Manin, 1987). Manin claims that the source of legitimacy in political decision making is not found in the predetermined will of individuals. People seldom have an already formed will, and the source of political legitimacy thus lies in the very process of will formation, that is, in deliberation itself. As Manin goes on to argue:

An individual's liberty consists first of all in being able to arrive at a decision by a process of research and comparison among various solutions. As political decisions are characteristically imposed on all, it seems reasonable to seek, as an essential condition for legitimacy, the deliberation of all or, more precisely, the right of all to participate in deliberation. (Manin,1987: 352)

As such, political legitimacy is predicated on an inclusive deliberation through which individuals form their political will and make joint political decisions based on their different wills.

A practical linkage between participation and deliberation emerges as a part of Nabatchi and Leighninger's typology of empirical forms of participation that distinguishes 'conventional participation' in public meetings and hearings and 'thin participation' in crowdsourcing and crowdfunding activities from 'thick participation' involving group-based interaction that enables people to learn, decide, and act together (Nabatchi & Leighninger, 2015: 14–22). Thick participation is deliberative. As such, participation is defined as 'the activities by which people's concerns, interests and values are incorporated in decisions and actions on public matters and issues' (2015: 14). While the participatory democrats paid little attention to how different concerns, interests, and values are integrated, deliberative democrats believed that their incorporation in public decisions was a result of deliberation, defined as 'a thoughtful, open, and accessible discussion about information, views, experiences, and ideas during which people seek to make a decision or judgment based on facts, data, values, emotions and other less technical considerations' (2015: 14).

We agree with Dryzek (2000) that democratic deliberation should facilitate discursive contestation and with Warren (2009) that deliberation is pervaded by power strategies that are implicit in the attempt to persuade other participants through a combination of logos, pathos, and ethos. The attempt to make room for power and contestation in the conceptualization of deliberation facilitates its combination with broad-based participation that may bring together a diverse set of actors with diverging views, different resources, and varying forms of expression (for further discussion of the combination of deliberation and participation see Della Porta, 2013).

The participatory and deliberative model of democratic governance not only provides an alternative to representative democracy but also criticizes its negative implications. Notwithstanding, the literature on participatory and deliberative democracy also recognizes the merits of representative democracy and the potential problems of its own preferred alternative (Hirst, 2000; Fung, 2009). Table 7.1 provides an overview of the merits and problems of the two models of democracy based on key contributions to the literature on participatory and deliberative democracy (Pateman, 1970; MacPherson, 1977; Barber, 1984; Young, 2000; Cohen, 2007; Gutmann and Thompson, 2009).

As indicated by Table 7.1, the two models of democracy complement and support each other. The problems of representative democracy are countered by the merits of participatory and deliberative democracy and vice versa. This discovery, however, begs the question of whether the two models could be integrated in order to achieve their combined merits while offsetting their respective problems.

One way to integrate the two models takes its inspiration from strategic planning. According to the strategic planning model (Bryson, 2011), public leaders – whether elected or appointed – must first identify problems, create a vision for the future, and define overall objectives. They may then use more or less formal mandates to instruct

Table 7.1 *Merits and problems of the two models of democracy*

	Representative democracy	Participatory and deliberative democracy
Merits	• Ensures formal participatory equality based on the 'one man one vote' maxim • Comprises a widely accepted procedure for conflict resolution (majority voting) • Produces relatively clear and determinate outcomes of the decision-making process • Contains an efficient mechanism for holding decision makers to account for their doings (regular elections)	• Helps to construct a 'we' and thus to counteract individualistic atomization and group-based fragmentation • Enables policy makers to elicit relevant information, experiences, and ideas through inclusion of relevant and affected actors in joint deliberation • Spurs the production of innovative solutions by stimulating processes of mutual and transformative learning • Builds joint ownership over new and bold solutions that helps to ensure their implementation
Problems	• By taking existing or minimally corrected preferences as given, it risks reinforcing existing distributions of power • By excluding large segments of the population from the actual decision-making process, it turns citizens into passive spectators • Lacks an efficient mechanism for transmitting relevant information, views, and ideas to the actual decision makers and for mobilizing resources in the implementation phase • Fails to produce broad ownership over new solutions and thus hampers implementation	• Fosters biased and unjust outcomes if participation is low and selective and power asymmetries among the participants are large • Leads to paralysis if destructive conflicts persist in the face of attempts to overcome or mediate conflicts • Results in nonimplementable outcomes when deliberation results in unclear and muddy compromises • Has no clear method for holding decision makers accountable for their decisions and their impact

and empower actors in participatory and deliberative arenas to reflect on the formulation of problems and objectives, develop creative strategies through processes of co-creation, and turn these strategies into concrete plans that will eventually achieve the desired strategic objectives. Finally, they may use their own organization and the assistance they can get from the participating actors to implement the new plans.

This is more or less the method applied in the process of issue-specific policy development in the Municipality of Gentofte in Denmark and the Municipality of Svelvik in Norway where the City Council mandates a number of so-called Task Committees to solve pressing societal problems. The Task Committees typically comprise ten citizens and five elected councilors who work closely together over three to six months to find innovative, yet feasible, policy solutions and to reflect on their implementation. The policy recommendations are submitted to the City Council that discusses, amends, and formally endorses the recommendations before they are passed on to the administration to implement, often with the involvement of relevant stakeholders (Sørensen & Torfing, 2019).

Another way to integrate representative democracy with participatory and deliberative democracy is more bottom-up and begins with a diverse group of private actors coming together to solve a common problem through deliberation and mutual learning. Sometimes they will manage to co-create a solution by themselves, but often they will need some kind of political support in order to finance their solution, receive administrative support, get the necessary permissions, or gain legitimacy. Direct contact to elected politicians and/or their administrative aides may help bottom-up co-creation initiatives to succeed in their mission.

To illustrate, a group of young radical environmentalists in Copenhagen were increasingly frustrated that they could not do anything about the environmental threats to the planet such as climate change, a thinning ozone layer, pesticide pollution in drinking water, and so on (Sørensen & Torfing, 2018). One of them saw an official poster saying that local citizens could get administrative help from a local Agenda 21 agency if they wanted to launch a local environmental initiative. The public consultants at Agenda 21 helped them to get the necessary permissions and some funding from local politicians so that they could build a green urban garden on top of an old concrete bunker from the Second World War. A network of young environmentalists, local citizens, public employees, and private gardening firms was formed and co-created a green and lush garden with flowers, vegetables, and green grass in the middle of Copenhagen.

Hybrid models of democracy may help alleviate the fundamental conflict in liberal democracy between the equal right to influence political decisions and the need for political leadership. This inherent tension between the egalitarian ethos of democracy and the exercise of political leadership is at the root of persistent legitimacy problems (Kane & Patapan, 2012). Whereas representative democracy has been preoccupied with ensuring democratic political leadership through electoral procedures, participatory and deliberative democracy has been preoccupied with fostering democratic interaction among citizens and lay-actors. The development of a hybrid model of democracy may simultaneously strengthen democratic political leadership and foster a more egalitarian and less elitist participation in public policy making by creating an ongoing interaction between the people and their elected representatives.

Nevertheless, hybrid democracy is bound to be riven by internal contradictions. Whereas participatory and deliberative democracy is premised on the willingness of the participants to revise their views and opinions in the face of persuasive arguments, representative democracy is premised on the ability to settle disputes through majority voting (Öberg, 2016). However, it is perfectly possible to combine deliberation and voting, if the latter provides the final confirmation of an agreement reached through well-informed discussions based on open exploration of problems and solutions.

Another contradiction is between the relatively equal access to voting in representative democracy and the risk of selective participation bias in participatory and deliberative democracy. Here, we should remember that participation in democratic elections is far from equal since citizens with low education and income are overrepresented in the group of nonvoters (Blais, 2007). Moreover, seen from a democratic viewpoint, selective involvement of relevant and affected actors as opposed to universal participation is perfectly legitimate. The definition of the relevant demos varies from case to case and inclusion may be determined by the degree of interestedness (Dahl, 1989). Finally, there are many ways of minimizing selective participation biases when it comes to involving relevant and affected actors. Instead of issuing an open call that is only heeded by the 'usual suspects,' such as the group of white middle-class seniors with plenty of time and resources and those with extremist viewpoints, elected politicians may recruit a broad range of interested actors with different voices simply by tapping them on the shoulder and inviting them personally.

Finally, representative democracy may tolerate more power inequalities than participatory and deliberative democracy. In representative democracy, an asymmetric distribution of power resources among the participants is counteracted by the fact that each vote counts just as much as any other vote. By contrast, in participatory and deliberative democracy, the weaker actors may be discouraged from participating in deliberative processes if they fear that the stronger actors have the power to ignore, dismiss, or patronize them, thus rendering them powerless. However, arguably, the participatory and deliberative model of democracy is more compatible with power asymmetries than we might expect. First, power differentials may spur deliberation because it is more rewarding to deliberate with and try to influence powerful actors. Second, if the stronger actors recognize their dependency on input and support from weaker actors, they might constrain their own display of power in order to keep the weaker actors onboard (Torfing, 2016).

7.7 Co-creating the Future Development of Democracy

For centuries, the development and deepening of democracy through democratic reforms has been spearheaded by social movements and political leaders. More recently, however, public administrators have aimed to solve complex problems by involving citizens and relevant stakeholders in collaborative governance and this deviation from the standard procedures of bureaucratic governance has indirectly contributed to expanding democratic participation and making democracy more interactive (Warren, 2009). Although collaborative interaction between public and private actors contributes to enhancing input and output legitimacy, the administrative recasting of democracy carries the danger that democracy is developed merely out of instrumental concerns for efficient problem-solving in a complex and fragmented society. Ideally, democratic reform should be a result of joint deliberation among politicians, administrators, citizens, and organized stakeholders. The future development of democracy is too important to be left to even the most well-intentioned administrators. Democratic reforms, whether intended or unintended, must enjoy broad-based political support in order for the result of the reforms to be accepted as a fair, meaningful, and legitimate framework for democratic participation, decision making and accountability.

As argued earlier, the recent participatory and deliberative expansion of democracy that has emerged as a by-product of the new and emerging forms of collaborative governance must be thoroughly linked to the traditional forms of representative democracy through the development of a hybrid democracy. However, there are no clear and uniform ideas about the form and functioning of hybrid democracy. Iterative rounds of discussion, experimentation, and evaluation involving a broad selection of social and political actors are important in order to build a shared ownership for new democratic procedures, arenas and processes. Co-creation provides a tool for securing such an ownership.

The attempt to co-create democratic innovation will constitute a kind of democratic metagovernance as it will construct the overall institutional framework for co-creation processes aiming to solve societal problems and respond to serious challenges. The British Columbia Citizens' Assembly (BCCA), which consisted of 160 randomly selected citizens and convened for eleven months in 2004, provides an interesting example of citizen involvement in the metagovernance of democratic innovation (Warren & Pearse, 2008). Not only did the Assembly demonstrate the reflexive capacity of democracy to reform itself in response to democratic deficits, but it is also the first example in history where ordinary citizens have been empowered to develop and present proposals for redesign of democratic institutions to their fellow citizens. The example has been followed in other countries such as Australia and the Netherlands, and it sets a new standard in terms of opening democratic reform processes up for ordinary citizens and facilitating public dialogue about how to reform democracy in the twenty-first century. From a co-creation perspective, the limitation of the Assembly is not only that it just focused on reform of the electoral system, but also that it did not create a constructive dialogue between the citizens and the elected politicians that could produce joint ownership over the final recommendation. As a result, the democratic reform proposal failed to reach the supermajority threshold of 60 percent of the overall vote in the 2005 referendum. Subsequent efforts to co-create democratic futures could heed this example by widening the democratic reform agenda and deepening deliberation in order to secure broad-based ownership over the reform.

8 | Mainstreaming and Scaling Co-creation

Chapter 3 demonstrated that "co-creation is everywhere" in the sense that we can find examples of co-creation across a wide variety of countries, levels, and policy fields. However, the chapter also argued that "co-creation is nowhere" in the sense that co-creation has not yet developed into a comprehensive strategy for improving service production, solving complex public problems, and developing innovative policy solutions. The two previous chapters have revealed the great potential for co-creation to enhance the production of public value outcomes and reinvent democracy. These findings prompt us to ponder how it is possible to mainstream co-creation so that it becomes a key part of the modus operandi of public organizations and how it can be scaled so that co-creation of service delivery, problem-solving, and policy making becomes a core rather a peripheral phenomenon. To answer these pertinent questions, this chapter aims to assess the conditions for expanding the scope, depth, and impact of co-creation and for gradually turning it into a core principle of public governance, thus adding flesh and blood to what is increasingly referred to as New Public Governance (Osborne, 2006, 2010).

Transforming the way that public governance is produced and delivered is tough given the combination of bureaucratic politics (Peters, 2002) and institutional path-dependence (Pierson, 2000). To imagine whether it is still possible, we will look at how public leaders can transform public institutions through intentional reform and what kind of change they must bring about in order to advance and support co-creation. First, we discuss how different forms of strategic management can help to spur the transition to co-creation. We then present four crucial conditions for enabling the future expansion of co-creation into a predominant mode of governance. As such, we argue that a public sector based on co-creation requires: 1) the creation of new institutional designs; 2) the cultivation of new forms of leadership and management; 3) the transformation of the role perceptions of key social and political actors; and 4) the development of new ways of measuring effects. The conclusion critically examines competing scenarios for the development of co-creation into a mode of governance and presents a five-step model for the transition to co-creation.

8.1 Strategic Management of the Transition to Co-creation

Reaping the fruits of co-creation requires that the public sector recasts itself from primarily being a legal authority or an efficient service provider to being a sponsor, champion, and facilitator of collaborative innovation, whether initiated by public leaders, managers, or societal actors. Bringing about such a transformation is a formidable task that requires the exercise of strategic management, defined as the attempt of institutionally situated actors to transform the modus operandi of their organization by formulating and implementing major goals, strategies, and plans based on analysis of internal and external environments (Nag, Hambrick, & Chen, 2007).

Despite the resilience and normative virtues of public bureaucracy (Du Gay, 2000; Meier & Hill, 2005), it tends to pay scant attention to the need for strategic reflection and development. Top-level managers are supposed to follow the political cues provided by their democratically elected principals while hierarchical control puts severe limitations on the operational autonomy and strategic renewal promoted at the lower levels of public bureaucracy. Finally, a low tolerance for uncertainty and risk tends to crowd out entrepreneurial behavior (Ferlie & Ongaro, 2015: 4). These inherent constraints of bureaucratic governance explain why the introduction of strategic management in the public sector, which was triggered by New Public Management reforms, took inspiration from the private sector where strategic management has had considerable impact (Pettigrew et al., 2006; Mintzberg et al., 2009).

A large number of theoretical schools of thought on strategic management have been developed (for a succinct and helpful overview, see Ferlie & Ongaro, 2015). A few of these schools of thought are particularly helpful for envisioning the process, content, and dynamics of a strategic transition to co-creation.

The first school of thought is known as the *strategic planning school*. It builds on the earlier design school that aimed to achieve a strategic fit between organizations and their internal and external environments

(Ansoff, 1965; Andrews, 1971). The design school is criticized for its binary split between the executive formulation of an organizational strategy and its subsequent implementation by the rank and file. This bifurcation tends to give rise to "paper plans" with no bearing on reality and limited effects due to the lack of ownership over the plan beyond the executive leadership group (Mintzberg, 1994). In an attempt to deal with this problem, Bryson (1988, 2018) developed a strategic planning model with several stages that are part of a "change cycle." First, a strategic planning group must foster agreement on the strategic planning process, identify organizational mandates, and clarify mission and values. It must then carefully assess the internal and external environment using stakeholder analysis as a key tool. This analysis leads to the identification of strategic issues that must be dealt with through the formulation of a planning strategy that must be technically feasible and politically acceptable. Effective implementation of the plan must be ensured through dialogue and collaboration with internal and external stakeholders and guided by an organizational vision of future success.

Building on these ideas, public organizations seeking to expand the use of co-creation as a governance tool might use the change cycle to develop and implement plans that detail what co-creation entails, why they should spur it, how it could be pursued, and finally where, when, and with whom they should co-create future governance solutions. The success of this approach will depend on the strategic planning group's ability to create a meaningful and implementable plan based on broad organizational ownership.

The *emergent strategy school* focuses less on the ability of top-level strategic managers to develop a well-aligned strategy and to secure support for its implementation. This school is critical of the ability of executive leaders to propel and control strategic planning processes from the top downwards and aims to involve a broader range of actors at lower levels of the organization and to stimulate their capacity for organizational learning (Mintzberg et al., 2009). The emergent strategy school tends to view strategy as a pattern in a stream of decisions at all levels of the organization. Strategy emerges as a result of processes of organizational learning in which the distinction between formulation and implementation is blurred. In these processes, the role of leadership is to manage strategic learning in order to allow new strategies to emerge and flourish (Ferlie & Ongaro, 2015: 32). Strategic managers become midwives helping organizational actors at all levels to reflect on their experiences and act strategically on what they learn from these reflections.

From this perspective, a strategic embrace of co-creation would emerge incrementally from the recognition of the failure of bureaucratic and market-led governance strategies to mobilize resources in the face of growing expectations for public performance and to produce the kind of innovative solutions needed to tackle more or less wicked problems (Head & Alford, 2015). The role of strategic managers in this context is to spur reflection on current practice, to encourage experimentation, and to enable and sponsor co-creation processes.

The *entrepreneurial school* moves further away from top-down management initiative by highlighting the proactive role of middle managers, such as school headmasters, police lieutenants, or social welfare managers, in creating enduring and alternative practices in local settings that are later imitated by other institutions in the same field (Sarason, 1974; Pettigrew, 1979). According to Mintzberg (1973), strategy making in entrepreneurial organizations is characterized by: (1) the predominance of the local leader who becomes the founder of new ways of doing things; (2) the search for exciting new possibilities rather than dealing with existing organizational problems; (3) change that takes the form of "bold strokes" with the possibility of high payoff rather than incremental adjustment of the existing strategy; and (4) strategic change driven by individual leaders' experience, intuition, and personal ambition to enhance growth and excellence in conditions marked by a high level of uncertainty and risk.

The entrepreneurial school would perceive the transition to co-creation as resulting from the visionary action of local entrepreneurs who disrupt their organizations in order to mobilize the collaborative advantage implicit in co-creation (Huxham & Vangen, 2013). While this kind of entrepreneurial leadership may inspire others to follow suit and spark large scale organizational change, the danger is that these new governance practices depend on the founder who is almost irreplaceable and often unwilling to delegate responsibilities, thus leading to overload and bottlenecks at the top (Ferlie & Ongaro, 2015: 37).

The *strategy as practice school* further decenters strategic management. According to Johnson, Melin, and Whittington, this approach to strategic management emphasizes "the detailed processes and practices which constitute the day to day activities of organizational life and which relate to strategic outcomes" (2003: 6). The focus is on micro-activities that are often invisible to traditional strategic management research but still may have important consequences for organizations and their modus operandi. The strategy as practice perspective is concerned with the "doing of strategy" by a broad range of people in and around public organizations, including middle managers, employees, and consultancy firms. This allows us to observe the strategic mutation at the local level that results from interactions between managers, employees, and external consultants who are hired to help solve organizational problems or to reorganize urban-planning processes or service production.

Today, a large number of esteemed consultancy houses perceive co-creation as an important governance tool and thus may inject local practices with ideas and discourses that support a transition to co-creation. It goes without saying that micro-level practices need to be understood in a wider context and that change agents are not acting in isolation from social and organizational logics. However, the recognition of how formal strategic planning at the macro-level conditions and influences micro-level practices does not make the strategy as practice school give up its pluralist everyday view on how situated actors are "doing strategy." Rather, it discounts the idea of a directive power center that controls the strategic renewal of the organization.

The final strategic management school to consider is the *public value management school* that we touched upon in Chapters 1 and 2. In its original formulation by Moore (1995), the public value management school criticizes New Public Management for failing to capture the uniqueness of the public sector, which consists in the tax-financed production of public value for society at large rather than private value validated by private consumers and appropriated as profits by private shareholders. Strategic management in the public sector aims to maximize public value production and this endeavor rests on the alignment of three fundamental tenets that Moore referred to as the strategic triangle: (1) public managers must clarify and specify the strategic goals of their organization by developing public value propositions that delineate the social purposes that the public sector should pursue and spend its public revenues on; (2) public managers must then go to their authorizing environment that consists of elected politicians and relevant public, private, and third sector stakeholders in order to get support for their public value propositions and the strategic actions necessary to realize these propositions; and (3) public managers must finally build the organizational capacity to maximize public value production by means of harnessing and mobilizing operational resources from inside and outside the organization.

Moore (1995, 2000) does recognize the role that private actors play in authorizing public value propositions and co-producing services, and Bennington and Moore (2011) also talk about the emergence of a "new pattern of co-creation" (2011: 15). However, on closer inspection, this perspective reduces the "co-creation" of public value outcomes to the "co-production" of predetermined public services. This reduction is particularly clear when we are told that "clients play a crucial role in co-production" and that the success of government agencies depends on "millions of individuals accepting the obligation and doing their duty" (Benington & Moore, 2011: 269). However, other researchers (Stoker, 2006b; Crosby, 't Hart & Torfing, 2017) have extended the public value perspective by criticizing the implicit managerialism of Moore (1995) and arguing that public value outcomes are not only endorsed by but also co-created by a broad range of public and private actors.

By extension, the argument is that a strategic focus on public value outcomes may help to mobilize and align relevant and affected actors from state, market, and civil society. This argument connects public value management with governance network theory by emphasizing the resource interdependency between public and private actors engaged in the formulation and realization of joint solutions that have public value and are valued by the public.

There is a striking complementarity between the five strategic management schools in the sense that they tend to focus on strategic work undertaken by different groups of actors operating at different levels both inside and outside the public sector. Top-level managers, middle managers, entrepreneurs, public employees, and cross-boundary networks that include elected politicians, stakeholder organizations, and user groups may all play a role in the strategic reorientation of public organizations. These different schools help us to understand how all these different actors may drive change, alone or together. Indeed, most of the above-mentioned strategic management schools also apply to third sector organizations that can engage different actors in order to secure a transition to co-creation. The dissemination and circulation of a new governance discourse may inspire both public and private nonprofit organizations to coevolve, thus creating interorganizational synergies.

In a public sector pervaded by conflicts and power struggles between bureaucratic actors and strong path-dependencies that make it costly to pursue a new path despite its long-term efficiency, intentional reform is difficult unless there is a strong coalition of actors that both recognize the problems of the existing path and believe there is something to gain from trying something new (Considine, 2013). Hence, strategic management requires the construction of broad alliances between leading politicians, top-level managers, entrepreneurial leaders of particular institutions, different professional groups, consultancy firms, external stakeholders, lead users, and so on. Such alliances may be kept together by resource interdependencies, story lines that motivate and give direction to the strategic work of the different actors, shared values and a common vocabulary that facilitate cross-boundary communication, strategic plans that set goals and provide tools for achieving them, reports about quick wins, and joint access to common resources and forms of knowledge. This change-coalition perspective cuts across the different strategic management schools and attempts to bring together actors that may play different roles in the transition to co-creation.

Sabatier and Weible (2007) tend to see dominant coalitions of like-minded actors that are working to solve particular problems as defenders of the status quo. Other theories argue that coalitions of interdependent actors have a capacity for bringing forth hidden alternatives or creating new ones, promoting such alternatives so that they are shared between different systems, and securing a form of political authorization that can resist the pitfalls of partisan alternation (Considine, 2013). It is these qualities of change coalitions that enable them to confront legacy effects and transform public organizations.

The limitation of the strategic management perspective is that it provides a generic view on how to change public organizations rather than a plan for bringing about a specific transformation. As such, it helps us to understand strategy as process and practice, but it does not say anything about the content of the strategic management of the transition to co-creation. The next four sections add flesh and blood to the strategic management perspective by pinpointing four crucial stepping stones on the road to co-creation.

8.2 Institutional Design

There are several reasons why the expansion of co-creation requires institutional design. First, networks of relevant and affected actors engaged in productive interaction and public problem-solving do not arise spontaneously when needed, but must be supported by institutional designs that help to reduce the transaction costs of networking and counteract collective action problems. Second, public bureaucracy's administrative silos, long chains of command and institutional insulation do not provide a suitable framework for co-creation, which needs to be enabled through the construction of spaces for cross-boundary collaboration between distributed actors from different organizations and sectors. Third, social and cultural diversity, interest conflicts and power asymmetries may prevent sustained interaction between interdependent actors, and this necessitates the development of institutional designs that attract relevant and affected actors, facilitate collaborative interaction, and spur mutual learning. Finally, realizing the democratic potential of co-creation while ensuring democratic accountability and anchorage may depend on the choice of institutional designs that secure broad-based participation, allow the tracking and evaluation of results and outcomes, and ensure close interaction with representative democracy.

Alexander defines institutional design as "the devising and realization of rules, procedures, and organizational structures that will enable and constrain behavior and action so as to accord with held values, achieve desired objectives, or execute given tasks" (2005: 213). This definition encompasses the accounts of institutional design held by different strands of the new institutionalism.

While the new institutionalism has been primarily interested in how institutions condition social and political action (Peters, 2019), it has also had a keen interest in how institutional design can shape outcomes. Rational choice institutionalism (Kliemt, 1990; Goodin, 1995) strongly believes that iterative rounds of institutional design can ensure desirable outcomes of rational action by individual actors. The conscious design of rules, formal contracts, and strategic games played by rational actors is supposed to generate socially desirable results of social and political action (Moe, 1984; Banks and Weingast, 1992; Scharpf, 1994; Steunenberg, 2000; Hertting, 2007).

Historical institutionalism has little to say about institutional design of spaces for distributed action as it claims that institutional rules, norms, and procedures are results of struggles and compromises between the participating actors and the gradual codification of reproduced actions. Although this view leaves limited space for deliberative design of institutions (Alexander, 2005), it is asserted that institutions are formed around a few formative ideas supported by a few rules and norms that will determine the subsequent development of the institution (Steinmo, Thelen, & Longstrech, 1992; Peters, 2019). Hence, at particular formative moments deliberative design may help shape future governance.

Given its focus on the normative integration of the actors (March & Olsen, 1995) and the search for legitimacy rather than efficiency (Powell & DiMaggio, 1983), sociological institutionalism focuses more attention on institutional design than historical institutionalism. By contrast to rational choice institutionalism, however, institutional design is depicted as a result of ongoing dialogue rather than a constitutive choice and motivated by the wish to create a normative fit between social and political actors and the institutional framework guiding their interaction and between the norms of the institution and those valued by the external environment (Alexander, 2005). We largely concur with this understanding of institutional design because the focus on internal and external legitimacy established through the use of "goodness of fit" evaluations helps us to understand the institutional design of spaces for co-creation that attract relevant and affected actors, support their interaction, and lead to outcomes compatible with the social and political environment.

A "goodness of fit" evaluation is an assessment of whether an institutional design is appropriate for the processes it is designed to support. We add the observation that institutional designs based on "goodness of fit" evaluations can arise from either dialogue between the actors involved in co-creation, reflections by a group of appointed leaders representing different groups and organizations, or the initiative of an external third party facilitator who gets the ball rolling and acts as a mediator (Provan & Kenis, 2008). Furthermore, there might be a difference between the institutional design of platforms and arenas. Institutional design of arenas tends to be negotiated among the participants themselves, whereas the design of platforms tends to be determined by external actors aiming to facilitate the emergence of arenas of co-creation. Platforms may provide standardized organizational templates that are easy to use in the initiation of co-creation, but these templates may be subsequently adapted based on "goodness of fit" evaluations (Ansell, Sørensen, & Torfing, 2020).

Institutional design for co-creation is a form of metagovernance (Torfing, et al., 2012). Hence, the creation of platforms and arenas is a way of governing emergent and tendentially self-governing co-creation processes without determining their form, content, and results by means of hierarchical command and control. In Chapter 4, we argued that platforms and arenas are critical structural and institutional supports for co-creation, and now we want to reflect on how choices about the design of platforms and arenas may affect processes and outcomes.

There are some hard choices when designing platforms and arenas for co-creation. As such, we are faced with a number of design dilemmas that call for context-sensitive reflections that may lead to an accommodating, yet uneasy, compromise between extremes.

The first design choice concerns the degree of inclusiveness. Co-creation processes can be designed to be inclusive in order to mobilize ideas and resources and gain democratic legitimacy, but more exclusive processes may sometimes help to secure alignment of the participants and facilitate intensive, high-quality interaction. A compromise between these extremes might combine a more exclusive group of core actors engaged in frequent interactions and decision-making processes with a wider and more inclusive group of participants who engage less frequently and typically in deliberation rather than decision making.

The second choice revolves around the relative degree of openness and closure. When a group of relevant and affected actors engaged in co-creation is formed, it can be difficult to open up for newcomers who might rock the boat and force the group to spend precious time and energy on realignment. On the other hand, newcomers may offer new forms of resources and expertise and prevent the network of co-creators from developing tunnel vision. As such, openness is sometimes difficult and costly, but may help to spur innovation. A compromise may be to create a procedure for an open search for participants that subsequently leads to the formation of a relatively more closed group that establishes its own rules about when to open up for newcomers.

The third choice concerns the relative degree of insulation from mainstream activities. Co-creation processes that are institutionally sheltered and operate on the margin of established organizations or existing activities (skunk works) may sometimes produce more innovative solutions because they are not bound by conventions and habits. On the other hand, making co-creation processes integral to the mainstream activities of existing activity fields will tend to enhance the visibility, take up, and the impact of co-created solutions, but this integration may also discourage the development of more disruptive innovation. The compromise here could be to begin by designing relatively insulated co-creation processes at the margins of existing structures and activities to maximize their innovativeness, and then upscale and mainstream these co-creation processes when they have found a suitable form and greater uptake and impact is called for.

The fourth design choice is whether to design purpose-built platforms and arenas that focus on solving a particular task or problem or whether to construct multi-purpose platforms that enable the formation of arenas that can deal with different sets of goals and tasks. Specialized purpose-built platforms and arenas might have a very strong profile that helps to attract and motivate actors by constructing a sense of urgency and articulating some attainable goals. By contrast, multi-purpose platforms and arenas with an open-ended agenda may be attractive for a wider range of actors seeking an opportunity to co-initiate processes of joint problem-solving around problems that have not yet entered the public agenda. A compromise might involve a modularization of platforms and arenas so that they provide a core module with a general usage and a plethora of additional modules that can be activated if the agenda moves in a specific direction.

The fifth design choice concerns the degree of formality through the use of explicit, authoritatively defined and publicly sanctioned rules, norms, and procedures. Formal platforms and arenas may enhance democratic legitimacy and ensure accountability, but might scare away citizens, civil society organizations, and private firms that fear being coopted and exploited by the public authorities. Informality may be preferred by nonpublic actors who will feel more at ease in an informal setting that is easier for them to control than a formal setting. However, informal networks of co-creating actors will be less visible and have problems recruiting the right actors and avoiding suspicion that they are engaging in clandestine and self-serving activities.

A compromise may be that formal platforms support co-creating networks that have a formal status but give room for informal interaction at the margins.

A sixth and final design choice concerns the question of accountability and ranges between transparency and seclusion. Some institutional designs will seek to enhance transparency in order to hold the network of co-creating actors to account for their actions and inactions. However, some studies show that seclusion may stimulate deliberation and compromise formulation as the participants do not have to lose face in public when granting concessions and revising their positions (Naurin, 2007). The compromise is to allow a certain degree of seclusion in the process of deliberation, while still requiring that co-creating networks produce accessible ex post accounts of their reflections over problems and solutions.

This short account of the dilemmas implicit to design choices demonstrates that the institutional design of spaces for co-creation of public value outcomes is a complicated balancing act and will tend to be based on trial and error and a lot of back and forth movement. It not so much a question of making the right design choice, but more a question of being prepared to adjust the balance between extremes in response to shifting conditions and contexts.

Advancing institutional design thinking is necessary in order to enhance public governance based on co-creation, but the barriers to hands-off metagovernance based on design thinking are considerable. First of all, we cannot assume that the different private actors are skilled in second-order governance reflections about how to design the arenas for co-creation of specific outputs and outcomes and third-order reflections about how to structure platforms enabling the formation, adaptation, and multiplication of arenas for co-creation. Private sector consultants and professional staffers in NGOs will soon learn the drill, but it takes a lot of experience to become skillful designers of spaces for co-creation. Second, while the ultimate responsibility for institutional design lies with the public actors sponsoring or participating in co-creation processes, there are some clear obstacles as public actors are socialized to think that they should be in charge of governing society and the economy and must single-handedly solve pressing problems and challenges by drawing on their own skills and resources and without involvement of external actors. This bureaucratic preference for unilateral action makes it hard for public actors to think in terms of institutional design for co-created problem-solving. Hence, significant cultural change is needed to convince public administrators that institutional design thinking will allow them to simultaneously enhance input and output legitimacy while mobilizing resources so as to ease dire budget constraints (Janssen & Estevez, 2013).

8.3 Leadership and Management of Co-creation Processes

Although we should be careful not to consider leadership as the universal solution to all public-sector problems, the cultivation of new forms of political and administrative leadership and management is decisive for the attempt to initiate, support, and reap the fruits of co-creation. The design of platforms and arenas creates an institutional framework that facilitates and channels action and prompts collaborative interaction, but the successful expansion of collaborative learning, innovation, and governance processes requires the exercise of hands-on metagovernance based on leadership that takes a diverse group of actors forward – toward new and better solutions and management – that ensures that actions are coordinated and things are getting done according to jointly developed plans.

Indeed, leadership and management of emergent forms of co-creation taking place in highly distributed contexts characterized by a low degree of institutionalization is even more important than in highly centralized and institutionalized settings where everyone is clear about their role and task, and there is a clear command structure. In co-creation, actors come together because they want to deal with a specific problem or challenge and perhaps have a vague idea of the public value outcomes that they can co-produce. From that point onward, the process takes the form of an open, perilous, and contingent journey into relatively unknown territory, and leaders and managers play a crucial role in keeping the actors on board, the process on track, and the goal in sight.

Co-creation requires political endorsement and financial and institutional support from high-level decision makers in order to secure a "license to innovate" and to engage a broad set of actors in developing new and perhaps disruptive solutions. It involves mobilization of the knowledge, resources, and energies of relevant and affected actors and thus requires recruitment and motivation of the right group of actors that together possess the skills and resources needed to solve the problem or challenge at hand. Next, getting actors with different agendas, interests, and values to collaborate requires development of arenas and common vocabularies, brokerage, conflict mediation, and creation of a joint purpose and direction. Finally, to avoid collaborative processes ending up as mere talking shops and, conversely, to stimulate the development and implementation of innovative solutions, leaders and managers must have a constant focus on the production of short- and long-term outputs as well as on tracking and evaluating processes and outcomes. In short, leaders and managers have a huge and complicated task, as they must simultaneously act as sponsors of co-creation, conveners of relevant and affected actors, facilitators of constructive interaction, mediators of conflicts, catalysts of disruptive thinking and innovative solutions, and implementors aiming to secure the production of public value outcomes. Table 8.1 briefly explains the leadership roles that may support co-creation.

Table 8.1 *Leadership roles necessary to support co-creation of public value*

Sponsors	Secure political, financial, and institutional support to the network of co-creating actors and promote its solutions and results (Bryson and Crosby, 2005)
Conveners	Bring together relevant and affected actors and protect the integrity of the process (Page, 2010)
Facilitators	Facilitate collaboration by building trust relationships, developing a common vocabulary and frame of understanding, and removing obstacles to collaboration (Weber, 2009)
Mediators	Enable co-creation by resolving, mitigating, or managing conflict, and arbitrating exchange between public and private stakeholders (Crosby & Bryson, 2010; Ansell & Gash, 2012)
Catalysts	Create an appropriate disturbance in order to spur disruptive thinking and the development of innovative solutions (Luke, 1997; Morse, 2010)
Implementors	Coordinate the action of many hands in order to create tangible results and track outcomes in order to improve performance (Crosby & Bryson, 2010)

Developing, refining, and exercising these crucial leadership roles requires a shift in the mindset of public leaders and managers. For decades, we have told public leaders to focus on effectively transforming their organizational inputs, including budget frames, infrastructures, and employees, into organizational outputs that can help to achieve a specific set of political objectives frequently defined in terms of key performance indicators. If public leaders are to support and encourage co-creation, this traditional conception of public leadership must change. The traditional leadership approach must give way to a new and more interactive leadership approach that supports co-creation of public value outcomes (Sørensen, 2020). Let's see what this shift entails.

The traditional leadership approach is *hierarchical* and constructs relations of superiority and subordination. At the apex of the public sector, we find political leadership that involves goal setting, budget allocations, and crafting legislation that ranges from detailed regulatory laws to broad framework laws. Political leadership focuses on leading parties, members of the government and voters. While interest organizations may try to influence political decisions, there is generally limited interaction between elected politicians and their constituency. Instead political leaders rely on executive administrators, policy experts, and personal advisors when defining problems, developing solutions, and mustering support for their realization (Svara, 2001; Mouritzen & Svara, 2002). These political leaders instruct public administrators to implement legislation, but delegate responsibility for the choice of administrative tools, budget control, and discretionary decisions about regulation and service provision to the administration.

Traditional forms of public leadership and management are *inward-looking*. Administrative leaders focus on the policy programs that their institution or organization are responsible for implementing and they scrutinize the means that they have at their disposal in order to fulfill predetermined policy goals. Hence, they look at their organization, budget, and employees in order to find efficient and effective ways of putting them to work that will lead to enhanced performance vis-à-vis the key performance indicators that measure the outputs of their organization. Administrative leaders use a mixture of transactional and transformational leadership to motivate employees and prevent opportunistic behavior. Conditional rewards and punishments aim to ensure that employees deliver what they are supposed to deliver by speaking to their self-interest, while the formulation and communication of organizational goals and values aims to build collective commitment and loyalty that go beyond individual utility maximization (Jensen et al., 2019).

The overall purpose of the traditional leadership approach is to *secure compliance with predetermined goals* and to make sure that administrative performance targets are reached within given resource constraints. The emphasis is on a linear transformation of inputs into outputs, often without much attention to processes or outcomes. Successful implementation of political goals requires clearly formulated goals, communication of a comprehensive plan for policy implementation, regular performance measurement, and the use of a broad range of positive and negative sanctions (Barber, 2008).

Administrative leaders must be agile and are expected to adjust administrative plans and procedures to new developments, but their task is to implement a given policy program, not to involve relevant and affected actors in the development of new and better solutions.

Finally, the power of public leaders to formulate and implement political decisions through intraorganizational resource mobilization and transformation of inputs into outputs rests on *formal authority*. Leaders higher up in the bureaucratic hierarchy can impose their will upon agencies and actors at lower levels. It is their formal position in the hierarchical command structure that authorizes leaders to lead subordinated actors.

Table 8.2 compares the traditional public leadership approach with a new co-creation leadership approach. Whereas the traditional leadership approach is based on hierarchy and creates a certain distance between leaders and followers, the co-creation leadership approach requires political and administrative leaders to *engage constructively* with those they are leading in order to define problems, set goals, design solutions, and coordinate their implementation. Leaders aim to reduce the distance between themselves and their followers and to exploit the proximity to engage in a constructive dialogue with the network of actors that they are leading and to which they perhaps belong. The interaction between leaders and followers is not primarily motivated by democratic egalitarian concerns but rather by the need of the leaders to learn from their active, competent, and critical followers while building joint ownership over goals and values. In the world of co-creation, leaders are not facing a group of subordinate

Table 8.2 *Traditional leadership approach and co-creation leadership approach*

Leadership dimensions	Traditional leadership approach	Co-creation leadership approach
Relation between leaders and followers	*Hierarchical relation* between leaders and followers based on distance	*Constructive dialogue* between leaders and followers based on proximity
Main focus of leaders	*Inward-looking focus* on reaching goals by using organizational resources such as budget, infrastructure, and employees	*Outward-looking focus* on solving problems by means of cross-boundary mobilization and exchange of resources
Main goal of leadership	Ensure *compliance* with predetermined goals and performance indicators	Facilitate *creative problem-solving* and the emergence of new and unexplored goals and solutions
Authority	*Formal hierarchical authority* based on position in command structure	*Informal horizontal authority* based on relational attributes and leadership capacity

actors, but a group of critical, competent, and resourceful allies that they must befriend and learn from in order to do a good job taking the co-creation process forward to secure the production of public value outcomes.

Whereas traditional leadership is inward-looking, the new co-creation leadership approach is *outward-looking*. It aims to transcend the boundaries of the institution or organization by mobilizing and orchestrating distributed action across administrative silos and across the public–private divide. Leaders of co-creation must lead emergent processes of cross-boundary collaboration by means of strategic inter-mediation that aims to empower and selectively activate the partici-pants, facilitate a constructive management of internal differences, mediate conflicts and disputes, encourage out-of-the-box thinking, enhance coordination and so on. When attempting to foster cross-boundary networks of co-creating actors, leaders will find themselves in a situation where they must lead external actors over whom they have limited or no formal authority.

Whereas the traditional leadership approach tends to focus on compliance with predetermined goals and seeks to motivate subordinate actors to deliver what they are supposed to deliver, the new co-creation leadership approach focuses on *creative problem-solving and innovation*. It aims to encourage the participants in co-creation arenas to further explore the problem or challenge at hand and to collaborate in bringing their different skills, competences, and ideas into designing, prototyping, and testing new innovative solutions. In this process, it is dangerous to focus too much on inputs and outputs. Each of the participating organizations have their own resources and goals and too much attention to these may generate collective action problems as the actors may start to wonder whether the other actors are chipping in and whether their own goals are achieved in and through the collective endeavor.

To address these challenges, leaders of co-creation processes should aim to put more emphasis on processes and outcomes. How can the network of co-creating actors together create processes that facilitate productive exchange of ideas? How can the network produce outcomes that have public value and solve the problems and challenges that the actors set out to tackle? Co-creation leadership requires a shift in mindset from a linear top-down model to a nonlinear model that focuses on processes of mutual learning and joint action and appreciates that solutions will be emergent and iterative. Goals and solutions are transformed as a part of the process and that means that the traditional idea of compliance no longer makes sense, although the leaders must ensure that the co-created outcomes are not violating existing laws and regulations.

Finally, whereas the traditional leadership approach tends to base the exercise of leadership on the leaders' formal hierarchical authority, the co-creative leadership approach argues that leadership depends on an informal horizontal authority. Leaders of co-creation might not even be formally appointed as leaders. They may simply be one of the actors in the co-creating network that undertakes a number of important leadership tasks. The authority of such a horizontal leadership builds on the co-creating actors' ongoing recognition of the knowledge, skills, and relational competences of the leader(s) and the actual display of leadership capacity through the orchestration of processes and the production of tangible outcomes. Leaders of co-creation may, to some extent, rely on their charisma and rhetorical skills to enable them to unify a diverse group of actors, but ultimately it is the results that count for the participants' acceptance of their leadership work.

The co-creation leadership approach summarized in Table 8.2 does not constitute an original approach to public leadership. Rather, it brings the previously described leadership roles (see Table 8.1) into view and highlights central insights from theories of distributed leadership, voluntary leadership, integrative leadership, and innovation management. Let's briefly consider some of these insights in order to gauge the dilemmas inherent to the co-creation leadership approach.

Distributed leadership (Gronn, 2002; Pearce & Conger, 2003; Spillane & Diamond, 2007; Bolden, 2011) aims to mobilize public and private actors as an active force in solving joint problems by means of distributing leadership responsibility to a broad range of local managers, public employees, voluntary organizations, private firms, citizens, and so on. As such, distributed leadership creates a shared or collective leadership that emerges through the interaction of multiple actors performing different leadership tasks (Uhl-Bien, 2006). However, distributed leadership is not merely the sum of the leadership work of many individual actors. It is "a group activity that works through and within relationships, rather than individual action" (Bennett et al. 2003: 3). Thus, distributed leadership offers a systemic perspective on leadership as a result of interaction between a broad set of actors that aim to achieve a particular set of objectives in and through their relation to others.

For public leaders, the distribution of leadership responsibilities and the acceptance of shared leadership means that they reflect on with whom they can share different leadership responsibilities. They must also find ways of communicating the emergent understanding of the mission and vision to distributed actors contributing to the shared or collective leadership. Coordination of leadership tasks is also important in order to avoid duplication or gaps. Finally, public leaders must sometimes coach the actors who are taking responsibility for particular leadership tasks without being formally appointed as leaders or having received any formal leadership training.

The dilemma confronting public leaders in a distributed leadership context is that they are expected to take full responsibility for the entire decision-making process and its different outputs and outcomes, but they must do so without undermining the distributed leadership actions of the public and private actors that assume responsibility for particular leadership tasks in relation to specific activities. Distributed leadership is a "post-heroic leadership" (Badaracco, 2001) that decenters and distributes leadership, but executive leaders, auditors, and mass media still want to place the responsibility for policy and innovation failures with a single administrative leader who is to be sacrificed if and when things go badly.

Voluntary leadership excised by public leaders aims to create a fruitful interaction between public agencies and employees and the many organized or unorganized volunteers that are engaged in co-production of services and co-creation of public service systems and societal solutions (Brudney & England, 1983; Bovaird, 2007; Needham, 2008; Brandsen, Steen, & Verschuere, 2018). There is a stubborn myth that volunteers engaged in co-production and co-creation will not and cannot be led since they are as free as the birds, come and go as they please, and just want to mind their own business while doing their altruistic deed (Huxham & Vangen, 1996a, 1996b; Brudney, 1999). However, while volunteers may have a strong preference for self-government, we must not forget that voluntary organizations are based on fairly classical forms of leadership. Moreover, when volunteers collaborate with public actors in order to co-create public value outcomes, they are subjected to public leadership of a more or less distributed character. The big challenge for voluntary leaders in the public sector is that volunteer leadership can neither rely on giving orders, since that may make volunteers leave the collaboration, nor on pecuniary incentives, since volunteer labor is defined as a self-chosen and unpaid activity (Brudney, 1999).

Public leadership of volunteers who are co-creating solutions with public actors is important because the co-creation process will have to respect political priorities and administrative rules and regulations. Moreover, the collaboration between public actors and volunteers will only lead to better results and solutions if there is a clear exercise of strategic leadership and an appropriate institutional design (Fischer & Cole, 1993). There are generic aspects of leadership such as facilitation of interaction and focus of goal attainment that will affect all the actors engaged in co-creation. Nevertheless, the literature on voluntarism tends to emphasize a special need for recruiting, motivating, coaching, coordinating, recognizing, and protecting volunteers engaged in co-production and co-creation (Sørensen & Torfing, 2012). These leadership tasks are often delegated to front-line personnel that have little experience and no formal training in volunteer leadership (Brudney, 1990a, 1990b). The special attention to volunteer leadership also has a strategic dimension as collaboration with volunteers requires political commitment on the part of elected politicians, dedicated administrative resources and an accepted strategic framework. Clear goals, intensive communication, and regular evaluation are also important dimensions of volunteer leadership (Huxham & Vangen, 1996a, 1996b). An important lesson from volunteer leadership is that it is often the worthy cause that attracts volunteers, but the social network and bonds that they develop that make them stay on and contribute to public value production.

The basic dilemma that public leaders are facing when trying to lead volunteers engaged in co-production and co-creation is they must lead the volunteers by orchestrating and giving direction to their contribution to public value production while at the same time recognizing and supporting their demand for self-organization. Distributed leadership may help public leaders to lead in a manner that both frames and directs the collaborative process and involves volunteers in the exercise of leadership.

Integrative leadership aims to bring diverse groups and organizations together in semi-permanent ways, and typically across sector boundaries, in order to solve complex problems by developing new solutions that aim to achieve the common good (Crosby & Bryson, 2005, 2010; Morse, 2010; Silvia & McGuire, 2010). Integrative leaders are likely to have the most success in bringing together public and private actors in cross-boundary collaboration when the environment is turbulent, when separate efforts to tackle the problems have failed, and when other problem-solving mechanisms such as hierarchical steering or market competition have been tried but have not worked.

The research on integrative leadership indicates that successful integrative leaders work to form an initial agreement about the problem to be solved and the nature and character of the collaborative process, including its mandate, participants, intensity, and duration. They draw on the different competences of the collaborators, are responsive to points raised by key stakeholders and avoid imposed solutions that prevent an open-ended search for joint solutions. Integrative leaders ensure that trust-building activities are continuous throughout the collaborative process and they make sure that the collaboration is flexible and open to new actors. They commit their time and energy to mitigate power imbalances, deal with emerging obstacles and external shocks, and reframe conflicts in ways that have appeal across sectors. Finally, they develop systems and methods for utilizing data in processes of creative problem-solving and keep track of inputs, outputs, and outcomes to ensure accountability (Crosby & Bryson, 2010).

Integrative leadership aims to create and sustain networks and partnerships and thus has many affinities with network management (Kickert, Klijn, & Koppenjan, 1997; Sørensen & Torfing, 2009, 2017). A crucial point shared by the literature on integrative leadership and network management is the effort of leaders and managers to build and sustain collaborative relations through different kinds of boundary spanning. According to Morse (2010), boundary organizations often provide the structural context for the creation of networks and partnerships that integrate actors across jurisdictions, levels, and sectors. Boundary experiences and boundary objects serve to bridge differences between the actors and create a common purpose. Finally, yet importantly, "boundary spanners exhibit entrepreneurial qualities and leverage relationship capital in order to facilitate integration" (Morse, 2010: 231). Boundary spanners are people-oriented rather than task-oriented as they focus their attention on trust-building in order to facilitate exchange and pooling of knowledge and resources between interdependent actors (Silvia & McGuire, 2010).

Leaders from boundary organizations that have network facilitation as a core task will be like fish in the water, but leaders of public organizations acting as integrative leaders in collaborative settings face a huge dilemma. They must lead their own organization with a clear focus on budget control, personnel management, and goal attainment while simultaneously leading complex collaborative processes that tend to dissolve the boundary between their organization and its environment. To cope with this dilemma, public leaders must be skilled in situational leadership, pay attention to the context in which they are leading, and be able to constantly switch to the appropriate leadership perspective. They must not only take care of their own organization and pursue and attain its goals but also have a keen eye for how their organization can support and benefit from co-creation of public solutions and be able to bracket the pursuit of organizational interests in favor of long-term collective gains.

Innovation management aims to spur collaborative innovation based on mutual learning, joint experiments, coordinated implementation, and ongoing adaptation (Windrum & Koch, 2008; Bason, 2010; Torfing, 2016). Public innovation managers are entrepreneurs driven by the desire to produce public value outcomes by changing the way that the public sector and society work (Windrum & Koch, 2008). They use their broad-ranging social networks and their wide access to broadcast new ideas and initiatives in order to convene public and private actors with the resources, ideas, and competences needed to develop and implement new and innovative solutions. They secure political and economic support for the search for innovative solutions, and they encourage interaction between a diverse set of actors, build relational trust, and facilitate collaboration by lowering transaction costs, creating a common purpose and mediating conflicts (Torfing, 2016). Innovation managers create open, inventive, and active search processes and use future workshops, brainstorming, scenario building, prototyping, and design experiments to stimulate divergent and convergent thinking and to make the future concrete (Bason, 2010). A core task for innovation managers is to build broad ownership for new and bold solutions, facilitate real-life testing, and coordinate their implementation while seeking to manage risks and secure a fair distribution of costs and benefits (Osborne & Brown, 2011). Finally, as true entrepreneurs, innovation managers have to keep up the collective spirit by maintaining the belief in the feasibility of innovative solutions in the face of severe setbacks and unforeseen events that threaten to prevent success (Windrum & Koch, 2008).

Public leaders aiming to manage collaborative innovation must deal with a tough dilemma: they must lead and manage in order to secure stable and efficient governance and service production while managing risk-prone innovation processes that threaten to result in failures and waste of time, energy, and resources. The co-creation of innovative solutions may, of course, help them to "do more for less" when new effective solutions are developed, implemented, and consolidated, but in the short run there is a danger that the stable operation of public organizations is jeopardized by their engagement in risky and disruptive co-creation processes. A possible coping strategy here is to create "skunk works" that aim to develop and test co-created innovations on a small scale at the margins of the organization, only scaling up the innovative solutions when they have demonstrated their worth.

Some scholars see the four forms of leadership discussed earlier as a part of a "post-transformative leadership" (Parry & Bryman, 2006) that aims to decenter leadership and provide a different leadership approach that offers middle and line managers a set of new tools for managing their relations to citizens, volunteers, and stakeholders in ways that add to the production of public value. The four leadership theories have much in common, especially when it comes to the importance of relational leadership work. However, they also complement each other in important ways by emphasizing: (1) the synergy emerging between many distributed leaders; (2) the special attention that must be paid to those actors who are participating on a voluntary basis; (3) the effort to bridge the differences between actors from different sectors; and (4) the importance of getting different actors to collaborate in order to develop and implement disruptive solutions. Public leaders may benefit from drawing on insights from the four different post-transformation leadership theories but, as noted earlier, they face a series of dilemmas that each call for different coping strategies.

8.4 Motivating Key Actors

The expansion of co-creation beyond the co-production of public services requires the elaboration of different motivational strategies. Co-creation takes place in collaborative spaces where the formal obligation to contribute actively toward joint solutions is weak and participation is voluntary and often driven by role perceptions and calculations of self-interest that work against involvement in what might turn out to be complex and demanding processes with uncertain outcomes. Nevertheless, the different arenas of co-creation must bring together a broad range of relevant and affected actors that together possess the skills, competences, and resources required to co-create innovative public solutions. The public and private actors brought up in a world dominated by public bureaucracy and New Public Management may lack both motivation and suitable mindsets to participate in and spur co-creation. Premiums placed on individual performance in relation to predetermined goals and service production based on competition between public and private providers tend to crowd out collaborative strategies, and the roles prescribed by the hierarchical chain of government and the supplementary forms of private entrepreneurialism do not leave much space for horizontal interaction based on collaboration.

There has been a longstanding debate in the social sciences about what motivates social and political actors. Rational action theories based on methodological individualism claim that discrete actors use available information about alternative options and the related costs and benefits to calculate the consequences of particular actions with a view to optimizing their net gain (Ostrom, 1991). Net gain is measured either against the actors' personal self-interest or in relation to the interests of their organization. Institutional theories tend to criticize the idea that social outcomes can be derived from the rational choice of unencumbered individuals. Instead, they emphasize the role of socialization and claim that individual and collective actors are rule-followers who act in accordance with what the institutional context prescribes as appropriate action for actors like them in the situation in which they are placed (March & Olsen, 1989, 1995). From this perspective, social and political action is scripted rather than calculated.

Rather than deepening the gulf between these competing theories of action, we assume that actors are driven by mixed motives as they combine consequential action based on a bounded rationality with appropriate action defined by rules, norms, procedures, and role perceptions. Indeed, both the logics of consequential and appropriate action are inherent to a practical rationality that sees institutionally embedded repertoires of action as highly sensitive to situation and context (Ansell & Bartenberger, 2019). A stockbroker at the London Stock Exchange is bound to act based on calculations of the pay offs of different options, whereas a social entrepreneur in a social economic enterprise will be willing to trade economic gain for social purpose and a caregiver in a nursing home will tend to be driven by professional norms and values. Later, we shall evaluate different public and private actors' motivations to engage in processes of co-creation. We shall, first, consider the question of how to spur participation in co-creation from a logic of appropriateness perspective and, then, consider the same question from a logic of consequences perspective.

The logic of appropriate action assumes that the motivation to act in one way or another is shaped by the actors' context-dependent perception of their role and identity (March & Olsen, 1995). The role perception of the actors is not set in stone but socially constructed by institutionally situated actors. Shifting public governance paradigms provide important contexts for understanding how actors perceive their role and identity and thus whether they will be motivated to engage in co-creation. As shown in Table 8.3, Classical Public Bureaucracy, New Public Management, and New Public Governance support the development of different institutionalized role perceptions for elected politicians, public managers, frontline personnel, citizens, and private for-profit and nonprofit organizations.

Table 8.3 *Role perceptions in three different public governance paradigms*

	Classical Public Bureaucracy	New Public Management	New Public Governance
Elected politicians should be concerned with ...	Making decisions, rules, and laws	Defining broad policy goals, service standards, and budget frames	Leading the political community consisting of competent and critical followers
Public managers are good at ...	Making sure that rules and laws are observed all the way down the hierarchy	Effective and efficient management of public service organizations that produce results	Leading cross-boundary collaboration in networks and partnerships
Frontline personnel are preoccupied with ...	Doing what is correct, fair and just	Serving the wants and needs of the citizens	Mobilizing available resources in the pursuit of public value outcomes
Citizens perceive themselves as ...	Subjects of the law and clients in public welfare systems	Customers with exit and voice options	Active citizens with rights and obligations vis-à-vis their community

Table 8.3 (*cont.*)

	Classical Public Bureaucracy	New Public Management	New Public Governance
Private for-profit and nonprofit actors see themselves as ...	Lobbyists aiming to influence public decisions	Service providers competing for public contracts	Partners in public–private collaboration

Source: Torfing, Sørensen, and Røiseland (2019)

Table 8.3 helps us to gauge the motivational barriers to co-creation that spring from the role perceptions associated with Classical Public Bureaucracy and New Public Management and the need to cultivate new role perceptions associated with New Public Governance.

Politicians who see themselves as sovereign decision makers in charge of law making and goal and framework steering will tend to find it difficult to share power with other actors, and spend time on problem-solving in and through processes of co-created policy making. By contrast, politicians that perceive themselves as organic leaders of the political community that consists of active, competent, and critical followers that can inspire their policy making may be inclined to develop an interactive political leadership style (Sørensen, 2020).

Public managers who see themselves as compliance officers and efficient managers in charge of stable, high-performing public service organizations will be terrified by the thought of collaborating with people from other organizations and sectors who they cannot control and who may pursue other goals. By contrast, public managers convinced that resource mobilization through cross-boundary collaboration is the way forward in a cash-strapped public sector that needs to do more with less will be keen to co-create solutions with relevant and affected actors.

Public employees who strongly identify with their role as administrative "rule followers" and professional "relievers" may not like the idea of mobilizing the resources of users, volunteers, and civil society actors. By contrast, public employees that perceive themselves as "enablers" will find co-creation to be a standard practice (Bovaird, 2007).

Citizens who either perceive themselves as subordinate clients to be rescued by the public knights in shining armor or as customers who have dutifully paid their taxes and therefore can lean back and expect the public and private providers to do their best to satisfy their needs are likely to oppose the idea of an active involvement in public service production and public problem-solving. By contrast, citizens that perceive themselves as active and engaged members of a community that both gives them rights and obligations to contribute to the production of public value outcomes will be ready to engage in the co-creation.

Last, but not least, private for-profit and nonprofit organizations that see themselves as lobbyists aiming to influence government policy and perhaps even as competitors fighting over public contracts will not want to engage in collaborative problem-solving based on knowledge exchange, joint decision making, and risk sharing. By contrast, private organizations perceiving themselves as partners in public–private collaboration will have no problem participating in co-creation of public solutions.

The bottom line is that the transition to co-creation requires significant shifts in the role perceptions of the key actors. While institutions and organizations are relatively easy to change, at least at the formal level, the institutionally embedded roles and identities of public and private actors are often rather difficult to transform. It is painful to redefine one's role because it provides a socially sanctioned guide for action and a sense of purpose and empowerment. As such, social and political actors often cling to their old role and identity perceptions and seem to be more inclined to add new elements to the former role than to replace it with a completely new one (Jæger & Sørensen, 2003). However, old role perceptions will tend to make it increasingly difficult for social and political actors to operate in a new environment based on a different governance paradigm. The clash between role and environment is likely to create irritation that over time may grow into a sizeable disruption that triggers role transformation. These role transformations will in turn create a mutually reinforcing dynamic between governance paradigms, role perceptions, and governance practices that will enable co-creation.

Seen from the perspective of the logic of consequences, the motivation to engage in co-creation depends on the time and effort that the actors think it will cost them to participate in co-creation compared to how much they are likely to gain from participating. Naturally the perceived gains depend on the value that social and political actors attribute to the solution. If they really care about the local environment, they will put a high price on a solution that secures access to clean air and water and green pastures with high biodiversity. The costs of participation and uncertainty about the future gains may, nevertheless, deter participation. This problem can be addressed in two ways.

The first strategy is to change the perception of what it requires to participate by making the co-creation process more ad hoc, flexible, and scalable, so that potential participants can see that they do not have to participate in all activities with the same intensity and over long periods of time that will tend to require more and more action. At least some actors will be persuaded by a clear process map (Straus, 2002) that shows them that participation can be temporary and vary in intensity over time.

The second strategy is to tactically produce small wins in the early days of the co-creation process and to ensure positive feedbacks from the process (hedonistic effects) and the interaction (network effects). Small wins may help to demonstrate the collaborative advantage of co-creating public solutions, but may "be in contradiction with the need to address major social issues rapidly or meet the requirements of external funding bodies for demonstrable output" (Huxham & Vangen, 2003: 16). Hedonistic effects can be obtained by letting people use their skills and competences, by designing creative processes, and by giving everybody the possibility to express and assert themselves. Co-creation processes that create enjoyment by empowering the actors and spurring learning and personal growth are likely to attract more people. Finally, network effects are about building relations that both make people feel that they belong and make them see all the things they can do in and through these relations.

In sum, the mixed motives perspective enables us to see that the transition to co-creation calls for broad-based motivational strategies that both seek to transform the roles and identities of the actors and to influence the calculations of the potential participants.

8.5 Assessing the Outcomes of Co-creation

In today's audit society (Power, 1997), activities that cannot be measured and proven to have a result will not be regarded as legitimate activities that are worthy of public interest and investment. Therefore, systematic evaluation of co-creation processes is essential to their expansion and mainstreaming. If we want to expand co-creation as a mode of governance, we have to demonstrate that it can be subjected to regular and efficient evaluation and does not create islands of unreported and unaccountable activity.

There are scores of empirical examples of co-creation that demonstrate the capacity of public and private actors to engage in fruitful collaboration that creates new and better solutions (Brandsen, Steen, & Verschuere, 2018). To illustrate, in 2012, the Surrey County Council in the United Kingdom commissioned a complete transformation of the services offered to disadvantaged young people. The new co-creation approach involved a broad range of stakeholders, including third sector organizations and the disadvantaged youth, and resulted in a dramatic decrease (60 percent) in the numbers of young people who were not in employment, education, or training, despite a 25 percent budget cut (Tisdall, 2015).

Unfortunately, there are few examples of systematic attempts to measure and document the actual and multiple effects of co-created solutions, and this may hamper the endeavor to spur co-creation in the current climate where legitimacy, in part, is derived from the auditability of public action (Loeffler & Bovaird, 2018). To solve this problem, we shall consider some well-known evaluation tools and discuss the prospect of developing an easy-to-use assessment tool that facilitates systematic evaluation.

Public leaders of co-creation are under pressure to subject the processes of collaborative innovation and public value production to the new performance management procedures associated with New Public Management. By contrast, the participants in co-creation tend to eschew systematic evaluation because they believe that the complex and multi-perspectival processes of goal formulation, mutual learning, creative problem-solving, and co-delivery of solutions do not lend themselves to evaluation and may even be stalled or suppressed by a rigorous measurement of inputs and outputs. We agree that subjecting co-creation to performance management based on a linear sequence of goal formulation, service production, and measurement of results will often be counterproductive or even damaging. Imagine volunteers helping out in hospital wards or public schools being subjected to registration of the hours they put in, or a group of community actors aiming to find new ways of fighting child obesity being asked to keep track of their attendance in meetings and the number of specific measures they come up with. This kind of performance management will most likely scare volunteers away.

That being said, we believe that co-creation both *should* and *can* be subjected to careful evaluation out of concern for legitimacy, learning-based improvement, and the production of important demonstration effects. Careful evaluation of activities that involve the use of public money is not only an important source of legitimacy. It also produces knowledge about the process and impact of co-creation that stimulates learning and enables joint reflection on how to improve outcomes through a proactive reshaping of the process. Co-creators should, therefore, welcome a more rigorous approach to evaluation as it helps to achieve their jointly formulated goals. Finally, on a broader scale, the advancement of co-creation depends on demonstrating that the mobilization of the resources of citizens, local communities, and organized stakeholders tends to produce more effective, democratic, and sustainable outcomes than other available governance tools.

The arguments in favor of systematic evaluation of co-creation begs the question of how this can be done in ways that respect the special character of co-creation practices that defy description in terms of a linear goal-tool-result model. Drawing on the work of Patton (2010), we shall briefly describe and compare three alternative evaluation methods.

Formative evaluation aims to improve a particular project or process through a regular assessment of whether planned activities have been carried out and milestones are reached. It also aims to solicit feedback on past activities from users and relevant stakeholders in order to improve future activities. Finally, it seeks to identify the strengths of the project and to delineate the room for improving it in order to increase its chances of realizing the overall goals at the end of the project. As such, formative evaluation aims to prepare projects or processes for the final assessment of their achievements.

Formative evaluation is typically followed by *summative evaluation* that takes place at the end of the project. Summative evaluation aims to evaluate whether a given set of goals have been achieved and whether the results can be ascribed to the project activities. It also aims to determine the conditions under which the project led to particular results in order to probe the possibility for generalization and scaling.

Formative and summative evaluation are often used in tandem, and the combination of the two evaluation methods is particularly useful when projects have clear, predefined goals, involve implementation of standardized program activities, and have a definite ending point. None of these requirements are fulfilled in emergent co-creation processes. Here the goals are subject to constant reformulation, the actors seek to design new and innovative solutions through ongoing experimentation, and the overall purpose is not to deliver a final standardized solution, but to pursue continued development, both now and in the future. The absence of predefined goals and activities to be evaluated through formative and summative evaluation calls for an alternative evaluation method that can be used to evaluate emergent co-creation processes.

Developmental evaluation offers such an alternative. According to Patton, "developmental evaluation is designed to be congruent with and to nurture developmental, emergent, innovative and transformative processes" (2010: 7). Developmental evaluation recommends that co-creators undertake a continuous reality-testing of their changing assumptions, propositions, and ideas and thus offers a strategy for evaluation of co-creation that is compatible with its emergent character that derives from the fact that problem definitions, goals, solutions, and project activities are subject to processes of multi-actor collaboration, mutual learning, and chance discoveries (Patton 2010).

Developmental evaluation takes place throughout the steadily evolving co-creation process and is usually carried out by one or more team members who encourage their fellow collaborators to ask evaluative questions. Are we sure that we understand what the problem is? What is it exactly that we want to accomplish? Do we walk the talk? Do the assumptions about preferred solutions hold up? How do we know that? Answering these and similar questions based on a systematic gathering of and reflection on evaluative data is bound to stimulate collaborative innovation.

Developmental evaluation aims to drive the co-creation process onward through a continuous questioning of joint perceptions, common wisdom, tacit knowledge, change theories, results, and impacts. The purpose is not to ensure accountability by allowing hierarchical authorities and funders to control the process and judge the results. The purpose is rather to stimulate mutual learning through a critical evaluation of the reasons and evidence for supporting the current problem diagnosis, the goal formulation, the proposed solutions, and the assessments of the outputs and outcomes. Developmental evaluation critically interrogates the goals, ideas, and propositions that emerge in the process of creative problem-solving by thinking through their implications and testing them through real-life experiments and systematic data collection. Goals that have no relevance for the attempt to solve the problem, ideas that cannot be realized, and solutions that do not produce the expected results are challenged, reformulated, and submitted to a new test. As such, developmental evaluation confirms the idea that the development of robust solutions through active engagement of relevant and affected actors requires iterative rounds of goal formation, trying out solutions, and evaluation of impacts (see Andrews, Pritchett, & Woolcock, 2013).

Developmental evaluation does not believe that there is a final solution or outcome of co-creation processes. Outcomes are always provisional, conditioned by turbulent environments and subject to ongoing innovation. Still, they must be systematically scrutinized and that constitutes a special challenge for the actors engaged in co-creation. Several problems arise when a network of co-creating actors attempt to assess the outcomes of their endeavors. First, despite joint agreement on the overall goals, the actors involved in co-creation may have different views on what constitutes a benefit or a cost vis-à-vis the overall goals. The co-creating actors may have different normative belief systems and their interpretation of the results and impact of co-creation may reflect their relative net gains.

Second, co-creation projects often have intangible goals and produce intangible outcomes such as public safety, resilient communities, attractive neighborhoods, holistic health care, sustainable consumption, democratic empowerment, democratic legitimacy, and so on, which are much more difficult to measure than the quantity and quality of discrete public services. This problem is intensified if the outcomes are only supposed to be detectable in the longer term (Loeffler & Bovaird, 2018: 272).

Third, the tendency of co-creation projects to focus on benefits may hide the public costs that include increasing time spent by public leaders and employees in setting up the framework for co-creation and participating in and managing processes, large investments in ICT-enabled platforms and tools supporting co-creation, heightened costs of informing, instructing, and training private actors engaged in co-creation in specialized areas such as wild fire prevention or prevention of flooding, and rising expenditure resulting from growing ambitions and more intensive forms of co-creation and co-production (Loeffler & Bovaird, 2018: 276–277)

A final complication when measuring outcomes of co-creation processes is the difficulty that emerges when assessing the trade-offs between different goals, or between benefits and costs. Although there might be some form of co-creation leadership, there will be no hierarchical authority to legitimately settle disputes and adjudicate the assessment.

Despite these complications, developmental evaluation offers a welcome alternative to formative and summative evaluation, one that is compatible with emergent forms of co-creation. Systematic application of developmental evaluation is important as it helps to ensure the legitimacy of co-creation in the context of political demands that public money, managers, and employees are not wasted on time-consuming collaborative processes that are nice and cozy, but never lead to any results.

Developmental evaluation is an embedded process that both evaluates and drives co-creation processes. However, there is a risk that the lack of transparency associated with the embeddedness of developmental evaluation prevents it from generating sufficient legitimacy. To solve this problem Torfing, Krogh, and Ejrnæs, (2017, 2020) have developed an easy-to-use self-assessment tool that co-creation projects in the field of crime prevention can use to evaluate the quality of collaboration, the level of innovation, and the impact of the crime preventive solutions in ways that both stimulate learning and secure transparency. The three key variables are each scored from 1–5 on four dimensions in order to construct composite scores that project participants can use to reflect on how they can improve outcomes, public managers can use in the allocation of public funding, and researchers can use to test the causal association between collaboration, innovation, and co-created outcomes.

8.6 Mainstreaming and Scaling Co-creation

For co-creation to grow into a new and predominant mode of governance, the ubiquitous but often scattered and somewhat marginal co-creation practices must be mainstreamed and scaled. This chapter has shown that such a mainstreaming and scaling of co-creation is predicated on the development of special institutional designs and forms of leadership and the attempt to motivate key actors and introduce new forms of evaluation accommodating the emergent and multilateral character of co-creation.

Depending on the successful provision of the enabling support described earlier, we may see the development of one of three scenarios for the transition to co-creation:

Scenario 1: Co-creation will continue to exist on the margins of existing governance practices with only a few and limited scaling attempts. In this scenario, the benefits are likely to remain limited while the costs will continue to be considerable. The result is that co-creation will not diffuse beyond the current level to become a mainstream governance tool.

Scenario 2: Ambitious goals for a transition to co-creation are formulated based on the most promising examples, but without introducing new supporting institutional designs, leadership strategies, role perceptions, and forms of evaluation. Such a development will tend to create high expectations while the benefits will be moderate and not exceed the immediate gains from picking the lowest hanging fruits. This scenario will lead to disappointment and hence fatigue with co-creation strategies, eventually fostering a sharp decline.

Scenario 3: Co-creation expands in a co-evolutionary manner along with the extension of a supporting framework of structures and strategies that are designed based on learning from prior attempts at co-creating public governance solutions. This scenario is likely to lead to a sustainable shift to co-creation, but requires careful attention to the need for the scaffolding of co-creation.

This book explores the conditions for realizing the third scenario. Many public leaders, local citizens, and organized stakeholders are disappointed with the ability of public bureaucracy and private markets to solve the pressing problems confronting local communities and society at large. They are prepared to move toward co-creation and may go all the way in making it a core governance principle. In order to bridge the gulf separating the present will to experiment with co-creation from the perhaps not so distant future in which scenario three is realized, we shall conclude this chapter by presenting an

Table 8.4 *Five steps to co-creation*

Step 1: The curious municipality

Impetus	Austerity and external inspiration put co-creation on the agenda
Extension	Individual agencies experiment with co-creation where appropriate
Organizational design	Administrative silos prevail and contact with external actors is sparse
Participation	Citizens are sporadically involved, but late in the process
Core principle	Curiosity as to how co-creation can help solve acute problems

Step 2: The involved municipality

Impetus	Initial experiences are positive and spur new efforts
Extension	Local experiments blossom as leaders openly support co-creation
Organizational design	Project groups cut across silos on an ad hoc basis
Participation	Citizens and NGOs are involved earlier to harness their resources
Core principle	Co-creation will enhance democratic legitimacy

Step 3: The ambitious municipality

Impetus	Mixed evaluations stimulate learning about how to co-create
Extension	Bottom-up initiatives are supplemented by top-down strategies
Organizational design	Employees drill holes in silos and co-create in mandated networks
Participation	Professional boundary spanners connect public and private actors
Core principle	Public and private actors can learn from each other to improve solutions

Step 4: The mature municipality

Impetus	Identification of problems and dilemmas heightens ambitions
Extension	Co-creation becomes a standard operational procedure

Table 8.4 (*cont.*)

Step 4: The mature municipality	
Organizational design	Cross-boundary collaboration is enhanced by new platforms
Participation	Relevant actors participate in co-creation steered by the municipality
Core principle	Public and private actors are co-responsible for public value outcomes

Step 5: The co-creating municipality	
Impetus	National Public Innovation Award turns the municipality into a beacon
Extension	The local councilors have begun to co-create policy solutions
Organizational design	Agile and fluid organizations design digital and physical platforms
Participation	Both public and private actors can initiate and lead co-creation
Core principle	The municipality increasingly sees itself as an arena for co-creation

idealized five-step model for transition to co-creation. To convey a familiar and relatable image, the model presented in Table 8.4 looks at a local municipality's road to co-creation. Municipalities have the advantage of being close to citizens and local stakeholders and often have a strong interest in mobilizing resources and enhancing innovation to make ends meet.

The model presented in Table 8.4 may both serve to make it easier for change-makers to imagine the transformation as a stepwise process and to facilitate discussion of where particular organizations are in the projected transition to co-creation and what the next step might be. Some organizations may never come very far as they lose momentum on the way. Others will go some of the way, or perhaps even all the way, despite stumbling blocks and severe setbacks, only to find that mastery of co-creation is work in progress.

9 | Handling Dilemmas, Avoiding the Dark Side, and Tackling Democratic Problems

Co-creation brings together a diversity of public and private actors in collaborative processes of creative problem-solving in which different resources, experiences, and ideas are exchanged, shared, enriched, and integrated. As we saw in Chapter 3, co-creation thrives in countries with consensual democracy, corporatist traditions for public–private collaboration and a high degree of devolution that motivates citizens to participate in local governance. Yet, the absence of these favorable societal conditions does not seem to prevent countries with different political and administrative traditions from experiencing a growth in co-creation that is stimulated by new digital means of communication, social and political empowerment of citizens, and increasing societal turbulence.

Co-creation is initiated by different actors, in different policy areas and at different levels of governance, and is equally relevant for service production, policy making and societal problem-solving. The actors who come together to co-create solutions are driven by a mixture of urgency, curiosity, and willful determination to produce new and better solutions that have value to a specific group of individuals as well as to society at large. Their hopes and aspirations might be shattered by political and institutional obstacles, including risk averse politicians, administrative inertia, group think, and conflicts of interest. Chapters 4 and 5 gave some ideas about how emerging barriers can be overcome by the construction of generative platforms and arenas and by using a broad range of practical management tools. However, as discussed in Chapter 8, co-creation remains a complex and perilous process in need of particular forms of leadership and management (see also Schlappa & Imani, 2018).

There are many exciting examples of how co-creation improves services, breaks policy deadlocks, and solves complex problems. However, this does not mean that the future belongs to co-creation. Along with the potential benefits and advantages that include social

empowerment, resource mobilization, effective and legitimate problem-solving, enhanced resilience, public innovation, and reinvigoration
of democracy, co-creation presents a series of dilemmas that may
hamper the expansion of co-creation as a core principle of governance.
In addition, co-creation has a dark side that we seldom talk about.
Finally, co-creation may jeopardize cherished norms and values of
liberal democracy. Our attempt to elevate co-creation to a key governance principle must look these challenges in the eye and reflect on the
possibilities for either circumventing them or mitigating their negative
effect. Consequently, this chapter aims to assess the acknowledged
governance dilemmas inherent to co-creation, shed light on the dark
side of co-creation, and consider the conflicts that may arise between
co-creation and some of the fundamental principles of liberal democracy. The chapter also reflects on the normative status of co-creation as
a way of democratizing public governance and insists that co-creation
is neither a settled concept nor a perfected ideal, but rather a work in
progress in need of further reflection and experiential learning.

In discussing dilemmas, dark sides and democratic perils, this chapter aims to respond to a number of actual and anticipated criticisms of
our attempt to advance co-creation as a new mode of governance that
supplements and supplants existing modes of governance. It is our
experience that critics of co-creation tend to invoke different kinds of
denial – for instance, by arguing that co-creation is a marginal and
negligible phenomenon; that even if it is becoming more prevalent, it is
by no means a new phenomenon that requires special attention; and
that even if it is a new, growing, and interesting phenomenon, it is not
for the good as it carries a number of ineradicable problems. In the
prior chapters, we have already aimed to rebut the two first denials. We
shall, therefore, focus on the criticisms embedded in the last denial and
respond to the dilemmas, dark sides, and democratic challenges of co-
creation in an appreciative but inquisitive way.

9.1 Handling Dilemmas Inherent to Co-creation

A number of dilemmas potentially confront co-creation. One dilemma
is that politicians and public administrators are expected to play
a proactive role in initiating, sponsoring, facilitating, and giving direction to co-creation of public solutions in areas where other actors are
unlikely to take the lead, while, at the same time, they should welcome

societal actors' attempts to initiate co-creation and be careful not to steer or dominate self-grown and self-organized processes too much. In other words, the dilemma is between proactive and accommodating leadership. For public leaders who are used to being in charge and steering through top-down command, it is difficult to lead without controlling the process. They will often be tempted to over-steer collaborative partnerships and networks in the hope of reducing uncertainty and risk while realizing their goals and targets (Harkin, 2018). However, control-fixated leadership will tend to hamper the process of creative problem-solving and may demotivate private actors. That being said, failing to lead processes of co-creation may also be fatal as both hands-off meta-governance through the construction of platforms and arenas and hands-on metagovernance based on facilitation, motivation, and conflict mediation are required to ensure collaborative progress and break through fixed behaviors (Newman, 2001). Nevertheless, in order to respect the self-organized character of co-creation, we should remember that the normative signpost for hands-on leadership is neither to do too little nor too much (Sørensen & Torfing, 2009). This dilemma can be handled by finding the middle way between under- and over-steering, but that may take a lot of trial and error.

A second dilemma arises in the tension between specialized professional expertise and experiential lay knowledge. In line with new ideas of "swarm creativity" (Gloor, 2006) and "collective intelligence" (Landemore, 2012), co-creation invites citizens and stakeholders to bring their different experiences, insights, and ideas into collaborative processes of creative problem-solving. The mobilization of alternative forms of knowledge from a broad array of lay actors may stimulate innovation, but it may also crowd out the specialized knowledge and expertise of public professionals. This poses us with a second dilemma since we want to both stimulate innovation by disrupting the potential group think of public professionals while making sure that the co-created solutions build on the knowledge and expertise of well-trained public professionals.

Professionals may tend to see themselves as experts with a monopoly on a particular form of knowledge and can have great difficulty interacting with actors that challenge their authority, status, and expert knowledge. However, studies show that there is a positive relationship between professionals' motivation to serve the public and their willingness to engage with lay actors who are experts on their own life

(Coursey, Yang, & Pandey, 2012; Huang & Feeney, 2016; see also Steen & Tuurnas, 2018). The big question remains, however, of how to create a fruitful meeting between different forms of knowledge that spurs creativity and joint problem-solving. A part of the answer is that professionals should insist on the relevance of their own professional knowledge while recognizing its limitations and the need to mobilize other forms of knowledge and experience. As such, they should not view themselves as infallible experts with a privileged access to the truth, but rather as lead partners in knowledge sharing processes that result in the formation of common problem definitions and joint solutions.

A third dilemma is located in the trade-off between cost-effectiveness and democratic quality in interactive forms of governance (O'Toole, 1997; Sørensen & Torfing, 2007). A small group of skillful and powerful actors who know each other from previous projects may co-create new and innovative solutions in a speedy, flexible, and efficient manner without wasting time on idle talk and meetings with little added value. However, the democratic quality measured in terms of the equality, inclusion, and transparency of the process will tend to be low. Conversely, the ambition to involve a broad group of actors in all parts of the co-creation process and ensure that everybody can monitor the process and influence the outcomes may enhance the democratic quality, while simultaneously it may increase the transaction costs of collaborating beyond the efficiency gains created by the new solution. So, while in the best of all worlds, co-creation is both efficient and democratic, real-world compromises have to be struck between the cost-efficiency and democratic quality of co-creation.

The formation of viable compromises is eased by the fact that up to a certain point inclusive participation in co-creation will both democratize public governance and result in new and better solutions. However, there are also situations where more participation will slow down the process and the search for quick and efficient solutions will undermine democracy. These situations with clear trade-offs call for joint reflection among the public and private stakeholders and the leaders and managers of the process in order to form acceptable compromises that, for example, can be achieved by letting the intensity of participation correlate with the intensity of relevance and affectedness.

The simultaneous quest for diversity and consensus in co-creation presents a fourth dilemma (Torfing, 2019). Diversity is needed to spur the development of innovative solutions, but it may prevent the actors from forging collaborative relations and agreeing on joint solutions. This dilemma poses a serious challenge for leaders and managers of collaborative innovation. They may want to recruit a group of public and private actors with highly different backgrounds, experiences, and forms of knowledge, but the question then becomes how to facilitate collaboration between these actors without eliminating their mutual differences and disputes that may stimulate innovation.

In handling this dilemma, innovation managers may use one of three strategies, or combine them as they see fit. The first strategy aims to emphasize the mutual dependency between the actors and seeks to convince them that they need to pool or share their different experiences, ideas, and resources in order to find an innovative solution that hopefully will make all of them better-off. Hence, a strong feeling of interdependency may keep a diverging set of actors together, despite their internal differences.

The second strategy makes use of temporal sequencing. Here actors are brought together and told that in the first phase of the co-creation process they should merely engage in divergent thinking and try to come up with as many possible solutions as they can without passing any form of judgment on the ideas. This is typically what happens in brainstorming. Divergent thinking should then be followed by convergent thinking that aims to integrate new ideas. In this sequencing of the process, the actors first exploit their differences to create a large number of ideas and then collaborate in order to combine and integrate the ideas into feasible solutions.

The third strategy is based on segmenting and aims to create different forums and arenas for different sets of more or less like-minded actors. Actors with very different worldviews, vocabularies, and interests are kept apart as each of them is invited to engage with other actors with whom they share core beliefs and vantage points. The challenge here is to integrate the different solutions developed by different groups of actors. Innovation managers may do this by anchoring the innovation process in a core group of collaborative innovators that is exposed to competing solutions produced in and by other forums and arenas. The risk is that radically different solutions are dismissed right away, but there is also a good chance that the core group of innovators will be sufficiently disrupted to avoid tunnel vision and groupthink.

A fifth dilemma can be identified in the tension between responsiveness and responsibility. Co-creation processes are open and inclusive and aim to be responsive to the needs, demands, and ideas of a broad range of actors, but the more actors contributing to shaping the ultimate solution through informal processes of decision making, the more difficult it becomes to see who is responsible for the solution and discern its positive and negative impacts. A rigid insistence on the ability to identify the responsible actors behind a co-created solution based on formally registered participation may seriously undermine the responsiveness of the design process. A way of handling this dilemma is to develop a system for tracking the inputs and results of co-creation in a transparent way. Here digital platforms may offer a solution. Another management strategy is to form a core leadership group that both processes and assesses the many different inputs and assumes responsibility for the results.

The penultimate dilemma is between the altruistic discourse pervading co-creation and the self-interested motivation of participants in co-creation. Co-creation brings together public and private actors in order to enhance the production of public value outcomes and thus tends to expect the participants to be public-spirited, whereas in reality they may pursue a particular set of private interests. Commitment to serving society at large will not prevent public actors from simultaneously having organizational or institutional interests that they are defending. Since in a pluralist society we have to accept the individual pursuit of interests as the starting point for any political interaction, the question becomes how self-interested actors can produce public value outcomes that both benefit a broad range of actors and society at large.

This dilemma can be handled through a combination of socialization and learning leading to a gradual formulation of joint solutions that take us beyond the least common denominator. When actors with vague, but diverging interests come together to co-create public solutions, there is little that binds them together except the ambition to solve a common problem or to respond to a certain challenge. However, over time, the manifold actors will develop a number of ground rules for how to interact and perhaps also some shared perceptions about the problem and the range of available solutions. The actors will learn from each other as well as from joint experimentation and they will gradually accumulate a common fund of knowledge that they will draw upon in their deliberations. Assuming that preferences are endogenous, shared rules, norms, and ideas will mold the actors' different preferences and interests, thus enabling the formation of new and innovative solutions that the somewhat self-interested parties will prefer over the absence of a joint solution.

The last in this list of co-creation dilemmas is that the quest for tailor-made solutions forged by co-creation carries the risk of a growing balkanization of public governance that may threaten its overall coherence. This problem calls for coordination, but retreating to hierarchical top-down ex ante coordination or relying on ex post market-based coordination will undermine co-creation. The solution is to advance what some researchers refer to as "pluricentric coordination" (Pedersen, Sehested, & Sørensen, 2011; Sørensen, 2014). Defying the idea of coordination based on either imposition or competition, pluricentric coordination involves all those who participate in shaping public sector solutions in coordination processes that: "a) aim to establish a plurality of interactive linkages between different levels and different institutions; b) that are adjusted to context (time, space, and problematic); c) in a way that promotes the construction of shared meaning through the exchange of storylines and story work; and d) facilitate the mutual adjustment of situated practices" (Pedersen, Sehested, & Sørensen, 2011: 390). Far from providing a unified and seamless coordination, pluricentric coordination offers a patchwork approach that aims to link, modify, and weave together a plurality of governance practices so that they are well-aligned, support each other, and perhaps even subscribe to the same overall story line. As such, coordination is neither ex ante nor ex post but is an emergent feature of public governance.

As summarized in Table 9.1, co-creation is no flawless diamond, but rather ridden by a series of dilemmas that must be dealt with for co-creation to work as a mode of governance.

As indicated earlier, dilemmas cannot be "solved," since opposed and related logics co-exist in a contradictory relationship. However, there are different ways of coping with these dilemmas, so that we are not impaled by one of two equally pointed horns (Lewis & Smith, 2014; Schad et al., 2016). Coping with dilemmas makes it possible for us to live with them and even to productively embrace the double binds that they create. As such, the dilemmas inherent to co-creation should not deter us from trying to reap the fruits of more multilateral forms of interactive governance.

Table 9.1 *Co-creation dilemmas and possible coping strategies*

Dilemma	Coping strategy
Proactive public leadership *v.* respect for self-grown processes	Find middle way between over-steering and under-steering through trial and error
The knowledge and insights of lay actors *v.* the specialized knowledge of well-trained professionals	Emphasize relevance and importance of professional knowledge but also its contingency and limits
Cost-effectiveness *v.* democratic quality in interactive forms of governance	Joint reflection on situations with trade-offs in order to form acceptable compromises
Diversity *v.* consensus	Stress mutual interdependence and use temporal sequencing and spatial segmentation
Responsiveness *v.* responsibility	Develop system for tracing inputs and outcomes, or form core leadership group that processes inputs and takes responsibility for outcomes
Altruistic public value orientation *v.* pursuit of private interests	Stimulate socialization and learning that mold the preferences and interests of the actors
Tailor-made solutions *v.* balkanization of public governance that undermines coherence	Develop new forms of pluricentric coordination

9.2 Avoiding the Dark Side of Co-creation

During the last decade, scholars have become increasingly aware of the dark side of co-creation (Larsson & Brandsen, 2016; Williams, Kang, & Johnson, 2016; Brandsen, Steen, & Verschuere, 2018). This dark side is made up of the unintended negative effects that arise from more or less successful attempts to co-create public value outcomes. The negative effects are the evils that we by all means should try to avoid, or at least counteract, mitigate, and compensate for so as to minimize the damage they might cause. Let us look at some of the negative effects that might potentially accompany a turn to co-creation of public governance and look for possible cures and remedial strategies.

The first negative effect is the risk that co-creation will lead to the co-destruction of public value. A growing number of scholars (Plé & Caceres, 2010; Echeverri & Skålén, 2011; Steen, Brandsen, & Verschuere, 2018) have drawn attention to the fact that collaborative interaction between public and private actors not only leads to the co-creation of public value but also has adverse consequences as it may foster co-destruction of public value. The involved actors may set out to solve social problems, meet socioeconomic challenges, and carry out important public tasks through the exchange and pooling of resources, but instead of – or perhaps in addition to – public value creation, they end up destroying public value.

There are several sources of the co-destruction of public value. For example, the involved actors might miss important opportunities to act by being unperceptive or slow to take action when the window of opportunity allows them to climate proof a local neighborhood or prevent social problems from getting out of control (see Williams, Kang, & Johnson, 2016). At other times, the actors may be perfectly attentive to the situation, but lack competence such that their combined effort to deal with important problems, challenges, or tasks ends up making everybody worse off. Moreover, strong or irresponsible actors may also abuse the power that they get when participating in co-creation. As such, co-creation of crime preventive solutions in a local neighborhood may result in violent vigilante action, and co-creation of social care for the elderly based on user participation may lead to collection and circulation of personal data that is not stored in a secure way. Last, but not least, co-destruction of public value may be a result of unintended negative externalities of an otherwise success-ful co-creation project. To illustrate, co-creation of nature preservation solutions may succeed in protecting pristine nature in order to enhance biodiversity, but the environmental restriction on clearing dead trees and bushes may fuel disastrous wildfires that destroy people's homes and kill animals. The only known cure to co-destruction of public value is education, training, and experiential learning combined with some form of oversight that can help to prevent the worst blunders and to right wrongs.

Another negative effect of co-creation is the risk of reinforcing existing inequalities. Despite the ability of co-creation to lower the bar for participation and involve a broader mixture of actors than those who are usually involved in politics and public governance

(Clarke, Brudney, & Jang, 2013; Alford & Yates, 2016), powerful actors with lots of social and cultural capital may dominate the co-creation process and use it to get an even bigger slice of the pie. Hence, co-creation may unintendedly give rise to the Matthew effect, according to which those who already have will receive more. Resource asymmetries are ubiquitous but can be compensated by empowering weaker actors and giving them the power to veto final decisions that may disadvantage them, although this presupposes that they can properly assess the distributive effects of co-created solutions, which is not always the case.

A third negative effect is the pressure on citizens to conform to the new ideal of co-creation propagated by public authorities. Public organizations that aim to transform themselves into arenas for co-creation will demand that the citizens contribute actively to the creation of services, policies, and societal solutions, and they may punish or stigmatize citizens that do not live up to the new standard (Loeffler & Bovaird, 2018). In times of severe budget constraints, public authorities may be tempted to step up the pressure on vulnerable groups of citizens to participate in co-creation by engaging in moral blackmail that describes participation as a "pay-back" for the services that they receive (McMullin & Needham, 2018). Participation in co-creation projects may even be presented as a condition for receiving public support. The best way to avoid that happening is to include local citizens, or at least experienced NGOs, in the leadership of co-creation projects, having them oversee the process so as to prevent co-creation from being an instrument of control and punishment.

A fourth negative effect is the risk of the suppression of difference in favor of unity. The urgency of public problems combined with public leaders' wish to achieve and demonstrate quick results creates a strong pressure on the participants in co-creation processes to agree on "joint solutions" that they might not really support. Hence, the emphasis on consensus-seeking may silence dissenting or oppositional actors, despite the official celebration of difference as the driver of innovation and the conceptualization of collaboration as the constructive management of difference. If public authorities control and fund the platforms and arenas for co-creation, they may be able to force an agreement and suppress difference. To illustrate, Davies recalls how "mildly dissenting citizen-activists were cast as troublemakers by network managers, showing how institutions promising 'democratic empowerment' can do symbolic violence to subaltern groups" (2011: 64). Again, shared leadership and insistence on the mutual dependency between public and private actors may offer a bulwark against the steamrolling of private actors.

A fifth unintended negative effect of co-creation is the increase in transaction costs as public managers spend a growing amount of time, energy, and resources on the creation and maintenance of platforms and arenas and the facilitation of collaborative processes in networks and partnership. The rising managerial costs may be offset by the reduction of implementation resistance and the mobilization of private resources in the implementation process. However, the precarious and temporary nature of co-created solutions means that there is a continuous need for addressing emerging problems and difficulties in the co-creation process and for motivating private actors to partici-pate. The managerial costs of doing this may crowd out the resources available for regular services. Co-creation may also be an increasing burden to civil society. Hence, if the same small group of civil society organizations is repeatedly invited to participate in a growing number of co-creation processes, the citizen-activists may become exhausted and eventually burned out (Birchhall & Simmons, 2004). While a slow and sustainable acceleration of co-creation as a mode of governance may prevent an overburdening of civil society, the only way to deal with the growing managerial costs is to factor them into the budget and see them as an investment in mobilizing private resources so as to alleviate the burden of the public sector.

This brings us to the sixth negative effect of co-creation. Co-creation may be used as a Trojan horse for cutback management in times of fiscal crisis. Hence, governments may apply British "Big Society" or Dutch "Participatory Society" rhetoric about engaging citizens and empowering local communities as a smoke screen for shedding respon-sibility for social problems that are difficult and/or costly to solve (Ishknian & Szreter, 2012). While resource mobilization is a legitimate goal of co-creation, the attempt to use co-creation rhetoric as an instrument for cutting back the welfare state and abdicating responsibility for public service production is a cynical strategy that should be stopped. When properly managed, co-creation can foster innovative solutions that are better and less costly than the old solu-tions and tend to make everybody better off. By contrast, political attempts to shed social responsibilities in the vain hope that poor and fragmented local communities will be able to shoulder the burden turns service users and local communities into big time losers. Abuse of co-creation can be curtailed by insisting that it is based on voluntary agreements by two or more parties who agree to work together to define problems, design solutions, and evaluate the results. Only a high degree of parity and a critical press can effectively prevent co-creation from degenerating into disparaging attempts to shift the burden from the public to the private sector.

Finally, one of the implicit criticisms in the current debates is that co-creation embarks on a dangerous path in which the responsibility for societal risks are individualized so that in the final instance the welfare state is dismantled and people are to create their own personal solutions. In Western European societies, with large universalistic welfare states that have aimed to socialize risks in the field of health, education and employment, there might be a need to adjust the balance between collective and individual responsibilities in order to avoid the dominance of blunt and inflexible systemic solutions associated with top-down control and spur social innovation that makes the solutions more needs-based while simultaneously enhancing local ownership of these solutions. Co-creation aims to create such an adjustment, while insisting that not only public agencies and private firms but also civil society organizations, volunteers, and the users themselves should contribute to solving socioeconomic and societal problems. Working together to solve common problems is not the same as individualizing problems with the danger that people with particular needs no longer receive proper help and support. On the contrary, it means that a plethora of relevant and affected actors – and not only different public agencies – will collaborate to invent and deliver solutions that are more needs-based, efficient, and humane than the status quo.

There is no point in denying the presence of a dark side of co-creation. Co-creation intends to create a whole series of positive effects, but may inadvertently produce negative effects due to the emergence of unforeseen developments, bad management, misconceptions, misuse, or direct abuse of co-creation. Awareness of these risks is the first step in preventing them. The next step is to devise counter strategies and to utilize available tools for alleviating the unintended negative effects. Some tools have already been described in Chapter 5 and additional tools have been described in this section.

9.3 Answering Criticisms that Co-creation Violates Liberal Democratic Norms

While the involvement of end users in the co-production of services at the output side of the political-administrative system is perfectly compatible with liberal representative democracy, the elevation of co-creation to a core principle of governance might be criticized for violating cherished norms of liberal representative democracy. Let us consider and answer some potential criticisms.

First, co-creation might be criticized for placing a totalitarian public demand on private actors who are urged to become actively involved in the joint pursuit of the common good rather than minding their own business and pursuing their own private interests. As such, it is not difficult to imagine critics portraying co-creation as the end of personal freedom that is sacrificed by public demands for everybody to take part in collective "do good" projects. Add the prospect that our behavior is monitored by public authorities in order to determine our social credit points and it begins to sound like an anti-liberal nightmare of Chinese proportions.

Fortunately, co-creation is not seeking to question or undermine our personal freedom, but rather aims to redefine and strengthen citizenship by reviving the tradition of civic republicanism that views citizenship as a bundle of rights and obligations. The liberal notion of citizenship as the legal right of individuals to enjoy a series of civic, political, and social rights tends to create a community that is too weak to defend and secure these very rights (Mouffe, 1993). The antidote is the cultivation of a citizenship that combines individual rights with obligations toward the community. As former President, John F. Kennedy said: "Don't ask what your country can do for you, but what you can do for your country." This famous statement echoes the civic republicanism of Tocqueville and is fully compatible with liberal democracy.

Co-creation hails citizens as resourceful and skillful actors who have a moral obligation to consider how, when and where they can contribute meaningfully to the creation of new and better solutions to problems that are important for themselves as individuals, their social community, and society as a whole. Some citizens will have more time, energy, and motivation than others when it comes to contributing to the co-creation of services, policies, and societal solutions. Nevertheless, those resources and energies that are mobilized and the very process of co-creation will strengthen the social bonds that society is made of and thus create the foundation for the exercise of our liberties. In other words, co-creation aims to embody in individuals and private actors the will to support and care for the community rather than leaving it to the state alone.

Second, co-creation might be criticized for shrinking the demos from the large group of voters with an equal right to vote to a small group of citizens and stakeholders that get to participate due to their relevance or affectedness. This criticism invokes the standard image of the open and egalitarian liberal representative democracy in which we can all participate and have an equal influence on who gets elected to govern on our behalf and a closed and non-egalitarian interactive democracy in which a small group of (self-) selected actors have a special access to decision making in a particular domain in which they get to have more influence than those who are not participating.

Let us leave aside the fact that we recommend the creation of a hybrid democracy in which interactive forms of democracy are linked to representative forms of democracy, and instead consider the argument in favor of the construction of democratic arenas in which actors with relevant knowledge and expertise and intensely affected actors have a privileged access to democratic decision making. The provision of extra channels of influence for intensely affected actors is by no means foreign to liberal democracy (Dahl, 1989). As such, it is well-established that people in a particular geographical area (local or regional) should have a special say when it comes to decisions about local conditions. This argument provides the foundation for local and regional government and the idea that elected local and regional assemblies can govern local issues within certain bounds defined by national governments.

In many parts of the Western world, it is also accepted that special interest groups should be able to affect decisions within a particular functionally defined area. Hence, corporatism invites unions and employer associations to discuss issues pertaining to labor-market policy because they have a strong stake in the issue, can provide valuable input to the decision-making process, and are capable of blocking the implementation of decisions that they are against. Given the acceptance of this mode of representation in local government and in certain policy sectors, it is strange that Western democracies have been less inclined to grant influence to relevant and affected actors who may contribute to the co-creation of solutions to emergent problems, such as climate change and immigration. President Macron of France might have prevented the rise of the "yellow vest" protest if he had been more inclined to listen and work more closely with relevant and affected actors in climate change policy.

Co-creation reactivates and extends democratic norms that for a century have supported local democracy and corporatist policy making, but in so doing, it forges arenas for creative problem-solving that, at least potentially, cut across levels and jurisdictions and widen the group of participants beyond the narrow confines of peak interest organizations. What is important, however, is to avoid closure and seclusion of problem-solving and policymaking arenas by ensuring that relevant and affected actors have ample possibilities for entering and exiting co-creation processes and have plenty of opportunities to voice their opinions. While self-selection of the participants and lack of transparency are endemic problems, the fate of co-created solutions will often depend on the ability of the lead actors to demonstrate that a broad range of actors have been involved in designing and supporting these solutions. It is also paramount to ensure that co-created solutions respect democratically sanctioned laws, rules, and norms and are aligned with the views and preferences of elected politicians, who in some cases may also formally endorse them. Such an alignment can be obtained through metagovernance that involves politicians in overseeing, framing, and communicating with co-creating networks and partnerships (Sørensen and Torfing, 2016). Political metagovernance of co-creation arenas is an important tool for connecting interactive democracy with representative democracy and facilitates the expansion of hybrid democracy.

Third, co-creation can be criticized for undermining established patterns of democratic accountability. Traditional accountability models assume that there is a strict separation between citizens, elected politicians, and public administrators and that accountability is ensured by agents who report their decisions and actions to their respective principals and subsequently face positive and negative sanctions based on their principals' judgments of their performance. These models are challenged by the fact that co-creation replaces the chain of government and its principal–agent relations with collaborative interaction between a plethora of public and private actors that are co-responsible for outcomes (Sørensen, 2012).

Chapter 7 responded to the "many-hands" accountability problem by recommending a combination of different forms of accountability. Hence, new forms of horizontal accountability that allow the co-creating actors to switch roles between being accountability holders and holdees should be combined with existing forms of vertical accountability where the participating actors are held to account by their respective principals, such as politicians, voters, and social communities including user groups, neighborhoods, and civic organizations. These accountability mechanisms should then be supplemented with a "whole network" accountability mechanism that obliges the networked co-creators to produce joint and publicly accessible accounts of how they ended up defining the problem at hand, the reasons for designing and choosing a particular solution and the impact it has had so far. The production of such accounts will permit metagoverning politicians and critical publics to assess and pass judgments on co-created public governance. In sum, the messiness of co-creation processes by no means eliminates the ability to ensure democratic accountability.

Finally, co-creation might be criticized for eroding the boundary between the public and private realms. This boundary is a key feature of both liberal representative democracy and classical Habermasian types of deliberative democracy. While the former aims to protect representative democracy from illegitimate interference from nonelected pressure groups based in the economy or civil society that may undermine the ability of the elected politicians to represent the people as a whole, the latter forms of deliberative democracy seek to protect civil society from systemic power logics inherent in either the state or private markets that threaten to distort the process of reasoned debate (Sørensen & Torfing, 2005). Hence, both the advocates of representative democracy at the level of the state and supporters of deliberative democracy in civil society are eager to maintain a clear separation of the public and private realms.

By encouraging cross-sector collaboration between public and private actors, co-creation deliberately blurs the boundary between the public and private realms. However, it is a long time since liberal democracy lost its innocence to the rise of public–private collaboration, a point readily accepted by both pluralist democracy and democratic corporatism. However, we will take one step further to argue that public–private collaboration is not only an accepted feature of modern democracy but actually good for democracy. Hence, the egalitarian logic of democracy has always had a problem with the exercise of sovereign leadership by elected politicians and their administrative aides that tends to concentrate power in the hands of a political-administrative elite (Kane & Patapan, 2012). The tension between democracy and political leadership is fueled by the fact that while the mass of voters are relatively homogenous despite its internal divisions based on class, race, and gender, this does not hold for political leaders who have to be special and stand out in order to become elected and therefore risk constituting a separate class of political decision makers separated from the people (Landemore, 2019). Co-creation alleviates this tension in modern democracy by bringing political (and administrative) leaders into contact with lay actors from the economy and civil society. As such, co-creation reminds the political and administrative elites that the voice of the people is fundamental in democratic decision making and that public solutions must serve the community. As such, we can conclude that the interpenetration of the public and private realm is both a vice and a virtue.

9.4 The Normative Status of Co-creation as a Democratic Project

As we discussed in Chapter 7, co-creation may help to reinvigorate democracy in the face of the current problems and challenges to liberal democracy, such as democratic disenchantment, anti-politics, ideological polarization, and counter-democracy. Both this bold justification for co-creation as a democratic problem-solver, and our defense of the democratic quality of co-creation in Section 9.3, prompts us to clarify the normative status of co-creation as a democratic project.

We have already emphasized that the advantage of co-creation does not merely lie in its ability to spur democratic participation beyond the occasional visit to the ballot box and the involvement of the usual suspects in elected school boards, citizen councils, and user panels. Stimulating democratic participation is definitely a good thing as it tends to enhance democratic legitimacy and trust in government, but participation for the sake of participation is not sufficient to justify the democratic value of co-creation as a core governance principle.

Therefore, we contend that the true democratic value of co-creation lies in its ability to produce better solutions that narrow the gap between what people need and what they get. Improved public problem-solving has for many years been considered as an important aspect of democracy, alongside the provision of opportunities for intensely affected actors to influence public decisions (Lindblom, 1965; Briggs, 2008; Ansell, 2011; Landemore, 2012). As a matter of fact, what is special about co-creation is that the enhancement of democratic input legitimacy tends to go hand in hand with democratic output legitimacy (Scharpf, 1999). Participation of a broad range of actors helps to find efficient solutions to problems that citizens and stakeholders find important.

Despite the democratic promise of co-creation to simultaneously improve democratic participation and public outcomes through collective wisdom and swarm creativity, we refrain from seeing co-creation as a new democratic ideal state that we should strive to realize in practice. As we have seen earlier, co-creation is accompanied by a series of democratic dilemmas and problems that we might be able to handle and mitigate, but that we cannot effectively eliminate. Hence, far from constituting a democratic ideal in line with visionary ideas about "associative democracy" (Hirst, 1984), "discursive democracy" (Dryzek, 1994) and "deliberative democracy" (Gutmann & Thompson, 2009), we see co-creation as offering a democratizing supplement to existing forms of liberal representative democracy.

A turn to co-creation as a core component of public governance will help to democratize our existing democracy in three different ways. First, it will create new participatory and deliberative arenas in which relevant and affected actors debate small and big problems, challenges, and tasks and put their brains together in designing, prototyping, and testing new solutions in processes that may not be governed by an overriding conception of the common good, but nevertheless produce public value outcomes. Second, in so far as elected politicians participate in the arenas of co-creation, it will allow them to get input to public governance and policy making between elections and explain the decisions they have taken to citizens and private stakeholders. Finally, it will transform the institutions of representative democracy as their role will not only be to make authoritative decisions based on deliberation between politicians themselves and advice from their executive team of administrators but also to initiate, govern, facilitate, and participate in co-creation processes that may or may not produce proposals, recommendations, or ideas that the elected politicians will be asked to endorse. In sum, co-creation will democratize liberal representative democracy by making it less gated and by qualifying and improving the outcome of democratic governance.

The argument about how co-creation may contribute to democratizing the current system of democratic governance, despite its problems and challenges, may sound weak when compared with the recent attempts to describe a new democratic ideal state that we should aspire to achieve. We would like to contest this view by arguing that a visionary description of a new democratic ideal state, for all its worth, will fail to bring about the democratic change that we urgently need. The problem is that no matter how well-intended a democratic ideal state model is and how well it is described and advocated for, it will always be criticized for being utopian, unachievable, biased in favor of a particular type of democracy and leading to unintended outcomes that hamper rather than enhance democracy. The hope and energy invested in formulating and seeking to realize democratic visions of a future ideal state therefore implodes and leaves people disillusioned and fighting an uphill struggle against a growing list of unanswered problems. The antidote to this negative prospect is to take a pragmatist approach to democratic renewal that aims to democratize existing forms of democracy based on a precise diagnosis of problems and opportunities and a thorough testing of context-sensitive democratic innovations that both complement and transform the existing forms of democratic governance. The advancement of co-creation as a core governance principle offers a new political imaginary that can spark such experimental democratizations.

9.5 Co-creation as Work in Progress

This chapter has demonstrated that there is no bulletproof protection against being trapped by tough dilemmas, transgressing into the dark side, and violating well-established democratic norms. As a model for public governance, co-creation is still a work in progress and thus requires further thinking, designing, and testing. We will pave the road as we drive and it might take a while before we get it right most of the time and the benefits clearly exceed the costs. Hence, just as it took many decades to institutionalize representative democracy, design some reasonably well-functioning public bureaucracies, and avoid the most blatant failures of market-based governance, it will take time and require a lot of experimentation, joint evaluation, and mutual learning before co-created governance will find ways of dealing with all of the above-mentioned problems and risks.

Striving for perfection in public governance is futile, but systematic research combined with practical processes of trial and error may over time provide a co-creation toolbox enabling us to deal with most problems in a satisfactory way and thus improve public governance. From a learning perspective, it is important that the search for and implementation of *best practice* for co-created governance does not prevent the development of *next practice* that seeks to problematize, transgress, and improve what is already considered as the best way of doing things. To illustrate, the copying of an award-winning project aiming to bring together prison authorities, NGOs, and private firms in co-creating rehabilitation solutions for inmates – who are offered training in building and construction work when they are inside in order to get a job outside – may discover that involvement of the inmates in running the program produces better outcomes. Exploiting such a chance discovery for designing next practice is paramount to the future success of co-creation but is easily prevented by funding agencies who want project leaders to stick to the original concept.

10 | *Where Are We Today, and Where to Go from Here?*

In a recent EU Commission report (Vesnic-Alujevic et al., 2019) on the future of government, a group of researchers and practitioners presents four different scenarios for how Western societies might respond to the pervasiveness of wicked problems and unmet social needs, the rapid growth of new digital technologies, and the increasing distrust in government.

The *first scenario* involves the creation of a "DIY democracy" in which the public sector fails to deliver proper services and forces groups of resourceful and empowered citizens to create local service solutions based on a new type of sharing and caring economy, frequently assisted by the formation of new digital platforms, while offline physical gatherings continue to be important. Political power is devolved to the local level in which citizens can either vote directly on different political issues or elect delegates to represent their views ("liquid democracy"). While co-creation is a key feature of this scenario, the provision of co-created services at the local level is likely to be patchy and incomplete as the system will tend to be atomistic and service provision will rely on the availability, commitment, and capacity of social entrepreneurs. Moreover, the local system of co-creation will not be scaled to the national and transnational levels as the public sector suffers from declining financial capabilities and legitimacy. Hence, there might be a lack of big collective solutions for big society-wide problems that often require massive investments in research and development and the construction of national consent and international cooperation. In this scenario, co-creation emerges by default due to the lack of state capacities and its full potential will not be realized.

The *second scenario* envisions the rise of a "private algocracy" in which monopolistic and relatively unregulated digital tech companies use artificial intelligence to collect and process individual data and construct algorithms that support global consumer industries and political and administrative decision-making processes in which the citizens' needs and wants are interpreted from their data profile. Private businesses play an increasing role in public service delivery and the role of democracy in public life diminishes, as power is concentrated in the hands of a few global corporations that control data integration in the Internet of Everything. In this scenario, co-creation plays a limited role as it is reduced to the co-production of services that are provided digitally via the internet.

The *third scenario* involves the development of a "regulatocracy" in which national governments take control of leading digital platforms and use big data and artificial intelligence in the production and delivery of high-quality welfare services and in technocratic attempts to solve major societal problems through protective legal regulations. As a result, government becomes ever more pervasive and paternalistic, thus further undermining the its legitimacy. It follows that democracy suffers from declining participation rates and the development of a generalized distrust in political institutions. In this scenario, co-creation is nonexistent as government institutions think they hold all the answers, and citizens are disempowered by the growth of bureaucratic red tape.

The *final scenario* is the emergence of a "super collaborative government" that aims to realize the full potential of digital government, open governance, and public-sector innovation. Government agencies use digital technologies to develop a real-time understanding of social, economic, and environmental problems, facilitate seamless participation of relevant and affected actors in public decision making via online platforms, and encourage public innovation based on citizen-centric design thinking. Government-sponsored co-production of services and co-creation of societal problem-solving empower citizens and enhance their support for democracy and political institutions by ensuring government transparency and accountability. In this scenario, citizens control their personal data but have access to a wide array of digital resources and services and participate actively in the co-design of the future society.

The researchers and practitioners behind the report have a clear preference for the fourth and final scenario that aims to make co-creation a core principle of public governance. They list four key drivers that may help realize it: (1) technical advancements in artificial intelligence and real-time data analytics; (2) a strong push for open and innovative government; (3) growing political support for data protection and privacy; and (4) increasing inclusion of citizens in public decision making. Since all four drivers must be present for the "super collaborative government" scenario to emerge, it is clear that the preferred scenario is highly contingent, although far from unlikely, in the context of recent developments in the European Union.

While this report tends to stress the technological component of a co-creation future more than we do in this book, we certainly feel that digital platforms can facilitate co-creation by making communication and distributed problem-solving easier. However, our primary position on co-creation focuses on the institutional design and leadership of inclusive processes and the public value outcomes they can generate.

In this book, we have outlined a broad vision for co-creation as a strategy and tool for democratic governance. We have introduced the notion of generativity in order to better understand the need for institutional scaffolding of co-creation processes and provided a detailed description of these processes – how they are initiated, how problems are defined and solutions are designed, how innovative strategies are implemented, and how they can be further consolidated, upscaled, and diffused. We have identified the causal pathways that connect co-creation with desirable outcomes, such as service improvement, innovative problem-solving, development of resilient communities, and greater input and output legitimacy. We have argued that co-creation can offer a much-needed reinvention of democracy in response to current challenges. Finally, we have pinpointed the conditions for mainstreaming co-creation and addressed the need for dealing with the problems and dilemmas that may arise from the adoption of co-creation as a core principle of public governance.

The kind of co-creation that we are advocating in this book is different from the traditional understanding of citizen participation as the occasional involvement of citizens in decision-making processes that are planned, carried out, and concluded by elected politicians and public managers. It is also different from the Ostrom and Arnstein vision of citizen participation as ideally involving the self-government of the people. In our view, co-creation is essentially about power-sharing and joint action based on the recognition of mutual dependence between a broad range of public and private actors.

The aim of this final chapter is to take stock of the current research on co-creation in the public sector and to assess the prospect for co-creation to become a core principle of public governance. The chapter will also set an agenda for future research and identify some disruptive steps that may help to advance co-creation.

10.1 How Far Have We Come in Studying Co-creation?

The continuation of fiscal austerity, the growing demand for services, and the declining interest in the New Public Management interpretation of citizens as consumers who expect high-quality services has given rise to a new focus on how citizens and users can use their resources to add value to the services they receive by co-producing these very services. Users can co-produce their own services, and citizens can become volunteers in co-producing services for their fellow citizens. There are many studies of different forms of public service co-production (Brandsen, Steen, & Verschuere, 2018). Some of these studies have begun to stretch the concept of co-production to cover the design of entire service systems and the development of innovative planning initiatives (Osborne & Strokosch, 2013). However, few studies have yet envisioned co-creation as a tool for solving complex societal problems and developing new policies, let alone as a mode of governance seeking to transform the public sector into a platform organization that engages public and private actors to work together to produce innovative public value outcomes.

This book has sought to provide the conceptual foundations for bringing this vision to fruition. Although our agenda is a departure from the prior research on co-production, our exploration of co-creation builds directly upon existing research and practice. In Chapter 2, we took a close look at the state of the art research on co-creation in the public sector by comparing and integrating the concepts, ideas, and arguments provided by leading scholars in the field. In Chapter 3, we found that there is extensive research on co-creation at different levels of government, in different parts of the world, and in different policy sectors. Still, most of these studies have focused on governance on the local level in Europe and North America, and often in policy fields such as urban planning and health.

In terms of thematic preoccupations, the emerging co-creation literature has focused on a variety of issues, including the social, political, and technological *preconditions* for co-creation to emerge and flourish; the *motivation* of citizens, stakeholders, and public agencies to participate in co-creation; the *institutional design* of platforms and arenas; the *collaborative process* itself; the impact of *leadership and management* on co-creation; and the positive and negative *outcomes* and implications of co-creation. Let's briefly look at a few examples of the findings from the literature to highlight each of these themes:

Preconditions: In a study of the technological preconditions for co-creation, Lember, Brandsen, and Tõnurist (2019) find that while digital technologies can enable collection and sharing of relevant data, lower the threshold for participation, and facilitate direct interaction, they may also have a negative effect on co-creation by bypassing citizens and stakeholders altogether.

Motivation: Eijk and Steen (2016) identify the importance of internal and external efficacy, along with self-centered motives, in shaping person and community-centered motivations to improve the quality of community life.

Institutional Design: Nambisan and Nambisan (2013) find that co-creation requires not only a strong public sector and a well-organized civil society, but also an ecosystem of actors that interact across sectors and the institutional design of platforms and arenas that can provide venues for cross-sector co-creation.

Collaborative Process: In a study of Danish police reform, Degnegaard, Degnegaard, and Coughlan (2015) show how design thinking and strategic visualization can be used as frameworks and tools for organizing co-creation processes. Design thinking emphasizes that the collaborative process begins with an empathic understanding and joint definition of problems and solutions and proceeds through ideation to the development and testing of prototypes. Strategic visualizations make use of spatio-visual narratives that aim to make the future concrete and function as boundary objects enabling the actors to engage in collaborative problem-solving.

Leadership and Management: Bason (2010, 2018) claims that stimulating co-creation in the public domain requires leadership that is at the same time visionary and enabling. He goes on to argue that effective co-creation requires public leaders to adopt a citizen-centric "design attitude" that questions assumptions, integrates different views and meanings, and uses concrete models to envision the future and focus on outcomes.

Outcomes: In a comprehensive meta-analysis, Voorberg, Bekkers, and Tummers (2015) find that many studies consider co-creation as a virtue in itself and do not look for other desirable outcomes, although some studies explore the contribution of co-creation to improved effectiveness, efficiency, and user satisfaction.

These and other related studies make an important contribution to our understanding of co-creation, but they only begin to scratch the surface of co-creation envisioned as a mode of public governance. To provide an adequate foundation for a more visionary agenda where co-creation is a core principle of public governance, a more ambitious research endeavor is necessary as there are still many unexplored issues and a general lack of empirical evidence. The study of co-creation is still in its infancy, but it already provides a starting point upon which to build a more expansive co-creation agenda.

10.2 Can Co-creation Become a Core Principle of Governance?

The soil for the future growth of co-creation is not equally fertile everywhere. In some political-administrative systems, institutional conditions weigh against successful introduction and expansion of co-creation as a mode of governance. Other political-administrative systems offer more favorable terrains. A number of existing typologies of political and administrative systems can provide insight into the opportunities and constraints for the prospect of an expanded use of co-creation in public governance.

Painter and Peters (2010) distinguish between four public administration (PA) traditions in advanced industrial societies: Anglo American, Napoleonic, Germanic, and Scandinavian. Each of these traditions can be interpreted as placing barriers in the way of a full-fledged rollout of co-creation.

While the pluralist and civic republican traits of the Anglo American PA tradition may support co-creation of public governance solutions, the overall preference for stateless society, limited government, weak local authorities, and the tendency for public agencies to become politicized can make it difficult for public actors to convene private for-profit and nonprofit actors, facilitate collaboration, ensure the integrity of the process, and guarantee the implementation of outcomes. Public actors simply tend to lack the organizational capacity, political mandate, and democratic legitimacy when interacting with societal actors.

The interventionism embedded in the Napoleonic PA tradition clearly sets an agenda for finding collective solutions to societal problems, but the hierarchical and centralized system of government, the elitist PA, and the weak civil society can discourage intersectoral collaboration and societal resource mobilization. The Jacobin State is expected to solve social and economic problems without participation of citizens and societal actors.

The organicist conception of State–Society relations and the Catholic principle of subsidiarity at the heart of the Germanic PA tradition encourage corporatist consultation in relation to key policy issues and thus prepare the ground for co-creation. However, the stress on formal legalism inherent to the *Rechtsstaat* may discourage the more informal and distributed interaction that is typically found in co-creation.

The Scandinavian preference for universal welfare and open government combined with extensive devolution of political power to local governments that are close to citizens provides the most fertile soil for the expansion of co-creation, but the strong emphasis on professional values and competences can run at cross purposes with co-creation efforts. Professional social workers may develop an overly paternalistic attitude toward users, citizens and the public.

Countries belonging to either the Latin American, postcolonial Asian and African, Soviet, or Islamic PA traditions may for different reasons prevent the advancement of co-creation. Many of these countries have strong authoritarian states, significant corruption problems and huge popular distrust in government, conditions that work against co-creation with societal actors, or they have weak institutions that can hardly orchestrate co-creation. However, some countries in Asia and Latin America provide promising terrains for the development of co-creation as they either strongly encourage public innovation (Singapore) or strongly encourage popular participation (Brazil).

Judging the future prospect for the growth of co-creation from the perspective of the different PA traditions can lead to a rather bleak and pessimistic conclusion: only a few countries will escape the institutional barriers inherent in their PA traditions, although there are remarkable exceptions where co-creation is developed either through a deliberate attempt to replace an old PA regime with a new one, or by adapting the existing PA tradition in ways that support multi-actor collaboration (see Voorberg et al., 2017a). In addition, each of the PA traditions contains gaps and opportunities that allow for the development of "pockets" of co-creation and governance innovation produced through interactions of public agencies with domestic and international civil society organizations or with developmental aid agencies. These pockets of successful innovation may gradually become upscaled and mainstreamed.

Moreover, while there are important institutional path-dependencies inherent in the various PA traditions, we should not forget that there are also important path-shaping forces that work in favor of co-created governance. Let us briefly look at some of the important political logics that seem to counter the institutional barriers created by the different PA traditions.

First, changing demographics and growing citizen expectations about public services, in combination with slow economic growth, means that public finances are under constant pressure. At the same time, the public sector is called upon to realize the United Nations' Sustainable Development Goals, which target complex problems such as underdevelopment and food insecurity, growing social inequality, the lack of opportunities for education and employment, the decline of biodiversity, the pollution of our oceans, and climate change. These pressures make it imperative for the public sector to work smarter and spur the development of innovative solutions by means of collaboration across public agencies and creative problem-solving with private and societal actors (Nambisan & Nambisan, 2013; Torfing, 2016). To engage a wider set of actors with new ideas, co-creation can be an essential tool for dealing with the cross pressure between fiscal constraints and a growing number of problems and tasks.

Second, while laws and regulations provide suitable tools for building a safe and well-ordered society and a well-functioning market economy, there are many policy areas where legal regulation is a dull instrument. In the area of preventive health care, sustainable living, culture and arts, crime prevention, anti-discrimination, and so on, the social outcomes that we are looking for cannot be achieved by laws and regulations alone (Trubek & Trubek, 2006). New policy instruments aiming to change social behaviors based on information campaigns and transformative learning, the development of common norms, role models, and voluntary standards, and the construction of networks and partnerships are in high demand (Salamon, 2002). These new tools of governance will often have little impact if they lack support from the relevant and affected actors. Here, co-creation offers a solution for securing broad-based participation in the development of new forms of soft governance.

Third, over the years there have been many examples of costly implementation failures where public solutions fail to meet the needs of the target group (May, 2014). More often than not, such failures result from the lack of empathy with the users and lack of understanding of the social and economic problems seen from the point of view of citizens. A key tool for preventing future implementation failures is to involve relevant and affected groups in defining public problems and designing solutions through processes of co-creation (Ansell, Sørensen, & Torfing, 2017).

Fourth, politicians can no longer close their eyes to the growing distrust in elected government and public institutions that seem to provide the conditions for the rise of a right-wing populism with little respect for the procedures and values of liberal democracy (Stoker, 2019). Winning back the trust of citizens in the wake of the global financial crisis and the emerging climate crisis is not easy, but may be spurred by the adoption of a co-creation approach to policy making that aims to reconnect elected politicians with relevant and affected groups of citizens (Dzur & Hendriks, 2018).

Fifth, wide sections of the population are becoming increasingly empowered and more assertive (Dalton & Wetzel, 2014). They want to be seen and heard and trust themselves to be able to contribute to steering society toward better solutions. However, there is a risk that these increasingly competent and assertive citizens will fall prey to the rhetoric of populist political leaders who seek to speak on their behalf, although not necessarily with them. To avoid this scenario, the alternative is to offer citizens new channels for effective participation. Co-creation may provide such a channel as the citizens are not only invited to support policy proposals offered by the political elites but also invited to actively engage in defining problems and designing and implementing solutions and thus to form a new sub-elite that can challenge the existing elites, whether they belong to the traditional political establishment or to the new populist alternatives (Etzioni-Halevy, 1993).

Sixth, political parties have lost their broad membership basis (Whitely, 2010), and the party leaders have increasingly allied themselves with the executive civil servants thus becoming cartel parties with only a weak direct connection to the electorate (Katz & Mair, 1995). Some political leaders aim to compensate for the lack of a broad membership by enhancing communication through social media or by hiring professional consultants to probe the opinions of focus groups, but these attempts to connect with the voters are tenuous and do not provide genuine opportunities for political deliberation and inter- action. Alternatively, new forms of "direct representative democracy" (Neblo, Esterling, & Lazer, 2018) may combine traditional forms of democratic representation with new forms of interactive democracy. Online dialogues between elected politicians and their local constitu- ents may develop into co-created policy making if the politicians begin to involve the citizens in the definition of problems and the design of solutions.

Seventh, the new media landscape provides citizens with the ability to post comments and blogs and participate in online discussions with each other. While this may help to provide valuable input to govern- ment, it may also spur unconstructive negative engagement whereby citizens subject government and other responsible governance actors to uncompromising and hateful criticism without any attempt to take responsibility for the provision of alternative governance solutions (Lutz & Hoffmann, 2017). Moreover, social media tends to create echo chambers where people only share their negative views with like- minded people. Alternatively, new social media may be used as plat- forms for involving skeptical citizens in constructive processes of co- creation that aim to find joint solutions to common problems by facilitating dialogue between a diversity of relevant and affected actors.

Eighth, trends toward multiculturalism create demand for more inclusive representation (Morales & Giugni, 2016). As a result of global migration, populations become increasingly diverse and this development undermines the provision of the standardized one-size- fits-all solution that characterized the public sector in industrial soci- eties. Public solutions must cater to the needs of different groups of citizens that demand to be represented and to be able to influence the alignment of policy solutions with community needs. Co-creation can both facilitate a more inclusive representation at the output side of the political system, and a new approach to service design that takes the diverse needs of citizens as a starting point.

Ninth, the rise of multilevel governance creates a risk that important governance decisions are taken by distant and unaccountable experts and technocrats who are providing smart and intelligent governance solutions but will never experience the local consequences of their decisions (Radaelli, 2017). As we have seen in the United Kingdom with the Brexit process, the growing distance between bureaucratic experts and elites of the European Union's complex system of multilevel governance, on the one hand, and increasingly frustrated citizens on the other, breeds a widespread distrust that forms the basis of anti-political and antiestablishment sentiments (Flinders, 2018; Marsh, 2018). Co-creation aims to reduce the distance between citizens and the different levels of public governance in order to restore trust in government.

All these new and emerging political logics push and pull governments in the direction of co-creation. On the pull-side, these political logics require all the different PA traditions to reinvent themselves in order to create opportunities for citizens to engage with the state in a new way. On the push-side, citizens demand new channels for active and direct participation in the making of public decisions that affect the quality of their lives. Ultimately, the fate of co-creation as a mode of governance, and the forms it may take in different countries, depends on the balance between the institutional path-dependencies created by the PA traditions and these path-shaping political logics.

10.3 Future Research Agenda

Given that the research on co-creation as a core principle of public governance is still in its infancy, there is an urgent need for more academic research and for practical design experiments that can lead the way by describing and cataloging different forms of co-creation, assessing the contingent effects of co-creation on the production of public value outcomes, and identifying drivers and barriers of co-created futures. All aspects of co-creation covered in this book require more in-depth analysis and deserve to be studied in greater detail using state-of-the-art theories and methods. However, to advance co-creation as a mode of governance, there are some critical issues that call for special attention. Here, we identify five major research tasks that have particular strategic importance for the future of co-creation.

The *first research task* is to gauge the range of variation in the relevance and use of co-creation across different contexts. Comparative studies are needed to understand which public tasks and processes lend themselves to co-creation and which do not. Is co-creation primarily relevant in areas concerned with the welfare of the population and the presence of clearly defined user groups, or can it also extend to areas pertaining to planning, economic regulation, security, and crisis management? Comparative studies may also offer insights into the variation of co-creation across countries with different political and administrative cultures, policy sectors with different prior experiences with collaboration, and levels of government with different degrees of proximity to citizens and civil society actors. In addition to comparing co-creation across tasks and contexts, it is also important to understand how it unfolds over time. In particular, we need to identify the patterns of diffusion across space and time in order to understand the conditions for its spread.

The *second research task* seeks to identify the conditions that may support or prevent the initiation and mainstreaming of co-creation in public governance. One key task is to study how the public sector can promote co-creation through strategic management and to assess the efficiency of different styles of strategic management. As a corollary to this point, we need to evaluate the conditions under which public agencies can and will support co-creation and analyze the prospects for citizens and civil society actors themselves to initiate co-creation by inviting public actors to participate in creative problem-solving. In continuation with this focus on the initiation of co-creation, we need to study how platforms and other generative governance mechanisms can efficiently support the formation and adaptation of co-creation arenas. The digital revolution has not only created new opportunities for distributed action but also carries a risk that face-to-face interaction is replaced by data harvesting. Therefore, we need to discern the conditions for effective use of digital tools to enable co-creation.

The *third research task* is to further explore how to structure and manage co-creation processes for success. Co-creation processes are not completely self-organized; they need institutional and managerial inputs to thrive. We know that the institutional structures may be less formal than is typically found in public bureaucracy and that the exercise of leadership and management will take a less directive form in co-creation arenas. However, we need to assess the impact of institutional design on the process and outcomes of co-creation and identify best practices for leadership and management to support distributed decision making in co-creation arenas.

The *fourth research task* concerns the efforts to ensure positive outcomes while avoiding negative ones. Co-creation is about producing public value outcomes and achieving public goals such as effectiveness, efficiency, resilience, trust, and legitimacy. However, we need to refine and deepen our understanding of the causal pathways that link co-creation to these outcomes. Co-creation also carries a risk of producing negative outcomes and thus may have a dark side. These negative outcomes may involve the co-destruction of public value and the imposition of high transaction costs for both public and private actors that must spend an increasing amount of time and energy to participate in meetings and deliberations. Empirical studies can help us to discover how to avoid the negative outcomes of co-creation. For example, how can we find new ways of recruiting and mobilizing wider publics that avoid a biased, self-selected participation favoring privileged actors? Nevertheless, the persistent risk that co-creation fails to solve urgent problems or produce negative outcomes prompts concerns for ensuring accountability. Future research could explore new forms of social accountability and how these can be backed by government sanctions.

The *final research task* is to gauge the possibility for scaling co-creation and reinvigorating democracy. Co-creation often begins with small local experiments designed to address specific problems or challenges. This book endeavors not only to build on but also to go beyond such scattered one-off problem-solving efforts and turn co-creation into the backbone of PA and governance. To do this, it is necessary to ponder how co-creation can be scaled upward from local to regional, national, and transnational levels of government – and across organizations and jurisdictions – and become a systematic and pervasive strategy for producing public value outcomes. Co-creation may not only have relevance for making public governance more efficient and effective but may also contribute to a much-needed renewal of liberal democracy. To further explore this democratic reform agenda, we call upon researchers to reflect on the democratizing mechanisms embedded in co-creation practices and to investigate how the participatory and deliberative forms of democracy associated with co-creation can be combined with established forms of representative democracy, thus establishing a hybrid form of democracy.

10.4 Five Disruptive Steps to Advance Co-creation

We have already talked about strategies for the mainstreaming and diffusion of co-creation in Chapter 8. We realize that many things need be done before the public sector becomes a platform for the formation of co-creation arenas that mobilize relevant and affected actors in the production of public value. Although the path forward is becoming visible, it is no doubt a bumpy road that lies ahead. We know that the change we are aiming for requires the development of new organizational strategies, new institutional designs, and new leadership practices together with a good deal of experimentation. But what are the immediate steps that scholars and practitioners can take to advance co-creation?

We shall identify five important steps that will help to advance co-creation in the present conjuncture by disrupting existing barriers that prevent key actors from wholeheartedly embracing co-creation as a mode of governance. The overall structures of the public sector are hard to change in the short-run, so we might start by transforming the worldviews and role perceptions of social and political actors who have a clear interest in improving the quality and effectiveness of societal solutions. If we can shift the mindset of these actors and engage them in experimentation with co-creation, the necessary structural scaffolding may slowly emerge from above and below.

Following this line of argument, we shall conclude this book by emphasizing the need for disrupting the thinking and doing of six key actors that all play a crucial role in the advancement of co-creation.

For politicians: They are increasingly "home alone" now that they lack party members and must increasingly lean on civil servants or lobbyists to understand policy problems and design and implement new solutions. To disrupt this predicament, politicians must see themselves as political leaders of social communities rather than public organizations, insist on being actively involved in policy development, and take the lead in orchestrating a much broader process of deliberation with experts, interest organizations, and lay actors representing relevant and affected citizens in civil society (Torfing & Ansell, 2017).

For public agencies: They tend to think of themselves as occupying a particular position in a hierarchical chain of command and a horizontal division of labor. There is a self-protective aspect of this positioning that leads to increasing isolation and a failure to learn from the experiences, knowledge, and ideas of lay-actors, including users, citizens, and civil society organizations who possess resources that can be mobilized in the implementation of new governance solutions. What is really disruptive is for public agencies to stop thinking of themselves as privileged guardians of the public interest and as unilateral suppliers of professional solutions to societal problems and social needs. Instead, they should open up the public sector by creating platforms and arenas of co-creation that can leverage ideas and resources across levels, organizations, and sectors (Bommert, 2010; Ansell & Miura, 2019).

For public employees: What really makes an impact at the level of public employees is for frontline personnel to quit thinking that it is the organizational structure that determines their problem-solving prerogatives and thus that the efforts to solve particular problems or tasks are confined to particular public organizations, departments, units, and employees. The way to disrupt this way of thinking about public problem-solving is to dare public employees to ask the key question of "who can help me to solve this problem or task?" and then get them to involve all the relevant and affected actors that they can think of in the co-creation of joint solutions. Inviting citizens and stakeholders to share power and contribute resources is the first step in co-creation (Crosby & Bryson, 2005).

For organized interests: Organized interests – whether interest organizations representing particular segments of the population or large private companies with political agendas – tend to focus on advancing their immediate short-term interests by putting pressure on public authorities through sophisticated media strategies, contacts to political and administrative policy makers, and participation in policy-relevant negotiations and networks. This kind of lobbyism needs to be disrupted by broadening the perception of organizational interests to include long-term goals such as the Sustainable Development Goals that are already impacting firm strategies in many countries (Zanten & Tulder, 2018). Instead of approaching public authorities with a wish list of specific economic, legal, or regulatory demands, organized interests may both benefit themselves and society at large by flagging goals that they want to solve together with other public and private stakeholders.

For citizens: While typically perceiving themselves as "takers," citizens must begin to see themselves as "makers" of public services and solutions. The traditional perception of citizens as either "subjects" of state regulation or "consumers" of public services must be disrupted in favor of the cultivation of an active citizenship based on rights and obligations. Active citizenship is not just about what people can do for their country, but rather about how they can contribute to solving the problems they face in their lives, their local community, and society at large. We're not asking people to sacrifice themselves to an abstract patriotic ideal, but rather to help mobilize resources and ideas to address public problems and co-create solutions that enhance their quality of life (Nabatchi, Sancino, & Sicilia, 2017).

For researchers: We should engage more in a "seek-and-enlarge" game that identifies co-creation practices that are working well and then improves and enlarges these practices to enhance their volume, scale, and impact. What we should disrupt is the traditional view that our job as social scientists is to identify and explain governance and policy failures. Instead, we should: (1) look for promising instances of collaboration and co-creation; (2) conduct design experiments in order to bring the potential to fruition; and (3) support the diffusion of well-tested models across organizations and countries. Hence, instead of proving our ability as researchers to identify governance mistakes and policy disasters and demonstrate that the glass is only half empty, we must use our theories and methods to seek out potentially successful instances of co-creation and show how the half-full glass can be filled (see 't Hart & Compton, 2019 for a new focus on successful governance).

Disruption of the traditional roles and worldviews of key actors and the development of new ones supportive of co-creation may either come from social and institutional entrepreneurs problematizing existing role perceptions in order to make new things possible or from individual and collective learning processes spurred by new collaborative practices that question and reframe the mindset of the participants. Such disruption is no doubt painful as it removes the normative scaffolding of social action that defines the logic of appropriate action. During this transition, we have to learn to live with a heightened sense of uncertainty until new roles and worldviews have sedimented and while we experiment with co-creation processes that may be risky and failure-prone. Hence, we should expect that the process of mainstreaming co-creation as a core governance tool will encounter failures and difficulties. However, there is much to gain from a successful transition to co-creation that may help to enhance efficiency, effectiveness and equity, build more resilient communities and reinvigorate our democracy.

References

Abrahamson, E. (1991). Managerial fads and fashions: The diffusion and rejection of innovations. *Academy of Management Review*, 16(3), 586–612.

Adekunle, A. A. & Fatunbi, A. O. (2012). Approaches for setting-up multi-stakeholder platforms for agricultural research and development. *World Applied Sciences Journal*, 16(7), 981–988.

Academy of Sciences (2014). *Building Community Disaster Resilience through Private–Public Collaboration*. Washington, DC: National Academies Press.

Ackermann, F. & Eden, C. (2011). Strategic management of stakeholders: Theory and practice. *Long Range Planning*, 44, 179–196.

Agger, A. & Jensen, J. O. (2015). Area-based initiatives – and their work in bonding, bridging and linking social capital. *European Planning Studies*, 23(10), 2045–2061.

Ahn, H. C. (2007). Design tools and three steps in participatory design processes: A proposal for better communications among residents and experts, based on a case project of neighborhood park in Seoul, Korea. In 6th Conference of the Pacific Rim Community Design Network. pp. 1–10. http://courses.washington.edu/quanzhou/pacrim/proceedings.html

Alexander, E. R. (2005). Institutional transformation and planning: From institutionalization theory to institutional design. *Planning Theory*, 4 (3), 209–223.

Alford, J. (2014). The multiple facets of co-production: Building on the work of Elinor Ostrom. *Public Management Review*, 16(3), 299–316.

Alford, J. (2010). Public value from co-production with clients. In M. H. Moore & J. Benington, eds., *Public Value: Theory and Practice*. Basingstoke: Palgrave Macmillan, pp. 144–157.

Alford, J. (2009). *Engaging Public Sector Clients: From Service-Delivery to Co-Production*. Basingstoke: Palgrave Macmillan.

Alford, J. (2002). Defining the client in the public sector: A social-exchange perspective. *Public Administration Review*, 62(3), 337–346.

Alford, J. (1998). A public management road less travelled: Clients as co-producers of public services. *Australian Journal of Public Administration*, 57(4), 128–137.

Alford, J. & Yates, S. (2016). Co-production of public services in Australia: The roles of government organisations and co-producers. *Australian Journal of Public Administration*, 75(2), 159–175.

Alves, H. (2013). Co-creation and innovation in public services. *The Service Industries Journal*, 33(7–8), 671–682.

Andrews, K. R. (1971). *Concepts of Corporate Strategy*. Homewood, IL: Irwin.

Andrews, R., Boyne, G. A., & Walker, R. M. (2006). Subjective and objective measures of organizational performance. In Boyne, G. A., Meier, K. J., O'Toole Jr, L. J., & Walker, R. M. eds., *Public Service Performance: Perspectives on Measurement and Management*. Cambridge: Cambridge University Press, pp. 14–34.

Andrews, M., Pritchett, L., & Woolcock, M. (2013). Escaping capability traps through problem driven iterative adaption (PDIA). *World Development*, 51, 234–244.

Ansell, C. (2019). Coping with conceptual pluralism: Reflections on concept formation. *Public Performance & Management Review*, 1–22, DOI:10.1080/15309576.2019.1677254

Ansell, C. (2016). Pragmatism. In C. Ansell & J. Torfing, eds., *Handbook of Theories of Governance*. Cheltenham: Edward Elgar, pp. 392–401.

Ansell, C. (2011). *Pragmatist Democracy: Evolutionary Learning as Public Philosophy*. Oxford: Oxford University Press.

Ansell, C. & Bartenberger, M. (2019). *Pragmatism and Political Crisis Management: Principle and Practical Rationality during the Financial Crisis*. Cheltenham: Edward Elgar.

Ansell, C. & Bartenberger, M. (2017). The diversity of experimentation in the experimenting society. In I. Poel, L. Asveld, & D. C. Mehos, eds., *New Perspectives on Technology in Society*. London: Routledge, pp. 36–58.

Ansell, C. & Bartenberger, M. (2016). Varieties of experimentalism. *Ecological Economics*, 130, 64–73.

Ansell, C. & Gash, A. (2017). Collaborative platforms as a governance strategy. *Journal of Public Administration Research and Theory*, 28 (1), 16–32.

Ansell, C. & Gash, A. (2012). Stewards, mediators, and catalysts: Toward a model of collaborative leadership. *The Innovation Journal*, 17(1), 2–21.

Ansell, C. & Gash, A. (2008). Collaborative governance in theory and practice. *Journal of Public Administration Research and Theory*, 18 (4), 543–571.

Ansell, C. & Geyer, R. (2017). "Pragmatic complexity" a new foundation for moving beyond "evidence-based policy making"? *Policy Studies*, 38(2), 149–167.

Ansell, C., Lundin, M., & Öberg, P. (2017). How learning aggregates: A social network analysis of learning between Swedish municipalities. *Local Government Studies*, 43(6), 903–926.

Ansell, C. & Miura, S. (2019). Can the power of platforms be harnessed for governance? *Public Administration*, 98(1), 261–276. https://doi.org/10.1111/padm.12636.

Ansell, C. & Torfing, J. (eds.) (2018). *How Does Collaborative Governance Scale?* Bristol: Policy Press.

Ansell, C. & Torfing, J. (2014). *Public Innovation through Collaboration and Design*. Abingdon: Routledge.

Ansell, C., Sørensen, E., & Torfing, J. (2020). The social embedding of generic governance instruments. In J. Meek, ed., *Handbook on Collaborative Public Management*. Cheltenham: Edward Elgar.

Ansell, C., Sørensen, E., & Torfing, J. (2017). Improving policy implementation through collaborative policymaking. *Policy and Politics*, 45(3), 467–486.

Ansell, C. & Trondal, J. (2017). Governing turbulence: An organizational-institutional agenda. *Perspectives on Public Management and Governance*, 1(1), 43–57.

Ansoff, H. I. (1965). *Corporate Strategy: Business Policy for Growth and Expansion*. New York: McGraw-Hill.

Anttiroiko, A. V. (2016). City-as-a-platform: The rise of participatory innovation platforms in Finnish cities. *Sustainability*, 8(9), 922.

Aragón, P., Kaltenbrunner, A., Calleja-López, A., Pereira, A., Monterde, A., Barandiaran, X. E., & Gómez, V. (2017). Deliberative platform design: The case study of the online discussions in Decidim Barcelona. In G. Ciampaglia, A. Mashhadi, & T. Yasseri, eds., *Social Informatics. SocInfo 2017. Lecture Notes in Computer Science, vol. 10540*. Cham: Springer.

Argyris, C. & Schön, D. A. (1978). *Organizational Learning: A Theory of Action Perspective*. Reading: Addison Wesley.

Arnstein, S. R. (1969). A ladder of citizen participation. *Journal of the American Institute of Planners*, 35(4), 216–224.

Autio, E. & Thomas, L. (2014). Innovation ecosystems: Implications for innovation management? In M. Dodgson, D. M. Gann, & N. Phillips, eds., *The Oxford Handbook of Innovation Management*. Oxford: Oxford University Press, pp. 204–228.

Bache, I. & Flinders, M. (2004). Multi-level governance and the study of the British State. *Public Policy and Administration*, 19(1), 31–51.

Bächtiger, A. (2014). Debate and deliberation in legislatures. In S. Martin, T. Saalfeld, & K. Strøm, eds., *The Oxford Handbook of Legislative Studies*. Oxford: Oxford University Press, pp. 145–166.

Badaracco, J. L. Jr. (2001). We don't need another hero. *Harvard Business Review*, 79(8), 120–126.

Banks, J. S. & Weingast, B. R. (1992). The political control of bureaucracies under asymmetric information. *American Journal of Political Science*, 36(2), 509–524.

Bang, H. (2005). Among everyday makers and expert citizens. In J. Newman, eds., *Remaking Governance: Peoples, Politics and the Public Sphere*. Bristol: Policy Press, pp. 159–178.

Bang, H. P. & Sørensen, E. (1999). The everyday maker: A new challenge to democratic governance. *Administrative Theory & Praxis*, 21(3), 325–341.

Banerjee, B. (2010). *Designer as Agent of Change*. Available at: https://upl oads-ssl.webflow.com/5a9898f92fa8fa00017acfa3/5c63e109cbc13 e075f6db2aa_Banny%20Banerjee-Designer%20as%20Agent%20of %20Change.pdf

Baptista, N., Alves, H., & Matos, N. (2019). Public sector organizations and co-creation with citizens: A literature review on benefits, drivers, and barriers. *Journal of Nonprofit & Public Sector Marketing*, 32(3), 217–214, DOI:10.1080/10495142.2019.1589623

Barber, B. (1984). *Strong Democracy: Participatory Politics for a New Age*. Berkeley: University of California Press.

Barber, M. (2008). *Instruction to Deliver: Fighting to Transform Britain's Public Services*. London: Methuen.

Barnes, M., Newman, J., & Sullivan, H. (2006). Discursive arenas: Deliberation and the constitution of identity in public participation at a local level. *Social Movement Studies*, 5(3), 193–207.

Barnes, M. (1999). *Public Expectations: From Paternalism to Partnership: Changing Relationships in Health and Health Services*. London: Nuffield Trust/University.

Bartenberger, M. & Sześciło, D. (2016). The benefits and risks of experimental co-production: The case of urban redesign in Vienna. *Public Administration*, 94(2), 509–525.

Bason, C. (2010). *Leading Public Sector Innovation: Co-Creating for a Better Society*. Bristol: Policy Press.

Behn, R. D. (1998). The New Public Management paradigm and the search for democratic accountability. *International Public Management Journal*, 1(2), 131–164.

Benington, J. (2009). Creating the public in order to create public value? *International Journal of Public Administration*, 32(3–4), 232–249.

Benington, J. & Moore, M. H. (2011). *Public Value: Theory & Practice.* Basingstoke: Palgrave Macmillan.

Bennett, N., Wise, C., Woods, P. A., & Harvey, J. A. (2003). *Distributed Leadership: A Review of Literature.* Nottingham: National College of School Leadership.

Benz, A. & Papadopoulos, I. (2006). *Governance and Democracy: Comparing National, European and International Experiences.* Abingdon: Routledge.

Beran, D., Lazo-Porras, M., Cardenas, M. K., Chappuis, F., Damasceno, A., Jha, N., Madede, T., Lachat, S., Leon, S. P., Pastrana, N. A., Pesantes, M. A., Singh, S. B., Sharma, S., Somerville, C., Suggs, S., & Miranda, J. J. (2018). Moving from formative research to co-creation of interventions: Insights from a community health system project in Mozambique, Nepal and Peru. *BMJ Global Health*, 3(6), e001183.

Bergvall-Kåreborn, B., Eriksson, C. I., Ståhlbröst, A., & Svensson, J. (2009). A milieu for innovation: Defining living labs. In *Proceedings of the 2nd ISPIM Innovation Symposium: Simulating Recovery.* New York: ISPIM.

Bhaskar, R. (2008). *A Realist Theory of Science.* London: Routledge.

Biljohn, M. I. M. & Lues, L. (2019). Citizen participation, social innovation, and the governance of local government service delivery: Findings from South Africa. *International Journal of Public Administration*, 43(3), 229–241, DOI:10.1080/01900692.2019.1628052

Birchall, J. & Simmons, R. (2004). *User Power: The Participation of Users in Public Services.* London: National Consumer Council. Available at: www.ncc.org.uk/nccpdf/poldocs/NCC071ft_ user_power.pdf.

Bisschops, S. & Beunen, R. (2019). A new role for citizens' initiatives: The difficulties in co-creating institutional change in urban planning. *Journal of Environmental Planning and Management*, 62(1), 72–87.

Blair, T. (1998). *The Third Way: New Politics for the New Century.* London: Fabian Society.

Blais, A. (2007). Turnout in Elections. In R. J. Dalton & H. Klingemann, eds., *The Oxford Handbook of Political Behavior.* Oxford: Oxford University Press, pp. 621–635.

Bobbio, L. (2003). Building social capital through democratic deliberation: The rise of deliberative arenas. *Social Epistemology*, 17(4), 343–357.

Bohmann, J. (2005). From demos to demoi: Democracy across borders. *Ratio Juris*, 18(3), 293–314.

Bolden, R. (2011). Distributed leadership in organizations: A review of theory and research. *International Journal of Management Reviews*, 13(3), 251–269.

Bommert, B. (2010). Collaborative innovation in the public sector. *International Public Management Review*, 11(1), 15–33.

Börzel, T. A. & Panke, D. (2007). Network governance: Effective and legitimate? In E. Sørensen & J. Torfing, eds., *Theories of Democratic Network Governance*. Basingstoke: Palgrave Macmillan, pp. 153–166.

Boudjelida, A., Mellouli, S., & Lee, J. (2016). Electronic citizens participation: Systematic review. In Proceedings of the 9th International Conference on Theory and Practice of Electronic Governance. New York: ACM.

Boudreau, K. (2010). Open platform strategies and innovation: Granting access vs. devolving control. *Management Science*, 56(10), 1849–1872.

Bourgoin, J., Castella, J-C., Pullar, D., Lestrelin, G., & Bouahoun, B. (2012). Toward a land zoning negotiation support platform: "Tips and tricks" for participatory land use planning in Laos. *Landscape and Urban Planning*, 104(2), 270–278.

Bourgon, J. (2009). New directions in public administration: Serving beyond the predictable. *Public Policy and Administration*, 24(3), 309–330.

Bovaird, T. (2007). Beyond engagement and participation: User and community co-production of public services. *Public Administration Review*, 67(5), 846–860.

Bovaird, T. & Loeffler, E. (2012). From engagement to coproduction: The contributions of users and communities to outcomes and public value. *Voluntas*, 23(4), 1119–1138.

Bovens, M. (2007a). New forms of accountability and EU governance. *Comparative European Politics*, 5(1), 104–120.

Bovens, M. (2007b). Analysing and assessing accountability: A conceptual framework. *European Law Journal*, 13(4), 447–468.

Bovens, M., Goodin, R. E., & Schillemans, T. (2014). *The Oxford Handbook of Public Accountability*. Oxford: Oxford University Press.

Bovens, M. & Schillemans, T. (2014). Meaningful accountability. In M. Bovens, R. E. Goodin and T. Schillemans, eds., *The Oxford Handbook of Public Accountability*. Oxford: Oxford University Press, pp. 673–682.

Bowen, S., McSeveny, K., Lockley, E., Wolstenholme, D., Cobb, M., & Dearden, A. (2013). How was it for you? Experiences of participatory design in the UK health service. *CoDesign*, 9(4), 230–246.

Bowler, S. & Glazer, A. (2008). *Direct Democracy's Impact on American Political Institutions*. New York: Palgrave Macmillan.

Boyle, D. & Harris, M. (2009). *The Challenge of Co-production: How Equal Partnership between Professionals and the Public Can Lead to Improved Public Services*. London: NESTA.

Boyne, G. A. & Walker, R. M. (2004). Strategy content and public service organizations. *Journal of Public Administration Research and Theory*, 14(2), 231–252.

Brabham, D. C. (2013). *Crowdsourcing*. Cambridge: MIT Press.

Braithwaite, J. (2006). 'Accountability and Responsibility through Restorative Justice', in M. Dowdle (ed.), *Public Accountability: Designs, Dilemmas and Experiences*. Cambridge: Cambridge University Press, 33–51.

Brandsen, T. & Helderman, J. K. (2012). The trade-off between capital and community: The conditions for successful co-production in housing. *VOLUNTAS: International Journal of Voluntary and Nonprofit Organizations*, 23(4), 1139–1155.

Brandsen, T. & Honingh, M. (2016). Distinguishing different types of co-production: A conceptual analysis based on the classical definitions. *Public Administration Review*, 76(3), 427–435.

Brandsen, T. & Pestoff, V. (2006). Co-production, the third sector and the delivery of public services: An introduction. *Public Management Review*, 8(4), 493–501.

Brandsen, T., Steen, T., & Verschuere, B. (2018a). *Co-Production and Co-Creation: Engaging Citizens in Public Services*. New York: Routledge.

Brandsen, T., Steen, T., & Verschuere, B. (2018b). How to encourage co-creation and co-production: Some recommendations. In T. Brandsen, B. Verschuere, & T. Steen, eds., *Co-Production and Co-Creation: Engaging Citizens in Public Services*. New York: Routledge, pp. 299–302.

Bressers, N. (2014). The impact of collaboration on innovative projects: A study of Dutch water management. In C. Ansell & J. Torfing, eds., *Public Innovation through Collaboration and Design*. London: Routledge, pp. 89–105.

Briggs, X. D. S. (2008). *Democracy as Problem-Solving: Civic Capacity in Communities across the Globe*. Cambridge: MIT Press.

Brink, E. & Wamsler, C. (2018). Collaborative governance for climate change adaptation: Mapping citizen–municipality interactions. *Environmental Policy and Governance*, 28(2), 82–97.

Brogaard, L., Sørensen, E., & Torfing, J., (2019). The impact of governance on the outcomes of contracting out. *Journal of Strategic Contracting and Negotiation*, 3(4), 215–233.

Brown, T. (2008). Design thinking. *Harvard Business Review*, 86(6), 84.

Brown, T. L., Potoski, M., & Slyke, D. M. (2006). Managing public service contracts: Aligning values, institutions, and markets. *Public Administration Review*, 66(3), 323–331.

Brudney, J. L. (1990a). Expanding the government-by-proxy construct: Volunteers in the delivery of public services. *Nonprofit and Voluntary Sector Quarterly*, 19(4), 315–328.

Brudney, J. L. (1990b). The availability of volunteers: Implications for local governments. *Administration and Society*, 21(4), 413–424.

Brudney, J. L. (1984). Local co-production of services and the analysis of municipal productivity. *Urban Affairs Review*, 19(4), 465–484.

Brudney, J. L. (1999). The effective use of volunteers: Best practices for the public sector. *Law and Contemporary Problems*, 62(4), 219-255.

Brudney, J. L. & England, R. E. (1983). Toward a definition of the co-production concept. *Public Administration Review*, 43(1): 59–65.

Bryson, J. (2018). *Strategic Planning for Public and Nonprofit Organisations: A Guide to Strengthening and Sustaining Organizational Achievement*. Hoboken: John Wiley and Sons.

Bryson, J. (2011). *Strategic Planning for Public and Nonprofit Organizations: A Guide to Strengthening and Sustaining Organizational Achievement*, 4th edn, San Francisco: Jossey-Bass.

Bryson, J. (2004.) What to do when stakeholders matter: Stakeholder identification and analysis techniques. *Public Management Review*, 6 (1), 21–53.

Bryson, J. (1988). Strategic planning: Big wins and small wins. *Public Money and Management*, 8(3), 11–15.

Bryson, J. M. & Crosby, B. C. (1993). Policy planning and the design and use of forums, arenas, and courts. *Environment and Planning B: Planning and Design*, 20(2), 175–194.

Bryson, J. M., Crosby, B. C., & Bloomberg, L (2014). Public value governance: Moving beyond traditional public administration and the new public management. *Public Administration Review*, 74(4), 445–456.

Bryson, J. M., Cunningham, G. L., & Lykkesmoe, K. J. (2002). What to do when stakeholders matter? The case of problem formulation for the African American Men Project of Hennepin County, Minnesota. *Public Administration Review*, 62(5), 568–584.

Bryson, J. M., Patton, M. Q., & Bowman, R. A. (2011). Working with evaluation stakeholders: A rationale, step-wise approach, and toolkit. *Evaluation and Program Planning*, 34, 1–12.

Bryson, J., Sancino, A., Benington, J., & Sørensen, E. (2017). Towards a multi-actor theory of public value co-creation. *Public Management Review*, 19(5), 640–654.

Buuren, A., Meerkerk, I., & Tortajada, C. (2019). Understanding emergent participation practices in water governance. *International Journal of Water Resources Development*, 35(3), 367–382.

Bushe, G. R. & Paranjpey, N. (2015). Comparing the generativity of problem solving and appreciative inquiry: A field experiment. *The Journal of Applied Behavioral Science*, 51(3), 309–35.

Campos-Matos, I., Chrysou, M., & Ashton, C. (2017). Co-creation of local smoking cessation services: An innovative public health intervention in times of austerity. *The Lancet*, 390, S31.

Canovan, M. (1999). Trust the people! Populism and the two faces of democracy. *Political Studies*, 47(1), 2–16.

Castiglione, D., Deth, J. W. V., & Wolleb, G. (2008). *The Handbook of Social Capital*. Oxford: Oxford University Press.

Cawson, A. (1985). *Organized Interests and the State: Studies in Meso-Corporatism*. London: Sage Publications.

Cepiku, D. & Giordano, F. (2014). Co-production in developing countries: Insights from the community health workers experience. *Public Management Review*, 16(3), 317–340.

Christensen, H. E. & McQuestin, D. (2019). Community engagement in Australian local governments: A closer look and strategic implications. *Local Government Studies*, 45(4), 453–480.

Clark, B. Y, Brudney, J. L., & Jang, S. G. (2013). Coproduction of government services and the new information technology: Investigating the distributional biases. *Public Administration Review*, 73(5), 687–701.

Clarke, N., Jennings, W., Moss, J., & Stoker, G. (2018). *The Good Politician: Folk Theories, Political Interaction, and the Rise of Anti-Politics*. Cambridge: Cambridge University Press.

Cockburn, C. (2007). *From Where We Stand: War, Women's Activism and Feminist Analysis*. London: Zed Books.

Cohen, J. (2007). Deliberative democracy. In S. W. Rosenberg, ed., *Deliberation, Participation and Democracy*. Basingstoke: Palgave Macmillan, pp. 219–236.

Compton, M. & 't Hart, P., eds., (2019). Great Policy Successes. Oxford University Press.

Conrad, E. (2015). Bridging the hierarchical and collaborative divide: The role of network managers in scaling up a network approach to water governance in California. *Policy & Politics*, 43(3), 349–366.

Considine, M. (2013). Governance networks and the question of transformation. *Public Administration*, 91(2), 438–447.

Corballis, M. C. (1992). On the evolution of language and generativity. *Cognition*, 44(3), 197–226.

Cornwall, A. & Coelho, V. S. (2007). *Spaces for Change? The Politics of Citizen Participation in New Democratic Arenas*. London: Zed Books.

Cottam, H. & Leadbeater, C. (2004). *Health: Co-Creating Services*. London: Design Council.

Coursey, D., Pandey, S. K., & Yang, K. (2012). Public service motivation (PSM) and support for citizen participation: A test of Perry and

Vandenabeele's reformulation of PSM Theory. *Public Administration Review*, 72(4), 572–582.

Crawford, M. J., Rutter, D., & Thelwall, S. (2004). *Service User Involvement in Change Management: A Literature Review*. London: National Coordinating Centre for Service Delivery and Organisation.

Crosby, B. & Bryson, J. M. (2005). *Leadership for the Common Good*. San Francisco: Jossey-Bass.

Crosby, B. C. & Bryson, J. M. (2010). Integrative leadership and the creation and maintenance of cross-sector collaborations. *The Leadership Quarterly*, 21(2), 211–230.

Crosby, B. C., 't Hart, P., & Torfing, J. (2017). Public value creation through collaborative innovation. *Public Management Review*, 19(5), 655–669.

Crozier, M., Huntington, S., & Watanuki, J. (1975). *The Crisis of Democracy*. New York: New York University Press.

Cruz-Coke, M. L. (2001). Between stability and crisis in Latin America. *Journal of Democracy*, 12(1), 137–145.

Cullen, B., Tucker, J., Snyder, K., Lema, Z., & Duncan, A. (2014). An analysis of power dynamics within innovation platforms for natural resource management. *Innovation and Development*, 4(2), 259–275.

Cuoto, R. A. (2014). Civic leadership. In R. A. W. Rhodes & P. 't Hart, eds., *The Oxford Handbook of Political Leadership*. Oxford: Oxford University Press, pp. 347–361.

Dahl, R. A. (1989). *Democracy and Its Critics*. New Haven: Yale University Press.

Dahl, D. W. & Moreau, C. P. (2007). Thinking inside the box: Why consumers enjoy constrained creative experiences. *Journal of Marketing Research*, 44(3), 357–369.

Dalton, R. J. (2007). Partisan mobilization, cognitive mobilization and the changing American electorate. *Electoral Studies*, 26(2), 274–286.

Dalton, R. J. (2004). *Democratic Challenges: Democratic Choices*. Oxford: Oxford University Press.

Dalton, R. J. (2002). The decline of party identifications. In R. J. Dalton & M. P. Wattenberg, eds., *Parties Without Partisans: Political Change in Advanced Industrial Democracies*. Oxford: Oxford University Press, pp. 19–36.

Dalton, R. J. (1999). Political trust in advanced democracies. In P. Norris, ed., *Critical Citizens: Global Support for Democratic Government*. Oxford: Oxford University Press, pp. 57–77.

Dalton, R. J. & Welzel, C. (2014). *The Civic Culture Transformed: From Allegiant to Assertive Citizens*. New York: Cambridge University Press.

Damgaard, B. & Lewis, J. M. (2014). Accountability and citizen participation. In M. Bovens, R. E. Goodin, & T. Schillemans, eds.,

The Oxford Handbook of Public Accountability. Oxford: Oxford University Press, pp. 258–272.

Davies, J. S. (2011). *Challenging Governance Theory: From Networks to Hegemony*. Bristol: The Policy Press.

Davis, A. & Andrew, J. (2017). Co-creating urban environments to engage citizens in a low-carbon future. *Procedia Engineering*, 180, 651–657.

De Winter, M. (2018). Implementing an integrated care system for chronic patients in Belgium: A co-creation process. *International Journal of Integrated Care*, 18(S2): 202.

Degnegaard, R. (2014) Co-creation, prevailing streams and a future design trajectory. *CoDesign: International Journal of CoCreation in Design and Arts*, 10(2), 96–111.

Degnegaard, R., Degnegaard, S., & Coughlan, P. (2015). How to design for large-scale multi-stakeholder co-creation initiatives: Reframing crime prevention challenges with the police in Denmark. *Journal of Design, Business & Society*, 1(1), 7–28.

Della Porta, D. (2013). *Can Democracy Be Saved? Participation, Deliberation and Social Movements*. Cambridge: Polity Press.

Delwit, P. (2011). Still in decline? Party membership in Europe. In E. Haute, ed., *Party Membership in Europe: Exploration into the Anthills of Party Politics*. Bruxelles: Editions de l'Université de Bruxelles, pp. 25–42.

Denis, J. L., Hébert, Y., Langley, A., Lozeau, D., & Trottier, L. H. (2002). Explaining diffusion patterns for complex health care innovations. *Health Care Management Review*, 27(3), 60–73.

Desouza, K. C. & Bhagwatwar, A. (2014). Technology-enabled participatory platforms for civic engagement: The case of US cities. *Journal of Urban Technology*, 21(4), 25–50.

Dobbin, F., Simmons, B., & Garrett, G. (2007). The global diffusion of public policies: Social construction, coercion, competition, or learning? *Annual Review of Sociology*, 33, 449–472.

Dobre, C. C., Ranzato, M., & Moretto, L. (2019). Citizen involvement in co-producing decentralised stormwater systems in Brussels. *CoDesign*, https://doi.org/10.1080/15710882.2019.1631356

Doig, J. W. & Hargrove, E. C. (1990). *Leadership and Innovation: Entrepreneurs in Government*. Baltimore: Johns Hopkins University Press.

Donetto, S., Pierri, P., Tsianakas, V., & Robert, G. (2015). Experience-based co-design and healthcare improvement: Realizing participatory design in the public sector. *The Design Journal*, 18(2), 227–248.

Dorf, M. C. & Sabel, C. F. (1998). A constitution of democratic experimentalism. *Columbia Law Review*, 98(2), 267–473.

Downs, A. (1967). *Inside Bureaucracy*. Boston: Little Brown.

Dreyfus, H. L. & Dreyfus, S. E. (1986). *Mind over Machine: The Power of Human Intuition and Expertise in the Era of the Computer*. New York: The Free Press.

Dryzek, J. S. (2000). On the prospects for democratic deliberation: Values analysis applied to Australian politics. *Political Psychology*, 21(2), 241–266.

Dryzek, J. S. (1994). *Discursive Democracy: Politics, Policy and Political Science*. Cambridge: Cambridge University Press.

Du Gay, P. (2000). *In Praise of Bureaucracy: Weber – Organization – Ethics*. London: Sage Publications.

Dunleavy, P. & Hood, C. (1994). From old public administration to New Public Management. *Public Money and Management*, 14(3), 9–16.

Dunleavy, P., Margetts, H., Bastow, S., & Tinkler, J. (2006). New Public Management is dead – long live digital-era governance. *Journal of Public Administration Research and Theory*, 16(3), 467–494.

Dunston, R., Lee, A., Boud, D., Brodie, P., & Chiarella, M. (2009). Co-production and health system reform: From re-imagining to re-making. *Australian Journal of Public Administration*, 68(1), 39–52.

Dzur, A. W. & Hendriks, C. M. (2018). Thick populism: Democracy-enhancing popular participation. *Policy Studies*, 39(3), 334–351.

Echeverri, P. & Skålén, P. (2011). Co-creation and co-destruction: A practice-theory based study of interactive value formation. *Marketing Theory*, 11(3), 351–373.

Eck, A. & Uebernickel, F. (2016). Untangling generativity: Two perspectives on unanticipated change produced by diverse actors. *24th European Conference on Information Systems (ECIS)*. www.researchgate.net/pro file/Alexander_Eck/publication/301295204_Untangling_Generativity_ Two_Perspectives_on_Unanticipated_Change_Produced_by_Diverse_ Actors/links/5751400108ae10d9336ec215.pdf

Eden, C. & Ackermann, F. (1998). *Making Strategy: The Journey of Strategic Management*. Thousand Oaks: Sage Publications.

Edenbolos, J., Buuren, A., & Schie, N. (2011). Co-producing knowledge: Joint knowledge production between experts, bureaucrats and stakeholders in Dutch water management projects. *Environmental Science and Policy*, 14(6), 675–684.

Edmondson, A. (1999). Psychological safety and learning behavior in work teams. *Administrative Science Quarterly*, 44(2), 350–383.

Eggers, W. D. (2016). *Delivering on Digital: The Innovators and Technologies that are Transforming Government*. New York: Rosetta Books.

Eijk, C. & Steen, T. (2014). Why people co-produce: Analysing citizens' perceptions on co-planning engagement in health care services. *Public Management Review*, 16(3), 358–382.

Eijk, C. & Steen, T. (2016). Why engage in co-production of public services? Mixing theory and empirical evidence. *International Review of Administrative Sciences*, 82(1), 28–46.

Eijk, C., Steen, T. & Verschuere, B. (2017). Co-producing safety in the local community: A q-methodology study on the incentives of Belgian and Dutch members of neighbourhood watch schemes. *Local Government Studies*, 43(3), 323–343.

Emerson, K., Nabatchi, T., & Balogh, S. (2012). An integrative framework for collaborative governance. *Journal of Public Administration Research and Theory*, 22(1), 1–29.

Engeström, Y. (1987). *Learning by Expanding*. Cambridge: Cambridge University Press.

Engeström, Y. (2008). *From Teams to Knots: Activity-theoretical Studies of Collaboration and Learning at Work*. Cambridge: Cambridge University Press.

Erikson, E. H. (1950). *Childhood and Society*. New York: Norton.

Etzioni-Halevy, E. (1993). *The Elite Connection: Problems and Potential of Western Democracy*. Cambridge: Polity Press.

Evans, R. (1996). *The Human Side of School Change: Reform, Resistance, and the Real-Life Problems of Innovation*. San Francisco: Jossey-Bass.

Fanjoy, M. & Bragg, B. (2019). Embracing complexity: Co-creation with retired immigrant women. *Gateways: International Journal of Community Research and Engagement*, 12(1), 1–16.

Faraj, S., Jarvenpaa, S. L., & Majchrzak, A. (2011). Knowledge collaboration in online communities. *Organization Science*, 22(5), 1224–1239.

Farr, M. (2016). Co-production and value co-creation in outcome-based contracting in public services. *Public Management Review*, 18(5), 654–672.

Fawcett, P., Flinders, M., Hay, C., & Wood, M. (2017). *Anti-Politics, Depoliticization and Governance*. Oxford: Oxford University Press.

Fenwick, J. & McMillan, J. (2013). Management development and co-production: Myths and realities. *Journal of Management Development*, 32(9), 971–983.

Ferlie, E. & Ongaro, E. (2015). *Strategic Management in Public Services Organizations: Concepts, Schools and Contemporary Issues*. Abingdon: Routledge.

Fernandez, S. & Rainey, H. G. (2006). Managing successful organizational change in the public sector. *Public Administration Review*, 66(2), 168–176.

Fisher, J. C. & Cole, K. M. (1993). *Leadership and Management of Volunteer Programs: A Guide for Volunteer Administrators*. San Francisco: Jossey Bass.

Fischer, G., Giaccardi, E., Eden, H., Sugimoto, M., & Ye, Y. (2005). Beyond binary choices: Integrating individual and social creativity. *International Journal of Human-Computer Studies*, 63(4–5), 482–512.

Fitzgerald, J. & Lenhart, J. (2016). Eco-districts: Can they accelerate urban climate planning? *Environment and Planning C: Government and Policy*, 34(2), 364–380.

Fledderus, J., Brandsen, T., & Honingh, M. (2014). Restoring trust through the co-production of public services: A theoretical elaboration. *Public Management Review*, 16(3), 424–443.

Fleischmann, K., Hielscher, S., & Merritt, T. (2016). Making things in fab labs: A case study on sustainability and co-creation. *Digital Creativity*, 27(2), 113–131.

Fleming, L., Mingo, S. & Chen, D. (2007). Collaborative brokerage, generative creativity, and creative success. *Administrative Science Quarterly*, 52(3), 443–475.

Flinders, M. (2018). The (anti-)politics of Brexit. In P. Diamond, P. Nedergaard, B. Rosamond & C. Lequesne, eds., *The Routledge Handbook of the Politics of Brexit*. London: Routledge, pp. 179–193.

Flinders, M. (2012). *Defending Politics: Why Democracy Matters in the 21st Century*. Oxford: Oxford University Press.

Flood, J., Minkler, M., Hennessey Lavery, S., Estrada, J., & Falbe, J. (2015). The collective impact model and its potential for health promotion: Overview and case study of a healthy retail initiative in San Francisco. *Health Education & Behavior*, 42(5), 654–668.

Floridia, A. (2017). *From Participation to Deliberation: A Critical Genealogy of Deliberative Democracy*. Colchester: ECPR Press.

Foerderer, J., Kude, T., Schütz, S., & Heinzl, A. (2014). Control versus generativity: A complex adaptive systems perspective on platforms. *35th International Conference on Information Systems*. https://aisel.aisnet.org/icis2014/proceedings/ServiceScience/4/

Fox, J. A. (2015). Social accountability: What does the evidence really say? *World Development*, 72, 346–361.

Frantzeskaki, N. & Rok, A. (2018). Co-producing urban sustainability transitions knowledge with community, policy and science. *Environmental Innovation and Societal Transitions*, 29, 47–51.

Franz, Y., Tausz, K., & Thiel, S. K. (2015). Contextuality and co-creation matter: A qualitative case study comparison of living lab concepts in urban research. *Technology Innovation Management Review*, 5(12), 48–55.

Fung, A. (2009). *Empowered Participation: Reinventing Urban Democracy.* Princeton: Princeton University Press.

Fung, A. (2004). *Empowered Participation: Reinventing Urban Democracy.* Princeton: Princeton University Press.

Fung, A. & Wright, E. O. (2003). *Deepening Democracy: Institutional Innovations in Empowered Participatory Governance.* London: Verso.

Galuszka, J. (2019). Co-production as a driver of urban governance transformation? The case of the Oplan LIKAS Programme in metro Manila, Philippines. *Planning Theory & Practice*, 20(3), 395–419.

Gascó, M. (2017). Living labs: Implementing open innovation in the public sector. *Government Information Quarterly*, 34(1), 90–98.

Gascó, M. & Eijk, C. (2018). Case study – the Spanish Project Pla BUITS. In T. Brandsen, B. Verschuere & T. Steen, eds., *Co-Production and Co-Creation: Engaging Citizens in Public Services.* New York: Routledge, pp. 77–79.

Gawłowski, R. (2018). Co-production of public services in terms of the Polish experience. *Polish Political Science Yearbook*, 47(1), 110–120.

Gebauer, H., Johnson, M., & Enquist, B. (2010). Value co-creation as a determinant of success in public transport services: A study of the Swiss federal railway operator (SBB). *Managing Service Quality: An International Journal*, 20(6), 511–530.

Genitsaris, E., Roukouni, A., Stamelou, A., Nalmpantis, D., & Naniopoulos, A. (2017). *Co-Creating Innovative Concepts to Address Crucial Trends and Challenges that Public Transport Faces in Thessaloniki.* University–Industry Links: Coproducing Knowledge, Innovation & Growth.

Gergen, K. J. (1978). Toward generative theory. *Journal of Personality and Social Psychology*, 36(11), 1344.

Giddens, A. (1994). *Beyond Left and Right: The Future of Radical Politics.* Cambridge: Polity Press.

Gloor, P. A. (2006). *Swarm Creativity: Competitive Advantage through Collaborative Innovation Networks.* Oxford: Oxford University Press.

Goldman, S. 2003. Assessing the Senate judicial confirmation process: The index of obstruction and delay. *Judicature*, 86, 251–258.

Goldsmith, S. & Eggers, W. D. (2004). *Governing by Network: The New Shape of the Public Sector.* Washington D.C.: Brookings Institution Press.

Goodin, R. E. (1995). *The Theory of Institutional Design.* Cambridge: Cambridge University Press.

Gouillart, F. & Billings, D. (2013). Community-powered problem solving. *Harvard Business Review*, 91(4), 70–77.

Gouillart, F. & Hallett, T. (2015). Co-creation in government. *Stanford Social Innovation Review*, 13(2), 40–47.

Graaf, S. (2018). Participation and platformization at play. In *ComMODify Dynamics of Virtual Work*. Cham: Palgrave Macmillan.

Granovetter, M. S. (1973). The strength of weak ties. *American Journal of Sociology*, 78(6), 1360–1380.

Graversgaard, M., Hedelin, B., Smith, L., Gertz, F., Højberg, A., Langford, J., Martinez, G., Mostert, E., Ptak, E., Peterson, H., Stelljes, N., Brink, C., & Refsgaard, J. C. (2018). Opportunities and barriers for water co-governance: A critical analysis of seven cases of diffuse water pollution from agriculture in Europe, Australia and North America. *Sustainability*, 10(5), 1634.

Gray, B. (1989). *Collaborating: Finding Common Ground for Multiparty Problems*. San Francisco: Jossey-Bass.

Gray, B. & Ren, H. (2014). The importance of joint schemas and brokers in promoting collaboration for innovation. In C. Ansell & J. Torfing, eds., *Public Innovation through Collaboration and Design*. London: Routledge, pp. 125–147.

Greenfield, E. A. & Marks, N. F. (2004). Formal volunteering as a protective factor for older adults' psychological well-being. *The Journals of Gerontology*, 59(5), 258–264.

Greenhalgh, T., Jackson, C., Shaw, S., & Janamian, T. (2016). Achieving research impact through co-creation in community-based health services: Literature review and case study. *The Milbank Quarterly*, 94 (2), 392–429.

Greenhalgh, T., Robert, G., Macfarlane, F., Bate, P., & Kyriakidou, O. (2004). Diffusion of innovations in service organizations: Systematic review and recommendations. *The Milbank Quarterly*, 82(4), 581–629.

Gronn, P. (2002). Distributed leadership as a unit of analysis. *The Leadership Quarterly*, 13(4), 423–451.

Grönroos, C. (2011). Value co-creation in service logic: A critical analysis. *Marketing Theory*, 11(3), 279–301.

Gutmann, A. & Thompson, D. F. (2009). *Why Deliberative Democracy?* Princeton: Princeton University Press.

Habermas, J. (1985). Civil disobedience: Litmus test for the democratic constitutional state. *Berkeley Journal of Sociology*, 30, 95–116.

Hajer, M. A. (2009). *Authoritative Governance: Policy Making in the Age of Mediatization*. Oxford: Oxford University Press.

Halmos, A., Misuraca, G., & Viscusi, G. (2019). From public value to social value of digital government: Co-creation and social innovation in European Union initiatives. *52nd Hawaii International Conference on System Sciences*, 2974–2983.

Hambleton, R. (2019). The new civic leadership: Place and the co-creation of public innovation. *Public Money & Management*, 39(4), 271–279.

Handberg, C., Mygind, O., & Johansen, J. S. (2018). Lessons learnt on the meaning of involvement and co-creation in developing community-based rehabilitation. *Disability and Rehabilitation*, 42(25), 3052–3060.

Hardyman, W., Daunt, K. L., & Kitchener, M. (2015). Value co-creation through patient engagement in health care: A micro-level approach and research agenda. *Public Management Review*, 17(1), 90–107.

Hargadon, A. B. & Bechky, B. A. (2006). When collections of creatives become creative collectives: A field study of problem solving at work. *Organization Science*, 17(4), 417–526.

Harkin, D. (2018). Community safety partnerships: The limits and possibilities of policing with the community. *Crime Prevention and Community Safety*, 20(2), 125–136.

Hartley, J. (2006). *Innovation and Its Contribution to Improvement: A Review for Policymakers, Policy Advisers, Managers and Researchers*. London: Department for Communities and Local Government.

Hartley, J., Alford, J., Hughes, O., & Yates, S. (2015). Public value and political astuteness in the work of public managers: The art of the possible. *Public Administration*, 93(1), 195–211.

Hartley, J. & Benington, J. (2006). Copy and paste, or graft and transplant? Knowledge sharing through inter-organizational networks. *Public Money and Management*, 26(2), 101–108.

Hartley, J., Sørensen, E., & Torfing, J. (2013). Collaborative innovation: A viable alternative to market competition and organizational entrepreneurship. *Public Administration Review*, 73(6), 821–830.

Hayes, A. F., Scheufele, D. A., & Huge, M. E. (2006). Nonparticipation as self-censorship: Publicly observable political activity in a polarized opinion climate. *Political Behavior*, 28(3), 259–283.

Head, B. W. & Alford, J. (2015). Wicked problems: Implications for public policy and management. *Administration and Society*, 47(6), 711–739.

Heclo, H. (1978). Issue networks and the executive establishment. *Public Administration Concepts Cases*, 413(413), 46–57.

Heerik, R. A., Hooijdonk, C. M., Burgers, C., & Steen, G. J. (2017). Smoking is sóóó. . .Sandals and white socks: Co-creation of a Dutch anti-smoking campaign to change social norms. *Health Communication*, 32(5), 621–628.

Heifetz, R., Grashow, A., & Linsky, M. (2009). *The Practice of Adaptive Leadership: Tools and Tactics for Changing your Organization and the World*. Boston: Harvard Business Review Press.

Hendriks, C. M. (2016). Coupling citizens and elites in deliberative systems: The role of institutional design. *European Journal of Political Research*, 55(1), 43–60.

Henfridsson, O. & Bygstad, B. (2013). The generative mechanisms of digital infrastructure evolution. *MIS Quarterly*, 37(3), 907–931.

Hermansson, H. M. L. (2017). Disaster management collaboration in Turkey: Assessing progress and challenges of hybrid network governance. *Public Administration*, 94(2), 333–349.

Hertting, N. (2007). Mechanisms of governance network formation: A contextual rational choice perspective. In E. Sørensen & J. Torfing, eds., *Theories of Democratic Network Governance*. Basingstoke: Palgrave Macmillan, pp. 43–60.

Heying, C. (1997). Civic elites and corporate delocalization: An alternative explanation for declining civic engagement. *American Behavioral Scientist*, 40(5), 657–668.

Hibbing, J. R. & Theiss-Morse, E. (2002). *Stealth Democracy: Americans' Beliefs About How Government Should Work*. Cambridge: Cambridge University Press.

Hilgers, D. & Ihl, C. (2010). Citizensourcing: Applying the concept of open innovation to the public sector. *International Journal of Public Participation*, 4(1), 68–88.

Hines, F. (2005). Viable social enterprise: An evaluation of business support to social enterprises. *Social Enterprise Journal*, 1(1), 13–28.

Hirst, P. (1994). *Associative Democracy: New Forms of Economic and Social Governance*. Hoboken: John Wiley & Sons.

Hirst, P. (2000). Democracy and governance. In J. Pierre, ed., *Debating Governance: Authority, Steering, and Democracy*. Oxford: Oxford University Press, pp. 13–35.

Hjelmar, U., Petersen, O. H., & Vrangbæk, K. (2013). Udlicitering af offentlige opgaver i Danmark-en forskningsoversigt over de hidtil dokumenterede effekter. *Politica*, 45(1), 60–79.

Hofstad, H. & Torfing, J. (2017). Towards a climate-resilient city: Collaborative innovation for a 'green shift' in Oslo. In R. Á. Fernández, S. Zubelzu & R. Martínez eds., *Carbon Footprint and the Industrial Life Cycle*, New York: Springer, 221–242.

Homsy, G. C. & Warner, M. E. (2013). Climate change and the co-production of knowledge and policy in rural USA communities. *Sociologia Ruralis*, 53(3), 291–310.

Hood, C. (1991). A public management for all seasons? *Public Administration*, 69(1), 3–19.

Hood, C. & Dixon, R. (2015). *A Government that Worked Better and Costed Less? Evaluating Three Decades of Reform and Change in UK Central Government*. Oxford: Oxford University Press.

Hooghe, L. & Marks, G. (2001). *Multi-Level Governance and European Integration*. Lanham: Rowman.

Hopkins, M. M., Tidd, J., & Nightingale, P. (2014). Positive and negative dynamics of open innovation. In J. Tidd, ed, *Open Innovation Research, Management and Practice*. London: Imperial College Press, pp. 417–443.

Horsbøl, A. (2018). Co-creating green transition: How municipality employees negotiate their professional identities as agents of citizen involvement in a cross-local setting. *Environmental Communication*, 12(5), 701–714.

House, F. (2018). Democracy in Crisis: Freedom in the World 2018. Washington DC: Freedom House.

Howlett, M. (2009). Policy analytical capacity and evidence-based policy-making: Lessons from Canada. *Canadian Public Administration*, 52(2), 153–175.

Huang, W. L. & Feeney, M. K. (2016). Citizen participation in local government decision making: The role of manager motivation. *Review of Public Personnel Administration*, 36(2), 188–209.

Huxham, C. & Vangen, S. (2013). *Managing to Collaborate. The Theory and Practice of Collaborative Advantage*. Abingdon: Routledge.

Huxham, C. & Vangen, S. (2003). Nurturing collaborative relations: Building trust in interorganizational collaboration. *The Journal of Applied Behavioral Science*, 39(1), 5–31.

Huxham, C. & Vangen, S. (1996a). Working together. *International Journal of Public Sector Management*, 9(7), 5–17.

Huxham, C. & Vangen, S. (1996b). Managing inter-organisational relationships. In S. P. Osborne, ed., *Managing in the Voluntary Sector: A Handbook for Managers in Voluntary and Non-Profit Making Organizations*. London: International Thompson Business Press, pp. 202–216.

Ibbotson, P. (2008). *The Illusion of Leadership: Directing Creativity in Business and the Arts*. Basingstoke: Palgrave Macmillan

IDEA (2016). *Voter Turnout Database*. Retrieved 5/12 2019 at: www .idea.int/data-tools/data/voter-turnout.

Ind, N. & Coates, N. (2013). The meanings of co-creation. *European Business Review*, 25(1), 86–95.

Ishkanian, A. & Szreter, S. (2012). *The Big Society Debate: A New Agenda for Social Policy?* Cheltenham: Edward Elgar.

Israilov, S. & Cho, H. J. (2017). How co-creation helped address hierarchy, overwhelmed patients, and conflicts of interest in health care quality and safety. *AMA Journal of Ethics*, 19(11), 1139–1145.

Iyengar, S. (2016). Editorial foreword: E pluribus pluribus, or divided we stand. *Public Opinion Quarterly*, 80(S1), 219–224

Iyengar, S., Sood, G., & Lelkes, Y. (2012). Affect, not ideology: A social identity perspective on polarization. *Public Opinion Quarterly*, 76(3), 405–431.

Jæger, B. & Sørensen, E. (2003). *Roller der rykker: Politikere og administratorer mellem hierarki og netværk*. Copenhagen: Djøf Publishing.

Jahdi, K. S. & Acikdilli, G. (2009). Marketing communications and corporate social responsibility (CSR): Marriage of convenience or shotgun wedding? *Journal of Business Ethics*, 88(1), 103–13.

Janssen, M. & Estevez, E. (2013). Lean government and platform-based governance – Doing more with less. *Government Information Quarterly*, 30(1), S1–S8.

Jehn, K. A., Northcraft, G. B., & Neale M. A. (1997). Why differences make a difference: A field study of diversity, conflict and performance in workgroups. *Administrative Science Quarterly*, 44(4), 741–763.

Jensen, U. T., Andersen, L. B., Bro, L. L., Bøllingtoft, A., Eriksen, T. L. M., Holten, A. L., ... & Westergård-Nielsen, N. (2019). Conceptualizing and measuring transformational and transactional leadership. *Administration & Society*, 51(1), 3–33.

Jensen, P. H. & Stonecash, R. E. (2005). Incentives and the efficiency of public sector-outsourcing contracts. *Journal of Economic Surveys*, 19 (5), 767–787.

Jessop, B. (2002). *The Future of the Capitalist State*. Cambridge: Polity Press.

Jetté, C. & Vaillancourt, Y. (2011). Social economy and home care service in Quebec: Co-production or co-construction?. *VOLUNTAS: International Journal of Voluntary and Nonprofit Organisations*, 22(1), 48–69.

Johnson, G., Melin, L., & Whittington, R. (2003). Micro strategy and strategizing: Towards an activity-based view. *Journal of Management Studies*, 40(1), 3–22.

Joshi, A. & Moore, M. (2002). *Organisations that Reach the Poor: Why Co-Production Matters*. Paper presented at the World Bank Symposium on Making Public Services Work for Poor People, Oxford.

Joshi, A. & Moore, M. H. (2004). Institutionalised co-production: Unorthodox public service delivery in challenging environments. *Journal of Development Studies*, 40(4), 31–49.

Kane, J. & Patapan, H. (2012). *The Democratic Leader: How Democracy Defines, Empowers, and Limits its Leaders*. Oxford: Oxford University Press.

Kania, J. & Kramer, M. (2013). Embracing emergence: How collective impact addresses complexity. *Stanford Social Innovation Review*, 1–7, January 21, 2013 (website), https://ssir.org/articles/entry/social_progress_through_collective_impact

Kania, J. & Kramer, M. (2011). Collective impact. *Stanford Social Innovation Review*, 9(1) 36–41.

Katz, R. S. & Mair, P. (1995). Changing models of party organization and party democracy: The emergence of the cartel party. *Party Politics*, 1(1), 5–28.

Keast, R., Brown, K., & Mandell, M. (2007). Getting the right mix: Unpacking integration meanings and strategies. *International Public Management Journal*, 10(1), 9–33.

Kemp, R. & Scholl, C. (2016). City labs as vehicles for innovation in urban planning processes. *Urban Planning*, 1(4), 89–102.

Kench, P. S., Ryan, E. J., Owen, S., Bell, R., Lawrence, J., Glavovic, B., Blackett, P., Becker, J., Schneider, P., Allis, M., Dickson, M., & Rennie, H. G. (2018). Co-creating resilience solutions to coastal hazards through an interdisciplinary research project in New Zealand. *Journal of Coastal Research*, 85(sp1), 1496–1500.

Khayyat, M. M. (2017). *Co-Creation with Open Government Data: A Constructivist Approach Using a Multiple Case Studies Strategy from an Information Systems Perspective*. PhD Thesis. The School of Computer Science and Statistics. Trinity College Dublin.

Kickert, W. J. M., Klijn, E. H., & Koppenjan, J. F. M. (1997). *Managing Complex Networks: Strategies for the Public Sector*. London: Sage Publications.

Kingdon, J. W. (1984). *Agendas, Alternatives, and Public Policies*. Boston: Little Brown.

Kjær, U. & Opstrup, N. (2016). *Variationer i udvalgsstyret*. Copenhagen: Kommuneforlaget.

Kliemt, H. (1990). The costs of organizing social cooperation. In M. Hechter, K. D. Opp & R. Wippler, eds., *Social Institutions*. New York: Aldine de Gruyter, pp. 61–80.

Klijn, E. H. & Koppenjan, J. F. M. (2014). Accountability and networks. In M. Bovens, R. E. Goodin & T. Schillemans, eds., *The Oxford Handbook of Public Accountability*. Oxford: Oxford University Press, pp. 242–257.

Klok, J. (2013). Participatory design and public space: Catalysts for community. Thesis presented to The University of Guelph. Guelph, Canada.

Kohler, T., Fueller, J., Matzler, K., Stieger, D., & Füller, J. (2011). Co-creation in virtual worlds: The design of the user experience. *MIS Quarterly*, 35(3), 773–788.

Koo, Y. & Ahn, H. (2018). Analysis on the utilization of co-design practices for developing consumer-oriented public service and policy focusing on the comparison with Western countries and South Korea. In *ServDes2018. Service Design Proof of Concept, Proceedings of the*

ServDes. 2018 Conference, 18–20 June, Milan, Italy, 150, Linköping University Electronic Press, 281–297.

Kooiman, J. (1993). *Modern Governance: Government-Society Interactions*. London: Sage Publications.

Kooiman, J. (2003). *Governing as Governance*. London: Sage Publications.

Koppenjan, J. & Klijn, E. H. (2004). *Managing Uncertainties in Networks: A Network Approach to Problem Solving and Decision Making*. Abingdon: Routledge.

Kornberger, M. (2017). The visible hand and the crowd: Analyzing organization design in distributed innovation systems. *Strategic Organization*, 15(2), 174–193.

Kouzmin, A., Loffler, E., Klages, H., & Korac-Kakabadse, N. (1999). Benchmarking and performance measurement in public sectors towards learning for agency effectiveness. *The International Journal of Public Sector Management*, 12(2), 121–144.

Laclau, E. (2005). *On Populist Reason*. London: Verso.

Laclau, E. & Mouffe, C. (1985). *Hegemony and Socialist Strategy: Towards a Radical Democratic Politics*. London: Verso.

Laitinen, I., Kinder, T., & Stenvall, J. (2018). Co-design and action learning in local public services. *Journal of Adult and Continuing Education*, 24 (1), 58–80.

Landemore, H. (2019), *Open Democracy: Reinventing Popular Rule for the 21st Century*. Princeton: Princeton University Press.

Landemore, H. (2012). Democratic reason: The mechanisms of collective intelligence in politics. In H. Landemore & J. Elster, eds., *Collective Wisdom: Principles and Mechanisms*. Cambridge: Cambridge University Press, pp. 251–289.

Landi, S. & Russo, S. (2019). Co-production as an interpretative framework in the creation of value in public services. Department of Management, Università Ca'Foscari Venezia Working Paper (1).

Larsson, O. S. & Brandsen, T. (2016). The implicit normative assumptions of social innovation research: Embracing the dark side. In T. Bandsen, S. Cattacin, A. Evers & A. Zimmer, eds., *Social Innovations in the Urban Context: Nonprofit and Civil Society Studies*. Cham: Springer, pp. 293–302.

Lasker, R. D. & Weiss, E. S. (2003). Broadening participation in community problem solving: A multidisciplinary model to support collaborative practice and research. *Journal of Urban Health*, 80(1), 14–47.

Layman, G. C. (1999). Culture wars in the American party system: Religious and cultural change among partisan activists since 1972. *American Politics Research*, 27(1), 89–121.

Layman, G. C., Carsey, T. M., & Horowitz, J. M. (2006). Party polarization in American politics: Characteristics, causes, and consequences. *Annual Review of Political Science*, 9, 83–110.

Leask, C. F., Sandlund, M., Skelton, D. A., & Chastin, S. F. (2017). Co-creating a tailored public health intervention to reduce older adults' sedentary behaviour. *Health Education Journal*, 76(5), 595–608.

Leask, C. F., Sandlund, M., Skelton, D. A., Altenburg, T. M., Cardon, G., Chinapaw, M. J., De Bourdeaudhuij, I., Verloigne, M., & Chastin, S. F. M. (2019). Framework, principles and recommendations for utilising participatory methodologies in the co-creation and evaluation of public health intervention. *Research Involvement and Engagement*, 5(2), 1–16.

Leendertse, W., Langbroek, M., Arts, J., & Nijhuis, A. (2016). Generating spatial quality through co-creation: Experiences from the Blankenburgverbinding (the Netherlands). *Transportation Research Procedia*, 14, 402–411.

Le Grand, J. (2003). From pawn to queen: An economics perspective. In A. Oliver, ed., *Equity in Health and Healthcare: Views from Ethics, Economics and Political Science*. Proceedings from a Meeting of the Health Equity Network. London: The Nuffield Trust, pp. 25–32.

Le Grand, J. (2003). *Motivation, Agency and Public Policy: Of Knights and Knaves, Pawns and Queens*. Oxford: Oxford University Press.

Lehmbruch, G. & Schmitter, P. C., eds. (1979). *Trends toward Corporatist Intermediation*. London: Sage Publications.

Lember, V., Brandsen, T., & Tõnurist, P. (2019). The potential impacts of digital technologies on co-production and co-creation. *Public Management Review*, 21(11), 1665–1686.

Lente, H., Hekkert, M., Smits, R., & Waveren, B. A. S. (2003). Roles of systemic intermediaries in transition processes. *International Journal of Innovation Management*, 7(3), 247–279.

Levine, C. H. & Fisher, G. (1984). Citizenship and service delivery: The promise of coproduction. *Public Administration Review*, 44, 178–189.

Levitsky, S. & Ziblatt, D. (2018). *How Democracies Die*. New York: Broadway Books.

Lewis, M. W. & Smith, W. K. (2014). Paradox as a metatheoretical perspective: Sharpening the focus and widening the scope. *The Journal of Applied Behavioral Science*, 50(2), 127–149.

Lewis, S., Pea, R., & Rosen, J. (2010). Beyond participation to co-creation of meaning: Mobile social media in generative learning communities. *Social Science Information*, 49(3), 351–369.

Leyenaar, M. H. & Niemöller, B. (2010). *European Citizens´ Consultations 2009: Evaluation Report*. Brussel: King Baudouin Foundation.

Lijphart, A. (1984). *Democracies: Patterns of Majoritarian & Consensus Government in Twenty-One Countries*. New Haven: Yale University Press.

Lindblom, C. E. (1965). *The Intelligence of Democracy: Decision Making Through Mutual Adjustment*. New York: Free Press.

Lindgreen, A. & Swaen, V. (2010). Corporate social responsibility. *International Journal of Management Review*, 12(1), 1–7.

Lipsky, M. (1980). *Street Level Bureaucracy: Dilemmas of the Individual in Public Services*. New York: Russell Sage Foundation. Littlefield Publishers.

Loeffler, E. & Bovaird, T. (2018). From participation to co-production: Widening and deepening the contributions of citizens to public services and outcomes. In E. Ongaro & S. Thiel, eds., *The Palgrave Handbook of Public Administration and Management in Europe*. London: Palgrave Macmillan, pp. 403–423.

London, M. & Sessa, V. I. (2007). The development of group interaction patterns: How groups become adaptive, generative, and transformative learners. *Human Resource Development Review*, 6(4), 353–376.

Long, J. C., Cunningham, F. C., & Braithwaite, J. (2013). Bridges, brokers and boundary spanners in collaborative networks: A systematic review. *BMC Health Services Research*, 13(158), 1–13.

Luke, J. S. (1997). *Catalytic Leadership: Strategies for an Interconnected World*. San Francisco: Jossey-Bass.

Lund, D. H. (2018). Co-creation in urban governance: From inclusion to innovation. *Scandinavian Journal of Public Administration*, 22(2), 3–17.

Lutz, C. & Hoffmann, C. P. (2017). The dark side of online participation: Exploring non-, passive and negative participation. *Information, Communication & Society*, 20(6), 876–897.

Lykkebo, O. B., Jakobsen, N., & Sauer, P. (2018). *Innovationsbarometeret: Nyt sammen bedre: En håndbog om innovative samarbejdr i den offentlige sektor*. Copenhagen: Dansk Psykologisk Forlag.

MacPherson, C. B. (1977). *The Life and Times of Liberal Democracy*. Oxford: Oxford University Press.

MacPherson, C. B. (1978). *Property, Mainstream and Critical Positions*. Toronto: University of Toronto Press.

Magno, F. & Cassia, F. (2015). Public administrators' engagement in services co-creation: Factors that foster and hinder organisational learning about citizens. *Total Quality Management & Business Excellence*, 26(11–12), 1161–1172.

Maiello, A., Viegas, C. V., Frey, M., & Ribeiro, J. L. D. (2013). Public managers as catalysts of knowledge co-production? Investigating knowledge dynamics in local environmental policy. *Environmental Science & Policy*, 27, 141–150.

Mair, P. (2013). *Ruling the World: The Hollowing of Western Democracy*. London: Verso.

Manin, B. (1987). On legitimacy and political deliberation. *Political Theory*, 15(3), 338–368.

Mann, T. E. & Ornstein, N. J. (2016). *It's Even Worse Than It Looks: How the American Constitutional System Collided with the New Politics of Extremism*. New York: Basic Books.

Mansbridge, J. J. (1983). *Beyond Adversary Democracy*. Chicago: The University of Chicago Press.

March, J. & Olsen, J. P. (1995). *Democratic Governance*. New York: Free Press.

March, J. G. & Olsen, J. P. (1989). *Rediscovering Institutions: The Organizational Basis of Politics*. New York: Free Press.

Marin, B. & Mayntz, R. (1991). *Policy Networks: Empirical Evidence and Theoretical Considerations*. Boulder: Westview.

Marschall, M. J. (2004). Citizen participation and the neighborhood context: A new look at the co-production of local public goods. *Political Research Quarterly*, 57(2), 231–244.

Marsh, D. (2018). Brexit and the politics of truth. *British Politics*, 13(1), 79–89.

Marsh, D. & Rhodes, R. A. W. (1992). *Policy Networks in British Government*. Oxford: Clarendon Press.

Martens, K. (2005). *NGO's and the United Nations: Institutionalization, Professionalization and Adaption*. Basingstoke: Palgrave Macmillan.

Maru, Y., Sparrow, A., Stirzaker, R. & Davies J. (2018). Integrated agricultural research for development (IAR4D) from a theory of change perspective. *Agricultural Systems* 165: 310–320.

Mayangsari, L. & Novani, S. (2015). Multi-stakeholder co-creation analysis in smart city management: An experience from Bandung, Indonesia. *Procedia Manufacturing*, 4, 315–321.

Mayena, S. B. (2006). The concepts of resilience revisited. *Disasters*, 30(4), 434–450.

May, P. J. (2014). Implementation failures revisited: Policy regime perspectives. *Public Policy and Administration*, 30(3–4), 277–299.

Mayo, E. & Moore, H. (2002). *Building the Mutual State: Findings from the Virtual Thinktank*. London: New Economic Foundation/Mutuo.

McBride, K., Aavik, G., Kalvet, T., & Krimmer, R. (2018). Co-creating an open government data driven public service: The case of Chicago's food inspection forecasting model. *Proceedings of the 51st Hawaii*

International Conference on System Sciences. https://scholarspace
.manoa.hawaii.edu/handle/10125/50197

McBride, K., Toots, M., Kalvet, T., & Krimmer, R. (2019). Turning open government data into public value: Testing the COPS framework for the co-creation of OGD-driven public services. In M. Rodríguez Bolívar, K. Bwalya & C. Reddick, eds., *Governance Models for Creating Public Value in Open Data Initiatives. Public Administration and Information Technology*, vol. 31. Cham: Springer, pp. 3–31.

McEvily, B., Perrone, V., & Zaheer, A. (2003). Trust as an organizing principle. *Organization Science*, 14(1), 91–103.

McGill, M. E., Slocum Jr, J. W., & Lei, D. (1992). Management practices in learning organizations. *Organizational Dynamics*, 21(1), 5–17.

McMullin, C. & Needham, C. (2018). Co-production in healthcare. In T. Brandsen, T. Steen & B. Verschuere, eds., *Co-Production and Co-Creation: Engaging Citizens in Public Services*. New York: Routledge, pp. 151–160.

McMullin, C. (2018). Case study – co-production and community development in France. In T. Brandsen, B. Verschuere & T. Steen, eds., *Co-Production and Co-Creation: Engaging Citizens in Public Services*. New York: Routledge, pp. 208–210.

Meerkerk, I. & Edelenbos, J. (2018). *Boundary Spanners in Public Management and Governance: An Interdisciplinary Assessment.* Cheltenham: Edward Elgar.

Meijer, A. (2012). Co-production in an information age: Individual and community engagement supported by new media. *VOLUNTAS: International Journal of Voluntary and Nonprofit Organizations*, 23(4), 1156–1172.

Meijer, A. J. (2011). Networked co-production of public services in virtual communities: From a government-centric to a community approach to public service support. *Public Administration Review*, 71(4), 598–607.

Meier, K. & Hill, G. (2005). Bureaucracy in the 21st century. In E. Ferlie, L. Lynn Jr. & C. Pollitt, eds., *The Oxford Handbook of Public Management*. Oxford: Oxford University Press, pp. 51–71.

Menny, M., Palgan, Y. V., & McCormick, K. (2018). Urban living labs and the role of users in co-creation. *GAIA-Ecological Perspectives for Science and Society*, 27(1), 68–77.

Mergel, I. (2017). Open innovation in the public sector: Drivers and barriers for the adoption of challenge.gov. *Public Management Review*, 20(5), 726–745.

Merickova, B. M., Nemec, J., & Svidronova, M. (2015). Co-creation in local public services delivery innovation: Slovak experience. *Lex Localis*, 13 (3), 521.

Meuleman, L. (2008). *Public Management and the Metagovernance of Hierarchies, Networks and Markets: The Feasibility of Designing and Managing Governance Style Combinations.* Heidelberg: Physica-Verlag.

Mezirow, J. (1991). *Transformative Dimensions of Adult Learning.* San Francisco: Jossey-Bass.

Mezirow, J. (2000). *Learning as Transformation: Critical Perspectives on a Theory in Progress.* San Francisco: Jossey-Bass.

Mikheeva, O. & Tõnurist, P. (2019). Co-creation for the reduction of uncertainty in financial governance: The case of monetary authority of Singapore. *Halduskultuur*, 19(2), 60–80.

Miller, C. A. & Wyborn, C. (2018). Co-production in global sustainability: Histories and theories. *Environmental Science & Policy*, 1–8, https://doi .org/10.1016/j.envsci.2018.01.016

Mintrom, M. & Norman, P. (2009). Policy entrepreneurship and policy change. *Policy Studies Journal*, 37(4), 649–667.

Mintzberg, H. (1994). The fall and rise of strategic planning. *Harvard Business Review*, 72(1), 107–114.

Mintzberg, H. (1973). Strategy making in three modes. *California Management Review*, 16(2), 44–53.

Mintzberg, H., Ahlstrand, B., Lampel, J. B., & Koch, R. (2009). *Strategy Safari: The Complete Guide Through the Wilds of Strategic Management.* London: Pearson Education.

Mitlin, D. (2008). With and beyond the state: Co-production as a route to political influence, power and transformation for grassroots organizations. *Environment & Urbanization*, 20(2): 339–360.

Moe, T. M. (1984). The new economics of organization. *American Journal of Political Science*, 28(4), 739–777.

Mogstad, A., Høiseth, M., & Pettersen, I. N. (2018). Co-creation in public service innovation: A review of how to encourage employee engagement in co-creation. DS 91: *Proceedings of NordDesign 2018*, Linköping, Sweden, August 14–17, 2018. www.designsociety.org/publication/409 07/Co-creation+in+Public+Service+Innovation%3A+A+review+of+ho w+to+encourage+employee+engagement+in+co-creation

Molen, F., Puente-Rodríguez, D., Swart, J. A., & Windt, H. J. (2015). The co-production of knowledge and policy in coastal governance: Integrating mussel fisheries and nature restoration. *Ocean & Coastal Management*, 106, 49–60.

Moore, M. H. (1995). *Creating Public Value: Strategic Management in Government.* Cambridge: Harvard University Press.

Moore, M. H. (2000). Managing for value: Organizational strategy in for-profit, non-profit, and governmental organizations. *Nonprofit and Voluntary Sector Quarterly*, 29(1), 183–204.

Morales, L. & Giugni, M. (eds.). (2016). *Social Capital, Political Participation and Migration in Europe: Making Multicultural Democracy Work?* Basingstoke: Palgrave Macmillan.

Morgan, D. & Cook, B. (2014). *New Public Governance: A Regime-Centered Perspective.* Abingdon: Routledge.

Morris, P., O'Neill, F., Armitage, A., Lane, R., Symons, J., Dalton, E., Gaines, M., Katz, A., & Reed, J. (2007). Moving from tokenism to co-production: Implications of learning from patient and community voices in developing patient centred professionalism. Conference paper presented at Professional Lifelong Learning: Critical Debates about Professionalism Conference. University of Leeds. https://d1wqtxts1xzle7.cloudfront.net/4 8170935/Moving_from_tokenism_to_co-production_im20160819-1999 8-obgwzp.pdf?1471601982=&response-content-disposition=inline%3B+ filename%3DMoving_from_tokenism_to_co_production_im.pdf&Expir es=1599677177&Signature=G4xEe66Vx6uGm5-2KNhtbXn7arE423W F5N04ya6oB5SYfGNpZkaC~vKna8rkbIzU8bMTwhSphQWE7mZh R39Bo7aaWQ9LxQWPUZGVyAQXkBKwrileATDbJsoBHCoS86w~w FRC8l-rwxSBLGu-FF-XUQPGNd00YAfjTSTeySqdo6WtfKJIrdsIxHE C2p-sRAYQNlHeOrhnqO097fR4yRCYOaSfyRvAc6flxYOo2bYGHh Z-S~Y6lYZb3BUGfRAlyUOgv6CDkWPEDVJ1-4dhyOzXqiFnq3A66cc p5jmCOmc4p5zh6YqkANFDaYPCIdFdtA9zSZvfZVBWLj31XxKCl~x Abg__&Key-Pair-Id=APKAJLOHF5GGSLRBV4ZA

Morse, R. S. (2010). Integrative public leadership: Catalyzing collaboration to create public value. *The Leadership Quarterly*, 21 (2), 231–245.

Mosquera, J. (2018). The power of co-creation in redesigning Valencia's waterfront. *Community, Culture, Economy, Cooperative City.* https:// cooperativecity.org

Moss, T., Medd, W., Guy, S., & Marvin, S. (2009). Organising water: The hidden role of intermediary work. *Water Alternatives*, 2(1), 16–33.

Mouffe, C. (2005). *On the Political.* London: Routledge.

Mouffe, C. (2000). *The Democratic Paradox.* London: Verso.

Mouffe, C. (1993). *The Return of the Political.* London: Verso.

Mouritzen, P. E. & Svara, J. H. (2002). *Leadership at the Apex: Politicians and Administrators in Western Local Governments.* Pittsburgh: University of Pittsburgh Press.

Moynihan D. P. (2008). *The Dynamics of Performance Management: Constructing Information and Reform.* Washington D.C.: Georgetown University Press.

Moynihan, D. P. (2003). Normative and instrumental perspectives on public participation: Citizen summits in Washington D.C. *The American Review of Public Administration*, 33(2), 164–188.

Mudde, C. & Kaltwasser, C. R. (2017). *Populism: A Very Short Introduction*. Oxford: Oxford University Press.

Mudde, C. (2006). Europe's populist surge: A long time in the making. *Foreign Affairs*, 95(6), 25–30.

Mulder, I. (2012). Living labbing the Rotterdam way: Co-creation as an enabler for urban innovation. *Technology Innovation Management Review*, 2(9), 39–43.

Munck, R. (1993). After the transition: Democratic disenchantment in Latin America. *European Review of Latin American and Caribbean Studies*, 55, 7–19.

Munoz, S., Steiner, A., & Farmer, J. (2014). Processes of community-led social enterprise development: Learning from the rural context. *Community Development Journal*, 50(3), 478–493.

Nabatchi, T. & Leighninger, M. (2015). *Public Participation for 21st Century Democracy*. Hoboken: John Wiley and Sons.

Nabatchi, T., Sancino, A., & Sicilia, M. (2017). Varieties of participation in public services: The who, when, and what of co-production. *Public Administration Review*, 77(5), 766–776.

Nag, R., Hambrick, D. C., & Chen, M. (2007). What is strategic management, really? Inductive derivation of a consensus definition of the field. *Strategic Management Journal*, 28(9), 935–955.

Nalmpantis, D., Roukouni, A., Genitsaris, E., Stamelou, A., & Naniopoulos, A. (2019). Evaluation of innovative ideas for public transport proposed by citizens using multi-criteria decision analysis (MCDA). *European Transport Research Review*, 11(1), 22.

Nambisan, S. (2009). Platforms for collaboration. *Stanford Social Innovation Review*, 7(3), 44–49.

Nambisan, S. & Nambisan, P. (2013). *Engaging Citizens in Co-Creation of Public Services: Lessons Learned and Best Practices*. Washington D.C.: The IBM Center for the Business of Government.

Nambisan, S. & Nambisan, P. (2008). How to profit from a better virtual customer environment. *MIT Sloan Management Review*, 49(3), 53–61.

Naurin, D. (2007). *Deliberation Behind Closed Doors: Transparency and Lobbying in the European Union*. Colchester: ECPR Press.

Neblo, M. A., Esterling, K. M., & Lazer, D. M. J. (2018). *Politics with the People: Building a Directly Representative Democracy*. New York: Cambridge University Press.

Nederhand, J. & Meerkerk, I. (2017). Activating citizens in Dutch care reforms: Framing new co-production roles and competences for citizens and professionals. *Policy & Politics*, 46(4), 533–550.

Needham, C. (2008). Realising the potential of co-production: Negotiating improvements in public services. *Social Policy and Society*, 7(2), 221–231.

Nelimarkka, M., Nonnecke, B., Krishnan, S., Aitamurto, T., Catterson, D., Crittenden, C., Garland, C., Gregory, C., Huang, C. C., Newsom, G., Patel, J., Scott, J., & Goldberg, K. (2014). Comparing three online civic engagement platforms using the "spectrum of public participation" framework. In *Proceedings of the Oxford Internet, Policy, and Politics Conference* (IPP) (pp. 25–6).

Nemec, J., Mikušová Meričková, B., & Svidroňová, M. (2016). Social innovations on municipal level in Slovakia. European Commission – 7th Framework Programme, LIPSE or Learning from Innovation in Public Sector Environments. www.muni.cz/en/research/publications/1212675

Network of European Foundations (2017). *Pooling Funds, Pooling Strengths: A Case Study of the European Programme for Integration and Migration*. Brussels: Network of European Foundations.

Neulen, S. (2016). *Co-Creation between Citizens and the Government Influence of Settings on Intention of Citizens to Join Co-Creation*. University of Twente M.A. Thesis.

Newman, J. (2001). *Modernising Governance: New Labour, Policy and Society*. London: Sage Publications.

Nicolini, D., Mengis, J., & Swan, J. (2012). Understanding the role of objects in cross-disciplinary collaboration. *Organization Science*, 23(3), 612–629.

Niitamo, V., Kulkki, S., Eriksson, M., & Hribernik, K. A. (2006). State-of-the-art and good practice in the field of living labs, *2006 IEEE International Technology Management Conference (ICE)*, Milan, 1–8, DOI:10.1109/ICE.2006.7477081.https://ieeexplore.ieee.org/abstract/document/7477081

Niskanen, W. A. (1971). *Bureaucracy & Representative Government*. Chicago: Aldine, Atherton.

Nooteboom, B. (2002). *Trust: Forms, Foundations, Functions, Failures and Figures*. Cheltenham: Edward Elgar.

Norris, P. (2011). *Democratic Deficit: Critical Citizens Revised*. New York: Cambridge University Press.

Norris, P. (1999). *Critical Citizens: Global Support for Democratic Government*. Oxford: Oxford University Press.

Nye, J. S. (2008). *The Powers to Lead*. Oxford: Oxford University Press.

OECD (2017). *Fostering Innovation in the Public Sector*. Paris: OECD Publishing, https://doi.org/10.1787/9789264270879-en.

OECD (2011). *Together for Better Public Services: Partnering with Citizens and Civil Society*, OECD Public Governance Reviews. Paris: OECD Publishing, https://doi.org/10.1787/9789264118843-en.

O'Flynn, J. (2007). From New Public Management to public value: Paradigmatic change and managerial implications. *The Australian Journal of Public Administration*, 66(3), 353–366.

Öberg, P. (2016). Deliberation. In C. Ansell & J. Torfing, eds., *Handbook on Theories of Governance*. Cheltenham: Edward Elgar, pp. 179–187.

Obstfeld, D. (2005). Social networks, the tertius iungens orientation, and involvement in innovation. *Administrative Science Quarterly*, 50(1), 100–130.

Oksman, V., Väätänen, A., & Ylikauppila, M. (2014). Co-creation of sustainable smart cities: Users, participation and service design. In the 8th International Conference on Mobile Ubiquitous Computing, Systems, Services and Technologies, UBICOMM 2014. International Academy, Research, and Industry Association, 189–95. www .thinkmind.org/download.php?articleid=ubicomm_2014_7_20_10039

Osborne, D. & Gaebler, T. (1992). *Reinventing Government*. New York: Penguin Press.

Osborne, S. P. (ed.) (2010), *New Public Governance*, London: Routledge.

Osborne, S. P. (2006). The New Public Governance? *Public Management Review*, 8(3), 377–387.

Osborne, S. P. & Brown, L. (2011). Innovation in public services: Engaging with risk. *Public Money and Management*, 31(1), 4–6.

Osborne, S. P., Radnor, Z., & Strokosch, K. (2016). Co-production and the co-creation of value in public services: A suitable case for treatment? *Public Management Review*, 18(5), 639–653.

Osborne, S. P., Radnor, Z., & Nasi, G. (2013). A new theory for public service management? Toward a (public) service-dominant approach. *The American Review of Public Administration*, 43(2), 135–158.

Osborne, S. P. & Strokosch, K. (2013). It takes two to tango? Understanding the co-production of public services by integrating the services management and public administration perspective. *British Journal of Management*, 24, 31–47.

Ostrom, E. (2000). Collective action and the evolution of social norms. *Journal of Economic Perspectives*, 14(3), 137–158.

Ostrom, E. (1996). Crossing the great divide: Coproduction, synergy, and development. *World Development*, 24(6), 1073–1087.

Ostrom, E. (1991). Rational choice theory and institutional analysis: Toward complementarity. *American Political Science Review*, 85(1), 237–243.

Ostrom, E. (1990). *Governing the Commons: The Evolution of Instutitions for Collective Action.* Cambridge: Cambridge University Press.

Ostrom, E. & Whitaker, G (1973). Does local community control of police make a difference? Some preliminary findings. *American Journal of Political Science*, 17(1), 48–76.

Ostrom, E., Parks, R. B., Whitaker, G. P., & Percy, S. L. (1978). The public service production process: A framework for analyzing police services. *Policy Studies Journal*, 7, 381–389.

O'Toole, L. J. (1997). Treating networks seriously: Practical and research-based agendas in public administration. *Public Administration Review*, 57(1), 45–52.

Page, S. (2010). Integrative leadership for collaborative governance: Civic engagement in Seattle. *The Leadership Quarterly*, 21(2), 246–263.

Painter, M. & Peters, B. G. (2010). Administrative traditions in comparative perspective: Families, groups and hybrids. In M. Painter & B. G. Peters, eds., *Tradition and Public Administration*. Basingstoke: Palgrave Macmillan, pp. 19–30.

Palumbo, R., Vezzosi, S., Picciolli, P., Landini, A., Annarumma, C., & Manna, R. (2018). Fostering organizational change through co-production: Insights from an Italian experience. *International Review on Public and Nonprofit Marketing*, 15(3), 371–391.

Pan, S. L. & Leidner, D. E. (2003). Bridging communities of practice with information technology in pursuit of global knowledge sharing. *The Journal of Strategic Information Systems*, 12(1), 71–88.

Pappers, J., Keserü, I., & Macharis, C. (2019). Using co-creation methods to solve mobility problems in Brussels. In Real Corp 2019 – Is this the Real World? Perfect Smart Cities vs. Real Emotional Cities. *Proceedings of 24th International Conference on Urban Planning, Regional Development and Information Society* 993–9. CORP–Competence Center of Urban and Regional Planning. www.corp.at/archive/CORP2019_103.pdf

Park, S. & Berry, F. (2014). Successful diffusion of a failed policy: The case of pay-for-performance in the US Federal Government. *Public Management Review*, 16(6), 763–781.

Parker, G. & Alstyne, M. (2018). Innovation, openness, and platform control. *Management Science*, 64(7), 2973–3468.

Parks, R. B., Baker, P. C., Kiser, L., Oakerson, R., Ostrom, E., Ostrom, V., Percy, S. L., Vandivort, M. B, Whitaker, G. P., & Wilson, R. (1981). Consumers as co-producers of public services:

Some economic and institutional considerations. *Policy Studies Journal*, 9(7), 1001–1111.

Parrado, S., Ryzin, G. G., Bovaird, T., & Löffler, E. (2013). Correlates of co-production: Evidence from a five-nation survey of citizens. *International Public Management Journal*, 16(1), 85–112.

Parry, K. W. & Bryman, A. (2006). Leadership in organizations. In S. Clegg, C. Hardy, T. Lawrence & W. R. Nord, eds., *The SAGE Handbook of Organization Studies*. London: Sage Publications, pp. 447–468.

Paskaleva, K., Cooper, I., & Concilo, G. (2018). Co-producing smart city services: Does one size fit all? In M. Rodríquez Bolívar, ed., *Smart Technologies for Smart Governments*. Cham: Springer, pp. 123–158.

Pateman, C. (1970). *Participation and Democratic Theory*. Cambridge: Cambridge University Press.

Pateman, C. (2012). Participatory democracy revised. *Perspectives on Politics*, 10(1), 7–19.

Patton, M. Q. (2011). *Essentials of Utilization-Focused Evaluation*. Thousand Oaks: Sage Publications.

Patton, M. Q. (2010). *Developmental Evaluation: Applying Complexity Concepts to Enhance Innovation and Use*. New York: The Guilford Press.

Pearce, C. L. & Conger, J. A. (2003). *Shared Leadership: Reframing the Hows and Whys of Leadership*. Thousand Oaks: Sage Publications.

Pedersen, A. R., Sehested, K., & Sørensen, E. (2011). Emerging theoretical understanding of pluricentric coordination in public governance. *The American Review of Public Administration*, 41(4), 375–394.

Pellicano, M., Calabrese, M., Loia, F., & Maione, G. (2018). Value co-creation practices in smart city ecosystem. *Journal of Service Science and Management*, 12(1), 34–57.

Percy, S. L. (1984). Citizen participation in the co-production of urban services. *Urban Affairs Quarterly*, 19(4), 431–446.

Pestoff, V. (2012). Co-production and third sector social services in Europe: Some concepts and evidence. *VOLUNTAS: International Journal of Voluntary and Nonprofit Organisations*, 23(4), 1102–1118.

Pestoff, V. (2006). Citizens and co-production of welfare services: Childcare in eight European countries. *Public Management Review*, 8(4), 503–519.

Pestoff, V. & Brandsen, T. (2008). *Co-Production: The Third Sector Sector and the Delivery of Public Services*. Abingdon: Routledge.

Pestoff, V., Osborne, S. P., & Brandsen, T. (2006). Patterns of co-production in public services. *Public Management Review*, 8(4), 591–595.

Peters, B. G. (2019). *Institutional Theory in Political Science: The New Institutionalism*. Cheltenham: Edward Elgar.

Peters, B. G. (2010). Meta-governance and public management. In S. P. Osborne, ed., *The New Public Governance?* London: Routledge, pp. 52–67.

Peters, B. G. (2002). *Politics of Bureaucracy*, London: Routledge.

Petersen, O. H, Hjelmar, U., & Vrangbæk, K. (2017). Is contracting out still the great panacea? A systematic review of studies on economic and quality effects from 2000–2014. *Social Policy and Administration*, 51 (2), 130–157.

Pettigrew, A. M. (1979). On studying organizational cultures. *Administrative Science Quarterly*, 24(4), 570–581.

Pharr, S. J., Putnam, R. D., & Dalton, R. J. (2000). A quarter century of declining confidence. *Journal of Democracy*, 11(2), 5–25.

Phillips, M. (2006). Growing pains: The sustainability of social enterprises. *The International Journal of Entrepreneurship and Innovation*, 7(4), 221–230.

Pierson, P. (2011). *Politics in Time: History, Institutions, and Social Analysis*. Princeton: Princeton University Press.

Pierson, P. (2000). Increasing returns, path dependence, and the study of politics. *American Political Science Review*, 94(2), 251–267.

Pirinen, A. (2016). The barriers and enablers of co-design for services. *International Journal of Design*, 10(3), 27–42.

Plé, L. & Cáceres, R. C. (2010). Not always co-creation: Introducing interactional co-destruction of value in service-dominant logic. *Journal of Services Marketing*, 24(6) 430–437.

Pollitt, C. & Bouckaert, G. (2011). *Continuity and Change in Public Policy and Management*. Cheltenham: Edward Elgar.

Pollitt, C. & Bouckaert, G. (2004). *Public Management Reform: A Comparative Analysis*. New York: Oxford University Press.

Pollitt, C. & Hupe, P. (2011). Talking about government: The role of magic concepts. *Public Management Review*, 13(5), 641–658.

Poocharoen, O. O. & Ting, B. (2015). Collaboration, co-production, networks: Convergence of theories. *Public Management Review*, 17 (4), 587–614.

Pope, J. G., Hegland, T. J., Ballesteros, M., Nielsen, K. N., & Rahikainen, M. (2019). Steps to unlocking ecosystem based fisheries management: Towards displaying the N dimensional potato. *Fisheries Research*, 209, 117–128.

Post, D. G. (2009). The theory of generativity. *Fordham Law Review*, 78(6), 2755–2766.

Powell, W. W. & DiMaggio, P. J. (1983). The iron cage revisited: Institutional isomorphism and collective rationality in organizational fields. *American Sociological Review*, 48(2), 147–160.

Power, M. (1997). *The Audit Society: Rituals of Verification*. Oxford: Oxford University Press.

Prahalad, C. K. & Ramaswamy, V. (2002). The co-creation connection. *Strategy+Business*, 27, 50–61.

Prahalad, C. K. & Ramaswamy, V. (2004). Co-creation experiences: The next practice in value creation. *Journal of Interactive Marketing*, 18(3), 5–14.

Pressman, J. L. & Wildavsky, A. B. (1973). *Implementation: How Great Expectations in Washington Are Dashed in Oakland*. Berkeley: University of California Press.

Provan, K. G. & Milward, H. B. (2001). Do networks really work? A framework for evaluating public-sector organizational networks. *Public Administration Review*, 61(4), 414–423.

Provan, K. G. & Kenis, P. (2008). Modes of network governance: Structure, management, and effectiveness. *Journal of Public Administration Research and Theory*, 18(2), 229–52.

Przeworski, A. (2010). *Democracy and the Limits of Self-Government*. Cambridge: Cambridge University Press.

Puerari, E., de Koning, J., Von Wirth, T., Karré, P., Mulder, I., & Loorbach, D. (2018). Co-creation dynamics in urban living labs. *Sustainability*, 10(6), 1893.

Putnam, R. D. (1995). Tuning in, tuning out: The strange disappearance of social capital in America. *Political Science and Politics*, 28(4), 664–683.

Quick, K. S. (2017). Locating and building collective leadership and impact. *Leadership*, 13(4), 445–471.

Quick, K. S. & Feldman, M. S. (2011). Distinguishing participation and inclusion. *Journal of Planning Education and Research*, 31(3), 272–290.

Radaelli, C. M. (2017). *Technocracy in the European Union*. London: Routledge.

Radnor, Z., Osborne, S. P., Kinder, T., & Mutton, J. (2014). Operationalizing co-production in public services delivery: The contribution of service blueprinting. *Public Management Review*, 16(3), 402–423.

Ramaswamy, V. & Ozcan, K. (2018). What is co-creation? An interactional creation framework and its implications for value creation. *Journal of Business Research*, 84, 196–205.

Rantamäki, N. J. (2017). Co-production in the context of Finnish social services and health care: A challenge and a possibility for a new kind of democracy. *Voluntas: International Journal of Voluntary and Nonprofit Organizations*, 28(1), 248–264.

Rashman, L. & Hartley, J. (2002). Leading and learning? Knowledge transfer in the beacon council scheme. *Public Administration*, 80(3), 523–542.

Reich, R. B. (2012). *Beyond Outrage: What Has Gone Wrong with Our Economy and Our Democracy, and How to Fix It*. New York: Vintage Books.

Renn, O. (2008). Concepts of risk: An interdisciplinary review – Part 2: Integrative approaches. *GAIA Ecological Perspectives for Science and Society*, 17(2), 196–204.

Rhodes, R. A. (1997). *Understanding Governance: Policy Networks, Governance, Reflexivity and Accountability*. London: Open University Press.

Rittell, H. W. J. & Webber, M. M. (1973). Dilemmas in a general theory of planning. *Policy Sciences*, 4(2), 155–169.

Roberts, N. (2004). Public deliberation in an age of direct citizen participation. *The American Review of Public Administration*, 34(4), 315–353.

Roberts, N. (2000). Wicked problems and network approaches to resolution. *International Public Management Review* 1(1), 1–19.

Roberts, N. C. & King, P. J. (1996). *Transforming Public Policy: Dynamics of Policy Entrepreneurship and Innovation*. San Francisco: Jossey-Bass.

Rogers, E. M. (1995). Lessons for guidelines for the diffusion of innovations. *The Joint Commission Journal on Quality Improvement*, 21(7), 324–328.

Rosanvallon, P. (2011). *Democratic Legitimacy: Impartiality, Reflexivity, Proximity*. Princeton: Princeton University Press.

Rosanvallon, P. (2008). *Counter-democracy*. Cambridge: Cambridge University Press.

Rosen, J. & Painter, G. (2019). From citizen control to co-production: Moving beyond a linear conception of citizen participation. *Journal of the American Planning Association*, 85(3), 335–347.

Rosenstone, S. J. & Hansen, J. M. (1993). *Mobilization, Participation and Democracy in America*. New York: Macmillan.

Rossi, U. (2004). The multiplex city: The process of urban change in the historic centre of Naples. *European Urban and Regional Studies*, 11(2), 156–169.

Runciman, D. (2018). *How Democracy Ends*. London: Profile Books.

Rutter, D., Manley, C., Weaver, T., Crawford, M. J., & Fulop, N. (2004). Patients or partners? Case studies of user involvement in the planning and delivery of adult mental health services in London. *Social Science & Medicine* 58(10), 1973–1984.

Ryan, B. (2012). Co-production: Option or obligation? *Australian Journal of Public Administration*, 71(3), 314–324.

Sabatier, P. A. & Weible, C. M. (2007). The advocacy coalition framework: Innovations and clarifications. In P. A. Sabatier, ed., *Theories of the Policy Process*, 2nd edn. New York: Routledge, pp. 189–220.

Sabel, C. F. & Zeitlin, J. (eds.). (2010). *Experimentalist Governance in the European Union: Towards a New Architecture*. Oxford: Oxford University Press.

Salamon, L. M. (2002). *The Tools of Government: A Guide to the New Governance*. Oxford: Oxford University Press.

Sanders, E. B. N. (2000). Generative tools for co-designing. In S. A. R. Scrivener, L. J. Ball & A. Woodcock, eds., *Collaborative Design*. London: Springer, pp. 3–12.

Sanders, E. B. N. & Stappers, P. J. (2008). Co-creation and the new landscapes of design. *Co-design*, 4(1), 5–18.

Sarason, S. (1974), *The Creation of Settings and the Future Societies*. San Francisco: Jossey-Bass.

Schachter, H. L. & Aliaga, M. (2003). Educating administrators to interact with citizens: A research note. *Public Organisation Review*, 3(4), 433–442.

Schad, J., Lewis, M. W., Raisch, S., & Smith, W. K. (2016). Paradox research in management science: Looking back to move forward. *The Academy of Management Annals*, 10(1), 5–64.

Scharpf, F. (1999). *Governing in Europe: Effective and Democratic?* Oxford: Oxford University Press.

Scharpf, F. W. (1997). Introduction: The problem-solving capacity of multi-level governance. *Journal of European Public Policy*, 4(4), 520–538.

Scharpf, F. W. (1994). Games real actors could play: Positive and negative coordination in embedded negotiations. *Journal of Theoretical Politics*, 6(1), 27–53.

Scharpf, F. W. (1993). *Games in Hierarchies and Networks: Analytical and Empirical Approaches to the Study of Governance Institutions*. Frankfurt a.M.: Campus Verlag.

Schillemans, T. (2008). Accountability in the shadow of hierarchy: The horizontal accountability of agencies. *Public Organization Review*, 8(2): 175.

Schillemans, T., Van Twist, M., & Vanhommerig, I. (2013). Innovations in accountability: Learning through interactive, dynamic, and citizen-initiated forms of accountability. *Public Performance and Management Review*, 36(3): 407–435.

Schlappa, H. & Imani, Y. (2018). Who is in the lead? New perspectives on leading service co-production. In T. Brandsen, B. Verschuere & T. Steen, eds., *Co-Production and Co-Creation: Engaging Citizens in Public Services*. New York: Routledge, pp. 99–108.

Schmidt, V. A. (2013). Democracy and legitimacy in the European Union revisited: Input, output and "throughput". *Political Studies*, 61(1), 2–22.

Schmitter, P. C. (1974). Still the century of corporatism? *The Review of Politics*, 36(1), 85–131.

Schön, D. A. & Rein, M. (1995). *Frame Reflection: Toward the Resolution of Intractable Policy Controversies*. New York: Basic Books.

Scott, D. M. (2015). *The New Rules of Marketing and PR: How to Use Social Media, Online Video, Mobile Applications, Blogs, News Releases, and Viral Marketing to Reach Buyers Directly*. Hoboken: Wiley.

Sedelmeier, U. (2014). Anchoring democracy from above? The European Union and democratic backsliding in Hungary and Romania after accession. *Journal of Common Market Studies*, 52(1), 105–121.

Sele, K. & Grand, S. (2016). Unpacking the dynamics of ecologies of routines: Mediators and their generative effects in routine interactions. *Organization Science*, 27(3), 722–738.

Self, R. O. (2005). *American Babylon: Race and the Struggle for Postwar Oakland*. Princeton: Princeton University Press.

Sell, M., Vihinen, H., Gabiso, G., & Lindström, K. (2018). Innovation platforms: A tool to enhance small-scale farmer potential through co-creation. *Development in Practice*, 28(8), 999–1011.

Serrat, O. (2010). Design thinking. Available at: www.adb.org/documents/information/knowledge-solutions/design-thinking.pdf

Sharp, E. B. (1980). Toward a new understanding of urban services and citizen participation: The co-production concept. *The American Review of Public Administration*, 14(2), 105–118.

Shinya, Y. (2017). 'I-nnovate for tomorrow': Co-creating solutions together with the Sudanese children. *UNICEF Stories of Innovation*, www.unicef.org/innovation/stories/innovate-creating-solutions-with-sudanese-children, visited December 23, 2019.

Siebers, V. & Torfing, J. (2018). Co-creation as a new form of citizen engagement: Comparing Danish and Dutch experiences at the local government level. *International Public Management Review*, 18(2), 187–208.

Silvia, C. & McGuire, M. (2010). Leading public sector networks: An empirical examination of integrative leadership behaviors. *The Leadership Quarterly*, 21(2), 264–277.

Simon, H. A. (1996). *The Sciences of the Artificial*, 3rd edn. Cambridge, MA: MIT Press.

Simon, H. A. (1957). *Models of Man: Social and Rational.* Oxford: Wiley.

Skelcher, C. & Torfing, J. (2010). Improving democratic governance through institutional design: Civic participation and democratic ownership in Europe. *Regulation and Governance*, 4(1), 71–91.

Skilton, P. F. & Dooley, K. J. (2010). The effects of repeat collaboraton on creative abrasion. *Academy of Management Review*, 35(1), 118–134.

Smith, P. H. & Ziegler, M. R. (2008). Liberal and illiberal democracy in Latin America. *Latin America Politics and Society*, 50(1), 31–57.

Smits, R. & Kuhlmann, S. (2004). The rise of systemic instruments in innovation policy. *International Journal of Foresight and Innovation Policy*, 1(1–2), 4–32.

Sol, J., Beers, P. J., & Wals, A. E. (2013). Social learning in regional innovation networks: Trust, commitment and reframing as emergent properties of interaction. *Journal of Cleaner Production*, 49, 35–43.

Sopjani, L., Hesselgren, M., Ritzén, S., & Janhager Stier, J. (2017). Co-creation with diverse actors for sustainability innovation. In *21st International Conference on Engineering Design, ICED17* (Vol. 8). www.designsociety.org/publication/39864/Co-creation+with+diverse+actors+for+sustainability+innovation

Sørensen, E. (2020). *Interactive Political Leadership: The Role of Politicians in the Age of Governance.* Oxford: Oxford University Press.

Sørensen, E. (2014). Conflict as a driver of pluricentric coordination. *Planning Theory*, 13(2), 152–169.

Sørensen, E. (2012). Measuring the accountability of collaborative innovation. *The Innovation Journal*, 17(1), 2.

Sørensen, E. & Torfing, J. (2020). Radical and disruptive answers to downstream problems in collaborative governance? *Public Management Review*, forthcoming.

Sørensen, E. & Torfing, J. (2019). Designing institutional platforms and arenas for interactive political leadership. *Public Management Review*, 21(10), 1443–1463.

Sørensen, E. & Torfing, J. (2018). Co-initiation of collaborative innovation in urban spaces. *Urban Affairs Review*, 54(2), 388–418.

Sørensen, E. & Torfing, J. (2017). Metagoverning collaborative innovation in governance networks. *The American Review of Public Administration*, 47(7), 826–839.

Sørensen, E. & Torfing, J. (2012). Introduction: Collaborative innovation in the public sector. In J. Torfing, ed., *Collaborative Innovation in the Public Sector*. Washington DC: Georgetown University Press, pp. 1–24.

Sørensen, E. & Torfing, J. (2011). Enhancing collaborative innovation in the public sector. *Administration and Society*, 43(8), 842–868.

Sørensen, E. & Torfing, J. (2009). Making governance networks effective and democratic through metagovernance. *Public Administration*, 87(2), 234–258.

Sørensen, E. & Torfing, J. (2007). *Theories of Democratic Network Governance*. London: Palgrave Macmillan.

Sørensen, E. & Torfing, J. (2005). Network governance and post-liberal democracy. *Administrative Theory & Praxis*, 27(2), 197–237.

Sørensen, E. & Torfing, J. (2003). Network politics, political capital, and democracy. *International Journal of Public Administration*, 26(6), 609–634.

Spillane, J. P. & Diamond, J. B. (2007). *Distributed Leadership in Practice*. Cheltenham: Hawker Brownlow Education.

Spinosa, C., Flores, F., & Dreyfus, H. L. (1997). *Disclosing New Worlds: Entrepreneurship, Democratic Action and the Cultivation of Solidarity*. Cambridge: MIT Press.

Stacey, R. D., Griffin, D., & Shaw, P. (2000). *Complexity and Management: Fad or Radical Challenge to Systems Thinking?* London: Routledge.

Stangel, M. & Szóstek, A. (2015). Empowering citizens through participatory design: A case study of Mstów, Poland. *Architecture Civil Engineering Environment*, 8(1), 47–58.

Star, S. L. & Griesemer, J. R. (1989). Institutional ecology, "translations" and boundary objects: Amateurs and professionals in Berkeley's Museum of Vertebrate Zoology, 1907–39. *Social Studies of Science*, 19(3), 387–420.

Steen, T., Brandsen, T., & Verschuere, B. (2018). The dark side of co-creation and co-production: Seven evils. In T. Brandsen, T. Steen & B. Verschuere, eds., *Co-Production and Co-Creation: Engaging Citizens in Public Services*. New York: Routledge, pp. 284–293.

Steen, M., Manschot, M., & De Koning, N. (2011). Benefits of co-design in service design projects. *International Journal of Design*, 5(2), 53–60.

Steen, T. & Tuurnas, S. (2018). The roles of the professional in co-production and co-creation processes. In T. Brandsen, T. Steen & B. Verschuere, eds., *Co-Production and Co-creation: Engaging Citizens in Public Services*. New York: Routledge, pp. 80–92.

Steinmo, S., Thelen, K. A., & Longstreth, F. (1992). *Structuring Politics: Historical Institutionalism in Comparative Analysis*. Cambridge: Cambridge University Press.

Steunenberg, B. (2000). Constitutional change in the European Union. In H. Wagenaar ed., *Government institutions: Effects, changes and normative foundations*. Dordrecht: Springer, pp. 89–108.

Steyaert, P. & Jiggins, J. (2007). Governance of complex environmental situations through social learning: A synthesis of SLIM's lessons for research, policy and practice. *Environmental Science & Policy*, 10(6), 575–586.

Stickdorn, M. & Schneider, J. (2011). *This Is Service Design Thinking: Basics, Tools, Cases.* Amsterdam: BIS Publishers.

Stiles, K. (2002). International support for NGOs in Bangladesh: Some unintended consequences. *World Development*, 30(5), 835–846.

Stoker, G. (2019). Can the governance paradigm survive the rise of populism? *Policy & Politics*, 47(1), 3–18.

Stoker, G. (2011). Anti-politics in Britain. In R. Heffernan, P. Cowley & C. Hay, eds., *Developments in British politics 9*. Basingstoke: Palgrave Macmillan, pp. 152–173.

Stoker, G. (2006a). Explaining political disenchantment: Finding pathways to democratic renewal. *The Political Quarterly*, 77(2), 184–194.

Stoker. G. (2006b). Public value management: A new narrative for networked governance? *The American Review of Public Administration*, 36(1), 41–57.

Stoker, G. & John, P. (2009). Design experiments: Engaging policy makers in the search for evidence about what works. *Political Studies*, 57(2), 356–373.

Stokes, S. C. (2005). Perverse accountability: A formal model of machine politics with evidence from Argentina. *American Political Science Review*, 99(3), 315–325.

Stoltz, P. G. (1997). *Adversity Quotient: Turning Obstacles into Opportunities.* Hoboken: John Wiley and Sons.

Stonecash, J. M., Brewer, M. D., & Mariani, M. D. (2003). *Diverging Parties: Social Change, Realignment, and Party Polarization.* New York: Westview Press.

Straus, D. (2002). *How to Make Collaboration Work: Powerful Ways to Build Consensus, Solve Problems, and Make Decisions.* San Francisco: Berrett-Koehler Publishers.

Svara, J. H. (2001). The myth of the dichotomy: Complementarity of politics and administration in the past and future of public administration. *Public Administration Review*, 61(2), 176–183.

Sześciło, D. (2018). Legal dilemmas of co-production and co-creation. In T. Brandsen, B. Verschuere & T. Steen, eds., *Co-Production and Co-Creation: Engaging Citizens in Public Services*. New York: Routledge, pp. 137–144.

Tait, L. & Lester, H. (2005). Encouraging user involvement in mental health services. *Advances in Psychiatric Treatment*, 11(3), 168–175.

Teder, M. E. (2018). Placemaking as co-creation: Professional roles and attitudes in practice. *CoDesign*, 15(4), 289–307.

Teubner, G. (1982). How the law thinks: Towards a constructivist epistemology. *Law and Society Review*, 23(5), 727–757.

Tisdall, C. (2015). *The Transformation of Services for Young People in Surrey County Council*. Birmingham: Governance International.

Tiwana, A., Konsynski, B. & Bush, A. A. (2010). Research commentary: Platform evolution: Coevolution of platform architecture, governance, and environmental dynamics. *Information Systems Research*, 21(4), 675–687.

Toots, M., McBride, K., Kalvet, T., & Krimmer, R. (2017). Open data as enabler of public service co-creation: Exploring the drivers and barriers. In *E-Democracy and Open Government* (CeDEM), 2017 Conference for (pp. 102–12). IEEE. https://ieeexplore.ieee.org/abstract/document/8046277

Torfing, J. (2019). Collaborative innovation in the public sector: The argument. *Public Management Review*, 21(1), 1–11.

Torfing, J. (2016). *Collaborative Innovation in the Public Sector*. Washington DC: Georgetown University Press.

Torfing, J. & Ansell, C. (2017). Strengthening political leadership and policy innovation through the expansion of collaborative forms of governance. *Public Management Review*, 19(1), 37–54.

Torfing, J., Krogh, A. H., & Ejrnæs, A. (2020). Measuring and assessing the effects of collaborative innovation in crime prevention. *Policy & Politics*. /doi.org/10.1332/030557320X15788414270675

Torfing, J., Krogh, A. H., & Ejrnæs, A. (2017). *Samarbejdsdrevet innovation i kriminalpræventive indsatser: Slutrapport om sammenhængene mellem samarbejde, innovation og kriminalpræventiv effekt og måling heraf*. Copenhagen: Det Kriminalpræventive Råd.

Torfing, J., Peters, B. G., Pierre, J., & Sørensen, E. (2012). *Interactive Governance*. Oxford: Oxford University Press.

Torfing, J., Sørensen, E., & Røiseland, A. (2019). Transforming the public sector into an arena for co-creation: Barriers, drivers, benefits, and ways forward. *Administration & Society*, 51(5), 795–825.

Torfing, J. & Triantafillou, P. (2016). *Enhancing Public Innovation by Transforming Public Governance*. Cambridge. Cambridge University Press.

Torfing, J. & Triantafillou, P. (2013). What's in a name? Grasping New Public Governance as a political-administrative system. *International Review of Public Administration*, 18(2), 9–25.

Tortzen, A. (2018). Case study – Enhancing co-creation through linking leadership: The Danish 'Zebra City' project. In T. Brandsen, B. Verschuere & T. Steen, eds., *Co-Production and Co-Creation:*

Engaging Citizens in Public Services. New York: Routledge, pp. 112–114.

Trechsel, A. H. & Kriesi, H. (1996). Switzerland: The referendum system and initiative as a centrepiece of the political system. In M. Gallagher & P. V. Uleri, eds., *The Referendum Experience in Europe*. Basingstoke: Palgrave Macmillan, pp. 185–208.

Trubek, D. M. & Trubek, L. G. (2006). New Governance & (and) legal regulation: Complementarity, rivalry, and transformation. *Columbia Journal of European Law*, *13*, 539–548.

Tucker, R. C. (1995). *Politics as Leadership*. Columbia: University of Missoury Press.

Tuurnas, S. (2015). Learning to co-produce? The perspective of public service professionals. *International Journal of Public Sector Management*, 28(7), 583–598.

Uhl-Bien, M. (2006). Relational leadership theory: Exploring the social processes of leadership and organizing. *The Leadership Quarterly*, 17 (6), 654–676.

Vamstad, J. (2012). Co-production and service quality: The case of cooperative childcare in Sweden. *VOLUNTAS: International Journal of Voluntary and Nonprofit Organisations*, 23(4), 1173–1188.

Van Ryzin, G. G. & Immerwahr, S. (2007). Importance-performance analysis of citizen satisfaction surveys. *Public Administration*, 85(1), 215–226.

Vargo, S. L. & Lusch, R. F. (2016). Institutions and axioms: An extension and update of service-dominant logic. *Journal of the Academy of Marketing Science*, 44(1), 5–23.

Vargo, S. L., Maglio, P. P., & Akaka, M. A. (2008). On value and value co-creation: A service systems and service logic perspective. *European Management Journal*, 26(3), 145–152.

Vesnic-Alujevic, L., Stoermer, E., Rudkin, J., Scapolo, F., & Kimbell, L. (2019). *The Future of Government 2030+: A Citizen-Centric Perspective on New Government Models*. EUR 29664 EN. Publications Office of the European Union, Luxembourg, DOI:10.2760/145751, JRC 115008.

Voet, J., Groeneveld, S., & Kuipers, B. S. (2014). Talking the talk or walking the walk? The leadership of planned and emergent change in a public organization. *Journal of Change Management*, 14(2), 171–191.

Von Hippel, E. (1986). Lead users: A source of novel product concepts. *Management Science*, 32(7), 791–805.

Voorberg, W., Bekkers, V., Flemig, S., Timeus, K., Tonurist, P., & Tummers, L. (2017a). Does co-creation impact public service delivery?

The importance of state and governance traditions. *Public Money & Management*, 37(5), 365–372.

Voorberg, W., Bekkers, V., Timeus, K., Tonurist, P., & Tummers, L. (2017b). Changing public service delivery: Learning in co-creation. *Policy and Society*, 36(2), 178–194.

Voorberg, W. H., Bekkers, V. J., & Tummers, L. G. (2015). A systematic review of co-creation and co-production: Embarking on the social innovation journey. *Public Management Review*, 17(9), 1333–1357.

Voorberg W., Tummers, L., Bekkers, V., Torfing, J., Tonurist, P., Kattel, R., Lember, V., Timeus, K., Nemec, J., Svidronova, M., Merickova, B. M., Gasco, M., Flemig, S., & Osborne, S. (n.d.). Co-creation and citizen involvement in social innovation: A comparative case study across 7 EU-countries. LIPSE research report #2. https://centerforborgerdialog.dk/wp-content/uploads/2017/10/Voorberg-2015-co-creation-and-citizen-involvement-comparative-study.pdf

Wang, W., Bryan-Kinns, N., & Ji, T. (2016). Using community engagement to drive co-creation in rural China. *International Journal of Design*, 10 (1), 37–52.

Warburton, J. (2006). Volunteering in later life: Is it good for your health? *Voluntary Action*, 8(2), 3–15.

Warren, M. E. (2014). Accountability and democracy. In M. Bovens, R. Goodin & T. Schillemans, eds., *The Oxford Handbook of Public Accountability*. Oxford: Oxford University Press, pp. 39–54.

Warren, M. E. (2009). Governance-driven democratization. *Critical Policy Studies*, 3(1), 3–13.

Warren, M. E. (2002). What can democratic participation mean today? *Political Theory*, 30(5), 677–701.

Warren, M. E. (1996). What should we expect from more democracy? Radically democratic responses to politics. *Political Theory*, 24(2), 241–270.

Warren, M. E. & Pearse, H. (2008). *Designing Deliberative Democracy: The British Columbia Citizens' Assembly*. Cambridge: Cambridge University Press.

Watson, G. (1995). *Good Sewers Cheap. Agency–Customer Interactions in Low-Cost Urban Sanitation in Brazil*. Washington D.C.: World Bank.

Weber, E. P. (2009). Explaining institutional change in tough cases of collaboration: "Ideas" in the Blackfoot Watershed. *Public Administration Review*, 69(2), 314–327.

Welch, E. W. (2012). The rise of participative technologies in government. In M. A. Shareef, N. Archer, Y. K. Dwivedi, A. Mishra & S. K. Pandey, eds., *Transformational Government through eGov practice: Socioeconomic, Cultural, and Technological Issues*. Bingley: Emerald Group Publishing, pp. 347–368.

Whiteley, P. F. (2010). Is the party over? The decline of party activism and membership across the democratic world. *Party Politics*, 17(1), 21–44.

Wiewiora, A., Keast, R., & Brown, K. (2016). Opportunities and challenges in engaging citizens in the co-production of infrastructure-based public services in Australia. *Public Management Review*, 18(4), 483–507.

Wiktorska-Święcka, A. (2018). Co-creation of public services in Poland in Statu Nascendi: A case study on senior co-housing policy at the urban level. *Polish Political Science Review*, 6(2), 26–54.

Wilkinson, A., Mayer, M., & Ringler, V. (2014). Collaborative futures: Integrating foresight with design in large scale innovation processes-seeing and seeding the futures of Europe. *Journal of Futures Studies*, 18(4), 1–26.

Willams, B. N., Kang, S. C., & Johnson, J. (2016). (Co)-contamination as the dark side of co-production: Public value failures in co-production processes. *Public Management Review*, 18(5), 692–717.

Williams, P. (2002). The competent boundary spanner. *Public Administration*, 80(1), 103–124.

Windle, G. (2011). What is resilience? A review and concept analysis. *Reviews on Clinical Gerontology*, 21(2), 152–169.

Windrum, P. & Koch, P. M. (eds.) (2008). *Innovation in Public Sector Services: Entrepreneurship, Creativity and Management*. Cheltenham: Edward Elgar.

Windrum, P., Schartinger, D., Rubalcaba, L., Gallouj, F., & Toivonen, M. (2016). The co-creation of multi-agent social innovations: A bridge between service and social innovation Research. *European Journal of Innovation Management*, 19(2), 150–166.

Won, K. K., Young-jun, K., & Jong-bae, K. (2018). The design of bus reservation system for the transportation vulnerable. RESNA Annual Conference. www.resna.org/sites/default/files/conference/2018/out comes/Kiwon.html

Woo, J. J. (2019). The politics of policymaking: Policy co-creation in Singapore's financial sector. *Policy Studies*, 1–18. https://doi.org/10 .1080/01442872.2019.1634185

Yasuoka, M. & Sakurai, R. (2012). Out of Scandinavia to Asia: Adaptability of participatory design in culturally distant society. In *Proceedings of the 12th Participatory Design Conference: Exploratory Papers*, Workshop Descriptions, Industry Cases-Volume 2 (pp. 21–24). ACM. https://doi .org/10.1145/2348144.2348152

Yin, L., Fassi, D., Cheng, H., Han, H., & He, S. (2017). Health co-creation in social innovation: Design service for health-empowered society in China. *The Design Journal*, 20(sup1), S2293–S2303.

Yoo, Y., Boland Jr, R. J., Lyytinen, K., & Majchrzak, A. (2012). Organizing for innovation in the digitized world. *Organization Science*, 23(5), 1398–408.

Young, I. M. (2000). *Inclusion and Democracy*. Oxford: Oxford University Press.

Zanten, J. A. & Tulder, R. (2018). Multinational enterprises and the sustainable development goals: An institutional approach to corporate engagement. *Journal of International Business Policy*, 1(3–4), 208–233.

Zittrain, J. L. (2006). The generative Internet. *Harvard Law Review*, 119(7), 1975–2040.

Index